Gay Men
and the Sexual History
of the Political Left

Gay Men and the Sexual History of the Political Left

Gert Hekma
Harry Oosterhuis
James Steakley
Editors

Gay Men and the Sexual History of the Political Left, edited by Gert Hekma, Harry Oosterhuis, and James Steakley, was simultaneously issued by The Haworth Press, Inc., under the same title, as special issues of *Journal of Homosexuality*, Volume 29, Numbers 2/3, and 4, John P. De Cecco, Editor.

Harrington Park Press
An Imprint of
The Haworth Press, Inc.
New York · London

ISBN 1-56023-067-3

Published by

Harrington Park Press, 10 Alice Street, Binghamton, NY 13904-1580 USA

Harrington Park Press is an imprint of the Haworth Press, Inc., 10 Alice Street, Binghamton, NY 13904-1580 USA.

Gay Men and the Sexual History of the Political Left has also been published as *Journal of Homosexuality*, Volume 29, Numbers 2/3 and 4, 1995.

The development, preparation, and publication of this work has been undertaken with great care. However, the publisher, employees, editors, and agents of The Haworth Press and all imprints of The Haworth Press, Inc., including The Haworth Medical Press and Pharmaceutical Products Press, are not responsible for any errors contained herein or for consequences that may ensue from use of materials or information contained in this work. Opinions expressed by the author(s) are not necessarily those of The Haworth Press, Inc.

Library of Congress Cataloging-in-Publication Data

Gay men and the sexual history of the political left / Gert Hekma, Harry Oosterhuis, James Steakley, editors.
  p. cm.
  "Simultaneously issued by The Haworth Press, Inc., under the same title as special issue of Journal of Homosexuality, Volume 29, Numbers 2/3, and Volume 29, Number 4."
  Includes bibliographical references and index.
  ISBN 1-56024-724-X (thb : alk. paper). – ISBN 1-56023-067-3 (hpp : alk. paper)
  1. Homosexuality–Political aspects. 2. Gay liberation movement–History. 3. Gay men–Political activity. 4. Right and left (Political science) I. Hekma, Gert. II. Oosterhuis, Harry. III. Steakley, James D.
HQ76.25.G418 1995
306.76'62–dc20   95-36547
                              CIP

INDEXING & ABSTRACTING

Contributions to this publication are selectively indexed or abstracted in print, electronic, online, or CD-ROM version(s) of the reference tools and information services listed below. This list is current as of the copyright date of this publication. See the end of this section for additional notes.

- *Abstracts in Anthropology*, Baywood Publishing Company, 26 Austin Avenue, P.O. Box 337, Amityville, NY 11701

- *Abstracts of Research in Pastoral Care & Counseling*, Loyola College, 7135 Minstrel Way, Suite 101, Columbia, MD 21045

- *Academic Abstracts/CD-ROM*, EBSCO Publishing, P.O. Box 2250, Peabody, MA 01960-7250

- *Applied Social Sciences Index & Abstracts (ASSIA) (Online: ASSI via Data-Star) (CD Rom: ASSIA Plus)*, Bowker- Saur Limited, Maypole House, Maypole Road, East Grinstead, West Sussex RH19 1HH England

- *Book Review Index,* Gale Research, Inc., P.O. Box 2867, Detroit, MI 48231

- *Cambridge Scientific Abstracts*, *Risk Abstracts*, Cambridge Information Group, 7200 Wisconsin Avenue #601, Bethesda, MD 20814

- *Criminal Justice Abstracts*, Willow Tree Press, 15 Washington Street, 4th Floor, Newark NJ 07102

- *Criminology, Penology and Police Science Abstracts*, Kugler Publications, P.O. Box 11188, 1001 GD-Amsterdam, The Netherlands

- *Current Contents* . . . . . see: *Institute for Scientific Information*

- *Digest of Neurology and Psychiatry*, The Institute of Living, 400 Washington Street, Hartford, CT 06106

(continued)

- *Excerpta Medica/Secondary Publishing Division*, Elsevier Science, Inc./Secondary Publishing Division, 655 Avenue of the Americas, New York, NY 10010

- *Expanded Academic Index*, Information Access Company, 362 Lakeside Drive, Forest City, CA 94404

- *Family Life Educator "Abstracts Section,"* ETR Associates, P.O. Box 1830, Santa Cruz, CA 95061-1830

- *Family Violence & Sexual Assault Bulletin*, Family Violence & Sexual Assault Institute, 1310 Clinic Drive, Tyler, TX 75701

- *HOMODOK/"Relevant" Bibliographic Database, Documentation Centre for Gay & Lesbian Studies, University of Amsterdam (selective printed abstracts in "Homologie" and bibliographic computer databases covering cultural, historical, social and political aspects of gay and lesbian topics)*, ILGA Archive, O. Z. Achterburgwal 185, NL-1012 DK Amsterdam, The Netherlands

- *Index Medicus/MEDLINE*, National Library of Medicine, 8600 Rockville Pike, Bethesda, MD 20894

- *Index to Periodical Articles Related to Law*, University of Texas, 727 East 26th Street, Austin, TX 78705

- *INFO-SOUTH Abstracts: contemporary, social, political, and economic information on Latin America; available on-line*, North-South Center Consortium, University of Miami, Miami, FL 33124

- *Institute for Scientific Information*, 3501 Market Street, Philadelphia, Pennsylvania 19104. Coverage in:
  a) Social Science Citation Index (SSCI): print, online, CD-ROM
  b) Research Alerts (current awareness service)
  c) Social SciSearch (magnetic tape)
  d) Current Contents/Social & Behavioral Sciences (weekly current awareness service)

(continued)

- *Inventory of Marriage and Family Literature (online and hard copy)*, National Council on Family Relations, 3989 Central Avenue NE, Suite 550, Minneapolis, MN 55421

- *Leeds Medical Information,* University of Leeds, Leeds LS2 9JT, United Kingdom

- *Mental Health Abstracts (online through DIALOG)*, IFI/Plenum Data Company, 3202 Kirkwood Highway, Wilmington, DE 19808

- *MLA International Bibliography,* Modern Language Association of America, 10 Astor Place, New York, NY 10003

- *PASCAL International Bibliography T205: Sciences de l'information Documentation*, INIST/CNRS-Service Gestion des Documents Primaires, 2, allée du Parc de Brabois, F-54514 Vandoeuvre-les-Nancy, Cedex, France

- *Periodical Abstracts, Research I (general and basic reference indexing and abstracting data-base from University Microfilms International (UMI), 300 North Zeeb Road, P.O. Box 1346, Ann Arbor, MI 48106-1346)*, UMI Data Courier, P.O. Box 32770, Louisville, KY 40232-2770

- *Periodical Abstracts, Research II (broad coverage indexing and abstracting data-base from University Microfilms International (UMI), 300 North Zeeb Road, P.O. Box 1346, Ann Arbor, MI 48106-1346)*, UMI Data Courier, P.O. Box 32770, Louisville, KY 40232-2770

- *PsychNet*, PsychNet Inc., P.O. Box 470250, Aurora, CO 80047-0250

- *Public Affairs Information Bulletin (PAIS)*, Public Affairs Information Service, Inc., 521 West 43rd Street, New York, NY 10036-4396

- *Religion Index One: Periodicals*, American Theological Library Association, 820 Church Street, 3rd Floor, Evanston, IL 60201

- *Sage Family Studies Abstracts (SFSA),* Sage Publications, Inc., 2455 Teller Road, Newbury Park, CA 91320

(continued)

- *Social Planning/Policy & Development Abstracts (SOPODA)*, Sociological Abstracts, Inc., P.O. Box 22206, San Diego, CA 92192-0206

- *Social Science Citation Index*. . . . see: *Institute for Scientific Information*

- *Social Sciences Index (from Volume 1 & continuing)*, The H.W. Wilson Company, 950 University Avenue, Bronx, NY 10452

- *Social Work Abstracts*, National Association of Social Workers, 750 First Street NW, 8th Floor, Washington, DC 20002

- *Sociological Abstracts (SA)*, Sociological Abstracts, Inc., P.O. Box 22206, San Diego, CA 92192-0206

- *Studies on Women Abstracts*, Carfax Publishing Company, P.O. Box 25, Abingdon, Oxfordshire OXI4 3UE, United Kingdom

- *Violence and Abuse Abstracts: A Review of Current Literature on Interpersonal Violence (VAA),* Sage Publications, Inc., 2455 Teller Rd., Newbury Park, CA 91320

Book reviews are selectively excerpted by the Guide to Professional Literature of the Journal of Academic Librarianship.

SPECIAL BIBLIOGRAPHIC NOTES

related to special journal issues (separates)
and indexing/abstracting

☐ indexing/abstracting services in this list will also cover material in any "separate" that is co-published simultaneously with Haworth's special thematic journal issue or DocuSerial. Indexing/abstracting usually covers material at the article/chapter level.

☐ monographic co-editions are intended for either non-subscribers or libraries which intend to purchase a second copy for their circulating collections.

☐ monographic co-editions are reported to all jobbers/wholesalers/approval plans. The source journal is listed as the "series" to assist the prevention of duplicate purchasing in the same manner utilized for books-in-series.

☐ to facilitate user/access services all indexing/abstracting services are encouraged to utilize the co-indexing entry note indicated at the bottom of the first page of each article/chapter/contribution.

☐ this is intended to assist a library user of any reference tool (whether print, electronic, online, or CD-ROM) to locate the monographic version if the library has purchased this version but not a subscription to the source journal.

☐ individual articles/chapters in any Haworth publication are also available through the Haworth Document Delivery Services (HDDS).

ABOUT THE EDITORS

Gert Hekma, Codirector of Homostudies within the Sociologisch Instituut of Universiteit van Amsterdam, has published widely on the history and sociology of sexuality and homosexuality. He coedited *The Pursuit of Sodomy: Male Homosexuality in Renaissance and Enlightenment Europe* (New York: The Haworth Press, Inc., 1989). His most recent books, in Dutch, deal with the gay history of Amsterdam (1993) and discrimination against homosexuals in the world of organized sports (1994).

Harry Oosterhuis, Assistant Professor of History at the Rijksuniversiteit Limburg in Maastricht, wrote a dissertation, now published as a book, on the history of Catholicism and homosexuality in the Netherlands (1992). He also edited and introduced *Homosexuality and Male Bonding in Pre-Nazi Germany* (New York: The Haworth Press, Inc., 1991). At present he is researching the work of the German-Austrian psychiatrist Richard von Krafft-Ebing.

James Steakley, Professor of German language, literature, and culture at the University of Wisconsin-Madison has been a guest professor at the Freie Universität Berlin and the Universität Hannover. Author of *The Homosexual Emancipation Movement in Germany* (New York: Amo, 1975), he has published on anarchism and labor, the German reception of Darwinism, and German music. He is at work on an intellectual biography of Magnus Hirschfeld.

CONTENTS

Leftist Sexual Politics and Homosexuality: A Historical Overview

Gert Hekma
Harry Oosterhuis
James Steakley

During the post-World War II years, homosexual rights groups revived or came into being for the first time across the Western world–in the United States, Holland, Germany, France, and the Scandinavian countries.[1] These 1950s organizations, often designated as "homophile" to distinguish them from post-Stonewall developments, were largely politically neutral, although their backgrounds were actually quite diverse: the American and Dutch organizations, Mattachine and COC, had originated on the left, while the French Arcadie circle sprang from the right.[2] Their neutrality arose from the necessity of negotiating inhospitable political terrain, for the rebuilding of Western Europe and the Cold War spawned governments that continued and even bolstered the erotophobic ethos of the immediately preceding decades.[3] In Europe, gays faced a chilling atmosphere of opprobrium and ostracism. In Germany, the constitutionality of the 1935 sodomy statute promulgated by the Nazis was upheld by the highest West German court in 1957, and gay concentration camp survivors were flatly denied any restitution.[4] In France, the pro-Nazi Vichy regime had raised the age of

[Haworth co-indexing entry note]: "Leftist Sexual Politics and Homosexuality: A Historical Overview." Hekma, Gert, Harry Oosterhuis, and James Steakley. Co-published simultaneously in *Journal of Homosexuality* (The Haworth Press, Inc.) Vol. 29, No. 2/3, 1995, pp. 1-40; and: *Gay Men and the Sexual History of the Political Left* (ed: Gert Hekma, Harry Oosterhuis, and James Steakley) The Haworth Press, Inc., 1995, pp. 1-40; and *Gay Men and the Sexual History of the Political Left* (ed: Gert Hekma, Harry Oosterhuis, and James Steakley) Harrington Park Press, an imprint of The Haworth Press, Inc., 1995, pp. 1-40. Multiple copies of this article/chapter may be purchased from The Haworth Document Delivery Center. [1-800-342-9678 9:00 a.m. - 5:00 p.m. (EST)].

consent for homosexual relations from thirteen to twenty-one, and this law remained unchanged until 1978. In Holland just after the war, the Christian Democrats forced their Social Democratic coalition partners to fire one of their cabinet ministers because he was gay.[5] In Britain, Guy Burgess's 1951 desertion to Moscow was used as evidence to argue that homosexuals were traitors, part of a shadowy "Homintern" (see the contribution in this volume by Fred Sommer); and Alan Turing–whose work in counterintelligence during World War II had helped England as much as Blunt had thwarted it–was led to suicide by his 1952 prosecution for homosexuality and court-ordered hormone injections.[6] In the United States, McCarthyism was a witch-hunt against both communists and homosexuals even though Joseph McCarthy and Roy Cohn, the chief agents of the purge, were whispered to be gay men themselves.[7]

It was not until the 1960s that a broader current of liberation and change enabled a new generation of young gays and lesbians to cut loose from the moorings of postwar homophile organizations–of which indeed they were often blithely unaware–and to chart a new course toward sexual freedom.[8] Most gay and lesbian liberation groups that sprang into existence in the wake of the 1969 Stonewall rebellion were radical, leftist, and utopian. Names such as Gay Liberation Front, Lavender Menace, Red Butterflies, Radicalesbians, and Street Transvestite Action Revolutionaries suggest the provocatively socialist leanings of these countercultural activists.[9] Early gay liberation demonstrations rang with slogans such as: "Ho, ho, homosexual–The ruling class is ineffectual"; "Two, four, six, eight–Smash the family, smash the state"; or in Germany, "*Brüder und Schwestern, ob warm oder nicht–Kapitalismus bekämpfen ist unsere Pflicht*" ("Brothers and sisters, whether gay or not–Fighting capitalism is our duty").[10]

Inspired by the "rediscovery" of classical Freudian-Marxist texts such as Wilhelm Reich's *The Sexual Revolution* (1936; English translation 1945) and Herbert Marcuse's *Eros and Civilization* (1955), activists of the Stonewall generation were certain that only radical change could bring about the conditions under which sexual diversity would be not just tolerated but embraced by society as a whole. Homosexuality represented such a transgression of prevailing norms, they argued, that it could never be integrated within the existing order. The leading slogan of this era was "Come out!"–a deed which, individually and above all collectively, was deemed sufficient to topple the entire edifice of bourgeois culture.

American feminists of this era coined the motto "the personal is the political," but when they and the newly emergent gay liberationists sought to advance this notion within existing leftist organizations, they were often rebuffed. The New Left may have challenged the Old Left for its single-minded focus on the "main contradiction"–capitalist relations of production and power in the age of imperialism–but deeply ingrained attitudes of male chauvinism and homophobia still prevailed in most leftist and anti-war groups. With a mixture of embarrassment and indignation, they were concerned that their political agenda would be sullied by any linkage with sexual deviance and therefore tended to dismiss the gay and lesbian challenge to bourgeois norms as a form of "lifestylism." Some gay men and lesbians involved in New Left organizations were purged by their comrades for making good on the "come out" slogan of that era, while others placed such a high priority on their role within leftist groups that they chose to remain in the closet (see the contribution by David Thorstad).[11] While a handful of gay leftists sought to build cadre organizations, such as the short-lived Lavender and Red Union (Los Angeles), others founded new, programmatic periodicals–*The Body Politic* (Toronto), *Gay Left* (London), *Emanzipation* (Berlin/Munich), *Mietje* (Amsterdam), and *Gai Pied* (Paris).

Despite their utopian goal of transforming society as a whole, the activists of the Stonewall generation turned out to have only limited success at changing the sexual politics even of socialist and left-wing groups. Instead, their impact was initially confined to the gay movement itself, where they launched debates on the revolutionary nature of homosexuality. But here, too, they were soon challenged and in most instances superseded by advocates of an integrationist, assimilationist, "one-issue" approach to gay rights; in New York, for example, the Gay Liberation Front yielded to the Gay Activists Alliance, and in Berlin, the Homosexuelle Aktion Westberlin lost ground to the Allgemeine Homosexuelle Arbeitsgemeinschaft.[12] Moreover, the dialectic of personal and political liberation often replaced militance with new and increasingly visible forms of gay culture, community-building, and consumerism that developed in metropolitan centers during the 1970s.[13]

This development was supported by, but also contributed to, a broader trend in the United States and Western Europe beginning in the 1960s that extended civil rights to minorities, including homosexuals. While the repeal of anti-gay laws in Europe was spearheaded by various socialist and labor party governments, for example in England (1967), West Germany (1969), Sweden (1978), and Spain (1978), it was not exclusively to their credit, for liberal and sometimes even Christian Democratic parties also backed these legal reforms, as in the Netherlands (1971).[14] In the United States, too, a patchwork of state governments and judiciaries began to repeal sodomy statutes, and while these actions were primarily backed by Democrats, Republicans were often involved as well. The American picture was further complicated by the action of state and local governments to extend protection to homosexuals under equal rights ordinances, even in states where the sodomy statute remained on the books.

Overall, leftist politicians (to say nothing of those of other parties) by no means aimed to encourage the development of a distinctive gay identity and culture. On the contrary, their goal–usually implicit rather than explicit–was the seamless social integration of homosexuality, indeed the domestication of homosexuals by drawing them into the fold of what would come to be known as "family values." Contrary to the politicians' intentions, however, these law reforms invariably led to greater public visibility of homosexuality and in some instances–West Germany, for example–were actually a precondition for the emergence of gay militancy. Authorities sometimes responded negatively: in England, for example, the decriminalization of sexual acts between consenting adults in private was followed by stepped-up prosecutions of homosexuals on charges of public indecency,[15] and in France, the government moved to ban *Gai Pied* on grounds of obscenity.[16]

While leftist politicians generally supported the extension of formal rights in the 1960s and 1970s, some of their leaders continued to harbor strong prejudices against homosexuality. In Germany, the Social Democratic senator of Hamburg Helmut Schmidt, who later rose to Federal Chancellor, was instrumental in police crackdowns on gay bars in 1966.[17] In France, the Socialist government of François Mitterrand fulfilled a campaign promise to gay voters by placing homosexuality on a legal par with heterosexuality in 1982, but only a few years later, when the government was implicated in covering up the police murder of Joseph Doucé, a pedophile, the Socialists tried to squelch gay protests.[18] France's Socialist government may have introduced anti-discrimination laws in 1985, but in 1991, when the Socialist Edith Cresson, France's first woman Prime Minister, was asked to comment on a British report that she had once characterized England as overrun by homosexuals, she begged the question by jocularly belittling lesbianism.

Taking the balance of ten years of Socialist government in France, the weekly *Gai Pied* concluded that it had been a mixed blessing: it had instituted some legal advances, but it had given scandalously little attention to AIDS–even though it was French scientists who had first detected the virus (see the contribution by Jan Willem Duyvendak). The inaction of the French Socialists when confronted with AIDS mirrored the response of conservative governments elsewhere: throughout the first world, pervasive homophobia and racism allowed the epidemic to run rampant among marginalized groups. AIDS was of concern only to the extent that it threatened to spread among the population at large–as if the straight, white population were the only group worth protecting.

Western European Social Democracy may have done little to advance gay liberation during the 1970s and 1980s, but Eastern European gays living under regimes installed by Moscow were faring far worse.[19] The Soviet Union and its satellites had an utterly negative attitude toward homosexuality, and in Cuba, gays were consigned with other "antisocialist delinquents" to labor camps (Unidades Militaries Para el Aumento de la Producción) beginning in 1965–at a time when many Western social revolutionaries held up Cuba as a paradisiacal model.[20] Even in the German Democratic Republic–the country with the strongest historical heritage of homosexual emancipation in the precommunist era–it was not until the 1980s that very circumspect gay discussion groups were able to come into existence under the protection of the Evangelical Lutheran Church (see the contribution by Denis Sweet). Elsewhere in

Eastern Europe, initiatives in this direction were even more constrained.[21] In most countries where the Communists have lost power in recent years, homosexual movements have quickly emerged, although their prospects remain unclear.[22] Concerning the situation of gays and lesbians under Communist regimes in Asia we have regrettably little information, but there are various indications that they have been subject to intense persecution.[23]

The foregoing examples have demonstrated two trends that can actually be traced back far earlier than the Stonewall rebellion: the policies of socialist and communist parties and regimes toward homosexuality have been at best ambivalent and often much worse; even so, many gay liberationists have espoused socialism. Indeed, from the first stirrings of homosexual emancipation, a number of its pioneers and most prominent advocates–Magnus Hirschfeld in Germany, André Gide in France, and Harry Hay in the United States, to name just three examples–placed their hopes for "liberty, equality, and fraternity" in socialism and resolutely adopted a leftist stance. At the turn of the century, the preeminent defender of homosexuals in England, Edward Carpenter, wrote prolifically on sexuality, democracy, and socialism.[24] For decades, his books enjoyed an international resonance and were enthusiastically received within the labor movement and intellectual circles. Carpenter's long-term relationship with a working-class man, George Merrill, in the English countryside struck such contemporary observers as E. M. Forster as an exemplary anticipation of a future utopia in which the boundaries between classes and between rural and urban life would be overcome for all, including gay people.

Although classical political liberalism was also heir to the legacy of the French Revolution and claimed to advance individual liberties, these early advocates of homosexual emancipation spurned it and instead embraced socialism as the sole political force that posed a comprehensive challenge to bourgeois society. To them, liberalism seemed limited to freedom of the marketplace; when it came to questions of sexual freedom, liberalism was too closely tied to bourgeois respectability to open up the perspective of radically restructuring all social relations. This promise was held out by both socialism and anarchism, and two contributions in this volume (by

Walter Fähnders and Richard Cleminson) deal with anarchist approaches to homosexuality in Germany and Spain.

The essays in this volume demonstrate that historically, socialist and anarchist support for homosexual rights has been at best half-hearted and often entirely absent. Of course, the same is true of other political tendencies, be they liberal or conservative. Despite the negative or at best mixed record of virtually all political currents on the issue of homosexuality, socialism is singled out for particular attention here because its project was, and is, to fulfil the emancipatory goal of the Enlightenment: the universal liberation of humankind from oppressive ideologies and exploitative social structures. In criticizing the left's failure to advance the cause of homosexual emancipation, we aim not to denounce it wholesale but to hold it to its own high ideals.

In the following, we will offer a brief historical overview of socialists' attitudes toward homosexuality, highlighting the contours and background of their profound ambivalence. "Socialism" is, of course, notoriously a catch-all term, encompassing movements, parties, and regimes of socialists, Communists, and Social Democrats as well as utopian socialists and anarchists. This historical survey does not pretend to be exhaustive and will focus instead on certain key issues:

1. The public-private dichotomy, central to liberal political thought, has long been a problem for socialism. Both the utopian socialists and classical Marxists criticized the public-private dichotomy, but the latter never advanced beyond this to develop a political theory of gender and sexuality.

2. The Marxist current of socialism has always differentiated itself from utopian socialism by claiming to be an objective, "scientific" endeavor, and socialist views on (homo)sexuality were crucially shaped by Enlightenment thinking about nature as well as nineteenth-century scientific (biological and medical) paradigms, particularly Darwinism. Although Marxism as a social theory recognizes that humans have no fixed nature and are a product of history, socialists (like liberals and others) have tended to view gender and sexuality as biological givens and thus essentially ahistorical.

3. Socialists have repeatedly ascribed homosexuality to the "class enemy," contrasting the "manly" vigor and putative purity of the working-class with the emasculated degeneracy and moral turpitude of the aristocracy and haute bourgeoisie. The socialist concept of progress has long envisioned a utopia in which homosexuality would have no place, indeed would automatically disappear as an outdated remnant of oppressive vice and social malaise.

It might be added, finally, that simple opportunism has played an important historical role in politics. Even those socialist parties and regimes that endorsed legal reforms concerning homosexuality proved willing in moments of political need to compromise their principles by invoking stereotypical images of homosexuality to smear their opponents.

PRIVATE VERSUS PUBLIC

The legal principles of both Enlightenment thought and, in the ensuing decades, of liberalism were based on the principle of non-interference by the state in citizens' private lives. In 1791, early in the course of the French Revolution, the Constituent Assembly acted to decriminalize sodomy, which had long been treated as a capital crime in the world of Christendom. Because they were opposed to the union of church and state, Enlightenment *philosophes* and jurists emphasized the distinction between sin–the province of the church–and crime–of concern to the state. They argued that any sexual practice which infringed upon the rights neither of individuals nor of society as a whole belonged to the sacrosanct sphere of private life in which the state was to intervene not by punishment but by prophylaxis.[25]

Beginning in the seventeenth century, politics was conceptualized as distinct from the private sphere. John Locke's formulation of the classical liberal viewpoint, for example, distinguished two fundamentally distinct institutions within society, the state and the family, each of which fulfilled different needs. The state, founded on a voluntary and rational contract, was to protect fundamental individual rights, above all that of property. In so far as they shared the same basic rational principles, (male) individuals were free and equal within the public arena. The purpose of the family, on the other hand, was reproduction and childrearing; as a private zone, it was the site of intimacy, affection, and mutual care, but it also teemed with irrational desires. Passion (broadly ascribed by Locke to women) had to be rigorously excluded from the political realm, for desire and emotion rendered people incapable of arriving at any uniform understanding of rights and benefits. Locke concluded that the family, unlike the state, could not be based on voluntary contract but instead required control by patriarchal authority.[26]

Since eighteenth- and nineteenth-century liberalism grounded the entire domain of public politics on "a passionless, deprivatized sameness of true understanding,"[27] it had scant interest in developing a political theory of gender, sexuality, or difference. When it came to the actual practice of non-interference in individuals' sexual lives, however, the liberal separation of private and public spheres quickly ran up against its limits and showed inconsistencies. Prostitution was a chronic concern because it transmitted venereal diseases, and same-sex practices–particularly in such institutional settings as barracks, prisons, orphanages, dormitories–were also worrisome.[28] Confronted with these obstacles, liberals vacillated uneasily between the principles of utilitarianism, seeking the greatest good for the greatest number, and laissez-faire, allowing individuals to pursue their own interests.[29] While it was widely agreed that public hygiene was a valid rationale for political and medical intervention within the sexual realm, advocates of utilitarianism debated the proper scope of the state's role.

Initially introduced by the Napoleonic regime, a police system of registering prostitutes was gradually implemented throughout Europe in the course of the nineteenth century. While the aim of registration was to control sexually transmitted diseases, it was of course also used for surveillance of the demimonde of prostitution, linked in many ways with the criminal underworld. Faced with the challenge to otherwise privatized sexuality posed by prostitution, liberal sexual ideology responded by upholding–if not creating–a double standard: bourgeois women were supposed to be protected, but promiscuity on the part of bourgeois men was tacitly condoned, with lower-class women providing a "necessary outlet" for the male sexual "drive." Moreover, while prostitutes were subjected to medical examinations, their customers were not, which meant that the regulations were far from effective in preventing the spread of venereal disease. Thus the issues around prostitution not only forced political liberals to compromise the principle of non-interference in sexual matters but also led to a policy that failed to meet its own modest goals. By the late nineteenth century, the registration of prostitutes faced mounting opposition from several quarters: religious groups denounced it, because the state was endorsing vice; feminists criticized it, because it condoned the aggressive sexuality of males; and socialists opposed it, because it promoted the exploitation of working-class women by the bourgeoisie.[30]

Concerning such areas as family, sexuality, and gender, nineteenth-century socialism had much in common with liberalism, for they were joint heirs of Enlightenment principles. But in contrast to liberalism, certain currents of utopian socialism, especially in France, espoused an ideal of sexual freedom so sweeping that it tended to erase the Enlightenment distinction between public and private spheres. The most prominent of these utopians, Charles Fourier, devoted attention not just to the organization of labor but also to sensual pleasure. He envisioned the ideal communal city, the phalanstère, as a place for non-monogamous sexual relations of all kinds, including the "sapphic" and the "pederastic" (see the contribution by Saskia Poldervaart). By granting such importance to sexual issues, the utopian socialists in a sense recognized that the personal is political, but their sexual radicalism was contemptuously dismissed by the scientific socialists, especially in Germany.

Karl Marx was keenly aware of the connection between politics, economy, and family, and he attacked liberal ideology for locating economic relations as well as the family in a private, apolitical zone. But Marx's critique of the distinction between public and private spheres stopped at the half-way point, for while he bared the connection between economic exploitation and other social relations, he did not extend his analysis to the family. When discussing German divorce legislation in his *Economic and Philosophical Manuscripts of 1844*, for example, Marx stoutly defended the integrity of the family against individual rights, and he went on to condemn

Fourier (along with Joseph Proudhon and Claude Henri Saint-Simon) in the following terms:

> ... [their] movement of opposing universal private property to private property finds expression in the animal form of opposing to marriage (certainly a form of exclusive private property) the community of women, in which a woman becomes a piece of communal and common property. It may be said that this idea of the community of women gives away the secret of this yet completely crude and thoughtless communism. Just as woman passes from marriage to general prostitution, so the entire world of wealth (that is, of man's objective substance) passes from the relationship of exclusive marriage with the owner of private property to a state of universal prostitution with the community.[31]

Marx could only imagine the sexual freedom advocated by Fourier as a form of prostitution tantamount to a relapse into a more primitive, "bestial" stage of social development.

To be sure, the hollowness of bourgeois family values was exposed in *The German Ideology* (1845-46), where Karl Marx and Friedrich Engels remarked: "The dissolute bourgeois evades marriage and secretly commits adultery."[32] And in *The Communist Manifesto* (1848), they charged the bourgeoisie with tearing apart families by forcing women as well as children to sell their labor power on the market. Responding to the charge that communism would make all women sexually accessible to all men, they mockingly exposed the universal promiscuity of capitalist society:

> Our bourgeois, not content with having the wives and daughters of the proletarians at their disposal, not to speak of common prostitutes, take the greatest pleasure in seducing each other's wives. Bourgeois marriage is in reality a system of wives in common and thus, at the most, what the Communists might possibly be reproached with, is that they desire to introduce, in substitution for a hypocritically concealed, an openly legalized community of women. For the rest, it is self-evident that the abolition of the present system of production must bring with it the abolition of the community of women

springing from that system, i.e., of prostitution both public and private.[33]

But *The Communist Manifesto*'s scathing attack on the hypocrisy of capitalism when it came to family values was by no means a critique of the family itself.

In *The Origin of the Family, Private Property, and the State* (1884), Friedrich Engels did advance to a more sophisticated analysis of family and gender. Engels's book was based on the research of the ethnologist Lewis Henry Morgan, whose evolutionary theory of the family held that there was a universal, progressive development from a primitive matriarchy, in which promiscuity reigned, to patriarchal authority, in which monogamy was the standard. Engels elaborated on Morgan's work by linking the origins of private property, the division of labor, and ultimately class differences with the historical oppression of women. However, he did not extend his insights to a critique of marriage as an institution. Indeed, neither Marx nor Engels ever questioned heterosexual monogamy. Blaming capitalism for secretly encouraging licentiousness, they argued that natural moral principles would finally be fulfilled in the socialist future, when "monogamy, instead of declining, finally becomes a reality–for the men as well."[34] Marx and Engels were convinced that once society was liberated from the deformities of class oppression, a natural, heterosexual, monogamous love would finally flourish.

It was also in *The Origin of the Family* that Engels set forth two brief remarks on the subject of same-sex practices–the only explicit treatments of the subject in the entire œuvre of Marx and Engels published during their lifetimes. Characterizing Athenian family life during classical antiquity, Engels noted that "the men . . . sank into the perversion [*Widerwärtigkeit*] of boy-love, degrading both themselves and their gods by the myth of Ganymede."[35] These repellent practices were by no means limited to the ancient Greeks, Engels continued, for centuries later the migrating Germanic barbarians succumbed to "moral degeneration" when some of the Goth tribesmen adopted "serious unnatural vices."[36] In their private correspondence, however, Marx and Engels employed far more jocular and smutty language when commenting on homosexual contemporaries (see the contribution by Hubert Kennedy).[37]

The sexual-political stance staked out by Marx and Engels was perpetuated and elaborated by leaders of the Second International in Germany and Austria. The lack of a coherent view on sexuality among the Social Democrats arose in part because they were forced into the defensive by their political opponents, especially the Christian Socialists in Austria, who blamed working-class women for prostitution and attacked the Social Democrats (and especially women party members) for allegedly promoting free love. The Social Democrats reacted by stressing their own morality, and some of them argued that they were morally superior to the bourgeoisie as well as the Christian Socialists. The female editor of a Social Democratic newspaper for working women wrote in 1896: "We want a different, a better morality than the prevailing one protected by the district attorney. We are working for marriage and morality that is pure in the truest sense of the word."[38]

In the eyes of such Social Democrats as August Bebel, Karl Kautsky, and Eduard Bernstein, the entire "sexual question" came about because young men could not afford to marry early and support a family. Capitalism not only caused economic exploitation and social inequality, it also facilitated immorality and sexual exploitation of working-class women by bourgeois men. Prostitution was a typical vice of class society, while marriage based on love was the precondition for the healthy sexual ethics of socialist society. The Social Democrats did attack prevailing sexual mores and Christian asceticism, but their critique remained highly ambivalent, for they never questioned either monogamous marriage or the family as such.[39] Like Marx and Engels, the Social Democrats of the Second International reproached bourgeois males for hypocritically violating their own moral principles and upholding a double standard for men and women; the solution was not to open up for women the same sexual opportunities available to men, but to advocate monogamy for everyone. In doing so, they actually endorsed the nineteenth-century ideal of bourgeois respectability.

Apart from broadening access to early marriage, Social Democratic writers on sexuality proposed moderation and abstinence as solutions for the "sexual question."[40] Sexual energy was to be sublimated and channelled into healthy outdoors activities, such as sports and hiking. They echoed contemporary medical opinion by regarding masturbation as harmful and something to be avoided.

Eduard Bernstein, for example, was convinced that self-abuse would result in homosexuality and sadomasochism.[41] Some Social Democratic leaders asserted that masturbation was an upper-class phenomenon and rare among the working class.[42]

Social Democratic attitudes toward contraception were at best ambivalent. In Germany, for example, Ferdinand Lassalle criticized neo-Malthusianism as a typically capitalist solution for overpopulation, and his standpoint was shared by many other leaders of the Second International. According to Lassalle, the problem was not so much population growth as the unequal distribution of goods between rich and poor. The adoption of contraceptive techniques by proletarians could easily lead them to a resigned acceptance of the capitalist system. And in Austria, Otto Bauer actually advocated a massive population increase precisely in the working class to gain more voters for the left.[43] Moreover, such Social Democrats as Lassalle, Bebel, and Wilhelm Liebknecht opposed contraception because it would lead, like masturbation, to "unproductive" sexuality. Those few Social Democrats who joined Karl Kautsky in supporting birth control simultaneously warned that it could be misused to promote licentiousness. In France as well, many socialists regarded neo-Malthusianism as a counterrevolutionary movement. They were suspicious of population planning not just because they associated contraception with the corrupt and frivolous aristocracy and haute bourgeoisie, but even more because they feared that its acceptance would substitute individual self-help for genuine social reform. For socialists, the question was not whether individuals should have a right to contraception, but whether birth control resulted in a harmful loss of self-discipline and social responsibility.[44]

The single work dealing with sexuality most widely read by rank-and-file members of the SPD was not Engels's *The Origin of the Family* but August Bebel's *Woman under Socialism* (1879). Bebel's remarks on same-sex practices went considerably beyond the scanty information offered by Engels by bringing the vice of classical antiquity into the present:

> Yet another evil, frequently met, must also be shortly touched upon. Excessive sexual indulgence is infinitely more harmful than too little. A body, misused by excess, will go to pieces, even without venereal disease. . . . But temperance seems

difficult to youth. Hence the large number of 'young old men,' in the higher walks of life especially. The number of young and old *roués* is enormous, and they require special irritants, excess having deadened and surfeited them. Many, accordingly, lapse into the unnatural practices of Greek days. This crime against nature is today much more general than most of us dream of: upon that subject the secret archives of many a police bureau could publish frightful information. But not among men only, among women also have the unnatural practices of old Greece come up again with force. Lesbian love, or Sapphism, is said to be quite general among married women in Paris; according to Taxil, it is enormously in practice among the prominent ladies of that city. In Berlin, one-fourth of the prostitutes are said to practice "tribady"; but also in the circles of our leading dames there are not wanting disciples of Sappho.[45]

Bebel's standpoint is notable for attributing same-sex practices solely to sexual excess as well as describing it an upper-class, metropolitan, and foreign vice.

It is clear that the nineteenth-century socialists associated with the Second International failed to integrate sexuality into their social and political philosophies in any coherent way. In Marxist theory, all issues concerning the family and sexuality were subsumed within the "superstructure" that rested upon a given society's economic "basis," and this is where Marxists have focused their attention.[46] This corresponded to a similar shortcoming of liberal ideology, and both liberalism and Marxism (including its revisionist variant in Social Democracy) implicitly made the same differentiation between the public/private and political/personal spheres. Socialism, however, and especially Marxism differed from liberalism by virtue of prioritizing the public and the political. Explicitly rejecting the radical individualism of their contemporary, Max Stirner, Marx and Engels held that the ideal of harmony between humankind and nature as well as among people required a total socialization of the individual.

Wherever Marxists have come to power in the twentieth century, the individual has had little value outside collective demands, and the personal has been rigorously subordinated to collectivist politics, opening the door to state intrusion. The private sphere has enjoyed far less protection under socialist regimes than under liberal ones, and in many instances the very notion of a protected private sphere was simply abandoned as soon as Communist parties came to power. Overall, socialist regimes have remained true to the credo first enunciated by Marx and Engels: heterosexual monogamy would prevail in the workers' state, and homosexuality would simply disappear.

ENLIGHTENMENT, NATURE, AND SCIENCE

The difficulty of integrating sexuality within the political theories of both liberalism and socialism can be traced back to Enlightenment thought. The *philosophes* had often characterized the Christian view of sin and virtue as "artificial" and sought to replace it with a new, secular notion. They attempted to locate morality within nature rather than in some spiritual realm, for they were convinced that unspoiled human nature offered the foundation for both moral behavior and harmonious relations between the individual and society. Sexuality played an important role in the development of the life sciences as well as in some influential social and political theories, such as that of Jean-Jacques Rousseau.[47] Taken as a "natural" phenomenon, however, sexuality was open to two distinct moral meanings. To the extent that it contributed to procreation and was connected to harmonious heterosexual relations and maternity, it was applauded; but if sexuality was premature, illicit, excessive, or motivated by sheer lust, it was considered socially subversive.[48]

Enlightenment thought on sexuality connected it to divergent interpretations of human nature and was thus ambivalent. Sexuality outside of the private sphere of heterosexual intimacy was regarded as part of "untamed" nature that challenged normative and optimistic readings of nature as a positive source of social order and virtue. Rousseau, for instance, both celebrated and condemned sexuality, while Donatien Alphonse François de Sade, Paul Henri Thiry d'Holbach, Pierre Choderlos de Laclos, and others argued that natural drives were ethically neutral or even blindly amoral and thus could not provide a foundation on which to build society. They shared a new sense of nature as profoundly riven by inner tensions, contradictions, and disruptive forces.[49] Above all, sexuality undermined the optimistic idea of moral nature, and as such it could not be integrated in schemes that sought to improve society by reason.

Scientific socialism remained deeply committed to the Enlightenment belief in progress. Marxists and Social Democrats attacked religious tradition and social customs in the name of reason and (positivistic) science. They presumed that the rationalization of human society was rapidly rendering the force of individual differences based on sex or irrational desires irrelevant. Convinced that harmony between the individual and society would come about by a radical transformation of society or social engineering, socialist intellectuals devoted scant attention to those areas of human experience that were contradictory or difficult to predict and control by reason. This outlook led many of them to regard sexuality not as a positive force in life but on the contrary as a basically irrational, unproductive, and egoistic drive that posed a potential risk to social harmony and therefore had to be brought under rational control.

The philosophy of Marx and Engels certainly was innovative because it was one of the first "sociological" theories. They held that humankind, far from having a fixed nature, is instead determined by the natural as well as the social environment; people form themselves in the process of transforming nature by work. This breakthrough stopped short, however, when Marx neglected to historicize sexuality, which he regarded as part of nature rather than of culture. Implicitly or explicitly elevating nature to a standard by which to judge sexual behavior, scientific socialists–like liberals– relied on biological notions of sexuality. Many Social Democrats were confident that science, medicine, education, and social hygiene would shape a healthy sexuality capable of being integrated into society and fulfilling collective needs. "Sexuality became an issue for the proletariat, because filth was to be turned into cleanliness, disease into health, degeneration into integration."[50] Adopting medical views current at that time, scientific socialists found the unleashing of passion abhorrent; in the interest of a rational ordering of sexual life, they relied on hygienist solutions and emphasized the beneficial effects of education, hard work, self-mastery, sublimation, and marriage. The idea of social responsibility, the interests and solidarity of the social body, and scientific social reconstruction took precedence over individual liberties. Ultimately, many socialists eagerly adopted the precepts of eugenics, which seemed to hold out the promise of rational mastery of the natural laws of evolution by linking genetics, demographics, and medicine.[51]

Because eugenics has come to be associated with the Nazi racial state, it is easy to lose sight of the fact that "racial hygiene" was long embraced far more ardently by the left than the right. From the fin de siècle onward, socialists and progressives–including Social Democrats, the Fabians, and even the women's movement–regarded it as a scientific and even humanitarian method for improving society. Among its more prominent leftist advocates over the ensuing decades were Karl Pearson, Beatrice and Sidney Webb, George Bernard Shaw, Havelock Ellis, Eden and Cedar Paul, H. G. Laski, Graham Wallas, H. G. Wells, Julian Huxley, Joseph Needham, C. P. Snow, Magnus Hirschfeld, and Emma Goldman. Although socialists regarded class distinctions as artificial and propounded equality among the classes, they nonetheless regarded differences among individuals within a particular class as an important natural given. Since the collective took precedence over the individual, they had no scruples about expanding state intervention into the reproductive and family sphere. To be sure, socialists held that it would be possible to distinguish between the effects of heredity and environment only in a country without class distinctions, and thus the Soviet Union would eventually be accorded the status of the best laboratory for a socially responsible eugenic program.

Socialists' endorsement of eugenics was fundamentally predicated on their acceptance of the Darwinian concept of evolution, which gained an increasingly broad following among Social Democrats and liberals from the 1870s onward–against embittered opposition from Christians and conservatives, who clung to the notion of creationism.[52] Far from seeming purely scientific and hence ethically neutral, the evolutionary hypothesis was fraught with moral and political implications.[53] For contemporaries, the main political problem with Darwinism was how to understand the axiom of the struggle for existence. Liberals saw it primarily as a mirror of competition within the capitalist marketplace and went on to develop the doctrine of Social Darwinism.[54] For scientific socialists, Darwinism was attractive for a different reason: it held out the prospect of ineluctable development toward a higher stage of evolution, which they interpreted as the emergence of socialism.[55] Marx himself may have criticized Darwin as a bourgeois thinker, but the paradigmatic breakthrough of Darwinism was so widely recognized that Engels sought to link Marx with it posthumously. In his eulogy for Marx in 1883, Engels stated: "Just as Darwin developed the law of the development of organic nature, so Marx discovered the developmental law of human history."[56] This understanding accelerated the emergence of revisionist Social Democracy, supplanting the perspective of Marx himself with evolutionary gradualism, revolution with reform.[57] With the goal not of class struggle but of elevating the working class morally and intellectually, the revisionists advocated proletarian hygiene, moderation, and self-control.

With its axioms of sexual selection and natural variation, Darwinism contributed importantly to the emergence of the discipline of sexology, or *Sexualwissenschaft*–a term first used in 1906, but based upon psychiatric and forensic studies going back to the 1850s; Darwinism became crucial in its development starting in the 1860s.[58] Prior to this time, medicine had taken the reproductive pairing of male and female to be the unquestioned norm and telos of sexual behavior, while same-sex practices were taken to be a manifestation of degeneracy resulting from poor social and moral conditions. Early sexology was primarily concerned with labelling deviant behaviors and bracketing them as perversions, and several doctors clung to Bénédict Auguste Morel's studies of degeneration (1857) and tried uneasily to integrate it with Darwinism. They argued that while (hetero)sexuality was a "natural" and healthy component of the evolutionary process, degeneracy was not per se "unnatural," for nature, by moving backwards in a sort of process of devolution, was capable of producing monsters; and indeed, the Austrian psychiatrist Richard von Krafft-Ebing characterized homosexuals as "nature's stepchildren."[59] As signalled by the European-wide reception of Max Nordau's *Degeneration* (1892), this concern became something of an obsession affecting many nations by the late nineteenth century.[60]

While various doctors tried to use Darwinism to prove that heterosexuality was a natural norm for higher forms of life and that homosexuality was necessarily degenerate, others suspected that

Darwinism undermined the conventional differentiation between male and female.[61] As early as 1868, Karl Heinrich Ulrichs, who introduced the notion of male homosexuality as being a sort of psychological intermediacy ("a female soul in a male body"), referred to Darwin–albeit rather fleetingly–to argue that natural species "mesh and merge imperceptibly." He invoked Darwinism to state that the existence of homosexuality itself throughout the plant and animal kingdoms was tantamount to a "law of nature."[62] Inspired by Ulrichs's pioneering work and synthesizing the work of Morel and Darwin, Richard von Krafft-Ebing began to argue as early as 1877–nine years before the first publication of his classic *Psychopathia sexualis*–that homosexuality is a kind of biological intermediacy between male and female and properly belongs within the realm of nature as a "twist of fate," typically inborn and caused by hereditary factors. Over the course of the 1880s, Krafft-Ebing increasingly challenged the criminalization and prosecution of homosexuals, and by the 1890s he directly supported the repeal of § 175, the German anti-sodomy statute.

The world's first homosexual emancipation organization, the Scientific-Humanitarian Committee (Wissenschaftlich-humanitäres Komitee) founded in 1897 by the physician Magnus Hirschfeld, began its work by circulating a petition for the repeal of § 175, and Krafft-Ebing was one of its first signatories. Hirschfeld was, if anything, even more profoundly indebted to Darwinian notions of evolution and gradualism than his predecessors.[63] Whereas Darwin had envisioned a gradual transformation of life forms over time, Hirschfeld applied this notion synchronically rather than diachronically, arguing that there was a seamless continuum of human sexual types ranging between fully male and fully female. Hirschfeld contested the categorical correlation of gender roles with sexual dimorphism by proposing a range of male-to-female "intermediacy" that remained within the domain of natural variation, anomalous yet nonpathological. He charted a spectrum of intermediacy comprising (but not limited to) hermaphroditism, androgyny, homosexuality, and transvestism.

From 1897 until Hitler's accession to power in 1933, Germany differed from all other countries by virtue of its homosexual emancipation movement, and socialist discussions of homosexuality were more frequent and outspoken here than anywhere else. Germany attached exceptional prestige to science, which enjoyed the special patronage of the government; as a result, striking advances were made in the natural and social sciences, and this country was the world center for the production of knowledge in the domain of sexuality, including medical as well as non-medical theories. Hirschfeld's arguments for the repeal of § 175 were based first and foremost on scientific knowledge, and although he appealed to all political parties to heed his message, the most positive response came precisely from the Social Democrats. Joining Krafft-Ebing among the first signatories of Hirschfeld's petition was August Bebel, the parliamentary leader of the Social Democracy, and he was the first politician to speak in favor of repealing § 175 in an 1898 Reichstag speech.

In the second half of the nineteenth century, professional medicine's challenge to the authority of the church advanced a paradigm shift in the understanding of homosexuality, transferring it from the realm of virtue and sin to the domain of health and illness. Called upon to deliver expert testimony in court, physicians increasingly held that certain categories of defendants should be sent to clinics rather than to prisons. In Germany, both the intellectual elite and the burgeoning socialist movement saw themselves as the cutting edge of social and political progress. There was a particular harmony between the homosexual emancipation movement and the Social Democrats, for both subscribed to the Enlightenment ideal of using scientific knowledge to improve society. While the Social Democracy appropriated for itself the Baconian motto "Knowledge is power" ("*Wissen ist Macht*"), Hirschfeld's personal motto was "Per scientiam ad justitiam" ("Through knowledge to justice"). His biologistic understanding of homosexuality was endorsed by socialists (and later Communists) beyond Germany's borders: commenting on the Bolshevik repeal of the tsarist anti-sodomy law, the *Great Soviet Encyclopedia* of 1929 explicitly cited Hirschfeld's research.[64]

Yet it must be noted that support for the repeal of § 175 was by no means universal in the socialist movement, and some Social Democratic Reichstag delegates distanced themselves firmly from Bebel. Moreover, the adoption of a biologistic understanding of homosexuality proved to be a mixed blessing: most socialists vacillated between seeing homosexuality as a natural phenomenon on the one hand and a pathological form of degeneracy on the other. When the Social Democrats did offer support, their allegiance to the principle of liberty, equality, and fraternity for all (and thus also for homosexuals) was mingled with the uneasy feeling that condoning homosexual behavior might lead to its increase. Thus some socialist politicians defended the right to be homosexual, but not the right to engage in homosexual conduct.

When homosexuality was dealt with by medical science at the turn of the century, many doctors argued that culture could actually promote such tendencies in individuals who were by no means homosexual by birth. In undisturbed nature, simple instinct directed all creatures toward procreation, but civilization introduced an element that often distorted the natural course of libidinal development. The child was sexually undifferentiated, and culture could mold its instincts to take any direction or form. In culture, so-called natural instincts often were twisted. Therefore, such doctors as Max Dessoir, Albert Moll, and Emil Kraepelin stressed that it was necessary to foster heterosexual relations in human society.[65] Heterosexuality and procreation had to be incited and encouraged, these doctors argued; otherwise the birth rate would fall–an issue that stirred increasing alarm throughout Western Europe in the years around World War I.[66]

The notion that homosexuality could be either inborn or acquired also contributed to the ambivalence toward the homosexual emancipation movement felt by socialists. It left them hoping that in the socialist state of the future, heterosexual relations would prevail because the incidence of inborn homosexuality would turn out to be as low as most scientists assumed (Hirschfeld spoke of a fixed minority of approximately 2.2% in all times and places),[67] and moreover even the born homosexual could perhaps be dissuaded from engaging in homosexual conduct. Acquired or culturally mediated homosexual behavior was unquestionably to be prevented. The legal situation in the Soviet Union during the 1920s reflected this outlook: homosexual acts in general were decriminalized, but sanctions were invoked where such practices abounded due to social and cultural circumstances, as in the Muslim parts of the country.[68] According to

Lenin, the very notion of sexual emancipation was typical of capitalist societies and a symptom of bourgeois degeneracy.[69] Above all, the class struggle required the suppression of individualistic sexual desires and self-sacrifice in the interests of the collective.

Those openly gay Russians who initially sided with the Bolshevik Revolution of 1917 because of its repeal of the tsarist antisodomy statute were to be disappointed, for the Communist Party of the Soviet Union became increasingly puritanical and homophobic under Stalin and finally promulgated a new anti-sodomy statute in 1934, closing a fifteen-year span in which it had been possible to cherish the hope of social and cultural advances (see the contribution by Laura Engelstein). Stalinist sexual politics, as propagated internationally through the Comintern, and Hitler's accession to power in 1933 signalled the eradication of the homosexual emancipation movement in Germany, the only country where it had really flourished; and the 1930s marked an epochal setback for homosexual rights. In a Europe under the sway of fascism and Stalinism, homosexual emancipation was ruthlessly removed from all political agendas. In Spain, even the anarchist movement took recourse to the most odious homophobic stereotypes (see the contribution by Richard Cleminson).

While their commitment to Darwinism may have led socialists to tilt toward the notion of inborn rather than acquired homosexuality up to World War I, the theories of Sigmund Freud gained growing influence in socialist discussions during the 1920s and 1930s.[70] Stressing psychological factors in human sexuality and positing the notion of the polymorphous perversity of infants, Freud explicitly rejected Hirschfeld's notion of sexual intermediacy, which held that each individual had a genetically fixed sexual disposition from the moment of conception. On the contrary, Freud argued, it was the successful or unsuccessful resolution of a universal Oedipus complex that determined whether an individual's fundamental bisexuality would be channelled into heterosexuality or homosexuality. The Communist psychoanalyst Wilhelm Reich, founder of Freudo-Marxism, sociologized but simultaneously simplified Freud's theory by arguing that oppressive conditions under patriarchal capitalism stifled and deformed the libido, thereby actually inducing homosexuality. Since Comintern doctrine defined fascism as capitalism in its most extreme and openly terroristic form, Reich was predisposed to diagnose Nazi society as rife with homosexuality tinged with sadism. Harkening back to Marx and Engels, he was convinced that homosexuality would automatically disappear under communism and that healthy heterosexuality would be practiced by everyone (see the contribution by Harry Oosterhuis).

This pattern of thought, resonant throughout the theory and practice of exiled and underground antifascists during the Nazi era, reached perhaps its greatest degree of refinement in the "Critical Theory" of the Frankfurt School (see the contribution by Randall Halle). As Stalinism asserted its authority throughout the Comintern, however, Freudo-Marxism fell increasingly into disfavor, and socialist discussions in the post-World War II era often reverted to biological notions of homosexuality, as shown by the endocrinological research of Günter Dörner in the German Democratic Republic (see the contribution by Denis Sweet).[71] On the other hand, a number of socialist and Communist regimes continued after 1945 to entertain the notion of homosexuality as a social form of "bourgeois decadence" fundamentally foreign to "really existing socialism" (see the contribution by David Thorstad), which somewhat paradoxically represents a reversion to the attenuated Freudianism of Reich's theories. In this way the notion of an underlying unspoiled (heterosexual) proletarian nature could more or less be saved.

Reich's writings enjoyed something of a renaissance during the sexual revolution of the 1960s and were even embraced by gay liberationists, although Reich had always been anything but supportive of homosexual emancipation. His legacy and that of the Frankfurt School were still quite evident in the writings of Reimut Reiche, a German leftist who wrote on sexual liberation in the late 1960s.[72] At this time, Herbert Marcuse was one of the few "classic" leftist thinkers who took a more positive view of homosexuality. Marcuse was more or less exceptional because he associated liberated sexuality with play and art. Celebrating "polymorphous sexuality" as a realm of release from labor, he valorized sexual pleasure as an alternative to the productivist ethos of both capitalism and communism.[73] Ultimately, however, the sexual revolution's cooptation by consumerism made even Marcuse increasingly skeptical about the prospects for sexual liberation under capitalism.[74]

MORAL PURITY

In the 1830s, at the zenith of Fourier's utopian phalanstères, socialism was radical in its sexual politics. But towards the mid-century, scientific socialism became more puritanical, accompanying the process of embourgeoisement as documented in Marx and Engels's attacks on prostitution and their ideology of monogamy for both women and men.[75] Social Democrats of the Second International, convinced that they needed to attain respectability in order to achieve their goals, became increasingly rigid on moral issues. Any hint of unconventionalism in the sexual domain was abhorrent to them, as it provided grist for the mills of their opponents. In Germany, this process was stimulated by the Anti-Socialist Laws promulgated in 1878, but perhaps even more so by their repeal in 1890. Bismarck's acceptance of forward-looking social security and health insurance legislation simultaneously integrated the proletariat more closely within the state and accelerated the shift from revolutionism to reformism within the Second International. But the Social Democratic Party itself also contributed to proletarian embourgeoisement by establishing Workers Education Associations in cities throughout Germany, where laborers were taught to admire and emulate the achievements of middle-class culture.[76] By the turn of the century, the socialists had become staunch supporters of marriage and monogamy as part of their mission of civilizing the proletariat.

From the perspective of the educated public, homosexuality had long been linked with aristocratic decadence, for example, with the late Roman Empire or France's ancien régime. At the fin de siècle, this stereotype was heightened by the often homoerotic perversity of the neo-romantic and decadent movements in European literary culture.[77] This literary current had tremendous appeal for homosexual writers and readers alike, for it was a form of thinly veiled protest against the norms of bourgeois respectability.[78] Among the most prominent adepts of *l'art pour l'art* were Paul Verlaine and Arthur Rimbaud in France, Oscar Wilde in England, Louis Couperus in the Netherlands, and Stefan George in Germany. Moreover, some leaders of the homosexual emancipation movement, such as Adolf Brand and Kurt Hiller, favored an "aristocracy of the spirit" over any purely democratic system, in part because they were convinced that the hoi polloi (and socialist voters) would never be in favor of advancing the interests of homosexuals.

Individualism and aestheticism, favored by many homoerotic artists, were loathed by most socialists and left-wing artists. Even though Wilde wrote an essay in favor of socialism, he became the prime example of the stereotyped image of the decadent, effeminate aesthete corrupting working-class boys.[79] The contemporary literary movement most frequently embraced by the socialist left, Naturalism, proved incapable of treating homosexuality despite its stunning frankness in the depiction of social and sexual misery, including alcoholism, prostitution, venereal disease, and incest. The failure of Naturalist writers to deal with homosexuality arose in part from its status as the unspeakable, but also because they were committed to portraying proletarians as victims of oppressive social conditions beyond their control. Later as well, during the 1920s, those artistic groups that came nearest to the socialist left, such as the French surrealists under André Breton, were strongly homophobic–even though it was the surrealists who rediscovered the Marquis de Sade, the homosexual without remorse, and the leading surrealist novelist, René Crevel, was openly gay.[80] In the late 1920s and 1930s, the proletarian writers' movement that hailed the achievements of the Soviet Union was also relentlessly heterosexist in orientation.[81] This turn toward homophobia in the proletarian writers' movements reflected a growing conviction that the supposed effeminacy of homosexual men was the very antipode of the healthy manliness of working-class males and symptomatic of both bourgeois decay and economic collapse. As the Great Depression intensified political antagonisms, both the Communist insurrectionists on the left and the "revolutionary" National Socialists on the right increasingly valorized militant manliness, with a concomitant emphasis on the alleged weakness, effeminacy, and political unreliability of homosexuals.[82]

The cornerstone of Hirschfeld's theory of inborn homosexuality, the notion of sexual intermediacy, challenged the notion of a rigid male-female dichotomy. While a certain number of homosexual men no doubt presented the very signs of effeminacy expected by Hirschfeld (and regarded as degenerate by the socialists), the "third-sex" model was always controversial even within the homosexual emancipation movement itself. Beginning in 1903, a group of German homosexuals organized in Adolf Brand's Community of the Special (Gemeinschaft der Eigenen) firmly rejected Hirschfeld's biologism and instead advanced social concepts of male bonding and pedagogical eros, stressing that homosexuality was inherently masculine. This was a politically eclectic group, comprising extreme nationalist right-wingers as well as Nietzschean and Stirnerian anarchists.[83] The masculinist, bisexual, and pedophile ideals of this group were also endorsed by such important anarchists as Erich Mühsam and Johannes Holzmann (see the contribution by Walter Fähnders). This group continued its attacks on Hirschfeld through the 1920s, and a similar revulsion for effeminacy was now also voiced by Friedrich Radszuweit, the leader of a third homosexual emancipation organization, the League for Human Rights (Bund für Menschenrecht), as well as by André Gide in his *Corydon* (1911; rev. ed. 1920). Moreover, Hirschfeld's "third sex" flew in the face of the new manly ideal held up by left- and right-wing parties alike. Although the vigorous masculinity of both the Communists and the Nazis may have been attractive to gay men and may even have allured many of them to vote for the Nazis (see the contribution by Manfred Herzer), it was by definition an ideal that excluded and indeed repressed homosexuality.

Rather than attacking bourgeois respectability and the ideal of masculinity, socialism supported them. There was a gap between the leaders of the left-wing formations and their followers, for the leaders tended to support sanitary movements and hygiene policies to "civilize" the proletariat. This socialist emphasis on respectability certainly bolstered the homophobia that already existed within the working classes and may even have created prejudices where none existed previously. The process of embourgeoisement gradually transformed an earlier culture of proletarian everyday life in which men had been "available."[84] There is some evidence to suggest that proletarian culture was less puritanical before socialist ideology was inculcated among workers by their leaders. Before the rise of medical theories of homosexuality, masculinity and femininity had been a matter of active versus passive sex roles. At least among certain nationalities and ethnic groups, working-class men were willing to engage in homosexual practices as long they penetrated their male sex partners—and all the more so when they found heterosexual sex difficult or expensive to obtain. But as sexology erased the line between active and passive acts, all same-sex practices became stigmatized as a sign of effeminacy; working-class men who might earlier have been engaged in homosexual practices on their own terms were now dishonored even if they took the active role. The ideal of masculinity promoted by socialist leaders was heteronormative, and it was contrasted to homosexuality. Considered effeminate and bourgeois, visible homosexuals were far removed from the socialist ideal of manhood. They even endangered it to the extent that they tried to seduce working-class men and were attracted by rugged masculinity, which was certainly a fascinosum for many bourgeois homosexual men such as Edward Carpenter, who were drawn to socialism because they were charmed by the rough "working-class beast."

Some socialist leaders nominally supported the goals of the homosexual emancipation movement, but in the absence of a worked-out theory of sexuality it was all too easy for them to relapse into "othering" discourse. Western Europe has a venerable tradition of attributing sexual depravity to the other–be it across national boundaries (the "French," "German," "English," "Italian" vice), confessional divides (the satanic cults of medieval heretics and Renaissance witches, Martin Luther's tirades against the sodomitical Vatican), or hemispheres (nineteenth-century Europeans saw the Orient as "a living tableau of queerness" that seemed to exude "perverse morality" and "dangerous sex").[85] In addition, the educated bourgeoisie associated homosexuality with social and political decline resulting from aristocratic vice, as recounted in Edward Gibbon's *Decline and Fall of the Roman Empire* (1776-83). In this vein, the socialist approach was to ascribe such widespread notions as degeneracy and decadence to their major opponents–the aristocracy, the clergy, and the capitalist class. Whenever a scandal revealed the homosexuality of members of the upper classes, the socialist press would intervene to denounce their corrupt morals and to trumpet the threat they posed to society, contrasting this with the healthy heterosexual life of the working class that predestined it to assume leadership. In their treatment of scandals involving sexual exploitation, prostitution, and pederasty, socialists certainly expressed their underlying anxieties about sexuality in general.

There has been a multitude of homosexual scandals over the past decades, and the socialist press has often played a leading role in publicizing them, certainly the more spectacular ones.[86] When socialist leaders or activists were involved–Johann Baptist von Schweitzer (1862) in Germany, for example, or Jacob Israël de Haan (1904) in the Netherlands–they felt the full force of their comrades' contempt (see the contributions by Hubert Kennedy and Gert Hekma). But in contrast to such cases, which often led to party purges, the socialists fanned the flames of scandals involving members of the aristocracy or the haute bourgeoisie in order to harden working-class indignation. Given the socialists' lip-service to homosexual emancipation, this was frequently an opportunistic ploy to set off the homosexual "oppressors" from the "authentic" victims, workers. The most spectacular of these scandals occurred in Germany and concerned Alfred Krupp (1902), the "cannon king" who consorted with Italian youths on the isle of Capri; Philipp zu Eulenburg (1907-09), a diplomat and close friend of the kaiser; Fritz Haarmann (1924), a serial murderer linked to the SPD-governed police; and Ernst Röhm (1931-32), the head of the Nazi paramilitary SA organization.

The Röhm affair is dealt with by two contributors to this volume who take contrary standpoints. Manfred Herzer maintains that the German left was entirely justified in reporting on the turmoil over Röhm's homosexuality within the ranks of the Nazi Party and that the Communists never compromised their pledge to support homosexual emancipation. Harry Oosterhuis, on the other hand, argues that the Social Democrats and Communists knowingly exploited widespread homophobic prejudice in order to discredit their political opponent, thus revealing a long-standing ambivalence that ultimately led them to excoriate homosexuality as a typically National Socialist vice throughout the years of the antifascist struggle.

It is noteworthy that during the years of Hitler's rise to absolute power, both the left and the right used homosexuality as a stereotype to tar their opponents. A particularly vivid instance of this left-right convergence came in 1933 with the case of Marinus van der Lubbe, who was pronounced guilty of setting fire to the Reichstag; he was denounced both by the Nazis as a left-wing arsonist and by the communists as a homosexual anarchist (see the contribution by Harry Oosterhuis). At the very time when the Nazis declared homosexuality a form of "sexual bolshevism" and, in 1934, executed Ernst Röhm, Maxim Gorky in the Soviet Union declared that wiping out homosexuality would lead to the end of fascism.[87] Stalinist homophobia caused an international panoply of left-wing writers such as W. H. Auden, Christopher Isherwood, Klaus Mann (see the contribution by Harry Oosterhuis), André Gide, and Jef Last (see the contribution by Patrick Pollard) to repudiate Soviet policy, and many of them were then castigated as homosexual cowards and traitors by their former comrades.

We have thus returned to our starting point, the perpetuation of fascist and antifascist homophobia in the post-World War II setting. With the breakup of the anti-Hitler alliance and the demarcation of a new adversarial relationship by the Iron Curtain, the Western and Eastern powers alike underscored their heteronormativity by linking the other with homosexuality. During the Cold War era, Guy Burgess's 1951 defection to the Soviet Union was exploited to heighten Western fears of a shadowy Homintern, and the attempted defection of Günter Liftin, the first person slain at the Berlin Wall in 1961, was denounced in the East German press as the desperate act of a male prostitute cut off from his customers in the Western sector.[88] All decent heterosexuals, it was implied, would be entirely content to remain in the workers' state.

CONCLUSION

For almost a full century now, the revolutionary prospect of socialism has fuelled opening forays first of the homosexual emancipation and later of the gay liberation movements, both in Europe and in North America. It inspired Edward Carpenter and Magnus Hirschfeld at the turn of the century; André Gide and Richard Linsert in the post-World War I years; Harry Hay and Jim Kepner in the post-World War II era; and the British and American Gay Liberation Front, the Italian Fuori!, the French FHAR, the German "Rotzschwule," and the Dutch Red Faggots following the Stonewall rebellion.[89] While the official socialist parties of Northwestern Europe may have made only limited contributions to homosexual emancipation, they certainly have a better record than conservative and Christian parties and even the liberals, who have consistently, if contradictorily, underlined the freedom of private life. Even so, parties across the entire political spectrum have gradually come to endorse at least some of the movement's goals. As it has advanced, the gay movement has changed as well, and it now finds itself pulled in divergent directions. Gay leftists who still subscribe to the ideals expressed in Marxist and utopian socialist writings now find themselves at demonstrations shoulder-to-shoulder with members of ACT UP and Queer Nation, to say nothing of gay conservatives and gay Christians.[90] The successes achieved by the contemporary gay movement despite or precisely because of its diversity support Foucault's argument that "there is no single locus of great Refusal, no soul of revolt, source of all rebellions, or pure law of the revolutionary. Instead there is a plurality of resistances, each of them a special case. . . ."[91]

At the close of the twentieth century, the welfare state has reached its apogee in Northwestern Europe. As blue-collar workers historically committed to class struggle have become relatively well-to-do and minoritarian, socialist parties have increasingly lost their traditional base of support and been forced into the defensive. Depending only on the socialists would mean relying on an ineffectual partner, for nowhere are they in a stable position of power. Long before the collapse of "really existing socialism" in Eastern Europe and the former Soviet Union, gay and lesbian movements began developing their own autonomous politics independent of parties. They moved in this direction in part because the coalition with leftism so frequently led to disappointment, particularly when gays and lesbians working within socialist parties were called upon to subordinate or abandon their own goals in favor of party platforms. In other cases the gay-left coalition failed to yield results because a single-minded reliance on one party placed limits on lobbying other parties and entering compromises.

We have reached a time when inherited ideologies are no longer capable of laying claim to the undivided loyalty of the gay movement, if indeed they ever were. As it has developed autonomous theories and practices, the gay movement's choice of coalition partners has increasingly come to be based on pragmatism and success in advancing the gay agenda. Indeed, the roles of the gay movement and political parties have undergone a notable switch in recent years, with parties currying the support of the gay movement rather than vice versa. This signals a shift from the desire for politics to a politics of desire, going far beyond traditional socialist ideologies.

NOTES

1. For an international overview of the homophile movement in the mid-1950s, see Marvin Cutler (i.e., W. Dorr Legg), ed., *Homosexuals Today: A Handbook of Organizations and Publications* (Los Angeles: Publication Division of One, Inc., 1956).

2. On Mattachine's radical beginnings, see John D'Emilio, *Sexual Politics, Sexual Communities: The Making of a Homosexual Minority in the United States, 1940-1970* (Chicago: University of Chicago Press, 1983), pp. 57-74. On the leftist origins of the COC, see Hans Warmerdam and Pieter Koenders, *Cultuur en ontspanning: Het COC 1946-1966* (Utrecht: NVIH, COC & Interfacultaire Werkgroep Homostudies, Rijksuniversiteit Utrecht, 1987), p. 58. Among the founders of Arcadie, André Baudry was a moderate while Jacques de Ricaumont and Roger Peyrefitte were conservatives. See Jacques Girard, *Le mouvement homosexuel en France 1945-1980* (Paris: Syros, 1981), pp. 39-73, especially pp. 56 and 71.

3. For an interesting collection of memoirs and other texts documenting the subjective sense of continuity during the mid-century decades, see *Keine Zeit für gute Freunde: Homosexuelle in Deutschland 1933-1969*, ed. Joachim S. Hohmann (Berlin: Foerster, 1982).

4. See Robert G. Moeller, "The Homosexual Man Is a 'Man,' the Homosexual Woman is a 'Woman': Sex, Society, and the Law in Postwar West Germany," *Journal of the History of Sexuality* 4 (1993-94): 395-429. The Federal Constitutional Court's 1957 ruling was reaffirmed by the entire West German Bundestag in 1986; see ibid., p. 427. See also Michael Sartorius and Christian Schulz, *Paragraph 175. (abgewickelt) / Wider Gutmachung* (Hamburg: MännerschwarmSkript, 1994).

5. On the dismissal of the economist Hein Vos, see Rob Tielman, *Homoseksualiteit in Nederland: Studie van een emancipatiebeweging* (Amsterdam and Meppel: Boom, 1982), pp. 162-63.

6. On Turing, see Andrew Hodges, *Alan Turing: The Enigma* (New York: Simon and Schuster, 1985), pp. 456-527.

7. On McCarthyism and homosexuality, see John D'Emilio, "The Homosexual Menace: The Politics of Sexuality in Cold War America," in idem, *Making Trouble: Essays on Gay History, Politics, and the University* (New York: Routledge, 1992), pp. 57-73; also in *Passion and Power: Sexuality in History*, ed. Kathy Reiss and Christina Simmons with Robert A. Padgug (Philadelphia: Temple University Press, 1989), pp. 226-40. For a collection of pertinent documents, see Jonathan Katz, *Gay American History* (New York: Thomas Y. Crowell, 1976),

pp. 91-105. On p. 101, Katz reports that "on January 14, 16, and 21, 1952, journalist Drew Pearson's private diary refers to unsubstantiated rumors, circulating among Congressmen, the FBI, and the White House, of Senator Joseph McCarthy's being involved in homosexual activity," citing as his source Drew Pearson, *Diaries, 1949-1959*, ed. Tyler Abell (New York: Holt, Rinehart and Winston, 1974), pp. 188-89, 190, 192. On Roy Cohn, see Nicholas von Hoffman, *Citizen Cohn* (New York: Doubleday, 1988).

8. See Dennis Altman, *Homosexuality: Oppression and Liberation* (New York: Outerbridge and Dienstfrey, 1971), and *Radical Records: Thirty Years of Lesbian and Gay History*, ed. Bob Cant and Susan Hemmings (London: Routledge, 1988).

9. For a contemporary account of the groups that emerged in the wake of the Stonewall rebellion, see Donn Teal, *The Gay Militants* (New York: Stein and Day, 1971).

10. The German slogan, used at a 1972 demonstration in Münster, appears in "Bekennt, daß ihr anders seid," *Der Spiegel* 27.11 (March 12, 1973): 46-62; quote on p. 48. The two American slogans, from the 1970 and 1971 Christopher Street marches in New York, are recalled by a participant (Steakley); the first was a take-off on the "Ho, ho, Ho Chi Minh–The Vietcong is going to win" of antiwar demonstrations. Similar slogans appear, for example, in Toby Marotta, *The Politics of Homosexuality* (Boston: Houghton Mifflin, 1981), p. 177.

11. On similar developments in Germany, see Andreas Salmen and Albert Eckert, *Zwanzig Jahre bundesdeutsche Schwulenbewegung 1969-1989* (Cologne: Bundesverband Homosexualität e.V., 1989), pp. 37-43.

12. See Marotta, pp. 139-47 et passim; Salmen and Eckert, p. 46; and Jeffrey Weeks, *Coming Out: Homosexual Politics in Britain, from the Nineteenth Century to the Present* (London: Quartet, 1977), pp. 185-206.

13. See Dennis Altman, *The Homosexualization of America, the Americanization of the Homosexual* (New York: St. Martin's Press, 1982).

14. For a historical survey of the pertinent laws, see Peter Tatchell, *Europe in the Pink: Lesbian and Gay Equality in the New Europe* (London: GMP, 1992).

15. See Weeks, p. 176.

16. See Jan Willem Duyvendak and Mattias Duyves, "*Gai Pied* after Ten Years: A Commercial Success, a Moral Bankruptcy?" *Journal of Homosexuality* 25.1-2 (1993): 211. The government's plan to ban *Gai Pied* was halted by massive protests.

17. See Manfred Herzer, "Helmut Schmidt und die Flutkatastrophe–das schwule Hamburg 1950-1970," in *Hamburg von hinten*, ed. Ernst Meibach (Berlin: Bruno Gmünder, 1982), pp. 65-81.

18. Joseph Doucé, a Baptist minister who gave pastoral care to sexually marginalized groups at his Christ the Liberator Center, was taken into police custody and found dead two months later. Gay organizations charged the police with slaying him, but a thorough investigation never took place and no one was indicted, implicating the Socialist government in the cover-up. See Françoise d'Eaubonne, *Le scandale d'une disparation: Vie et œuvre du Pastor Doucé* (Paris: Editions du

Libre Arbitre, 1990) and Jan van Kilsdonk et al., *Voor alles pastor: De zorg van Joseph Doucé voor sexuele minderheden* (Aalsmeer: Dabar, 1993).

19. See Jürgen Brockmann, "Antihomosexualität in Osteuropa," in *Seminar: Gesellschaft und Homosexualität*, ed. Rüdiger Lautmann (Frankfurt a.m.: Suhrkamp, 1977), pp. 447-60. For a survey of the relevant East European laws, see *Rosa Liebe unterm roten Stern: Zur Lage der Lesben und Schwulen in Osteuropa*, ed. HOSI Wien/Auslandsgruppe (Hamburg: Frühlings Erwachen, 1984).

20. On Cuba, see Luis Salas, *Social Control and Deviance in Cuba* (New York: Praeger, 1979), pp. 150-77; Allen Young, *Gays under the Cuban Revolution* (San Francisco: Grey Fox Press, 1981); and Marvin Leiner, *Sexual Politics in Cuba: Machismo, Homosexuality, and AIDS* (Boulder, CO: Westview, 1994). For a vivid memoir by one of the roughly 15,000 gay men who left Cuba in the 1980 Mariel boatlift, see Reinaldo Arenas, *Antes que anochezca* (Barcelona: Tusquets, 1992), available in English as *Before Night Falls*, trans. Dolores M. Koch (New York: Viking, 1993); Arenas also authored a poetic report, *El Central* (Barcelona: Seix Barral, 1981), available in English as *El Central: A Cuban Sugar Mill*, trans. Anthony Kerrigan (New York: Avon, 1984). The Cuban regime has also found its defenders; see, for example, Lourdes Arguelles and B. Ruby Rich, "Homosexuality, Homophobia, and Revolution: Notes toward an Understanding of the Cuban Lesbian and Gay Male Experience" in *Hidden from History: Reclaiming the Gay and Lesbian Past*, ed. Martin Duberman, Martha Vicinus, and George Chauncey, Jr. (New York: New American Library, 1989), pp. 441-55.

21. For developments in Hungary, Yugoslavia, Poland, Czechoslovakia, and the German Democratic Republic, see Raelynn Hillhouse, "Communist Politics and Sexual Dissidents," in *Sexual Minorities and Society: The Changing Attitudes toward Homosexuality in the 20th Century Europe*, ed. Udo Parikas and Teet Veispak (Tallinn: Institute of History, 1991), pp. 66-77. See also Sergej Shcherbakov, "On the Relationship between the Leningrad Gay Community and Legal Authorities in the 1970s and 1980s," ibid., pp. 94-104.

22. See Harry Oosterhuis, Jan Willem Duyvendak, and Gert Hekma, "The European Post-War Gay and Lesbian Movement," *Homologie* (Amsterdam) 16.4 (July-August 1994): 22-28.

23. For a historical survey of the status of homosexuality in China, see Fang Fu Ruan and Molleen Matsumura, *Sex in China: Studies in Sexology in Chinese Culture* (New York: Plenum, 1991), pp. 107-44; contemporary attitudes are treated on pp. 159-80. Significantly, homosexuality goes entirely unmentioned in *Sexual Behaviour in Modern China–A Report of the Nation-Wide "Sex Civilisation" Survey on 20,000 Subjects in China* (Shanghai: Joint Publishers, 1992); the authors, Liu Dalin, Ng Man Lun, and Zhou Li Ping, were reportedly eager to treat homosexuality in this 866-page study but prevented from doing so. See also YanHong Krompacky, "Gay Life in China: A Closet Within a Closet," *Harvard Gay & Lesbian Review* 1.4 (Fall 1994): 15-17.

24. See Sheila Rowbotham and Jeffrey Weeks, *Socialism and the New Life: The Personal and Sexual Politics of Edward Carpenter and Havelock Ellis* (London: Pluto, 1977).

25. See Jacob Stockinger, "Homosexuality and the French Enlightenment," in *Homosexualities and French Literature*, ed. George Stambolian and Elaine Marks (Ithaca: Cornell University Press, 1979), pp. 161-85, and Gert Hekma, *Homoseksualiteit, een medische reputatie: De uitdoktering van de homoseksueel in negentiende-eeuws Nederland* (Amsterdam: Sua, 1987), pp. 26-31.

26. See Jean Bethke Elshtain, *Public Man, Private Woman: Women in Social and Political Thought* (Oxford: Martin Robertson, 1981), pp. 117-32. See also Linda J. Nicholson, *Gender and History: The Limits of Social Theory in the Age of the Family* (New York: Columbia University Press, 1986), pp. 133-66.

27. Elshtain, p. 119.

28. See Frank Mort, *Dangerous Sexualities: Medico-Moral Politics in England since 1830* (London: Routledge and Kegan Paul, 1987), and Jeffrey Weeks, *Sex, Politics and Society: The Regulation of Sexuality since 1800* (London: Longman, 1981), pp. 84-93.

29. On the sexual politics of two leading utilitarian philosophers, see Wendy Donner, "John Stuart Mill's Liberal Feminism," *Philosophical Studies* 69 (1993): 155-66, and Miriam Williford, "Bentham on the Rights of Women," *Journal of the History of Ideas* 36 (1975): 167-76. In a 1785 text, Bentham argued for reforming the English sodomy law: Jeremy Bentham, "Offenses against One's Self: Pederasty," ed. Louis Crompton, *Journal of Homosexuality* 3 (1977-78): 389-405, 4 (1978-79): 91-107. On the historical background, see also L. Crompton, *Byron and Greek Love* (Berkeley: University of California Press, 1985).

30. See Hekma, *Homoseksualiteit, een medische reputatie*, pp. 149-60; Annet Mooij, *Geslachtsziekten en besmettingsangst: Een historisch-sociologische studie, 1850-1950* (Amsterdam and Meppel: Boom, 1993), pp. 28-80; Judith Walkowitz, *Prostitution and Victorian Society: Women, Class, and the State* (Cambridge: Cambridge University Press, 1980); David J. Pivar, *Purity Crusade: Sexual Morality and Social Control, 1868-1900* (Westport, CT: Greenwood, 1973).

31. Karl Marx, *Economic and Philosophic Manuscripts of 1844*, ed. Dirk J. Struik, trans. Martin Milligan (Moscow: Progress; New York: International, 1964), p. 133.

32. Karl Marx and Friedrich Engels, *The German Ideology* (Moscow: Progress; London: Lawrence & Wishart, 1964), p. 195.

33. Karl Marx and Friedrich Engels, *Manifesto of the Communist Party*, trans. Samuel Moore, in idem, *Selected Works in One Volume* (Moscow: Progress; New York: International, 1968), pp. 50-51.

34. Friedrich Engels, *The Origin of the Family, Private Property, and the State*, trans. Alec West, in ibid., p. 511.

35. Ibid., p. 502.

36. Ibid., p. 506.

37. See Andrew Parker, "Unthinking Sex: Marx, Engels, and the Scene of Writing," in *Fear of a Queer Planet: Queer Politics and Social Theory*, ed. Michael Warner (Minneapolis: University of Minnesota Press, 1993), pp. 19-41.

38. *Arbeiterinnenzeitung*, quoted by Karin J. Jusek, *Auf der Suche nach der Verlorenen: Die Prostitutionsdebatten im Wien der Jahrhundertwende* (Ph.D. dissertation, Rijksuniversiteit Groningen, 1993), p. 165.

39. See Gunter Runkel, *Sexualität und Ideologien* (Weinheim: Beltz, 1979), pp. 148-62.

40. See Werner Thönnessen, *The Emancipation of Women: The Rise and Decline of the Women's Movement in German Social Democracy 1863-1933*, trans. Joris de Bres (London: Pluto, 1973); Richard J. Evans, *The Feminist Movement in Germany, 1894-1933* (London: Sage, 1976); and Annette Mühlberg, "Arbeiterbewegung und Sexualität im deutschen Kaiserreich," *Mitteilungen aus der kulturwissenschaftlichen Forschung* (Berlin) 15.31 (November 1992): 119-73.

41. See R. P. Neuman, "The Sexual Question and Social Democracy in Imperial Germany," *Journal of Social History* 7 (1974): 271-86, here p. 274.

42. The notion that masturbation was relatively rare among the working class was supported by the findings of the Kinsey Institute several decades later. See Alfred C. Kinsey et al., *Sexual Behavior in the Human Male* (Philadelphia: W. B. Saunders, 1948), pp. 339-43, and idem, *Sexual Behavior in the Human Female* (Philadelphia: W. B. Saunders, 1953), pp. 148-50.

43. See Doris Byer, "Sexualität–Macht–Wohlfahrt: Zeitgemäße Erinnerungen an das 'Rote Wien,'" *Zeitgeschichte* 14 (1987): 444.

44. Angus MacLaren, "Some Secular Attitudes toward Sexual Behavior in France, 1760-1860," *French Historical Studies* 8 (1974): 622-23.

45. August Bebel, *Woman under Socialism*, trans. Daniel De Leon (New York: New York Labor News Press, 1904), pp. 164-65. After becoming the first German parliamentarian to speak out in favor of reforming § 175, Bebel modified this text by adding a single clause conceding that homosexuality was in some cases "inborn"; in a footnote added in 1909, he remarked that the Eulenburg scandal "proved" that homosexuality was widespread in the upper classes. A. Bebel, *Die Frau und der Sozialismus* (Berlin: Dietz, 1974), p. 238.

46. Raymond Williams, "Base and Superstructure in Marxist Cultural Theory," in idem, *Problems in Materialism and Culture* (London: Verso, 1980), pp. 31-49.

47. See Ludmilla J. Jordanova, "Naturalizing the Family: Literature and the Bio-Medical Sciences in the Late Eighteenth Century," in *Languages of Nature: Critical Essays on Science and Literature*, ed. Ludmilla J. Jordanova (London: Free Association Books, 1986), pp. 86-116, and Joel Schwarz, *The Sexual Politics of Jean-Jacques Rousseau* (Chicago: University of Chicago Press, 1984).

48. See Théodore Tarczylo, *Sexe et liberté au siècle des Lumières* (Paris: Presses de la Renaissance, 1983).

49. See Anthony Pilkington, "'Nature' as Ethical Norm in the Enlightenment," in *Languages of Nature*, pp. 51-85, and Norman Hampson, *The Enlightenment* (Harmondsworth: Penguin, 1979), pp. 97-127, 186-217.

50. See Byer, p. 447.

51. See Rudolf Vecoli, "Sterilization: A Progressive Measure?" *Wisconsin Magazine of History* 43 (1959-60): 190-202; Loren R. Graham, "Science and Val-

ues: The Eugenics Movement in Germany and Russia in the 1920s," *American Historical Review* 82 (1977): 1133-64; Michael Freeden, "Eugenics and Progressive Thought: A Study in Ideological Affinity," *Historical Journal* 22 (1979): 645-71; Mark Adams, "From 'Gene Fund' to 'Gene Pool': On the Evolution of Evolutionary Language," *Studies in the History of Biology* 3 (1979): 241-85; Diane Paul, "Eugenics and the Left," *The Journal of the History of Ideas* 45 (1984): 567-90; Atina Grossmann, "The New Woman, the New Family and the Rationalization of Sexuality: The Sex Reform Movement in Germany 1928 to 1933" (Ph.D. dissertation, Columbia University, 1984), especially chapter 2, "Motherhood-Eugenics Consensus: The Discourse of Social Health," pp. 334-457; Paul Weindling, "Weimar Eugenics: The Kaiser Wilhelm Institute for Anthropology, Human Heredity and Eugenics in Social Context," *Annals of Science* 42 (1985): 303-18; idem, "Die Verbreitung rassenhygienischen/eugenischen Gedankengutes in bürgerlichen und sozialistischen Kreisen in der Weimarer Republik," *Medizinhistorisches Journal* 22 (1987) 352-68; idem, *Health, Race and German Politics between National Unification and Nazism, 1870-1945* (Cambridge: Cambridge University Press, 1989); and Carl N. Degler, *In Search of Human Nature: The Decline and Revival of Darwinism in American Social Thought* (New York: Oxford University Press, 1991), pp. 42-43.

52. See *The Comparative Reception of Darwinism*, ed. Thomas F. Glick (Chicago: University of Chicago Press, 1988).

53. See James Rachels, *Created from Animals: The Moral Implications of Darwinism* (Oxford: Oxford University Press, 1990).

54. See *Social Darwinism: Selected Essays*, ed. William Graham Sumner (Englewood Cliffs, NJ: Prentice-Hall, 1963).

55. See Alfred Kelly, *The Descent of Darwin: The Popularization of Darwinism in Germany, 1860-1914* (Chapel Hill: University of North Carolina Press, 1981).

56. Friedrich Engels, "Speech at the Graveside of Karl Marx," in *Selected Works* (see note 33), p. 435. See also Margaret Fay, "Did Marx Offer to Dedicate 'Capital' to Darwin? A Reassessment of the Evidence," *Journal of the History of Ideas* 39 (1978): 133-46.

57. See *Marxism and Social Democracy: The Revisionist Debate 1896-1898*, ed. and trans. by H. Tudor and J. M. Tudor; and Roger Fletcher, *Revisionism and Empire: Socialist Imperialism in Germany, 1897-1914* (Boston: G. Allen & Unwin, 1984).

58. See Gert Hekma, "'A Female Soul in a Male Body': Sexual Inversion as Gender Inversion in Nineteenth-Century Sexology," in *Third Sex, Third Gender: Beyond Sexual Dimorphism in Culture and History*, ed. Gilbert Herdt (New York: Zone Books, 1994), pp. 213-39.

59. Richard von Krafft-Ebing, *Psychopathia sexualis, mit besonderer Berücksichtigung der conträren Sexualempfindung*, 2nd ed. (Stuttgart: Ferdinand Enke, 1887), p. vi.

60. See, for example, Robert A. Nye, *Crime, Madness, and Politics in Modern France: The Medical Concept of National Decline* (Princeton: Princeton University Press, 1984).

61. Lawrence Birken, *Consuming Desire: Sexual Science and the Emergence of a Culture of Abundance, 1871-1914* (Ithaca: Cornell University Press, 1988), pp. 57-71.

62. Karl Heinrich Ulrichs, *"Memnon." Die Geschlechtsnatur des mannliebenden Urnings. Eine naturwissenschaftliche Darstellung. Körperlich-seelischer Hermaphroditismus*, 1868 (Leipzig: Max Spohr, 1898), pp. 126, 134.

63. See Magnus Hirschfeld, "Ernst Haeckel und die Sexualwissenschaft," in *Was wir Ernst Haeckel verdanken–Ein Buch der Verehrung und Dankbarkeit*, ed. Heinrich Schmidt (Leipzig: Unesma; Hamburg: Paul Hartung, 1914), vol. 2, pp. 282-84.

64. M. Sereiskii, "Gomoseksualizm," *Bol'shaia sovetskaia entsiklopediia*, vol. 17 (Moscow: Sovetskaia entsiklopediia, 1930), cols. 593-96.

65. See Emil Kraepelin, *Psychiatrie: Ein Lehrbuch für Studierende und Ärzte*, vol. 4: *Klinische Psychiatrie*, 8th ed. (Leipzig: J. A. Barth, 1915), pp. 1971-72, and Manfred Herzer, "Albert Moll," in *Homosexualität: Handbuch der Theorie- und Forschungsgeschichte*, ed. Rüdiger Lautmann (Frankfurt a.M.: Campus, 1993), pp. 60-65.

66. See Emil Kraepelin, "Geschlechtliche Verirrung und Volksvermehrung," *Muenchener medizinische Wochenschrift* 65 (1918): 117-20.

67. Magnus Hirschfeld, *Die Homosexualität des Mannes und des Weibes* (Berlin: Louis Marcus, 1914), p. 493.

68. See Simon Karlinsky, "Russia's Gay Literature and Culture: The Impact of the October Revolution," in *Hidden from History: Reclaiming the Gay and Lesbian Past*, ed. Martin Duberman, Martha Vincinus, and George Chauncey, Jr. (New York: New American Library, 1989), pp. 347-64.

69. See Clara Zetkin, *Erinnerungen an Lenin* (Berlin/GDR: Dietz, 1975), p. 67, and Fannina W. Halle, *Women in Soviet Russia*, trans. Margaret M. Green (New York: Viking, 1933), pp. 112-14.

70. It should be noted that Freud was cited alongside Hirschfeld in the *Bol'shaia sovetskaia entsiklopediia*. See also Manfred Herzer, "Wilhelm Reich und Magnus Hirschfeld–gescheiterte Konzepte sozialistischer Sexualpolitik und Faschismus," *Mitteilungen der Magnus-Hirschfeld-Gesellschaft* 2 (1983): 9-16.

71. See also James Steakley, "Gays under Socialism: Male Homosexuality in the German Democratic Republic," *The Body Politic* (Toronto), no. 29 (December 1976): 15-18.

72. See Reimut Reiche, *Sexuality and Class Struggle*, trans. Susan Bennett (New York: Prager, 1971); Reiche's book appeared originally as *Sexualität und Klassenkampf: Zur Abwehr repressiver Entsublimierung* (Frankfurt a.M.: Neue Kritik, 1968).

73. Herbert Marcuse, *Eros and Civilization: A Philosophical Inquiry into Freud* (Boston: Beacon Press, 1955).

74. Herbert Marcuse, *One Dimensional Man: Studies in the Ideology of Advanced Industrial Society* (Boston: Beacon Press, 1964).

75. See Robert Miklitsch, "Troping Prostitution: Two or Three Things about (Post-) Marxism/Feminism," *Genders*, no. 12 (Winter 1991): 120-39.

76. See Hans Wolf Butterhof, *Wissen und Macht: Widersprüche sozialdemokratischer Bildungspolitik bei Harkort, Liebknecht und Schulz* (Munich: Ehrenwirth, 1978); Dietger Pforte, *Von unten auf: Studie zur literarischen Bildungsarbeit der frühen deutschen Sozialdemokratie und zum Verhältnis von Literatur und Arbeiterklasse* (Giessen: Anabas, 1979); and Eckhard Dittrich, *Arbeiterbewegung und Arbeiterbildung im 19. Jahrhundert* (Bensheim: Pädagogik extra Buchverlag, 1980).

77. Mario Praz, *The Romantic Agony*, trans. Angus Davidson (London: Oxford University Press, 1933).

78. See Gert Mattenklott, *Bilderdienst: Ästhetische Opposition bei Beardsley und George* (Munich: Rogner & Bernhard, 1970).

79. See Ed Cohen, *Talk on the Wilde Side* (New York: Routledge, 1993), and Alan Sinfield, *The Wilde Century: Effeminacy, Oscar Wilde and the Queer Movement* (London: Cassell, 1994).

80. See Michel Carassou, *René Crevel* (Paris: Payard, 1989), pp. 75-100.

81. See Michael Rohrwasser, *Saubere Mädel, starke Genossen: Proletarische Massenliteratur?* (Frankfurt a.M.: Roter Stern, 1975).

82. See George L. Mosse, "Die Idee des 'Neuen Mannes' in modernen revolutionären Bewegungen," *Mitteilungen der Magnus-Hirschfeld-Gesellschaft* 14 (1989): 9-13.

83. See *Homosexuality and Male Bonding in Pre-Nazi Germany: The Youth Movement, the Gay Movement, and Male Bonding before Hitler's Rise: Original Transcripts from Der Eigene, the First Gay Journal of the World*, ed. Harry Oosterhuis and Hubert Kennedy (simultaneously published as the *Journal of Homosexuality* 22.1-2) (New York: The Haworth Press, Inc., 1991).

84. See George Chauncey, *Gay New York: Gender, Urban Culture, and the Making of the Gay Male World, 1890-1940* (New York: Basic Books, 1994), pp. 65-97.

85. Edward Said, *Orientalism* (New York: Vintage, 1979), pp. 103, 166-67.

86. See Alex Hall, *Scandal, Sensation and Social Democracy: The SPD Press and Wilhelmine Germany 1890-1914* (Cambridge: Cambridge University Press, 1977).

87. See Maxim Gorki, "Gegen den Faschismus: Proletarischer Humanismus," *Rundschau über Politik, Wirtschaft und Arbeiterbewegung*, no. 34 (1934): 1298; the Russian original is reprinted in Vladimir Kozlovskii, *Argo russkoi gomoseksual'noi subkul'tury: Materialy k izucheniiu* (Benson, VT: Chalidze, 1986), p. 152. For a Nazi condemnation of Hirschfeld and the sexual reform movement of the Weimar Republic as an aspect of "cultural bolshevism," see, for example, Adolf Ehrt and Julius Schweikert, *Entfesselung der Unterwelt: Ein Querschnitt durch die Bolschewisierung Deutschlands* (Berlin and Leipzig: Eckart-Verlag, 1932), pp. 181-205.

88. See Dieter Berner, "Wie die SED-Propaganda das Stigma Homosexualität zum Rufmord an einem Maueropfer benutzte," *Capri* (Berlin), no. 10 (1990):

38-41; reprinted with additional documentation in *Gay News* (Leipzig) 2.4 (March-June 1991): 1-3.

89. Guy Hocquenghem, *Le desir homosexuel* (Paris: Editions Universitaires, 1972), available in English as *Homosexual Desire*, trans. Daniella Dangoor (London: Alison & Busby, 1978); *Tuntenstreit: Theoriediskussion der Homosexuellen Aktion Westberlin* [ed. Egmont Fassbinder] (Berlin: Rosa Winkel, 1975); Mario Mieli, *Elementi di critica omosessuale* (Turin: G. Einaudi, 1977), also available as *Homosexuality and Liberation: Elements of a Gay Critique*, trans. David Fernbach (London: Gay Men's Press, 1988); *Homosexuality: Power and Politics*, ed. Gay Left Collective (London: Allison & Busby, 1980); *Flaunting It! A Decade of Gay Journalism from* The Body Politic, ed. Ed Jackson and Stan Persky (Vancouver: New Star; Toronto: Pink Triangle Press, 1982).

90. The literature on homosexuality and Christianity has taken on vast proportions, but John Boswell, *Christianity, Social Tolerance, and Homosexuality: Gay People in Western Europe from the Beginning of the Christian Era to the Fourteenth Century* (Chicago: University of Chicago Press, 1980), has had a particularly strong impact. In the Netherlands of the 1950s and 1960s, Catholic clergy and laity played a crucial role in the social acceptance of homosexuality; see Harry Oosterhuis, *De smalle marges van de Roomse moraal; Homoseksualiteit in katholiek Nederland 1900-1970* (Ph.D. diss., Universiteit van Amsterdam, 1992); English summary on pp. 289-300. Andrew Sullivan, editor of the *New Republic*, has as a practicing Catholic played an important role in shaping recent discussions of gay politics. A conservative gay position has underpinnings in the works of Roger Scruton, *Sexual Desire: A Philosophical Investigation* (London: Weidenfeld and Nicholson, 1986), and Richard A. Posner, *Sex and Reason* (Cambridge, MA: Harvard University Press, 1992), while a libertarian position is staked out in Richard D. Mohr, *Gays/Justice: A Study of Ethics, Society, and the Law* (New York: Columbia University Press, 1988). An explicitly anti-utopian voice is Bruce Bawer, *A Place at the Table: The Gay Individual in American Society* (New York: Poseidon, 1993). See also Marvin Liebman, *Coming Out Conservative* (San Francisco: Chronicle, 1992), and Mel White, *Stranger at the Gate: To Be Gay and Christian in America* (New York: Simon & Schuster, 1994).

91. Michel Foucault, *The History of Sexuality*, vol. 1: *An Introduction*, trans. Robert Hurley (New York: Pantheon, 1978), pp. 95-96.

Theories About Sex and Sexuality in Utopian Socialism

Saskia Poldervaart

Universiteit van Amsterdam

SUMMARY. It was the utopian socialists of the period 1800-50 (Fourier, Saint-Simon, and the Saint-Simonians in France, as well as the Owenites in Great Britain) who not only challenged the imperialism of reason but sought to rehabilitate the flesh by valuing its pleasure and incentives. Sex and sexuality were central issues for the first socialists, who were scorned as "utopian" by Marx and Engels for seeking to improve the status of all members of society through peaceful means. Because Marxism has played a greater role in the history of socialism, the utopian socialist discussions have been largely disregarded. This essay analyzes the works of the utopian socialists Fourier, Saint-Simon, and the Saint-Simonians, arguing that resurgences of the utopian socialist tradition can be discerned around 1900 and again circa 1970.

It is one of the greatest defeats of civilization . . . that all men and women are similar in their sexual needs. This "erotic Jacobinism" is closely related to the claim that the "natural" form of sexuality is the monogamous couple, comprising

---

Correspondence may be addressed: Vakgroep Vrouwenstudies, Universiteit van Amsterdam, O. Z. Achterburgwal 237, 1012 DL Amsterdam, Netherlands.

[Haworth co-indexing entry note]: "Theories About Sex and Sexuality in Utopian Socialism." Poldervaart, Saskia. Co-published simultaneously in *Journal of Homosexuality* (The Haworth Press, Inc.) Vol. 29, No. 2/3, 1995, pp. 41-67; and: *Gay Men and the Sexual History of the Political Left* (ed: Gert Hekma, Harry Oosterhuis, and James Steakley) The Haworth Press, Inc., 1995, pp. 41-67; and *Gay Men and the Sexual History of the Political Left* (ed: Gert Hekma, Harry Oosterhuis, and James Steakley) Harrington Park Press, an imprint of The Haworth Press, Inc., 1995, pp. 41-67. Multiple copies of this article/chapter may be purchased from The Haworth Document Delivery Center. [1-800-342-9678 9:00 a.m. - 5:00 p.m. (EST)].

41

woman and man. . . . Forcing all sexual needs into the one harness of monogamy . . . results only in pain and frustration.

Fourier, *Le Nouveau Monde amoureux* (1818)

I

The "utopian" socialists, Marx and Engels scoffed, "want to improve the condition of every member of society. . . . They reject all political, and especially all revolutionary action; they wish to attain their ends by peaceful means . . . and . . . by small experiments, necessarily doomed to failure."[1] Precisely because violent class struggle was rejected by the first socialists (Henri Saint-Simon, the Saint-Simonians, and Charles Fourier in France as well as Robert Owen in England), the new social science they developed was dismissed as "utopian." Their theories were derided by Engels as mere "germs of thought" issuing in "phantasies, which today only make us smile."[2]

In this essay I aim to take seriously the allegedly amusing phantasies of the utopian socialists, analyzing how their theories gave equal weight to economic relationships and changes in private life. If one removes Marxist-tinted lenses when studying the history of socialism, it becomes apparent that sexuality and the problematic of femininity/masculinity were disowned as legitimate issues as Marxism came to dominate. Utopian socialism's methods–changing the relationships of production as well as relations between the sexes by problematizing sexuality, the family, and the public/private distinction–were narrowed by Marxism to class struggle; utopian socialism's goal–new social relationships between people–was restricted to a new economic order and redistribution of material goods.

It was the Owenites and Saint-Simonians who, around 1830, coined the terms "socialism" and "social science," notions that were largely synonymous until 1850.[3] These concepts were developed to challenge "individualism," which they understood as an orientation toward financial profit and a perpetuation of differences in status and privilege. Yet they did not attach a negative value to "the individual" per se; on the contrary, they emphasized a social and creative concept that presupposed a mutual influence between the individual and society rather than seeing them in opposition. These early socialists advanced their theories as an alternative to the ideology that had prevailed during the Enlightenment. It is also worth noting that all of the early socialists explicitly rejected what they defined as "utopianism."[4]

These early socialists will nonetheless be characterized as "utopians" here, for I use the term without implying any negative connotations. It should be understood in the sense not that they were designing rigid blueprints for the future, but instead that they were living out ideals formulated on the basis of the present, with a non-deterministic view of history. The utopian socialists regarded social critique and the development of alternatives as a social science, presupposing the future as contingent and incapable of being mapped out in advance. They assumed that the alternatives they proposed would undergo change over the course of the historical process; in this way they differed from Marx and Engels, who saw history as guided by inexorable laws. Their strategy was likewise quite different: the utopian socialists were looking for common values, and tried to live up to them; they aimed at an enjoyable life in the here and now. Marxism entirely repudiated putting ideals directly into practice, holding instead that the entire capitalist system had to be utterly vanquished before future ideals could be lived.[5] In view of this disparity, utopian socialism ought not to be seen as a predecessor of Marxism; in my opinion, it suggested (and perhaps still suggests) a very different way of thinking and living.

A second reason for terming the early socialists "utopians" is that they belong to a specific tradition. This utopian strain has figured prominently during certain eras of Western history, enabling us to speak of various "utopian periods." The first, at about the beginning of our era in Palestine, was initiated by the Essenes and Jesus. These utopians envisioned a society which placed a priority on communal life as opposed to egoistic and individual living. The next period can be dated to the twelfth and thirteenth centuries, which witnessed the emergence of groups that sought to realize the Christian utopia of solidarity and equality by sharing all goods communally. Attacking the hypocrisy of the often debauched life of the clergy, these heretical groups abolished the family structure; and arguing that no one was to be the property of another, many of them practiced celibacy or free sexual relations between "brothers and sisters."[6] The sixteenth and seventeenth centuries brought forth not just utopian movements but also utopian designs, propounded by Thomas More, Francis Bacon, Tommaso Campanella, Gabriel Foigny. Although the movements and the designs had little to do with each other, their ideals were more or less the same: they aspired to a community in which all was honestly divided, housework carried out collectively (by the women), and private property abolished. Throughout this tradition, a harmonious community was always predicated on the notion that family arrangements could not be placed outside the political realm.

The first utopian socialists differed from the movements and designs of preceding centuries by developing theories which posited the ideal outcome as a distinct possibility within the historical process rather than proposing static designs for some remote future. They shared with the Western utopian tradition an attack on private property and prevailing family arrangements as well as a similarity in historical context: utopianism tends to emerge in times of "uncertainty," when many groups criticize their society.[7] Typical for the utopian socialist period (1800-50) is their attack on "the" Enlightenment and the (violence of the) French Revolution. However, conservatives (e.g., Edmund Burke and Joseph de Maistre) and romantics (e.g., August Wilhelm Schlegel and Percy Shelley) preceded the utopian socialists in this attack. All three critiques rejected the sterile rationality of French Enlightenment thought and the *philosophes'* concept of "the autonomous individual," the emphasis on "rights," and the public/private dichotomy. Whereas the ideas of the conservatives and romantics were opposed to the rational thinking of the *philosophes,* the utopian socialists tried to advance beyond this dualism. In this sense the utopian socialists marked a real innovation.[8] They tried to combine reason with a rehabilitation of feelings and the flesh. Because the dualistic oppositions which have structured mainstream Western thought are closely allied with sexual polarity and hierarchy, it follows that sexual equality necessarily involves a challenge to all related antitheses.

In the following I will comment first on the works of the utopian socialists Fourier and Saint-Simon, then on the Saint-Simonians and the women's journal that was connected with this movement. The Owenites will not be treated in this essay, as I have not yet studied them in depth.[9] In the conclusion, I will relate utopian socialist ideas about sex and sexuality to the critique of science and propose that one can speak of a utopian socialist period around 1900 (and another around 1970).

II

Charles Fourier (1772-1837) was a contemporary of Saint-Simon, but they were unacquainted with each other's work. Nonetheless, Fourier's formulation of a new paradigm, called by him "the theory of the passions," shows many similarities with the "moral science" developed simultaneously by Saint-Simon. Seeking harmony between unique individuals, Fourier aimed at a theory based not upon what he called "chimeras," such as freedom and equality, but instead upon observations. Labor and love took a central position in this theory, which was directed against the *philosophes*. Rejecting the self-imposed asceticism of these rationalist philosophers, he proposed a new vision of humankind, arguing that the Enlightenment principle of self-regulation had blocked any insight into the working of the passions and had led only "to highfalutin pronouncements, with the hypocritical authors never putting their moral stands into practice."[10] To overcome all forms of suppression, Fourier argued, it was necessary to see the interconnectedness of economic and emotional-sexual suppression and also to grasp the restrictiveness and hypocrisy of marriage.

Throughout his publications,[11] Fourier fulminated against "civilization" and the *philosophes*, countering the unmovable sciences ("les sciences fixes") of the Enlightenment with the uncertainty of sciences ("les sciences incertaines").[12] His view of knowledge replaced absolute truth and the primacy of rationality with "absolute doubt" and "absolute distantiation."[13] In light of social reality, Fourier charged, the vaunted concepts of freedom and equality meant nothing; freedom was illusory if unavailable to common people. They would be truly free only if they could live without masters, without the ethos of work, and without suppressing passions. Disgust at uniformity made Fourier emphatically reject equality between individuals, and he characterized the notion of utopia most often advanced up until then–a visionary society of equals, common property, and strong restrictions on luxury–as "the virtuous republic of cabbage and gruel."[14] He constantly emphasized the inherent variety and pluriformity of ways of living, which would finally find expression in Harmony–his ideal society.

Fourier's theory posited that suppression of the passions was immediately harmful to the individual and in the long run destructive for society. He distinguished among twelve basic passions, each of which had to be satisfied (one person attaching more importance to certain passions than another, depending on their personalities). These were divided into three categories: sensual passions (five in all), affective passions (friendship, ambition, love, parenthood), and distributive passions (the cabalist passion for intrigue and rivalry, the butterfly passion for variety and contrasts, and the composition passion for a mixture of physical and spiritual pleasure). With this final category of passions, Fourier explicitly acknowledged the role of conflict and rivalry, recognizing that people have a need to be continuously challenged.

In the Phalanx (the name for Fourier's community of the future), people would be divided into groups of seven to nine who shared a particular passion. The members of each group would cooperate and compete with other harmonic groups. Because people, according to Fourier, wanted to have all their passions addressed, individuals would repeatedly join in ever-changing coalitions, in which distinctions in age, wealth, sex, character, and intelligence would be forgotten. As every individual would be a member of various groups and people would continuously change their labor, they would in the course of a single day assume different roles in shifting groups of associates. By turns boss and subordinate, whether male or female, they would discover that a rival in one group could be an ally in another. Antagonisms would thus obtain between rival groups, not between individuals. Although the theory of passions was concerned with the development of individual needs and Fourier emphasized that all kinds of differences among people (including wealth) would continue in Harmony, his overriding goal was social integration. Alongside the social and sexual minimum (discussed below), he attached importance first and foremost to the unifying

education, which–like the mingling of the "serie passionelle"–
would replace class rivalry with intrigue and group competition.
With this system Fourier felt he had found the solution to the conflict of individual versus society.

We can discern in this theory of passions a notion about "the
unconsciousness," which Fourier termed "l'engorgement" (block-
ing).[15] Like water held back by a dike, passions suppressed at a
certain point would always reappear at another time.[16] Dammed-up
passion would make its demands felt more urgently, thereby becoming more destructive. In his *Le Nouveau Monde amoureux*,
Fourier illustrated through a number of examples just how destructive the suppression of passions could be. An oft-cited instance was
provided by Ms. Stroganoff, a princess from Moscow, who was in
love with her slave girl. Due to prevailing sexual prejudice, Stroganoff knew nothing about the existence of lesbian love (termed
"sapphism" by Fourier) and thus suppressed her own passion.[17] As
her desire pressed for consummation, she tortured and humiliated
the girl instead of enjoying her love.

Applying his theory of passions to two issues that he considered
of central importance for every human being, labor and love, Fourier worked out two minima.

The social minimum. According to Fourier, labor was not a duty
but a need. People could realize themselves totally in labor, provided that this labor was chosen of their own free will. And that
would be possible only if labor were made attractive. Fourier's
theory of labor aimed to organize work in such a way that every
socially necessary task (and he emphatically included domestic
chores and caretaking) could be carried out enthusiastically by at
least some members of the Phalanx. Tasks therefore needed to be
continuously exchanged, along with the composition of groups
executing those tasks. Furthermore, it was necessary for the circumstances of labor to be aesthetically satisfying, and the right to work
had to be assured for every man, woman, and child. But the single
most important precondition, according to Fourier, was a guaran-
teed income for all people: the social minimum. Only when men
and women were freed from the necessity to work would it be
"psychologically" possible for them to see their work as an attractive activity.[18]

The sexual minimum. From his first publications on, Fourier made it clear that he was solely interested in developing a society in which not only material restrictions would be removed, but people would no longer have to repress their passions. To this end, social relations would have to be completely altered, and this required abandoning the prevailing restrictions on emotional and erotic life. Because private mutual relationships undermined social solidarity, love had to become not a private affair but an essential part of collective life. His *Le Nouveau Monde amoureux* in particular is one extended paean to the importance of love, both spiritual and physical. "Precisely in the intoxication of love, man feels that he is ascending to heaven and sharing God's happiness."[19] "Nowadays man laughs about these follies ('les manies') but forgets that love is the domain of unwisdom and that the less rational something is, the more compatible it is with love."[20] "It is love that helps the individual to change inwardly."[21] Like Saint-Simon, Fourier drew a connection between love and art: "Eroticism and the creation of art . . . spring forth from the same vitality. . . . Desire's movement finds its fulfillment in works of art."[22]

Fourier worked out in this book how the most varied erotic passions could be satisfied while at the same time enhancing social integration. For this he proposed the Court of Love ("Court de l'amour"), presided over by an older woman well versed in amorous intrigue.[23] The task of this court was to organize parties and orgies for all members of the Phalanx and to bring together people with specific erotic preferences.

A first prerequisite for the birth of the new amorous world was, according to Fourier, acceptance of the fact that sexual needs differed enormously. Most people were not monogamous, and furthermore their sexual desires were both various and changing. During different stages of their lives, individuals had very different urges. Nor did a uniform need prevail within specific age-groups: while some people tended to sensualism, others were primarily sentimentalists; some loved the "sexe opposite," others "la monosexie."[24] Fourier mentioned "sapphisme," "pédérastie" (homosexuality between men), "flagellantisme," "l'amour céladonique" (purely spiritual love–heretofore overly neglected, according to Fourier, including by de Sade), "l'androgénité," "bissexué," and "trissexueté."[25] In Fourier's utopia, all sexual expressions would be permitted so long as people were not abused. Precisely the repudiation of taboos would enhance the social integration and at the same time strengthen individuality ("l'individualisation"). Fourier talked about "affirming one's difference":[26]

> Sexual integrity brings the sexes closer to each other; if nothing is forbidden or suppressed anymore, there would be a bridging of sexual identities, of sapphic and pederastic loves, and this bridging of less common sexual preferences is necessary for Harmony.[27]

Fourier notably excluded children up to the age of fifteen-and-a-half years, claiming that children had no sexual desire at all, only the passions for friendship and ambition. Incest between adults was not rejected by Fourier, who held that it was more widespread in civilization than people were ready to admit. Because the social taboo against it was so strong, incest between adults would remain forbidden during the transitional phases toward the final Harmony–a period estimated by Fourier to require three generations.

A second prerequisite for the new amorous world was a radical change in the position of women. It was necessary to recognize that women had the same sexual needs as men: "Woman is not a subject of lust, but an active participant."[28] Only when this was acknowledged could both sexes enter a new amorous world. Fourier described lesbian love with special warmth: "Sapphism is an exalted virtue, because it creates ties that did not exist until now. It is a precious amalgam of love and friendship."[29]

The third prerequisite formulated by Fourier was the sexual minimum. Much as the social minimum was a condition for self-expression and freedom of being, so would the sexual minimum transform amorous relationships by ridding them of any sort of constraint or need. Only after the fear of sexual deprivation had disappeared would men and women be free to develop their full sexual potential. Referring to his "composition passion," Fourier considered love as more than a physical act: it did not end with orgasms. By assuring each individual a sexual minimum of orgasmic fulfillment (regulated by the Court of Love),[30] Fourier wanted to free people from their fixation on coitus and genitals. He was ultimately concerned with the more subtle and complicated relationships between people that would become possible once sexual hunger was satisfied.

The ideal community would thus emphasize the enjoyment of both labor and love and an enjoyable public life. Repeatedly castigated for his advocacy of overt sexual gratification, Fourier shifted his emphasis from sexuality to the pleasure of a good meal. This, too, he saw as a public event. Next to attractive labor and amorous relationships, fine and abundant food figured as one of the three most pleasurable features in Fourier's Phalanxes.[31] To cultivate forms of life "between public/private," Fourier envisioned specially arranged salons as meeting places for a special "passion series" as well as a number of smaller salons where subgroups could indulge their cabalistic inclinations. The Court of Love would see to it that no one was excluded. News bulletins in the reception hall of the splendid central building would continuously announce upcoming festivities. The playful element of public life would be encouraged on all sides, and the boundary between the public and the private would be moved to the individual bedroom. Fourier took it for granted that after such lively daytimes and evenings, any individual above fifteen-and-a-half years of age would want to spend the remaining short nights alone, in his/her own room.[32]

Following a schism within the Saint-Simonian movement in late 1831 (described below), key adherents defected to the small group of Fourier disciples, leading to the birth of a new Fourierist movement. In the many lectures given by various leaders of this movement, however, Fourier's ideas about the abolition of the family and the range of possible sexual relationships were increasingly forsaken. Many people were won over as the "social sentiment" was increasingly limited to economic relationships alone, and the Fourierist movement gained a considerable following.[33] Followers began to put Fourier's proposals into practice, and Phalanxes were founded throughout Europe from the mid-1830s on; Fourierism also spread to North America between 1840 and 1850.[34] But the movement's exclusive emphasis on economic issues and its replacement of Fourier's phantasies with bourgeois "decency" had effectively removed the sting of sexual and feminist liberation.

III

Henri Saint-Simon (1760-1825) wrote little about sex and nothing about sexuality. His theories nonetheless prepared the ground for the sexual and feminist critique advanced by his pupils. Saint-Simon's views, like those of Fourier, were directed against the Enlightenment *philosophes*. The new, positive science he envisioned would no longer be based upon metaphysical concepts, such as equality and freedom, but instead upon observations and their relationships. Moral and historicizing, Saint-Simon's science aimed not at attaining universal equality, but at improving the position of "the most numerous and poorest class," whom he spoke of in 1824-25 as "les proletaires."[35]

In opposition to the Enlightenment concept of equality, Saint-Simon asserted that people were by nature unequal, because each individual was unique and had different capacities. All humans should have the chance to develop their own personalities, be it in the area of science, art, or in any form of industry ("l'industrie").[36] Precisely these differences formed the basis of his utopia, which envisioned a maximal application of uniquely individual capacities. By abolishing the right of inheritance, guaranteeing a good upbringing and education, and reserving the executive functions of professional groups for those best qualified, a real but nonidentical equality between people would come into existence.

Saint-Simon criticized the public/private distinction and aimed to integrate the state into society. He rejected the notion that public and private spheres could coexist, with the public sphere restricted by law from impinging on the private sphere and leaving the individual to live in liberty. Saint-Simon countered the atomistic, egalitarian society of the *philosophes* with an organic society in which relationships would be emotionalized to prevent social disintegration. He, too, saw the individual as a social, unique, and creative being, one in continuous interaction with society. In the future, people would not shirk their social tasks, for they would realize that to do so would violate their own interests.

According to Saint-Simon, scientists never worked autonomously, independent of society. Moreover, scientists were never purely rational, for their sentiments always played a part. As there was no certainty about anything, no abstract truths could exist. The proper role of the scientist was not to produce truth, but to work in cooperation with the artist and "l'industriel" for the progress of society. This would only be possible if all people were addressed not only as rational and active beings, but also as religious, sensitive, and caring. Exactly these qualities of sensitivity and care were the most important human attributes for social betterment.

The year of Saint-Simon's death fell in the post-Napoleonic Restoration, an era characterized not just by a restrictive system of public moral behavior but also by the flowering of the French Romantic movement. A number of young intellectuals felt drawn to the teachings of Saint-Simon because they were rebelling against the hypocritical codes of their contemporaries, who glorified monogamy while closing one eye toward prostitution and adultery and being entirely blind toward the poverty endured by a large part of the French population. Among the most important disciples of Saint-Simon were Benjamin Rodrigues, Saint-Armand Bazard, and Barthélmy Enfantin. Apart from publishing a monthly journal, the Saint-Simonians gathered to discuss such issues as love, property, and the law of inheritance. Because these issues were intertwined with the family, they also debated more and more heatedly related subjects, e.g., sexuality and male-female relationships. Given the division of society into families, domestic love ranked above love for one's fellow beings and property was passed on within the family, leading to the perpetuation of inequality by birth. From 1827 up unto about 1832, weekly meetings organized by Saint-Simonians drew hundreds of interested young men (women would only join in large numbers beginning around 1829), constituting a highly significant social movement. As one historian has commented: "In an era when individualism imagined it had achieved complete triumph, when liberalism assumed it had assured social progress, . . . the Saint-Simonians invoked *social ideas.*"[37] Guided by Saint-Simon's final work, *Le Nouveau Christianisme*, his disciples followed the example of early Christian communities by living their ideals while at the same time expanding and concretizing Saint-Simon's theories. "Saint-Simonism remained one of the most potent emotional and intellectual influences in nineteenth-century society, inchoate, diffuse, but always there, penetrating the most improbable places. . . . Piercing insights into the nature of love and sexuality . . . now have a greater appeal than [their] economic doctrines which have become rather commonplace."[38]

In their first lecture series from 1828 through the summer of 1829, the Saint-Simonians rejected the notions of "laissez-faire," abstract equality, and privilege. "The mass of workers is exploited by those whose property they serve. . . . The workers are being exploited *materially, intellectually,* and MORALLY, . . . but our political theorists still speak of liberty, the love of man, and equality."[39] In addition, they adamantly criticized the current methods of political economics: "The economists believe that they can isolate homogeneous facts from other facts. But we know that it is impossible to separate knowledge from economic facts, knowledge from political and legal institutions. Therefore we know that no eternal laws exist, as Adam Smith and his disciples believed. They believed in an 'order natural des sociétés,' but social facts and especially economic facts are variable."[40] Faced by the rise of philosophical positivism, they defended their own version of positivist science: "The pragmatists of our time state that a very large distance must exist between the methods of science and those of religion. But does not every science presuppose a belief? . . . Is not sentiment a source of deep inspiration even in scientific explication?"[41] "The positive method can be known by means other than rationality alone; because all sciences presuppose axioms, elements of belief and conviction also belong to scientific argumentation."[42]

Beginning with their sixth lecture, they discussed the oppression of women, critiquing paternalism and misogyny.[43] From this lecture on, women and discussions about "the feminine" would play an ever larger role in their theories and their movement.

A second lecture series from late 1829 to late 1830 thematized the "rehabilitation of the flesh": "Christianity has presupposed a separation between the spirit and the flesh, attributing men's weakness to the flesh. And the Church still condemns all that is of the flesh and all that is material. Poverty is portrayed as the highest good, while luxury and beauty are considered evil. But the condemnation and cursing of the material and the physical has no real foundation, not even in the pronouncements of early Christianity. Both the spirit and the flesh are an expression of God's love. The desire to be happy here below and to enjoy is justified."[44] All Saint-Simonians initially seemed to agree with this rehabilitation, but when Enfantin elaborated it one year later by presenting "the erotic challenge" as a positive quality, a schism in the movement ensued.

The Saint-Simonians presupposed that "love," not reason, was singularly capable of providing a strong and stable bond needed for a peaceful society, and that the future direction of the new era could be entrusted only to especially gifted individuals—women, priests, artists. They also ultimately agreed that the inequality of women was expressed in two ways: exclusion from public life, and oppression by men in private life.[45] Because they wanted to live the good example themselves so as to realize their ideals for the future here and now, all Saint-Simonian associations were headed from mid-1829 till the end of 1831 by a man and a woman.[46] But as evidenced in his many letters, Enfantin increasingly struggled with the question whether or not women in this way were not simply adapting to a male world. In November 1831, he launched his new theory of morals, proposing a utopia of sexual equality necessitating a new sexual morality. Enfantin subverted the Christian theory of morality by ascribing a positive value to "the sin of the flesh." "Until now coquettishness, frivolity, fickleness, beauty, and gracefulness have given rise only to guile, trickery, hypocrisy, wantonness, adultery, etc., for society has been incapable of regulating, or satisfying, or using [these] human qualities. They therefore have become sources of disorder rather than sources of joy and happiness, as they should be. People who are *inconstant, fickle, volatile* are therefore damned by the law of Christ (and note well that woman, more so than man, possesses these qualities) and must use their power . . . to corrupt rather than construct. This explains very well the anathema pronounced against *physical* pleasures and against *woman*."[47]

Enfantin thus related femininity to a kind of sexual challenge, called for this feminine quality to be more highly valued, and argued that woman possessed this quality more then men. But he did not interpret masculinity and femininity as opposites, nor did he link femininity to women, firstly because he considered man capable of acquiring this quality and secondly because exactly what constituted a woman was unknown.

Because he thought that no man could grasp what it was to be a woman, Enfantin proclaimed an *Appèl à la Femme* as a second part of his new moral law. It would take a particular woman, a priestess, to relate what women wanted, and the Saint-Simonian women were called upon to organize themselves until the coming of the Female Messiah. In the upshot, these women did organize themselves in a separate way, but this step also led to a schism among Saint-Simonian men, with the departure of those who regarded Enfantin's new theory as immoral.

Yet most men stayed. In their public lectures (in Paris and elsewhere in France), the Saint-Simonians recognized that being caring and sensitive were qualities that every individual should strive for, and the importance of domestic chores was also discussed. While they had mainly discussed what constituted "femininity" prior to the schism, they now set out to discuss their own behavior in a larger way, thus questioning masculinity itself. Men who attended these meetings were enjoined to scrutinize and modify their own intimate lives so that they could learn to acquire "feminine" qualities; there was crying, and an intimate feeling of belonging developed.[48]

These public "consciousness-raising sessions" frequently turned on the subject of love, because–according to Enfantin–society had heretofore emphasized only the spiritual. "Why can one not speak openly, with dignity, about love; why can one never talk about it, though everyone thinks about it?"[49] The frankness of these meetings became too much for the government, which was coming to regard the movement as an assault on public morality. In early 1831, the Saint-Simonian center was closed by law, with the intervention of the police and the army.[50] Other houses and associations were likewise banned, and the Saint-Simonian daily *Le Globe* was forced into financial liquidation. Together with about forty male disciples, Enfantin withdrew to an inherited house in Ménilmontant near Paris, where they awaited the caring but unknown Female Messiah and prepared themselves for a new life.

The Saint-Simonian men wanted primarily to deepen their insight into "what it is to be a woman" by practicing celibacy, opening up their personal feelings by means of continuous introspection and discussions, and handling all domestic chores themselves.[51] They wanted to prove that they took seriously their claim that all forms of work were equally important.[52] For French public opinion, the execution of household chores by men was perhaps even more "contrary to nature" than their celibacy. Cartoons and satirical songs ridiculing the Saint-Simonians were distributed on a large scale throughout France. The cartoons showed men washing dishes and kitchen utensils, scraping carrots, and doing the laundry.[53] The best-known cartoon shows them fastening each other's waistcoats, the buttons being at the back side. This image referred to the suit designed by Enfantin in accordance with the Saint-Simonian principle that honest socialists should "associate," even when they dressed or undressed.[54] On weekends the Saint-Simonians adhered to an open-door policy, performing symbolic ceremonies that attracted thousands of Parisians. But once again the police, supported by the army, intervened. In August of 1832, Enfantin and Michel Chevalier, another Saint-Simonian leader, were sentenced to a one-year prison term in a widely publicized trial.[55]

Communal life under Enfantin's leadership had lasted nine months. During his imprisonment, the other men left one after the other, and the Ménilmontant commune ceased to exist. This signalled the end of the effort of the Saint-Simonian men to live "femininity."[56]

In response to Enfantin's call for women to organize themselves, the Saint-Simonian women had in the meanwhile founded their own publication, *La Femme Libre* (August 1832-spring 1834). Because this title was subjected to ridicule, the editors changed it to *La Femme Nouvelle* and later to *Tribune des Femmes*. This paper never mentioned homosexuality, but it did provide a platform for an impassioned discussion about the importance of sexuality and avoided assigning a fixed meaning to femininity. Recognizing and embracing differences among women, the editors did not pretend to speak for all women and avoided giving prescriptions. The status of the housewife and the dominance of the family were criticized vehemently in the paper. "Society should at long last stop distorting the finest work of God, that is, pluriformity . . . by forcing us women to adapt ourselves to a universally similar, compulsory image, to a uniform model."[57]

The paper carried an extensive discussion about how to live "the rehabilitation of the flesh." One contributor asserted: "I have never believed in 'Christian' morality. Yearning for pleasure as I do, this morality means only suffering."[58] Another: "We shall love without hypocrisy and laugh about prejudices."[59] Finally: "For us the body is as holy as the spirit. Christian abstinence to us is completely ridiculous, even godless, because we cannot believe that the goal of God is to destroy His own work."[60] On the other hand, hesitance was expressed, particularly by the editors Susanne and Jeanne-Désirée: "Will not women in a society based purely on physical attraction be losers again?"[61] Yet the latter also called out: "Women, discover your potentiality for pleasure!" And Susanne pleaded for variety, declaring her disbelief in lifelong happiness with one man. "Such happiness seems to me merely to lead to boredom and monotony. For God's sake, a bit of uncertainty in life!"[62]

When in February 1834 the government passed a bill forbidding all organizations of an oppositional nature, the sole remaining editor (others having joined the Fourierist movement) was compelled to shut down the paper.[63]

IV

In examining utopian socialist theories and movements, this essay has scarcely had occasion to mention male homosexuality explicitly. I nonetheless hope to have indicated four elements important for a critique of the apparently unquestionable status of heterosexuality:

1. Recognition of the importance of sexuality.
2. Abandonment of fixed, "natural" ideas concerning masculinity and femininity—in current terminology: the acceptance that masculinity and femininity are constructions.
3. Recognition that love, sexuality, and sexual relations fall within the domain of social science, causing this discipline to be, in the words of Fourier, necessarily an "uncertain science"[64]—in Saint-Simonian terminology: recognition that

feeling always plays a part in science, and that no social "laws" can be constructed.
4. Endeavoring to live the formulated ideals in order to counter hypocrisy. It is characteristic of the utopian socialists that they put into practice a slogan of far more recent vintage: "The personal is the political."[65]

Taken in isolation, however, none of these factors is sufficient to put into question the self-evident status of heterosexuality:
1. Thus Wilhelm Reich pleaded on the one hand for recognition of the importance of sexuality, but his theory (and therapy) maintained the goal of reaching a "better, more natural family organization" and the ideal of "natural relationships between husband and wife." Tellingly, he declared his "sex economy" to be a "rational revolution" based upon "the functional laws of biological energy."[66]
2. Nor is criticism of the traditional male-female relationship sufficient, as shown by the history of the prevailing feminist traditions. With Olive Banks I presuppose that it is possible to distinguish three such lines of thought.[67] There is first a feminist theory of differentiation, placing "female" values above the effort to be equal with men. This tradition has its roots in evangelical thought and in Romanticism. Whether these values are biologically, psychically, or culturally determined remains a point of contention within this tradition. A second theoretical tradition emphasizes the potentiality of equality between the sexes and attributes differences solely to external factors. Rooted in the rationality of the Enlightenment, this tradition has been continued in the political liberalism of the nineteenth and twentieth centuries. A third, socialist-feminist tradition is founded in utopian socialism. It differs from both preceding ones because it values feeling as much as rationality, without attributing sentiment to women and reason to men.

In my view a kinship between feminism and the gay movement can exist only when the issues of masculinity and femininity are decoupled from gender and sexuality is recognized as a political issue, implying the rejection of such dichotomies as female/male, sentiment/rationality, private/public, housewife/breadwinner, difference/equality. The seeming self-evidence of heterosexuality has been thematized more explicitly in utopian socialist feminism than in other feminist traditions. Traditional Marxist feminism has taken sex as a given fact, disregarding the ramifications of femininity, masculinity, sexual preference, etc.

3. There is always a connection between prevailing scientific opinion and contemporaneous discussions about femininity/masculinity and heterosexuality. Thus Kolakowski discerns a clear relationship between the decline of utopian socialism around 1850 and the rise of the positivist philosophy of science.[68] With its notions of objectivity, cause-and-effect, and knowledge equalling prediction, positivism would remain a dominating force up to about 1880-90. The decades from 1890 to 1920, on the other hand, have been described as a "utopian period" marked by a "revolt against positivism."[69] It was a time when the subjectivity of the researcher was rediscovered and renewed emphasis was placed on passion and inspiration as part of the scientific terrain.[70] This did not, however, mean that everyone involved with this revolt was prepared to engage in a discussion of heterosexuality and femininity. Yet self-described socialist groups that differentiated themselves from Marxism did advance a range of views strongly resembling those of the first socialists. (One can likewise observe that in the 1960s, criticism of so-called bourgeois society with its rationality, neopositivism, and "freedom of values" initially led to an openness to other options and ideas.)[71]

4. The utopian socialist effort to live according to formulated ideals led to an appreciation of sexuality, love, and the distribution of domestic chores as political issues. Although only Fourier explicitly mentioned homosexuality, the utopian attitude to life appears to render people more open to all possible forms of love and sexuality. Of and by itself, however, insight into the relationship between the personal and the political does not automatically lead to a discussion of heterosexuality and masculinity/femininity, as shown by the commune movement of the 1960s, for example.[72]

Yet it is no coincidence that homosexuality was discussed and/or openly put into practice by many groups of the period 1890-1920 that called themselves socialist and sought to live according to their ideals. As examples I would cite:

The Fellowship of the New Life (ca. 1885-95): included among others Edward Carpenter, Havelock Ellis, Olive Schreiner, and Karl Pearson. Carpenter played a key role in this Fellowship, which emphasized the formation of new personal relationships and developed schemes for communities that would divide household chores equally between classes and sexes. With its ideas about "New Life Socialism," the Fellowship aimed to liberate men as well as women from the stunting effects of sex-based hierarchies and contested the rigid enforcement of heterosexual self-identification.[73]

The League of Progressive Women's Associations (Verband Fortschrittlicher Frauenvereine, 1891-1919): founded by Lily Braun among others. This League challenged the moral double standard for men and women, called for both a boycott of marriage and the enjoyment of sexuality, and aimed to organize "unprotected" working-class women–female homeworkers, shop assistants, domestic servants, and prostitutes. It also supported the right to abortion and the abolition of criminal penalities against homosexuality.[74]

The Feminism of Greenwich Village (1910-1920): comprising a large number of women and a smaller number of men who–equipped with higher education, a sense of humor, and self-confidence–tried to live their ideals in a pleasurable way. Their demands regarding women's rights were tied to the expectation that socialism was inevitable in America and also to the right to decide for themselves what was feminine and what was masculine. Then as today, the Village had a reputation as a "safe haven" for lesbians and homosexual men. It was too early for lesbian and gay political activism; no formal or even informal organizational structure had yet evolved in America for lesbians or gay men. But as part of this Village feminism, female couples in the Heterodoxy women's club were accorded the same status as male-female couples, and lesbian couples received strong emotional support from other Heterodoxy members.[75]

Although utopian socialism seemed to disappear after 1850, its ideas of course continued to exist. In these conclusions I have tried to point out that the utopian socialist intellectual tradition is still alive, that it tends to be open toward all expressions of and experiments with sexual preference, and that it has maintained a critical attitude vis-à-vis the self-evidence of heterosexual monogamy. This persistence becomes more comprehensible if, following Paul Ricoeur, one views it as a function of utopianism to provide direct or indirect criticism of society through an exploration of ideas and desires.[76] Or, according to Oscar Wilde: "A map of the world that does not include Utopia is not even worth glancing at, for it leaves out the one country at which Humanity is always landing. And when Humanity lands there, it looks out, and, seeing a better country, sets sail. Progress is the realization of Utopias."[77]

AUTHOR NOTE

Saskia Poldervaart works at the Department of Women's Studies of the Universiteit van Amsterdam. She has been active in various women's organizations, the ABVA (the civil servants' union), and in the Third World Center in Nijmegen, Netherlands. A member of the Utopian Studies Society (Bristol, England) and of the International Communal Studies Association (Yad Tabenkin, Israel), she has published on feminism, utopian socialism, and commune movements, and is the author of *Vrouwenstudies, een inleiding* (1983; 3rd ed., 1991).

NOTES

1. Karl Marx and Friedrich Engels, *Manifesto of the Communist Party* (1848), in Marx and Engels, *Selected Works in One Volume* (New York: International Publishers, 1968), p. 60.

2. Friedrich Engels, *Socialism: Utopian and Scientific* (1882), in Marx and Engels, *Selected Works in One Volume*, p. 403.

3. See Gregory Clays, "Individualism, Socialism and Social Science," *Journal of the History of Ideas* 47 (1986): 81-93.

4. Utopians were considered by them to be "dreamers," designers of a static image of society, while they on the contrary were concerned with scientific processes. See, among others, Vincent Geoghegan, *Utopianism and Marxism* (New York: Methuen, 1987), p. 8.

5. On this strategy difference, see Benjamin D. Zablocki, *Alienation and Charisma: A Study of Contemporary American Communes* (New York: Free Press, 1980), Introduction. He mentions communitarian and revolutionary movements.

6. One example of the groups with free sexual relations was the "Brethren and Sistern of the Free Spirit." On these heretical groups and their ideas about sexuality, see (among others) Georges Duby, *Le Chevalier, la femme et le prêtre: Le mariage dans la France féodale* (Paris: Hachette, 1981); Kenneth Rexroth, *Communalism: From Its Origins to the Twentieth Century* (London: Peter Owen,

1975); Karl Kautsky, *Die Vorläufer des neuen Sozialismus*, vol. 1: *Kommunistische Bewegungen im Mittelalter* (Stuttgart: J.H.W. Dietz, 1895); Siegfried B. J. Zilverberg, *Ketters in de middeleeuwen* (Weesp: Fibula-Van Dishoeck, 1968; 2nd ed., 1985); Theun de Vries, *Veertien eeuwen ketterij, volksbeweging en kettergedicht* (Amsterdam: Querido, 1984).

7. On these utopian periods and their distinguishing features, see (among others) Zablocki. Socialists and anarcho-communists regarded the early utopian movements and designs as their heritage and termed them socialist, communist, or libertarian, as well as utopian. Zablocki argues that because Marxism was a revolutionary theory and movement rather than communitarian, it does not belong to this utopian tradition. Anarchism was mostly revolutionary but occasionally (especially as advocated by the Christian anarchists around 1900) communitarian. Whereas the ideas of the utopian socialists may be seen as a reaction against the Enlightenment as well as the puritanism and violence of the revolution, Marx and especially Engels glorified the materialist *philosophes* and the French Revolution.

8. See Diana Coole, *Women in Political Theory* (Sussex: Wheatsheaf; Boulder, CO: L. Rienner, 1988), p. 5.

9. On the Owenites, see Barbara Taylor, *Eve and the New Jerusalem: Socialism and Feminism in the Nineteenth Century* (New York: Pantheon, 1983).

10. See Frank E. Manuel and Frizie P. Manuel, *Utopian Thought in the Western World* (Cambridge, MA: Belknap, 1979), p. 651.

11. *Theorie des quatre mouvements et des destinées générales* was published in 1808; *Traité de l'association domestique-agricole*, afterwards known as *Theorie de l'unité universelle*, in 1822; and *Le Nouveau Monde industriel* in 1829. During the years 1816-18, Fourier wrote *Le Nouveau Monde amoureux*, but neither he nor his pupils ever dared to publish it. Some 150 years later Simone Debout published it together with a very comprehensive analysis (Paris: Éditions Anthropos, 1967). But in his first published works as well, Fourier expounded his ideas about love life of the future, and this is what the critics attacked: his work would incite to lust and promiscuity. As primary sources I studied *Theorie des quatre mouvements* and *Le Nouveau Monde amoureux*.

12. Fourier, *Le Nouveau Monde amoureux*, pp. 416 and 426.

13. See Jonathan Beecher and Richard Bienvenu, *The Utopian Vision of Charles Fourier: Selected Texts on Work, Love, and Passionate Attraction* (Boston: Beacon, 1971), p. 34; J. Beecher, *Charles Fourier: The Visionary and His World* (Berkeley: University of California Press, 1986), p. 198; Debout, p. vii. Here Fourier was similar to Nietzsche; see Frank E. Manuel, *The Prophets of Paris* (Cambridge, MA: Harvard University Press, 1962), pp. 209-10.

14. Beecher, p. 247.

15. See Fourier, *Le Nouveau Monde amoureux*, p. 391.

16. Fourier in *Le Nouveau Monde industriel*, p. 409, from Beecher, p. 238; Nicholas V. Riasanovsky, *The Teaching of Charles Fourier* (Berkeley: University of California Press, 1969), p. 215.

17. Fourier, *Le Nouveau Monde amoureux*, p. 391.

18. To find the right person for each task, all people belonging to a Phalanx would plan their activities for the next day during the sessions of the "Bourse of Exchange." Unattractive work had to be avoided, remunerated at a higher rate, or carried out by a special group of children.

19. Fourier, *Le Nouveau Monde amoureux*, p. 15.

20. Ibid., p. 388.

21. Debout, p. lviii.

22. Fourier, *Le Nouveau Monde amoureux*, pp. 146 and following.

23. For another elaboration of the "Court de l'amour," see Beecher, p. 307. See also J. Beecher, "Parody and Liberation in The New Amorous World of Charles Fourier," in *History Workshop Journal*, no. 20 (Autumn 1985): 125-33, arguing that this Court of Love was a magnificent parody of the Catholic Church.

24. Fourier, *Le Nouveau Monde amoureux*, pp. 206-7.

25. Fourier introduces these terms on pp. 389, 391, 429, 458, 459, 462, and 463, respectively.

26. Debout, p. lxii.

27. Ibid., p. lix.

28. Ibid., p. cxi.

29. Ibid., p. li. Debout quotes Fourier's *Theorie des unité universelle*, p. 135. It is not clear why Fourier does not mention here male homosexuality. It is Beecher's conclusion that Fourier maintained many more intimate friendships with women than with men.

30. Fourier had constructed an elaborate system for the Court of Love to take care of this. Every Phalanx would include one or more ideal, beautiful, and respected bisexual "couples" (Narcisse and Psyché), who, apart from their love for each other, would see it as part of their calling to give others their physical love. By experimenting with love and sexuality, all people would be able to formulate their needs and make them known to the Court of Love, which consequently would select one or more appropriate persons or call for Narcisse or Psyché. By organizing love in this way, ugly, handicapped, and old people would no longer have to fear sexual deprivation.

31. Beecher, p. 250.

32. Children up to fifteen years of age slept in the children's home, where their parents, biological or not, could always visit them. Both men and women could adopt them, and biological mothers who did not want them did not need to care for them; men were encouraged to have a strong relationship with the children. This passion for parenthood was not connected to biological parenthood by Fourier.

33. Apart from the moral doctrine of Enfantin, this was one of the reasons why the Saint-Simonians "deserted" to the Fourierist movement. They wanted to act rather than waiting for "La Mère," or, as the "deserter" Transon formulated it: "Fourier delivered the means to put into practice the goal of Saint-Simonism." See Beecher, pp. 424-26.

34. Phalanxes were founded in France, Germany, Spain, Italy, Rumania, and especially in Russia, where Aleksandr Herzen and Fyodor Dostoyevski (among others) connected for a while. For Fourierism in North America, see Mark Hollo-

way, *Heavens on Earth: Utopian Communities in America 1680-1880*, 2d rev. ed. (New York: Dover, 1966), pp. 134-59.

35. Saint-Simon published a prodigious amount of work, his first article appearing in 1803 (five years before Fourier), his last in 1825. For the analysis of Saint-Simon's theory I used as primary sources *La pensée politique de Saint-Simon*, ed. Ghita Ionescu (Paris: A. Montaigne, 1976), and *Der Frühsozialismus: Quellentexte*, ed. Thilo Ramm (Stuttgart: Alfred Kröner, 1968), pp. 22-122. As secondary sources: Frank E. Manuel, *The New World of Henri Saint Simon* (Cambridge, MA: Harvard University Press, 1956); F. E. Manuel, *The Prophets of Paris* (Cambridge, MA: Harvard University Press, 1962), pp. 103-48; Rolf P. Fehlbaum, *Saint-Simon und die Saint-Simonisten: Vom Laissez-Faire zur Wirtschaftsplanung* (Tübingen: J. C. B. Mohr, 1970); Sébastian Charléty, *Histoire du Saint-Simonisme (1825-1864)* (1896) (Paris: P. Hartmann, 1931), pp. 1-23; Emile Durkheim, *Le socialisme: sa définition, ses débuts, la doctrine Saint-Simoniennne* (1928) (Paris: Presses universitaires de France, 1971), pp. 111-230; George D. H. Cole, *A History of Socialist Thought*, vol. 1: *The Forerunners, 1789-1850* (New York: St. Martin's, 1953), pp. 37-50; Hendrik P. G. Quack: *De socialisten*, vol. 2 (Amsterdam: P. M. van Kampen, 1921), pp. 12-111; Keith Taylor, *The Political Ideas of the Utopian Socialists* (London: Cass, 1982), pp. 39-68.

36. By "l'industrie" and "l'industriel," Saint-Simon meant everyone engaged in a profession or enterprise, including farmers. He drew a distinction between the former and scientists and artists.

37. Quack, vol. 3, p. 13.

38. Manuel and Manuel (see note 10), p. 616.

39. *Expositions de la doctrine de Saint-Simon. Première Année (1829)*, ed. Célestin Bouglé and Élie Halèvy (Paris: M. Rivière, 1924), Sixth lecture (February 25, 1929), pp. 239-41, emphasis by the Saint-Simonians.

40. Ibid., Préface, p. 40.

41. Ibid., pp. 179-202.

42. Ibid., pp. 341-42.

43. Ibid., pp. 242-43.

44. Quack, vol. 3, pp. 39-40.

45. Charléty, p. 126; Claire Goldberg Moses, *French Feminism in the Nineteenth Century* (Albany: State University of New York Press, 1984), p. 46.

46. Among these associations were "family houses," production cooperatives, and the Saint-Simonian "clubs." A communal life was led in the "family houses," which were visited by many well-known artists, including Thomas Carlyle, Franz Liszt, George Sand, Victor Hugo, and Heinrich Heine. The "clubs" were organized in the quarters of Paris, where they provided free education as well as medical care for the workers. Some 2,000 people were active there in the years 1829-31.

47. Letter from Enfantin to his mother, August 18, 1831, quoted by Moses, p. 467; Helga Grübitzsch and Loretta Lagpacan, *"Freiheit für die Frauen–Freiheit für das Volk!" Sozialistische Frauen in Frankreich 1830-1848* (Frankfurt a.M.: Syndikat, 1980), pp. 74-75; Robert B. Carlisle, *The Proffered Crown: Saint-*

Simonism and the Doctrine of Hope (Baltimore: Johns Hopkins University Press, 1987), p. 165; Charléty, p. 128; Quack, vol. 3, p. 67.

48. Quack, vol. 3, pp. 73-81; Carlisle, pp. 107-16.

49. Marguerite Grepon, *Une Croisade pour un meilleur amour: Histoire des Saint-Simoniennnes* (Brussels: Sodi, 1967), p. 60.

50. Charléty, p. 155.

51. Carlisle, p. 189; Grepon, p. 83. Consider also the similarity with the late 1960s, when young intellectuals took factory jobs in an attempt to become "workers"–the class destined (in their view) to change the world.

52. Fehlbaum, p. 131.

53. For these cartoons, see Grübitzsch and Lagpacan, pp. 140-41.

54. Carlisle, p. 190; Moses, p. 50; Edith Thomas, *Les Femmes de 1848* (Paris: Presses universitaires de France, 1948), pp. 8-9; Laure Adler, *A l'aube de féminisme: Les premières journalistes (1830-1850)* (Paris: Payot, 1979), p. 38; Manuel, *Prophets*, pp. 154-55. Only Adler states that this had an eroticizing function.

55. On this much-discussed trial, see among others Charléty, pp. 176-83. Enfantin defended himself with the words: "God will put an end to the misery of this world by woman–men lack the ability for it. That is why the Saint-Simonians declared openly the freedom of women and called for their revelation, because God will lead them step by step nearer to happiness, peacefully, without any violence or meanness."

56. After his release from prison, Enfantin along with other Saint-Simonist men and some women went to Egypt, aiming to execute the plan for international "industrial" politics designed by Chevalier. They felt that by organizing large public works, one could form a "peace corps" founded upon financial means rather than being absorbed by ministries of war, and this "army" would produce wealth and peace for nations. But the Saint-Simonian plan for digging the Suez canal resulted in failure. Most Saint-Simonians returned to France, often achieving fame–and wealth–by activities in the area of public works. Quack, vol. 2, p. 109: "In doing so they aimed to put into practice at least one aspect of Saint-Simonian theory, as it had turned out to be so difficult to found a new religion that aimed at the emancipation of women and 'brotherhood' and love among men."

57. Jeanne Désirée, in *La Femme Nouvelle*, pp. 37-38.

58. Josephine-Félicité, in *La Femme Nouvelle*, pp. 65-66.

59. Isabelle, in *La Femme Nouvelle*, p. 91; see also pp. 115-16.

60. Signed by "Les Femmes Nouvelles," in *La Femme Nouvelle*, p. 159.

61. *La Femme Nouvelle/Tribune des Femmes*, p. 237.

62. Ibid. She added: "I don't say *vary much*, but *vary in the right way*. This is the condition of happiness and by consequence of progress." ("Je ne dira pas *beaucoup varier*, mais *bien varier*. C'est la condition du bonheur et par consequent du progrès.")

63. Yet some former *Tribune* women regrouped after the February revolution of 1848 around the daily *Voix des Femmes* (March-June 1848). This paper was banned by the French government after the Paris June uprising. The *Tribune* was

widely read, as shown by letters and contributions of women not only from the whole of France, but also from England and even from the United States.

64. It is not insignificant that Marx and Engels left these social elements out of their theory: in their era, when positivism was a dominant force, laws had to be formulated if one wanted to be taken seriously. See also *The Left and the Erotic*, ed. Eileen Phillips (London: Lawrence and Wishart, 1983), p. 26: "The problem remains of how to develop a continuum from the rational ordering of a socialist economy, which overcomes the excesses and chaos of the market and provides democratic control, to rationalist sexual politics when sex and the erotic appear to thrive on irrationalism, on excess and chaos and lack of control."

65. This slogan has been used by feminists against (Marxist) socialism. Briefly, this entails that the way one wants to live should be related to one's dealing with people and the struggle for social change. See also: Saskia Poldervaart, "Feminisme, romantiek, socialisme. Romantiek als bemiddelende factor?" *Tijdschrift voor Vrouwenstudies*, no. 37 (1989): 37-51.

66. Wilhelm Reich, *The Sexual Revolution*, trans. Therese Pol (New York: Farrar, Straus & Giroux, 1974), Preface to the Third Edition (1945), pp. xviii-xix.

67. Olive Banks, *Faces of Feminism* (New York: St. Martin's, 1981). Although her classification of feminist intellectual traditions was an "eye-opener" for me, she hardly dealt with the utopian socialist tradition. She does indicate that this tradition is recognizable again around 1900 and 1970.

68. Leszek Kolakowski, *Positivist Philosophy from Hume to the Vienna Circle*, trans. Norbert Guterman (Harmondsworth: Penguin, 1972), p. 90. See also Walter Michael Simon, *European Positivism in the Nineteenth Century: An Essay in Intellectual History* (Ithaca: Cornell University Press, 1963), p. 139.

69. For the "Revolt against Positivism," see H. Stuart Hughes, *Consciousness and Society: The Reorientation of European Social Thought, 1890-1930* (New York: Random House, 1964). For a classification into utopian (also communitarian) periods, see Zablocki (note 5), Introduction. See also Christopher Lasch, *The New Radicalism in America, 1889-1963: The Intellectual as a Social Type* (Ithaca: Cornell University Press, 1988). Lasch calls this era "the progressive period" and thereby draws a distinction between the progressive movement and the new radicals. According to Lasch, the radicals influenced the progressive movement but at the same time this movement was purely political, while the new radicals were more interested in the reform of education, culture, and sexual relationships than raising political issues in the strict sense of the term.

70. See also Wolf Lepenies, *Between Literature and Science: The Rise of Sociology*, trans. R. J. Hollingdale (Cambridge: Cambridge University Press, 1977), pp. 244-45.

71. Influenced by Fourier, Marcuse (among others) searched for socialist manifestations in a society not yet socialist and emphasized the role of the human psyche—especially its erotic side. He viewed work as a game, recognized the revolutionary character of sexuality, and was convinced that the dealings of individuals on a sexual and interpersonal level are fundamentally tied to

their behavior on other, also political, levels. See Herbert Marcuse, *Eros and Civilization* (Boston: Beacon, 1953), and also Vincent Geoghegan, *Reason and Eros: The Social Theory of Herbert Marcuse* (London: Pluto, 1981). In this way Marcuse expanded the concept of politics that would play a large role in many of the movements of the 1960s up to the "proletarian shift," when a large number of students restricted themselves to an analysis of class. An analysis of the utopian character of the sixties is regrettably beyond the scope of this essay.

72. On this, see Saskia Poldervaart, "Woongroepen en de communautaire traditie," in *Woongroepen: Individualiteit in groepsverband,* ed. Tony Weggemans, Saskia Poldervaart, and Harrie Jansen (Utrecht: Spectrum, 1985), pp. 20-53. In "living groups" (as communes are nowadays termed in the Netherlands), compulsory heterosexuality remained undiscussed until the pretense was abandoned that communal living was the best way for everybody to live. Members came to realize that people are different in their desires and that the point is that everyone must have a choice how to live. Only after this was grasped did the heterosexual norm become an important discussion topic in "living groups."

73. See Taylor, p. 286, and especially Sheila Rowbotham and Jeffrey Weeks, *Socialism and the New Life: The Personal and Sexual Politics of Edward Carpenter and Havelock Ellis* (London: Pluto, 1977). See also Elaine Showalter, *Sexual Anarchy: Gender and Culture at the Fin de Siècle* (New York: Viking, 1991).

74. On the history of this League, see Ute Gerhard, *Unerhört: Die Geschichte der deutschen Frauenbewegung* (Reinbek bei Hamburg: Rowohlt, 1990), especially pp. 216-68. These socialist feminists focused upon "unprotected" working women because they did not work under "proletarian" conditions and had therefore been disregarded by the Marxist socialist movement.

75. On Greenwich Village feminism, see among other works June Sochen, *The New Woman: Feminism in Greenwich Village, 1910-1920* (New York: Quadrangle, 1972). For additional information and a critique, see also Judith Schwarz, *Radical Feminists of Heterodoxy: Greenwich Village, 1912-1940* (Lebanon, NH: New Victoria, 1982), pp. 30-31. Schwarz reproaches Sochen for not being open about the lesbianism of many women within Greenwich Village feminism.

76. Paul Ricoeur, *Lectures on Ideology and Utopia,* ed. George M. Taylor (New York: Columbia University Press, 1986).

77. Oscar Wilde, "The Soul of Man under Socialism" (1891), in *The Essays of Oscar Wilde* (New York: Albert and Charles Boni, 1935), p. 28.

Johann Baptist von Schweitzer:
The Queer Marx Loved to Hate

Hubert Kennedy

San Francisco State University

SUMMARY. Despite his conviction on a morals charge involving a boy, the early German Social Democrat Johann Baptist von Schweitzer went on to have a successful political career. His life furnishes the context to present remarks by his political opponents Marx and Engels, which reveal their deep-seated homophobia. It is pointed out that this has been glossed over by the translations of the recently published Marx/Engels *Collected Works*. Some remarks on boy-love and anarchism are appended.

In an attempt to analyze homosexuality from the viewpoint of dialectical or historical materialism, an effort would of course be made to learn the opinions of Marx and Engels. But the classics of Marxism are remarkably silent on the subject. Marx appears to assert the naturalness of heterosexuality in his statement, "The relation of man to woman is the *most natural* relation of human being to human being,"[1] while Engels twice condemns pederasty in the ancients: "In the course of their migrations the Germans had morally much deteriorated, particularly during their southeasterly

---

Correspondence may be addressed: 3475 16th St., Apt. 12, San Francisco, CA 94114.

[Haworth co-indexing entry note]: "Johann Baptist von Schweitzer: The Queer Marx Loved to Hate." Kennedy, Hubert. Co-published simultaneously in *Journal of Homosexuality* (The Haworth Press, Inc.) Vol. 29, No. 2/3, 1995, pp. 69-96; and: *Gay Men and the Sexual History of the Political Left* (ed: Gert Hekma, Harry Oosterhuis, and James Steakley) The Haworth Press, Inc., 1995, pp. 69-96; and *Gay Men and the Sexual History of the Political Left* (ed: Gert Hekma, Harry Oosterhuis, and James Steakley) Harrington Park Press, an imprint of The Haworth Press, Inc., 1995, pp. 69-96. Multiple copies of this article/chapter may be purchased from The Haworth Document Delivery Center. [1-800-342-9678 9:00 a.m. - 5:00 p.m. (EST)].

wanderings among the nomads of the Black Sea steppes, from whom they acquired not only equestrian skill but also gross, unnatural vices [*arge widernatürliche Laster*], as Ammianus expressly states of the Taifali and Procopius of the Heruli,"[2] and with regard to the Greeks, "The men, who would have been ashamed to show any love for their wives, amused themselves by all sorts of love affairs with *hetaerai*; but this degradation of the women was avenged on the men and degraded them also till they fell into the abominable practice of boy-love [*Widerwärtigkeit der Knabenliebe*] and degraded alike their gods and themselves with the myth of Ganymede."[3]

It is perhaps this near silence that has encouraged gay Marxists to believe that an analysis sympathetic to homosexuality can be made on the basis of Marxist principles.[4] This may indeed be possible, but it will have to be done without the personal opinions of Marx and Engels. Not that their opinions cannot be known; they were expressed to one another in their correspondence, and they were distinctly unsympathetic. This will be illustrated here by comments found in a search for references to Johann Baptist von Schweitzer (1833-75), whom they regarded as a boy-lover.[5]

Schweitzer was an important figure in the workers' movement in Germany during most of the 1860s. His political career began in 1859, but was interrupted briefly in 1862 by his conviction on a morals charge. With the help of Ferdinand Lassalle and his own very real abilities, Schweitzer was able to make a political comeback and went on to become in 1867, as a deputy to the North German Reichstag, the first outspoken Social Democrat to be elected to any European parliament.

For various reasons Schweitzer has been forgotten by the movement to which he contributed so much. To rescue him from this unjust silence is one reason for retelling his story. Another reason is to furnish the context for the remarks of Marx and Engels concerning him. Their views are important, for while the name Schweitzer quickly lapsed into obscurity, the mention of Marx and Engels would call on the loyalty of millions throughout the word. This context must also include the great pioneer of homosexual emancipation, Karl Heinrich Ulrichs, who personally intervened in the court case of Schweitzer and whose writings were known to Marx and Engels.

MARX, ENGELS, AND ULRICHS

In 1869, Marx sent Engels one of Ulrichs's booklets. Engels replied on June 22:

The *Urning* you sent me is a very curious thing. These are extremely unnatural revelations. The paederasts are beginning to count themselves, and discover that they are a power in the state. Only organisation was lacking, but according to this source it apparently already exists in secret. And since they have such important men in all the old parties and even in the new ones, from Rösing to Schweitzer, they cannot fail to triumph. *Guerre aux cons, paix aus trous-de-cul* [War to the cunts, peace to the assholes] will now be the slogan. It is a bit of luck that we, personally, are too old to have to fear that, when this party wins, we shall have to pay physical tribute to the victors. But the younger generation! Incidentally it is only in Germany that a fellow like this can possibly come forward, convert this smut into a theory, and offer the invitation: *introite* [enter], etc. Unfortunately, he has not yet got up the courage to acknowledge publicly that he is 'that way,' and must still operate *coram publico* 'from the front', if not 'going in from the front' as he once said by mistake. But just wait until the new North German Penal Code recognises the *drois du cul* [rights of the asshole]; then he will operate quite differently. Then things will go badly enough for poor frontside people like us, with our childish penchant for females. If Schweitzer could be made useful for anything, it would be to wheedle out of this peculiar honourable gentleman the particulars of the paederasts in high and top places, which would certainly not be difficult for him as a brother in spirit.[6]

The author of the booklet that Engels so contemptuously dismissed was Karl Heinrich Ulrichs (1825-95), an early theorist of homosexuality and a courageous fighter for the rights of homosexuals, religious and ethnic minorities, and women.[7] He was also a partisan of the movement of the 1840s that sought to unify Germany–though not by force: by 1869, when Engels wrote the above letter, Ulrichs had twice been imprisoned for publicly protesting the annexation of his homeland, Hannover, by Prussia in 1866.

Grandson of a Lutheran superintendent and son of an architect in the employ of the state (who died when Ulrichs was ten years old), Ulrichs studied law at the universities of Göttingen and Berlin. After only six years of administrative and legal service in the kingdom of Hannover, his homosexual activity came to the attention of the Ministry of Justice. Although such acts were not illegal in Hannover, as a civil servant of the state Ulrichs could be "disciplined," and would surely have been dismissed from state's service in disgrace had he not learned of this and quickly resigned in 1854. This act forestalled any disciplinary proceeding, but did not prevent vindictive officials from using their information to keep him from earning his living as a lawyer. Ulrichs lived on a small inheritance from his mother and money earned as private secretary and as reporter for the *Allgemeine Zeitung* of Augsburg.

By 1862 Ulrichs had begun to formulate a biological theory of homosexuality and in a series of twelve booklets from 1864 to 1879 he set forth his "third sex" view of homosexual men, whom he called "Urnings" (the term "homosexual" was coined later by the Hungarian writer Karl Maria Kertbeny and was never used by Ulrichs), championing their equal legal and civil rights as a distinct minority. Ulrichs saw Urnings as a sort of intermediate sex, which he summed up in the catch phrase "a woman's soul in a man's body" (with the opposite true of homosexual women).

Although Ulrichs used a pseudonym (Numa Numantius) at first, he used his real name after he publicly spoke out for his cause at the Congress of German Jurists in Munich on August 29, 1867, an event that made him notorious in the German legal profession. Psychiatrists, too, reported his theory, if only to reject it as the self-justification of a man of dubious mental stability. They preferred to view homosexuality as an illness (as seen in the title of the 1886 best seller *Psychopathia sexualis* of Richard von Krafft-Ebing, who was first interested in the subject by Ulrichs's writings), an illness in need of *their* treatment of course.

The booklet that Marx sent Engels was identified by the editors of the *Marx Engels Werke* as Ulrichs's *Argonauticus*,[8] and this identification has been repeated in the *Karl Marx, Frederick Engels: Collected Works*, whose translation of Marx's letter is given here.[9] But this cannot be correct, since *Argonauticus* was not completed until late September 1869. The reference to "introite," which Engels wanted to read as an invitation to anal intercourse, instead suggests some knowledge of Ulrichs's *Memnon* (1868), for it appears in that booklet's epigraph: "Introite! nam et hoc templum naturae est" ("Enter! for this is also a temple of nature"), which is rather a reference to the edifice of Ulrichs's theory.[10] (This is a variation of a phrase that goes back to Heraclitus and would have been known to Engels through its use as an epigraph to Lessing's play *Nathan der Weise*.)

More probably the booklet that Engels read was *Incubus*, which was completed on May 4, 1869. This is confirmed by several indications, the most important of which is Ulrichs's use of "von vorn hinein" for "von vorn herein," which Engels puns on and which occurs twice in *Incubus*. (The idiomatic phrase "von vorn herein" means "from the beginning.") That Ulrichs admits he is not "from the front" is clear enough in *Memnon*, in which he several times refers to himself as an example of an Urning,[11] but is not apparent in *Incubus*. The reference to Johannes Rösing, a merchant in Bremen who was active in the democratic movement in Germany in the 1830s and 1840s, may also be pointed out here, since he was mentioned in *Incubus*, but Engels could well have known about him from other sources. The "personal details" about Schweitzer, of course, were known to all.

That Engels mentioned "introite" does suggest, however, some knowledge, perhaps indirect, of *Memnon*. We know that, as a result of Ulrichs's sending copies of the first part of *Memnon* to private individuals, there was a lecture on the subject in London in early 1868 at the Anthropological Society; that booklet and his five earlier booklets were then added to the group's library. Marx may have heard of *Memnon* as a result of the lecture; he may even have heard the lecture. At any rate, he remembered the booklet he sent Engels and spoke of it to others, for on December 17, 1869, he wrote to Engels: "Strohn will be returning from here to Bradford, and desires you to send him the *Urnings* or whatever the paederast's book is called."[12] Marx was generally more moderate in his remarks than Engels and despite his political opposition to Schweitzer, he several times noted the latter's very real abilities.

SCHWEITZER AND LASSALLE

Schweitzer was born on July 12, 1833, to parents who belonged to the small group of socially prominent Catholics in largely Protestant Frankfurt am Main.[13] He grew up, however, in the home of his maternal grandparents until age thirteen, when he was sent to a Jesuit boarding school. After completing law studies in Berlin and Heidelberg, he returned to Frankfurt to begin a law career in which he was never very active. This left him time for philosophical, historical, and political studies as well as his own writing. The most important publication of this early period was *Der Zeitgeist und Christentum* (The Spirit of the Times and Christianity, 1861), in which he defended revealed religion, noting that it was not so much the findings of science as its method that had led to the undermining of belief in dogmatic religion.

As early as 1861, Schweitzer was prominent in several workers' clubs in Frankfurt and was elected president of the Gymnastics Club (Turnverein) as well as of the Workers' Educational Association (Arbeiterbildungsverein), which he founded in November. The Gymnastics Club and the Rifleman's Club (Schützenverein), which he helped to found in 1860, served Schweitzer's political goals. He hoped to unite the many such clubs throughout Germany as a way of strengthening national feeling and developing a genuine people's defense force. The spring of 1862 was a high point of his effectiveness. On May 25, at a Workers' Day gathering, he preached the class struggle in a speech that may be taken as the beginning of Social Democracy in the Frankfurt area. For several reasons, much of the press was opposed to him, but the workers were solidly behind him. A member of the executive committee of the Rifleman's Club, Schweitzer was also corresponding secretary of the central committee of the General German Riflemen's Festival (Allgemeines Deutsches Schützenfest) in Frankfurt in July 1862. Ulrichs, who reported on the festival to the Augsburg *Allgemeine*

Zeitung, almost certainly met him then, if not before. Then in August came the catastrophe, Schweitzer's arrest in a Mannheim park. (Schweitzer's biographer Gustav Mayer gives the date as August 7, 1862, but reports another date in the quotation given below.)

The story of this incident, which is the only hard evidence we have that Schweitzer was a boy-lover, was raked up time and again by his political opponents, no doubt with many embellishments. By the time Mayer wrote his biography, the records of the trial no longer existed. In a brief note he gives a summary of a police report of 1867 that was based on the Mannheim records:

> It was stated there that between nine and ten on the morning of August 4, 1862, the accused was arrested in the Mannheim Palace Park for having there seduced a boy under fourteen years of age into undertaking an indecent act. But since the boy ran away and his age could not therefore be ascertained, the sentence that resulted was not for a crime against morality [*Verbrechen gegen die Sittlichkeit*], but only for the giving of public offense through the public perpetration of an indecent act [*Erregung öffentlichen Ärgernisses durch öffentliche Verübung einer unsittlichen Handlung*].[14]

On September 5, Schweitzer was given a sentence of two weeks' confinement, which was served immediately in the jail in Bruchsal. In 1869, Ulrichs recalled the event:

> It is notorious that the Lassallean Social Democrat Dr. von Schweitzer of Berlin was given a criminal sentence on September 5, 1862, by the court in Mannheim, because by an unimportant bit of fooling around with a young lad in the Palace Park he gave "public offense" through simple carelessness, i.e., he was overheard by two no longer young women.[15]

In 1864, without naming Schweitzer, Ulrichs had mentioned his imprisonment in 1862, adding: "As early as that time I put together a kind of defense for him and sent it to the prisoner in two letters. One letter got through to him–but only by an oversight. The examining magistrate added the other to his file on the case."[16] That appeared to end the matter, for Ulrichs's argument was not used in

Schweitzer's defense; indeed Schweitzer denied that the incident with the boy ever happened.

On returning to Frankfurt, Schweitzer met with almost total ostracism on the part of his fellow citizens and former friends. In the preface to a pamphlet published the following year, he wrote:

> When those in my hometown who called themselves my friends believed that the time had finally come when they could let loose their pent-up envy, when so many credulously repeated what a few had invented, I asked myself in astonishment, "How have you deserved this?" But that was only the first quick moment–and it occurred to me that it was always like that and would remain so forever.[17]

Schweitzer was briefly in Vienna in the first half of 1863, lecturing on Schopenhauer, with whom he was acquainted sometime before the philosopher's death in 1860. He first read a brochure by Ferdinand Lassalle (1825-64) shortly before going there. When it seemed that Schweitzer's political career was ended forever, Lassalle's appearance on the scene was a godsend.

Lassalle was born in the Silesian city of Breslau of moderately affluent Jewish parents. As a boy he was "keenly conscious of his Jewish descent."[18] "It was not long, however, before he realized that race oppression is only a phase of the universal condition of social injustice and that the 'Jewish problem' can only be solved as part of a larger social problem. At the age of eighteen the insurgent Jewish nationalist became a revolutionary Socialist internationalist."[19]

According to Marx, "After fifteen years of slumber, Lassalle– and this remains his immortal service–re-awakened the workers' movement in Germany."[20] Lassalle had great success as an agitator, including a trip to the Frankfurt area in May 1863, and on the 25th of that month he founded in Leipzig the General Association of German Workers (Allgemeiner Deutscher Arbeiterverein, or ADAV). At about this time Schweitzer wrote a novel and asked if he might dedicate it to Lassalle. Noting the value of Eugène Sue's novels in France, Lassalle quickly agreed, and when the first volume of *Lucinde, oder Kapital und Arbeit* (Lucinde, or Capital and Labor) was published in September at Schweitzer's expense, Lassalle immediately recognized its propaganda value. When the second volume appeared in December, he was even more delighted.

Meanwhile, the Frankfurt branch of the ADAV refused to accept Schweitzer as a member or let him speak, and his appearance at the Gymnastics Club in November was cut short by cries of "Get out!" But at Lassalle's request he was accepted into the ADAV in Leipzig. In December, Schweitzer announced that he would speak at the next meeting in Frankfurt. This caused Abraham "Fritz" Strauss, who was in charge of the Frankfurt ADAV, to write to Lassalle and ask for a "Cesarean section": "We cannot use him as a person, even though a large number know how to value his abilities. He is dead here."[21] Lassalle was put on the spot, but wrote diplomatically to Schweitzer:

> I have to write a very embarrassing request to you today. . . . You are familiar with the facts that lie at the base of the dissension against you. I know only what I read at that time in the newspaper and do not know what is true in it and what not. But if what the newspapers at that time reported about the reason for your conviction is true, I know one thing: the regrettable and to my taste incomprehensible fondness imputed to you belongs to those offenses that have not the least to do with a man's political character. Such behavior, in a political organization, against a man of your character and your intelligence only proves how confused and narrow-minded the political ideas of our people still are. I, for my part at least, whatever the Frankfurt members of our Association may say, will never hide the fact that I have the highest respect for you and set the highest value on yours, and I therefore leave it to you to show this letter to whomever you wish. I have written in this vein to Frankfurt, have not kept back my disapproval, and I hope that this letter will have for the future the desired result. With all this you realize that for a while and at the moment there is nothing to do but avoid that conflict and a possible split. . . . Having already brought so great and so essential an offering, you will therefore also know how to bring the further offering of avoiding . . . this conflict. You will rightly feel upset by this–but . . . as little as I will you let yourself stray from serving and giving yourself to the common cause.[22]

Lassalle wrote Strauss that he had fulfilled the latter's wish, though he scolded him for it, and he added that at his next visit to Frankfurt he would appear in Schweitzer's company at the public session of the ADAV. He also noted:

> The abnormality attributed to Dr. von Schweitzer has nothing whatever to do with his political character. I need only remind you that, however incomprehensible such unnatural tastes appear to us, the tendency of which Dr. von Schweitzer is accused was the general rule among the ancient Greeks, their statesmen and their philosophers. Ancient Greece saw nothing wrong in it, and I consider the great Greek philosophers and the Greek people knew the meaning of morality. . . . I could understand your not wishing Dr. von Schweitzer to marry your daughter. But why not think, work, and struggle in his company? What has any department of political activity to do with sexual abnormality?[23]

Schweitzer also received a copy of the letter to Strauss and he wrote Lassalle on December 11 to thank him, adding: "Besides, I give you my word of honor that I have unjustly acquired the reputation for the fondness in question."[24] Lassalle was probably unconvinced by this, since Bernhard Becker had written him only three days earlier: "It is not just the Mannheim incident that has brought Schweitzer such a bad reputation. A similar incident is said to have occurred earlier in Sachsenhausen and then been hushed up."[25] But true to his word, Lassalle asked Schweitzer to represent him at the first anniversary of the founding of the ADAV in Leipzig, and during the first week of July 1864 they were always together, arm in arm through the busiest streets of Frankfurt.

All of this, however, was not enough to rehabilitate Schweitzer with the Frankfurt ADAV, and when Schweitzer turned to Lassalle for help, it was too late, for Lassalle had left on his fateful trip to Switzerland, already under the spell of Helene von Dönniges. (But Lassalle showed his trust in Schweitzer by appointing him to the board of directors of the ADAV.) Schweitzer next moved to Berlin where, with the financial help of his friend Johann Baptist von Hofstetten and with Lassalle's approval, he planned to publish a newspaper for the ADAV. Then tragedy struck him a second time;

just when he seemed to be making a return to political life, his protector died on August 31, 1864, as a result of a duel fought over Fräulein Dönniges. Schweitzer now had only his acumen to support him.

MARX, ENGELS, AND SCHWEITZER

Schweitzer knew of and respected Marx, and he had already met Marx's protégé, Wilhelm Liebknecht, in Berlin. On receiving the news of Lassalle's death, he immediately went to Liebknecht to suggest Marx as president of the ADAV. Knowing Marx would not accept, Liebknecht made the counterproposal of doing away with the presidency and having only a board of directors that would also be responsible for the paper. (Neither knew that Lassalle had left a will, naming Bernhard Becker as his successor.) But Schweitzer wanted the paper, the *Social-Demokrat*, to be independent of the organization and asked Liebknecht, Marx, and Engels for their collaboration, writing to Marx on November 11, 1864.

At first Marx did collaborate, but he soon learned that Lassalle had been in contact with Bismarck and of course suspected that Schweitzer knew of this. He warned Schweitzer to break with Bismarck. Then, when Schweitzer wrote a series of articles praising Bismarck, Marx withdrew. Schweitzer, anticipating this, wrote Marx on February 15, 1865:

If you wish to enlighten me, as in your last letter, on theoretical questions, I would gratefully accept such instruction on your part. But as regards the practical questions of immediate tactics I beg you to consider that in order to assess these things one must be in the centre of the movement. You are therefore doing us an injustice if you express your dissatisfaction with our tactics anywhere and anyhow. You should only do this if you were absolutely familiar with conditions.[26]

Marx wrote Engels on February 18, 1865: "I consider Schweitzer to be incorrigible (probably has a secret arrangement with Bismarck)."[27] Engels replied: "Schweitzer's letter is 'rotten to the core.' The fellow has the job of compromising us, and the longer we have our dealing with him, the deeper we'll sink into the mire. So, the sooner the better!"[28] On March 10, 1865, Marx wrote to Engels: "The impudence of Mr Schweitzer, who knows perfectly well that all I need to do is publish his own letters, is fantastic. Though what else can the shitty cur do? . . . You must arrange for a few jokes about the fellow to reach Siebel, for him to hawk around to the various papers."[29]

Later in the year, in the *Social-Demokrat*, Schweitzer's attacks on the government led on November 24, 1865, to his conviction for "press crimes, disturbing the peace, lese majesty, and slander of government officers." Marx laconically remarked to Engels: "Bismarck seems to have realised how powerless they are and therefore to have thrown them out, so at last there's a trial and Schweitzer has been sentenced to one year of imprisonment."[30] In May 1866, Schweitzer was temporarily released from prison for health reasons, and after the Austro-Prussian war of 1866 he was amnestied.

Although Schweitzer lost his bid for election to the constitutional convention of the new North German Confederation in the spring of 1867, he was elected president of the ADAV, and on September 7, he won election to the new parliament. Engels commented to Marx: "The great Schweitzer has been happily elected with the assistance of the pietists of Elberfeld and Barmen, and will now have the opportunity to bowdlerise various points from your book in the 'Reichstag.' You may wager your life that he will do so."[31] (Engels was referring to volume one of Marx's *Capital*.) He believed his wager won after a long speech by Schweitzer in the North German Reichstag on October 14, 1867, a report of which was published in the *Social-Demokrat*. Engels wrote Marx: "Schweitzer has shown himself to be a vain jackass and phrasemonger. He's finished now."[32] But on the contrary, Schweitzer was one of the few people in Germany to show real insight into Marx's writings.

In 1868, Schweitzer published in the *Social-Demokrat* a popular account of Marx's *Capital* in twelve installments (from January 2 to May 8). In the middle of this Marx wrote to Ludwig Kugelmann on March 17: "Did you see that my personal enemy Schweitzer has heaped eulogies on my head in six numbers of the *Social-Demokrat* on account of my book? Very harrowing for that old harlot Hatzfeldt."[33] To Engels he wrote: "Whatever secondary motives

Schweitzer may have (e.g., to annoy old Hatzfeldt, etc.), one thing must be admitted. Although he makes a mistake here and there, he has studied the stuff really hard, and knows where the centres of gravity lie."[34]

Schweitzer had invited Marx as "guest of honor" to the general meeting of the ADAV in August 1868, but Marx declined, giving as his excuse preparations for the September 9 congress in Brussels of the International Working Men's Association (The "First International," founded in London on September 28, 1864). On September 15, Schweitzer wrote him: "I consider you to be the head of the European working-class movement–not only through democratic election but by the will of God. You can also be assured that I will promote your intentions as best I can."[35] Marx sent the letter to Engels, asking, "What answer should I give the cunning Schweitzer?"[36] Engels returned the letter with the comment: "The man is an idiot to believe that he can bribe you with such a letter."[37] Marx wrote back: "As for the 'warm fraternal' letter from Schweitzer to me, this is explained simply by his fear that following the Nuremberg decision I might now publicly speak up for Wilhelm [Liebknecht] and against him."[38]

Comment: In all the above quotations I have followed the translations of the letters in *Karl Marx, Frederick Engels: Collected Works*, even though they tend to gloss over the colorful language of Marx and Engels. But a protest is necessary at this point. Readers with a knowledge of German will have guessed that in describing Schweitzer's letter Marx used the term "warmbrüderlich," which, with or without quotation marks, does *not* mean "warm fraternal" in English. It means "queer" (in America, also "faggoty"), and indeed in a pejorative sense.[39]

The translator has similarly bowdlerized their use of the term "schwül." For example, in 1868 Marx sent Engels the book of Dr. Karl Boruttau, *Gedanken über Gewissens Freiheit* (Thoughts on Freedom of Conscience), which, although it does not discuss homosexuality, does promote sexual freedom in general. Engels inquired on July 21: "Wer ist dieser Schwüle Dr. Boruttau der ein so empfindliches Organ für die Geschlechtsliebe an den Tag legt?"[40] Our translator gives this as "Who is this sultry Dr Boruttau, who displays such a sensitive organ for sexual love?"[41] But Engels certainly used "Schwüle" in a pejorative sense, which is also reflected in Marx's reply: "Von dem Dr. Boruttau, dem Schwanzschwülen, weiß ich weiter nichts, als . . . ,"[42] which our translator gives as "About Dr Boruttau, the man with the sultry prick, I know nothing except . . ."[43] Today a clear distinction is made between "schwul" ("queer"–and not necessarily in a pejorative sense in the current gay movement) and "schwül" ("sultry"), but this distinction was not so clear in the mid-nineteenth century. I believe that Marx and Engels used the term "schwül" with the connotation of "queer"; not that they believed Boruttau to be homosexual, but that "queer" expresses the pejorative way they wished to refer to him.[44]

Returning to the story of Schweitzer: The ADAV had been dissolved by police order, but in September 1868 Schweitzer helped found and was elected president of a new General German Workers' Union (Allgemeiner Deutscher Arbeiterschaftsverband). He thought that Marx would approve his policies and wrote him on October 8. Marx wrote Engels: "As regards the letter from Schweitzer, it is clear that he does not feel quite happy in his boots. . . . Above all it emerges from the whole letter that Schweitzer still cannot drop his fixed idea that he has 'his own workers' movement.' On the other hand, he is unquestionably the most intelligent and most energetic of all the present workers' leaders in Germany. . . . My plan is not to use diplomacy but to tell Schweitzer the unvarnished truth about my view of his dealings, and make it clear to him that he must choose between the 'sect' and the 'class.' "[45] But Engels, who had long since given up on Schweitzer, replied: "His ambitions exceed his strength, or, as the Italians put it, *vuol petare più alto del culo* [he wants to fart higher than his asshole], and on this internal contradiction he will work himself to death."[46]

On October 11, 1868, Schweitzer was able to call the ADAV back to life, with headquarters in Berlin and just enough changes to avoid another dissolution by the police. In parliament, he was unable to get a bill passed that would forbid Sunday work, limit the workday to ten hours, and establish a system of factory inspectors, but he was able to bring a vote to have Fritz Mende released from jail, even though Bismarck spoke against it. Besides being a fellow

Reichstag member, Mende was president of the splinter group of the ADAV supported by Countess von Hatzfeldt, and on June 18, 1869, Schweitzer and Mende announced the fusion of their two parties. On June 22, Engels commented: "So that is Wilhelm's entire success: that the male-female line and the all-female line of the Lassalleans have united!"[47] (Mende's group was called the "all-female" line because it was under the influence of Sophie von Hatzfeldt; Schweitzer, of course, was the "male-female." This was in the same letter in which Engels commented on Ulrichs's *Incubus*; thus the play on words here by Engels is probably a reflection of Ulrichs's terminology.)[48]

Because of the war with France in 1870, Schweitzer again moved further from the views of the party of Liebknecht and August Bebel that had been formed at the congress of August 1869 in Eisenach. Schweitzer was able to accept the idea of a defensive war and voted for the war appropriations bill; Bebel and Liebknecht opposed "Prussia's war" and were arrested for treason in December. In the Reichstag election on March 3, 1871, only a few days after the preliminary peace of Versailles, Schweitzer and all other Social Democrats lost, and before the end of the month he announced his retirement as president of the ADAV, effective as soon as the next general meeting in May could elect a successor. In the meantime his money was running out.

SCHWEITZER'S FINAL YEARS

Schweitzer's financial situation was indeed bad; he lived on borrowed money most of his life. Long before his death, Schweitzer's father had stopped helping him, and Schweitzer got most of his money by anticipating the inheritance from his father, whom he made out to be a millionaire. But when his father died in December 1868 and the inheritance was divided, Schweitzer got only a relatively small amount. The *Social-Demokrat* would probably have folded then, except that the father of the printer of the paper lent him money against the inheritance from his mother. But he charged such a high rate of interest that even though Schweitzer's later earnings from his plays were considerable, he was never able to get out from under debt.

In January 1871, before his retirement from politics, Schweitzer's play *Canossa* opened in Berlin and had a success in the press and with the public. He had begun writing plays much earlier and already in 1858 had gained recognition for his *Alkibiades oder Bilder aus Hellas* (Alcibiades, or Pictures from Hellas). This play was probably influenced by his experience as a boy-lover and by his acquaintance with Antonie Menschel. Although Alcibiades (who may be identified with Schweitzer) rejects the eloquent Aspasia (Antonie) in favor of a slave who attracts him sexually, Aspasia vows to be faithful to him. The play proved to be prophetic when, fourteen years later, Schweitzer married the faithful Antonie.

During his political career, Schweitzer wrote propaganda pieces (*Der Schlingel* [The Rascal], 1867; *Die Gans* [The Goose], 1869), but now he wrote for money, as he himself said, and he was enormously successful.[49] In the last four years of his life no less than twenty of his plays were presented on the Berlin stage, and several of them (*Epidemisch* [Epidemic], 1873; *Die Darwinianer* [The Darwinians], 1874; *Großstädtisch* [Metropolitan], 1875) played throughout Germany. During this period his social contacts, too, were mainly with the theatrical crowd.

Although Schweitzer no longer wished to discuss politics, he was naturally still interested in the ADAV, and he attended the general meeting in Berlin in May 1872. There he was attacked by Tölke, the party secretary, who accused him of having hindered the progress of the ADAV by involving it in the trade union movement. He even succeeded in having Schweitzer ousted from the meeting and got a resolution passed declaring that Schweitzer was unworthy of ever being admitted as a member. But there were still those who valued him and asked for his advice, and Schweitzer's last political act was to write an open letter in November 1872 "to my personal friends in the ADAV." In it he declared the union of the ADAV with the Eisenach party to be a necessity that could not be put off. Union finally came at the congress in Gotha, May 22-27, 1875. There, despite Marx's criticism of the platform drawn up by Liebknecht, the two groups were united in a new party, called Socialist Workers' Party of Germany (Sozialistische Arbeiterpartei Deutschlands). With the introduction in 1878 of Bismarck's *Sozialistengesetz*, the law forbidding socialist activity, the party ceased to function in

Germany and the executive committee emigrated to Switzerland. When this law was allowed to lapse in 1890, the party was reestablished in Germany as the Social-Democratic Party of Germany (Sozialdemokratische Partei Deutschlands), of which the current SPD is a descendant.

Schweitzer hardly lived to see the union he had urged. He died on July 28, 1875, in Giessbach, Switzerland, of pneumonia, leaving only debts to his wife, whom he had married just three years before. As a result of his insolvency, even the copyrights to his plays were put up for auction, but they were acquired for his widow by the German Schiller Foundation. Schweitzer's remains were finally laid to rest in Frankfurt, in the same cemetery as Schopenhauer. The burial was attended by Karl Franz von Schweitzer, mayor of Frankfurt, and other relatives. Catholic clergy, whose downfall he had predicted, were there, too. According to Gustav Mayer, his biographer, not one worker was there, not a flower from them for the man who gave the best years of his life to their cause.

Schweitzer's wife is said to have had the impression that his drive for recognition was stronger than for political activity and that inwardly he held himself above all party struggles. Mayer believed that the one thing directing his life was an ambition increased by a drive for activity and pleasure, and unbridled by any categorical imperative. There seems to be truth in all this. Schweitzer was indeed a remarkable man, who can also be admired for not accepting and internalizing society's concepts of right and wrong, for not yielding to that self-oppression which is the most successful of all oppressions. Given the time in which he lived, we certainly cannot fault him for not "coming out" as a boy-lover; not even Magnus Hirschfeld ever publicly admitted to being homosexual.

PEDERASTY AND POLITICS

I have more than once referred to Schweitzer as a boy-lover, since he was "arrested in the Mannheim Palace Park for having there seduced a boy under fourteen years of age into undertaking an indecent act." It is unlikely, however, that Marx and Engels distinguished boy-lovers from adult "pederasts," the term they both used in referring to Ulrichs's *Incubus*. In that booklet Ulrichs used the term "pederast" to mean someone attracted to a boy under the age of puberty–and he clearly disapproved of seducing such a child. But in popular speech–and, no doubt, for Marx and Engels as well–the term "pederasty" meant homosexual anal intercourse, the term perhaps also being influenced by the similarity to the word of Latin origin "pedication," which is precisely anal intercourse and was so used by Ulrichs. Hirschfeld, in a footnote to his edition of Ulrichs's writings, called attention to this by referring to "pederastic acts in the usual sense," meaning anal intercourse.[50] But whereas Hirschfeld insisted that it was rare among homosexuals, Marx and Engels probably shared the common belief that it was their usual activity.[51]

By the time of Hirschfeld, the age of the loved one had taken on a new significance. Whereas earlier the age of fourteen had been taken as representative of attaining puberty, so that legal distinctions were made in judging sexual activity with those above and below that age, in his petition for a revision of the sodomy statute § 175 (first presented to the Reichstag in 1897), Hirschfeld suggested the age of sixteen as the new age of consent. This led to his revision of the Schweitzer incident. In typical propagandistic fashion, Hirschfeld twice mentions Schweitzer's "Mannheim scandal" in his *Die Homosexualität des Mannes und des Weibes* (1914), but avoids mentioning the age of the other person and even goes so far as to invent an adult occupation for him, that of brick-layer, which he states twice.[52] By the time of this publication, homosexuality had been widely discussed, especially as a result of the so-called Eulenburg affair, beginning in 1906, during which all the usual prejudices against homosexuality, including of course the danger for youth, occupied the media for months.[53]

ANARCHISM

When Hirschfeld mentioned Schweitzer, he noted that the "Mannheim scandal . . . gave Lassalle occasion to show himself very tolerant of the same-sex inclination."[54] Indeed, Lassalle was head and shoulders above Marx and Engels in this regard; their homophobia is clear enough. Still, Engels and, especially, Marx were able to appreciate Schweitzer's very real abilities, despite their distaste for his sexual inclination. In another situation, that regarding the anarchist Mikhail (or Michael) Bakunin (1814-76), their attitude may have been similar. Günter Dworek may be near the mark about them when, in his review of the *Encyclopedia of Homosexuality* (1990), he writes:

Sometimes the mixing of the general with the specific descends into the grotesque, homosexualizing history in the process. In this manner the argument between Marxists and liberation anarchists at the First International, essential to the history of the European workers' movement, is reduced in Dynes' encyclopedia to the personal aversion of the notably quite homophobic gentlemen Marx and Engels toward the anarchist leader Bakunin and his alleged love for the dubious young Russian revolutionary Nechaev. Such crude personalizing would no doubt make the two key authors of historical materialism roll over in their graves.[55]

But Dworek has misread the article "Anarchism" by Charley Shively (the only place Nechaev is mentioned in the *Encyclopedia*), which says Marx "used Bakunin's relationship to Nechaev as an *excuse* for expelling the anarchists from the International in 1872" (my emphasis).[56] Marx was quite willing to use his knowledge of such relationships to attack his opponents—witness his instruction to Engels regarding Schweitzer: "You must arrange for a few jokes about the fellow to reach Siebel, for him to hawk around to the various papers."[57] There can be no doubt about the kind of jokes Marx had in mind.

In the case of Bakunin the jokes were ready at hand. According to E. H. Carr:

Bakunin was infatuated at first sight, as others had so often been infatuated with him. He began to call young Nechaev by the tender nickname of "Boy" (for Bakunin had retained a few words of English from his year's stay in London). The most affectionate relations were established. A queer story afterwards circulated among the Russian *émigrés* in Switzerland that Bakunin had given Nechaev a paper promising his implicit obedience "even to the point of forging bank notes," and had signed it, in token of complete submission, with a woman's name, "Matrena." This declaration is alleged to have been found among Nechaev's papers after his arrest. But the story is too lightly attested to warrant credence. If any document bearing such a signature existed, "Matrena" was probably an example of Michael's predilection for the childish mystification of code names, and was not invested with the significance which rumor attached to it.[58]

Nechaev's biographer Philip Pomper commented on this: "The rumors circulating in the émigré community about Bakunin's use of the woman's name 'Matrena' in a document given to Nechaev may be more significant than E. H. Carr, for example, believes, although it is virtually certain that no open homosexual relationship existed."[59] But their relationship reminded George Woodcock of "other disastrous relationships between men of widely differing ages: Rimbaud and Verlaine, or Lord Alfred Douglas and Oscar Wilde," and he adds: "There certainly seems to have been a touch of submerged homosexuality; indeed, it is hard to find any other explanation for the temporary submissiveness of the usually autocratic Bakunin to this sinister youth."[60]

Indeed, how else is one to read the statements in Bakunin's long letter to Nechaev of June 2, 1870, following the break between them: "I loved you deeply and still love you, Nechaev. . . . [German Lopatin] would not have judged me quite so severely had he known how deeply, how passionately, how tenderly I loved you and believed in you!"[61]

Marx used two incidents involving Nechaev to have Bakunin expelled from the First International at the 1872 congress in The Hague. Using evidence submitted by Marx, the investigating committee "found that 'Bakunin has used fraudulent means for the purpose of appropriating all or part of another man's wealth—which constitutes fraud—and further, in order to avoid fulfilling his engagement, has by himself or through his agents had recourse to menaces.'"[62] The first finding refers to money from the so-called Bakhmetev fund, for which Nechaev refused to sign a receipt when it was passed on to him by Bakunin, leading to rumors that Bakunin had appropriated the money for himself. The second refers to the fact that Bakunin accepted an advance of 300 rubles for the translation of volume one of Marx's *Capital*, but never completed the task. Nechaev persuaded him to devote his time instead to the "cause," saying that he would "settle the matter."[63] This he did by writing a threatening letter to the student Lyubavin, the publisher's middleman, requiring that Bakunin be freed of all obligations. This letter found its way into the hands of Marx and was used by him as the most incriminating evidence against Bakunin (although it is not at all clear that Bakunin knew how Nechaev intended to "settle the matter"). Thus it was Bakunin's infatuation with Nechaev–and no doubt the homophobic perception of it–which led to the action of the congress in The Hague: "They voted heavily for the expulsion of Bakunin."[64]

Of course Marx and Engels were not alone in using the common prejudice against homosexuality for political purposes; this was common to all political parties. Ulrichs gave several examples of this, including his own case, in *Incubus*, the booklet Marx and Engels read:

> How the *Kreuzzeitung* and the *Norddeutsche Allgemeine* slandered the Guelphs when, on taking me away to [prison in] Minden . . . the Prussian police found at my house an extraordinary collection of papers on Urning love! And how the Liberal papers are full of slander since in the circle of precisely those two papers the pious Preus has suddenly turned out to be an Urning![65]

But Schweitzer's past was dredged up constantly. Mayer points out that at the election for the constitutional assembly of the North German Confederation, Schweitzer urged the workers in Düsseldorf to support the Progressive candidate Groote. But for the parliament he urged the election of the Liberal candidate Michaelis–who was in fact elected. The Progressive candidate was Heinrich Bürgers, who then published in his *Rheinische Zeitung* the text of Schweitzer's verdict in Mannheim. Sweet revenge![66]

If there was concrete evidence against Schweitzer, rumors about the anarchist Bakunin may have been fueled by a widespread perception that a disproportionately large number of anarchists was homosexual. Indeed, the leading individualist anarchist in Germany at the end of the nineteenth century was the boy-lover John Henry

Mackay (1864-1933). Emil Szittya, who appears to have been the first to disclose in print that Mackay was also the pseudonymous Sagitta,[67] author of the *Books of the Nameless Love*, was of the opinion: "Very many anarchists have this tendency. Thus I found in Paris a Hungarian anarchist, Alexander Sommi, who founded a homosexual anarchist group on the basis of this idea."[68] The extravagant Szittya is not always to be trusted, but here his view is confirmed by Magnus Hirschfeld: "In the ranks of a relatively small party, the anarchist, it seemed to me as if proportionately more homosexuals and effeminates are found than in others."[69] But whereas Szittya reported the reasonable explanation of the Italian anarchist Bertoni (himself homosexual, according to Szittya)–"Anarchists demand freedom in everything, thus also in sexuality. Homosexuality leads to a healthy sense of egoism, for which every anarchist should strive"[70]–Hirschfeld had his own arbitrary, even bizarre explanation:

> Whether from ideological enthusiasm, or because they generalize the feeling of being unjustly deprived of rights, whether from sexual preference for the lowest social strata, or whether they love the brutal force of others out of passivist masochism is hard to say and will probably only be decided when someone bothers to subject a large series of anarchists to an exact psychoanalysis.[71]

Of course, not all anarchists who defended homosexuality were homosexual themselves. Robert Reitzel (1849-98), editor of *Der arme Teufel* (Detroit), was decidedly heterosexual, but: "From the beginning of the 1890s Robert Reitzel was one of the first in America to speak positively of homosexuality," according to Reitzel's biographer, who also suggests: "It was probably also Mackay who first drew Reitzel's attention to the problematic of homosexuality."[72] (I think this unlikely, but it is possible; the two became good friends when they met in Europe in 1889, and when Mackay visited the United States in 1893 he traveled to Detroit to see Reitzel.) And Hirschfeld was lavish in his praise of the American anarchist Emma Goldman, whose "open letter" regarding an article on Louise Michel he printed in the *Jahrbuch für sexuelle Zwischenstufen* in 1923. In a preface to it he wrote:

In her periodical, *Mother Earth*, and in countless speeches given over several decades across the breadth of the United States, Goldman has campaigned boldly and steadfastly for individual rights, and especially for those deprived of their rights. Thus it came about that she was the first and only woman, indeed the first and only American, to take up the defense of homosexual love before the general public.[73]

At the turn of the century individualist anarchists were particularly outspoken in the defense of homosexuality. For example: "A sharply outlined figure of the Berlin individualist anarchist cultural scene around 1900 was also the precocious Johannes Holzmann (pseudonym Senna Hoy). . . . Holzmann, an adherent of free love, celebrated homosexuality as a 'champion of culture' and engaged in the struggle against § 175."[74] Ewald Tschek, who wrote under the anagram pseudonym St. Ch. Waldecke, may also be mentioned in this connection. A frequent contributor to the Berlin homosexual journal *Der Eigene* (The Self-Owner), his 1932 brochure *Gedanken über Anarchie* (Thoughts on Anarchy) is a forceful summary of individualist anarchist thought.[75]

Today much of the socialist left appears to tolerate homosexuality, if not entirely accept it–at least for "consenting adults." And again it is the anarchists who are in the vanguard of those who accept the rights of people of all ages to determine their own lives.[76]

AUTHOR NOTE

Hubert Kennedy is Adjunct Professor, Human Sexuality Studies, and Research Associate, CERES, San Francisco State University. He is grateful to Manfred Herzer and James Steakley, who read a draft of this article and offered valuable suggestions.

NOTES

1. Karl Marx, *Early Writings*, trans. and ed. T. B. Bottomore (New York: McGraw-Hill, 1964), in the *Economic and Philosophical Manuscripts* (Third manuscript, section on private property and communism), p. 154.

2. Frederick Engels, *The Origin of the Family, Private Property and the State* (New York: International, 1972), pp. 61-62. That Engels meant pederasty by "un-

natural vices" is shown by his references. "Ammianus Marcellinus, writing ca. A.D. 380 and, more ambiguously, Procopius, writing ca. 550, expressed disgust that Germanic tribes, Taifales and Heruls, practiced pederasty." William A. Percy, "Indo-European Pederasty," in *Encyclopedia of Homosexuality*, ed. Wayne R. Dynes (New York: Garland, 1990), pp. 595-97, here p. 596.

3. Engels, p. 57. I have, however, put "boy-love" in place of the translator's interpretive "sodomy." But in light of the remarks of Engels to Marx regarding a booklet by Ulrichs (quoted below), sodomy may indeed be what Engels had in mind. The original German in brackets is taken from Friedrich Engels, *Der Ursprung der Familie, des Privateigenthums und des Staats* (Stuttgart: J. H. W. Dietz, 1900), pp. 51 and 57, respectively.

4. See, for example: Gay Left Collective (London), *Homosexuality: Power and Politics* (London: Allison and Busby, 1980); Bob McCubbin, *The Gay Question: A Marxist Approach* (New York: World View, 1976).

5. The present article is an elaboration of my "J. B. Schweitzer, the Faggot Marx Loved to Hate," *Fag Rag* (Boston), no. 19 (Spring 1977): 6-8.

6. *Karl Marx, Frederick Engels: Collected Works*, vols. 42, 43 (New York: International,1988), 43: 295-96; hereafter cited as MECW. All letters from Marx and Engels are given here in the translations of the MECW: letters dated 1867 or earlier were translated by Christopher Upward; letters dated 1868 or later were translated by John Peet. My exceptions to them will be noted. Here, in the translation from French, I have replaced "arse-hole" with "asshole."

For another view of this letter from Engels to Marx, see Andrew Parker, "Unthinking Sex: Marx, Engels and the Scene of Writing." *Social Text*, no. 29 (= 9.4) (1991): 28-45. There Parker finds that when Engels distances Ulrichs from himself and Marx ("poor frontside people like us"), this is "a strategy that allows him the freedom to experience vicariously the anal eroticism he seems to condemn" (p. 39). Similarly, Parker notes that the correspondence of Marx and Engels "is smeared liberally with excremental imagery," and he points out that "shit can acquire significance only by activating an economy of anal pleasure, desires, and attachments" (p. 40). I am grateful to James Steakley for calling this article to my attention.

7. For Ulrichs, see Hubert Kennedy, *Ulrichs: The Life and Works of Karl Heinrich Ulrichs, Pioneer of the Modern Gay Movement* (Boston: Alyson, 1988); in German, with additional information, as *Karl Heinrich Ulrichs: Sein Leben und sein Werk*, trans. Menso Folkerts (Stuttgart: Ferdinand Enke, 1990).

8. *Marx Engels Werke*, vols. 31, 32 (Berlin: Dietz, 1965), 32: 768; hereafter cited as MEW.

9. MECW, 43: 295.

10. Ulrichs also used the phrase earlier in his *Formatrix* (1865), where he notes: "I ask the reader to try to transport himself here to a medical auditorium. Sexual expressions are just as unavoidable here as in an actual medical lecture. Yet I touch on what is to be said only reluctantly and only because it just has to be said." See *Formatrix*, p. 5, in the collected edition, Karl Heinrich Ulrichs, *Forschungen über das Räthsel der mannmännlichen Liebe*, ed. Hubert Kennedy, 4

vols. (Berlin: Rosa Winkel, 1994); the writings are paginated separately. All references to Ulrichs's writings will be to this edition. It was perhaps this mention of "introite" by Engels that led Manfred Baumgardt to assert that *Memnon* was the booklet that Marx sent Engels. See Manfred Baumgardt, "Berlin, ein Zentrum der entstehenden Sexualwissenschaft und die Vorläufer der Homosexuellen-Bewegung," in *Eldorado. Homosexuelle Frauen und Männer in Berlin 1850-1950. Geschichte, Alltag und Kultur,* ed. Michael Bollé (Berlin: Frölich & Kaufmann, 1984), p. 15.

11. See, for example, Ulrichs, *Memnon,* pp. 54-56, in which he describes the awakening of his own love interest.

12. MECW, 43: 403. Here, I have replaced the translator's "return" with "send"; the original German is: "Strohn . . . wünscht, daß Du ihm die Urnings . . . zuschickst" (MEW, 32: 421). Wilhelm Strohn, a member of the Communist League and a friend of Marx and Engels, may have had a personal interest in Ulrichs's booklet: in the same letter Marx notes that Strohn "looks very poorly and is very peevish. The doctors recommend him to marry" (MECW, 43: 403). I am grateful to Manfred Herzer for pointing out the implications of the doctors' advice "to marry."

13. Biographical information on Schweitzer is taken from Gustav Mayer, *Johann Baptist von Schweitzer und die Sozialdemokratie, ein Beitrag zur Geschichte der deutschen Arbeiterbewegung* (Jena: Gustav Fisher, 1909).

14. Mayer, pp. 432-433. Unless otherwise indicated, all translations from the German are mine.

15. Ulrichs, *Incubus,* p. 14. The last phrase was shortly after revised to: "two snooping old maids" (Ulrichs, *Argonauticus,* p. 17).

16. Ulrichs, *Vindicta,* p. xvii.

17. Quoted in Mayer, p. 72.

18. George Brandes, *Ferdinand Lassalle* (New York: Bernard G. Richards, 1925), p. 8.

19. Morris Hillquit, "Introduction," in Brandes, p. ii.

20. MECW, 43: 132.

21. Quoted in Mayer, p. 91.

22. Ibid.

23. Quoted in David Footman, *Ferdinand Lassalle, Romantic Revolutionary* (New Haven, Yale University Press, 1947; reprint, New York: Greenwood, 1969), p. 182.

24. Ferdinand Lassalle, *Nachgelassene Briefe und Schriften,* ed. Gustav Mayer, vol. 5, *Lassalles Briefwechsel aus den Jahren seiner Arbeiteragitation 1862-1864* (Stuttgart and Berlin: Deutsche Verlags-Anstalt, 1925; reprint, Osnabrück: Biblio, 1967), p. 265.

25. Ibid., p. 262.

26. MECW, 42: 608, n. 144.

27. MECW, 42: 95.

28. MECW, 42: 98-99.

29. MECW, 42: 120. Our translator had "the wretched cur" for the German "der beschissene Hund" (MEW, 31: 95), which is rather "the shitty cur."
30. MECW, 42: 204-5.
31. MECW, 42: 426.
32. MECW, 42: 450.
33. MECW, 42: 553. Sophie, Countess von Hatzfeldt (1805-81), a friend and supporter of Lassalle, supported a splinter group of the ADAV.
34. MECW, 42: 556.
35. MECW, 43: 589.
36. MECW, 43: 105.
37. MECW, 43: 107.
38. MECW, 43: 115.
39. MEW, 32: 167. The use of "warmer Bruder" (warm brother) in the sense of "homosexual" is attested as early as 1669, in Grimmelshausen's *Simplicissimus* (personal communication from James Steakley), and this use continues today. See also the comment of Magnus Hirschfeld in note 44, below.
40. MEW, 32: 123.
41. MECW, 43: 71.
42. MEW, 32: 124.
43. MECW, 43: 72.
44. The doublet "schwul/schwül" has an interesting etymology: "The adjective was taken over in the form 'schwul' from Low German into High German in the 17th century. . . . The New High German form arose in the 18th century, probably under the influence of 'kühl.' The form 'schwul' has been used since the 19th century as colloquial speech for 'homosexual' (note in this regard 'warmer Bruder,' colloquial for 'a homosexual')." *Der Große Duden*, vol. 7, *Etymologie* (Mannheim: Bibliographisches Institut, 1963), p. 632.

Magnus Hirschfeld, as usual, has a biological explanation: "In general the skin of the Urning is warmer to the touch than that of persons around him. It appears that the designation 'warmer Bruder,' which is widespread in popular usage, has its physiological foundation in this phenomenon (also the word 'schwul' = 'schwül' has a similar meaning)." Magnus Hirschfeld, *Die Homosexualität des Mannes und des Weibes* (Berlin: Louis Marcus, 1914), p. 146.

The use of "schwul" in the sense of "homosexual" is attested as early as 1847. See Heinz Küpper, *Wörterbuch der deutschen Umgangssprache*, 6 vols. (Hamburg: Claasen Verlag, 1963-70), 2: 264, where Küpper also states: "In Austria the spelling *schwül* predominated." That the word "schwül" retained this ambiguity in Germany as late as the first third of the 20th century may be seen in the dissertation *Homosexualität und Strafrecht* (Homosexuality and Penal Law, 1937) of the Nazi lawyer Rudolf Klare. After noting "the pornographic literature on this theme which truly flooded over the regions of Germany" in the Weimar Republic, he singles out the homosexual writings of John Henry Mackay for special mention: "The language presented here is of such a disgusting and *schwül* kind that the reader becomes nauseated" (p. 33). The context makes it clear that "queer" is meant.

45. MECW, 43: 127-28.

46. MECW, 43: 129. My translation of the Italian; the MECW translator has "backside" for "culo."

47. MECW, 43: 295.

48. I am grateful to Manfred Herzer for pointing out this apparent influence of Ulrichs on Engels.

49. Schweitzer's propaganda pieces are discussed in Peter von Rüden, "Das Arbeitertheater zwischen politischer Aufklärung und Anpassung an den bürgerlichen Kulturbetrieb," in *Beiträge zur Kulturgeschichte der deutchen Arbeiterbewegung 1848-1918*, ed. P. von Rüden (Frankfurt a.M.: Büchergilde Gutenberg, 1981), pp. 223-60. I am grateful to James Steakley for this reference.

50. For a thorough discussion of terminology on the subject, see Hirschfeld (see note 44), Chapter 1.

51. In a footnote in his 1898 edition of Ulrichs's writings, Hirschfeld wrote: "The latest medical researchers in this field, particularly Krafft-Ebing, have been able to abundantly confirm this statement, that pederastic acts in the usual sense belong to the greatest rarities and exceptions in contrary-sexual intercourse" (*Formatrix*, p. 27, in Karl Heinrich Ulrichs, *Forschungen über das Rätsel der mannmännlichen Liebe*, ed. Magnus Hirschfeld, 12 vols. in 1, paginated separately [Leipzig: Spohr, 1898; reprint, New York: Arno Press, 1975]). Hirschfeld later gave the statistic that eight percent of Germany's practicing homosexuals carry out anal intercourse. See Hirschfeld, pp. 287-88.

52. Hirschfeld, pp. 522, 983. Hirschfeld cited an article by Hugo Friedländer in the *Frankfurter Zeitung* of January 9, 1910, as quoted in part in the *Jahrbuch für sexuelle Zwischenstufen* 11 (1910/1911): 426-27. There Schweitzer's partner is described as a "young man," with no mention of an occupation. Hirschfeld may have been misled by the statement of Ulrichs: "In August [1869] the *Frankfurter Zeitung* again jeered, 'It is not astonishing that von Schweitzer has a hand in the Berlin brick-layers' strike. The Mannheim court records very well know how to tell of his preference for young journeyman brick-layers'" (*Argonauticus*, p. 113).

53. For an excellent presentation of this affair, see James Steakley, "Iconography of a Scandal: Political Cartoons and the Eulenburg Affair," *Studies in Visual Communication* 9:2 (Spring 1983): 20-51. See also the revised and expanded versions of this article in *Hidden From History: Reclaiming the Gay and Lesbian Past*, ed. Martin Bauml Duberman et al. (New York: New American Library, 1989), pp. 233-63, and in *History of Homosexuality in Europe and America*, ed. Wayne Dynes (New York: Garland, 1992), pp. 323-85.

54. Hirschfeld, p. 522.

55. Günter Dworek, review of the *Encyclopedia of Homosexuality* (see note 56), *Magnus*, 1991, no. 4, p. 56; quoted (and translated) by Les Wright in his review of the same work in *OurStories* (Newsletter of the Gay and Lesbian Historical Society of Northern California) 6.3-4 (Spring/Summer 1991): 16.

56. Charley Shively, "Anarchism" in *Encyclopedia of Homosexuality*, ed. Wayne Dynes (New York: Garland, 1990), p. 51.

57. MECW, 42: 120.

58. E. H. Carr, *Michael Bakunin* (New York: Vintage, 1961), p. 392.

59. Philip Pomper, *Sergei Nechaev* (New Brunswick, NJ: Rutgers University Press, 1979), p. 231, n. 34.

60. George Woodcock, *Anarchism: A History of Libertarian Ideas and Movements*, New Edition (New York: Penguin, 1986), p. 143.

61. Michael Confino, ed., *Daughter of a Revolutionary: Natalie Herzen and the Bakunin-Nechayev Circle*, trans. Hilary Sternberg and Lydia Bott (LaSalle, IL: Library, 1974), pp. 273, 275.

62. Woodcock, p. 150.

63. Confino, p. 400.

64. Woodcock, p. 150.

65. Ulrichs, *Incubus*, p. 13.

66. Mayer, p. 202.

67. Emil Szittya, *Das Kuriositäten-Kabinett* (Konstanz: See, 1923; reprint, Berlin: Clemens Zerling, 1979), p. 155.

68. Ibid., p. 156.

69. Hirschfeld, p. 522.

70. Szittya, p. 156.

71. Hirschfeld, p. 522.

72. Ulrike Heider, *Der arme Teufel: Robert Reitzel–vom Vormärz zum Haymarket* (Bühl-Moos: Elster, 1986), pp. 79, 101.

73. Quoted in Jonathan Katz, *Gay American History: Lesbians and Gay Men in the U.S.A.* (New York: Thomas Y. Crowell, 1976), p. 378; translated by James Steakley.

74. Ulrich Linse, "Individualanarchisten, Syndikalisten, Bohémiens," in *Berlin um 1900*, ed. Gelsine Asmus (Berlin: Berlinische Galerie, 1984), p. 442. See also the essay by Walter Fähnders in this volume.

75. Ewald Tschek, *Gedankan über Anarchie* (1932); reprinted in *Beiträge aus der Reihe: Lernziel Anarchie*, ed. Kurt Zube, no. 16 (Freiburg/Br.: Mackay-Gesellschaft, 1981), pp. 35-46. *Der Eigene*, which was openly homosexual from 1898, began in 1896 as an anarchist journal in the direction of the philosopher of egoism Max Stirner, whose meaning of the word "eigen" is in the journal's title. For a full explanation of my translation of the journal's title as "The Self-Owner," see my note no. 10 in *Homosexuality and Male Bonding in Pre-Nazi Germany: The Youth Movement, the Gay Movement, and Male Bonding Before Hitler's Rise: Original Transcripts from Der Eigene, the First Gay Journal in the World*, ed. Harry Oosterhuis, trans. Hubert Kennedy (New York: Harrington Park Press, 1991) (published simultaneously as *Journal of Homosexuality* 22.1-2), pp. 22-23.

76. "So long as this society assigns women a second-class status, so long as children are held hostage as the 'possession' of nuclear-family tyrants, no one is free." Jochen Knoblauch, "Warum ich Anarchist bin–Gedanken nachhängend," in *"Anarchie ist Gesetz und Freiheit ohne Gewalt": Uwe Timm zum 60. Geburtstag* (Berlin: OPPO-Verlag, 1993), p. 25. See also the special issues "Children's Sexuality" and "Children & Anarchy" of *Anarchy: A Journal of Desire Armed* (Columbia, MO), no. 26 (Fall 1990) and no. 27 (Winter 1990-91), respectively.

Homosexuality and the Left in the Netherlands: 1890-1911

Gert Hekma

Universiteit van Amsterdam

SUMMARY. The attitudes of the Dutch socialist left toward homosexuality are examined, drawing upon a wide range of sources. At the end of the nineteenth century, a political debate on prostitution heightened social interest in sexuality in its diverse forms. Medical literature on sexual perversion was another starting point for the growing discussion of homosexuality. These debates were joined by Dutch socialists of divergent opinions. Whereas some of them wanted to acknowledge the right of homosexuals who were born that way to express themselves, only one exceptional author defended the right to homosexual sex. But most socialists were prejudiced against homosexuality and generally endorsed Frank van der Goes's proposal to eliminate homosexual behavior while accepting the notion of an inborn homosexual orientation.

Beginning in the 1890s, homosexuality became a topic of public debate in the Netherlands. Medical doctors, journalists, politicians, and novelists discussed it openly, albeit cautiously. A wide range of

---

Correspondence may be addressed: Voetboogstraat 7, 1012 XK Amsterdam, Netherlands. Email: hekma@sara.nl.

[Haworth co-indexing entry note]: "Homosexuality and the Left in the Netherlands:1890-1911." Hekma, Gert. Co-published simultaneously in *Journal of Homosexuality* (The Haworth Press, Inc.) Vol. 29, No. 2/3, 1995, pp. 97-115; and: *Gay Men and the Sexual History of the Political Left* (ed: Gert Hekma, Harry Oosterhuis, and James Steakley) The Haworth Press, Inc., 1995, pp. 97-115; and *Gay Men and the Sexual History of the Political Left* (ed: Gert Hekma, Harry Oosterhuis, and James Steakley) Harrington Park Press, an imprint of The Haworth Press, Inc., 1995, pp. 97-115. Multiple copies of this article/chapter may be purchased from The Haworth Document Delivery Center. [1-800-342-9678 9:00 a.m. - 5:00 p.m. (EST)].

views was expressed, from extremely conservative to rather libertarian. It was initially an open debate in which many viewpoints were heard. In 1911, the criminalization of homosexual "lewdness" with minors ended two decades of effervescent discussions.[1]

Dutch socialists took a very ambivalent position in this debate. By 1890, the anarchosocialist Social Democratic League (Sociaaldemocratische Bond) of Ferdinand Domela Nieuwenhuis was losing ground among the electorate. To my knowledge, it never took a public position on the issue of homosexuality. The year 1894 brought the founding of the Social Democratic Workers Party (Sociaaldemocratische Arbeiders Partij, or SDAP), which quickly regained the lost left votes. Many of its leaders, including Frank van der Goes, Florentius Marinus Wibaut, Louis Heijermans, Louis Maximiliaan Hermans, Willem Adriaan Bonger, and Pieter Jelles Troelstra, also discussed homosexual love.

When considering the statements made by Dutch socialists on homosexuality, we must recall two key concerns of the fin de siècle. First, sexuality had emerged as a social question, largely through the national debate on prostitution, and this debate strongly influenced the perception of homosexuality at the turn of the century. Next, we should also bear in mind that homosexuals themselves as well as psychiatrists developed a new theory of male love, also coining at this time a new terminology with such concepts as "homosexuality," "uranism," and "sexual inversion." Moreover, we need to ask what an educated public could even know about homosexuality. I will therefore introduce some information on homosexuality in literary circles and on the level of press coverage in various periodicals that dealt extensively with sexual questions.

THE DEBATE ON PROSTITUTION

Recent publications have thrown a clear light on the debate on prostitution in nineteenth-century Western Europe. Health professionals sought to prevent venereal diseases through the medical control of prostitution, but these efforts were generally unsuccessful from both medical and political points of view.[2] The incidence of venereal disease failed to decrease appreciably, and the political support that liberals contributed to such efforts diminished as Christian political parties, feminists, and socialists began to question the ethical side of the medical control of prostitution. The Christian parties were opposed to it because they considered any such measures tantamount to the tacit legalization of sin; feminists were opposed to it because hygienic measures implied stigmatization of and discrimination against women; and socialists were opposed to it because it meant sacrificing lower-class women to bourgeois immorality. Christians, feminists, and socialists thus united in the struggle against prostitution, regarding it as a manifestation of atheistic, liberal immorality, of male chauvinism, and of capitalist decadence, respectively. In the Netherlands, this broad coalition defeated the liberals and the medical profession. National policy was changed, and free clinics for venereal diseases were instituted in the place of medical control of prostitutes.[3]

One important issue in the debate centered on male and female sexuality. Liberals and medical practitioners tended to regard male sexuality as simply irrepressible. From this perspective, males had to be granted sex in the precincts of prostitution, for otherwise their desires would endanger bourgeois daughters and female servants–or would find another outlet, such as masturbation and other vices. Dutch abolitionists, on the other hand, stoutly maintained that men could and should live in sexual abstinence, following the example of most women. The solution to the problem of male sexuality, they argued, was not legalized prostitution but improved possibilities for marriage, especially among the lower classes, as well as sex education. One Christian merchant marine captain wrote to the abolitionist *Het Maandblad: Getuigen en Redden* (The Monthly: Confess and Save)–which immediately exploited his remarks by publishing his letter as a pamphlet–that sailors were certainly able to practice sexual abstinence for long periods and indeed did so, as he and his colleagues could attest from their experience on board ships.[4] Quite a different viewpoint was advanced by a regulationist doctor who had been a naval surgeon for many years: he reported that many men sinned alone or with a same-sex shipmate.[5] A confirmation of the latter viewpoint was provided by the first autobiographical case study by a Dutch homosexual, which appeared in 1893 in *Psychiatrische Bladen* (Psychiatric Papers): here a naval officer confessed to having had numerous homosexual contacts on board ships, both with other "urnings" and with normal sailors.[6]

Contrary to many published studies interpreting the fin de siècle as a period of sexual revolution, we can only state that in the Netherlands the liberal cause went down to defeat; the future would bring not sexual liberation, but male abstinence and heterosexual married life. This development seemed to fulfill Friedrich Engels's prediction for the future under socialism: man will be monogamous as woman already is.[7] Socialists supported the heterosexual policy wholeheartedly.

THE MEDICALIZATION OF HOMOSEXUALITY

Another effect of the debate on prostitution was the emergence of public discussion on homosexuality. Once the abolitionists had achieved their primary goal, they broadened their campaign and started to specify new sexual problems such as abortion, pornography, child abuse, incest, and unnatural vices. Queer love and sex certainly had flourished under the cover of normal prostitution, which meant that these pleasures also came under attack in the course of the abolitionist campaign of the 1890s. It is entirely likely that young men with homosexual preferences entering the sexual scene embraced the abolitionist critique of sexual promiscuity. They may have rejected sexual pleasures in favor of sexual abstinence, as did their socialist and feminist friends;[8] but they had no future in marriage.

A new theory and a new reality of homosexuality came into being in the nineties. What had been regarded as licentious practices of inverted lovers addicted to sodomitical pleasures due to decadence or advanced age was now transformed into the biological destiny of born homosexuals. Male-male lust had been part and parcel of libertine lifestyles; now it became a personal identity, explainable in terms of innate factors. Parallel to hermaphroditism, homosexual preference was regarded as the psychic side of a physiological peculiarity. As defined by the German jurist Karl Heinrich Ulrichs, a male homosexual was a female soul in a male body.[9] Ulrich's paradigm had many practical consequences, but the most significant for socialist theory was the possibility of differentiating a way of acting–this man carries out homosexual practices–from a state of being–this man is a homosexual. Basing their pleas on the state of being, the advocates of homosexual emancipation were rather unclear as to whether or to what extent being a homosexual even meant having homosexual sex. The socialists would later follow this lead with their apologetics for the right to be a homosexual while simultaneously affirming the necessity of sexual abstinence outside of marriage. This captures the fundamental ambivalence of socialism toward homosexuality.

SOCIALISTS' ACQUAINTANCE WITH HOMOSEXUALS

Finally, we must consider the actual presence of homosexuals and homosexuality in socialist circles. From the outset, some socialist leaders–notably Van der Goes and Wibaut–were deeply involved in Aestheticism, the modernist literary current of the eighties which aspired to a renewal of the arts in the Netherlands. Van der Goes was coeditor of *De Nieuwe Gids* (The New Guide), the leading journal of this movement, and Wibaut wrote for it. In 1890, Van der Goes, Lodewijk van Deyssel (pseudonym of Karel Alberdingk Thijm), and Frederik van Eeden engaged in a heated debate on socialism and art. The leader of the movement, Willem Kloos, was a tormented homosexual whose finest poetry was inspired by affairs of passion. The veiled love lyrics he exchanged with Albert Verwey, another Aestheticist poet, were published at that time, Verwey's part under the title "Of a Love Named Friendship."[10] Van Deyssel's second novel, *De kleine republiek* (The Little Republic, 1888), was clearly homoerotic and foregrounded the theme of special friendship in a boarding school. This book was decidedly autobiographical, for Van Deyssel himself had been expelled from the renowned Catholic boarding school Rolduc because of his involvement in a special friendship.[11]

Arnold Aletrino, a physician and a novelist who was both a friend of Van der Goes and a regular contributor to *De Nieuwe Gids*, emerged as the first spokesman of homosexual emancipation in the Netherlands in 1897.[12] Aletrino was probably not a homosexual but a sexual sadist.[13] His friend and pupil Jacob Israël de Haan was to be far more open about his sexual preferences. De Haan is perhaps best described as a sadomasochistic and pedophile homosexual, and from 1904 onwards he was at the center of major scandals.[14] Lucien Sophie Albert Marie von Römer, almost certainly a bisexual, was the second and most important advocate of homosexual emancipation in the first decade of the twentieth century; he also participated in progressive and socialist circles and wrote on homosexuality for socialist journals.[15] Finally, the leading socialist poet Carel Steven Adama van Scheltema was a bisexual, but his preference was closely guarded. Thus, Dutch socialists may well have known homosexuals personally; but as documented by the correspondence of Adama van Scheltema with his best friend, the mathematician Luitzen Egbertus Jan Brouwer, the subject of homosexual practices was absolutely taboo.[16] De Haan alone took a public stand in defense of his homosexual desires.

Beginning in the 1880s, the Dutch press occasionally mentioned pederastic and sodomitic scandals. Based on such reports in the daily press, brief articles in *Het Maandblad: Getuigen en Redden* served up such scandals with considerable regularity.[17] And as we will see in the following section, socialist-oriented journals also exploited this sort of press coverage, which inevitably conveyed a negative image of inverted lovers. These accounts were thus brought to the attention of a broad socialist readership. Moreover, sexual perversions were also treated from 1887 onwards in books and pamphlets, mostly translations from the French.[18] Although these publications had a semischolarly tone, they certainly targeted a reading public interested in pornography, as did the periodical press.

SOCIALISTS AND HOMOSEXUALITY

In the following, I will describe in some detail four contexts in which socialists devoted attention to homosexuality. First, in the 1890s, the socialist-oriented yellow press exposed and denounced inverted lovers. Second, in 1904, De Haan was discharged as editor of the children's column of the socialist daily *Het Volk* (The People) after publishing an outspokenly homosexual novel, *Pijpelijntjes* (Pipelines). Third, from 1904 on, advocates of homosexual emancipation and socialists discussed homosexuality in several socialist journals. And finally, in 1911, the Christian government introduced new sex laws that penalized, among other things, "lewdness" with same-sex minors. Dutch socialists played a prominent role in the parliamentary debates on these laws.

THE YELLOW PRESS

The socialist yellow newspaper *De Roode Duivel* (The Red Devil) edited by Louis Maximiliaan Hermans, who later became a socialist delegate to the parliament, took a stance opposed to crown, church, and capital. Late in 1893, it mentioned two noblemen from The Hague apprehended in an act of "unnatural fornication" and commented ironically: "Unnatural fornication and the rape of innocent girls have a good chance of becoming civic virtues, for the nobility and clergy are cultivating them assiduously."[19] Some weeks later, the rape of several boys by a Catholic priest was mentioned.[20] Jokes linking pederasty and Catholicism appeared in several other issues of the year 1894.[21] One of these issues also pilloried a "child rapist, baronet Van Heeckeren."[22] In 1897, when a Protestant teacher had been accused of pederasty, the famous Calvinist leader Abraham Kuyper was implicated in a joke; *De Roode Duivel* suggested that he had learned these sins from close reading of the Bible.[23] Some weeks later, after the police closed a male bordello in Arnhem, *De Roode Duivel* commented: "Several high-ranking men are leaving the city in a hurry, fearing involvement in the scandal of pederasty and male love. Numerous large mansions stand empty as an advertisement of the morals of our highest classes."[24] New jokes on this case followed a week later.[25] In the summer of the same year, the doctor of the Amsterdam prison was the object of a sneer: his rectal temperature was said to have risen enormously since he learned he could return to his job in prison.[26] At the end of the year, the journal announced that it was ceasing publication because of its linkage with a new weekly, *De Amsterdamsche Lantaarn* (The Amsterdam Lantern), which was even more scandalous.[27] Aiming at heightened respectability, the socialists now had to abandon the terrain of yellow journalism, and Hermans himself became a member of parliament.

Bram Cornelisse, the editor of *De Amsterdamsche Lantaarn*, another socialist-oriented yellow newspaper, started his journalistic career in 1897 with a leaflet entitled "Ontmaskering! Geen genade!

Onthullingen uit de Sodom-Sociëteit" (Unmasking! No Mercy! Revelations from the Sodom-Society) concerning a beerhouse where sodomites gathered. According to Cornelisse, the owner, one George Hermans, was a sodomite who sold quack cures for venereal diseases, providing him with the opportunity "to give rein to his dissolute passions." Any normal visitor who happened into this bar would be sickened by the caresses exchanged among males, and as a socialist Cornelisse declared his indignation at portraits of the royal family prominently displayed here. (Royalism appears to be a longstanding feature of the Dutch gay world.) Cornelisse went on to recount the story of one young man who had been asked by George Hermans whether he was willing to serve as secretary to a rich man: as soon as he had discerned the debauched intentions of this male procurer, the youngster had fled in utter disgust.[28]

Beginning with the first issue of *De Amsterdamsche Lantaarn* on September 17, 1897, Cornelisse launched a series entitled "In the Pillory." The first victim selected for exposure was George Hermans.[29] The same issue mentioned an inquiry in the Amsterdam City Council concerning indecent publications that were being freely distributed in the city, presumably the aforementioned pamphlet. Cornelisse indeed considered himself a target of this inquiry, for he immediately responded by asking whether the City Council intended to defend the pederasts and child abusers he was denouncing.[30] The third issue brought a confirmation of the effectiveness of Cornelisse's pillory: the windows of Hermans's beerhouse had been smashed–as would soon be revealed–by Cornelisse himself![31] He ultimately received a one-week jail sentence for this offense.[32] Subsequent issues continued to excoriate many inverted lovers in a somewhat veiled manner, and yet another sodomites' bar was placed in the pillory.[33] Cornelisse's anti-pederastic scandal mongering continued throughout 1898. The next year, he joked about the possible foundation of a "pederasts' club" which would certainly obtain royal assent.[34] (Royal assent was in fact finally granted to a Dutch homosexual emancipation organization in 1973, sixty-one years after the movement was founded.) Although Cornelisse's weekly continued to appear for five more years, no copies have survived, so we can no longer trace the course of its anti-homosexual crusade.

Just as *De Roode Duivel* had denounced pederasts among the clergy, nobility, and upper bourgeoisie, Cornelisse frequently pilloried inverted lovers in *De Amsterdamsche Lantaarn*. His attacks were not limited to high-ranking men, for his main target was the gathering places of pederasts in Amsterdam. All the while, he was also exposing bordellos, prostitution, and incest. Whereas *De Roode Duivel* had been more interested in political scandals, Cornelisse made sexual scandals his trademark. We do not know what happened to George Hermans and his bar after Cornelisse's exposé, but the second bar that he denounced was closed a short time later. All in all, the socialist yellow press participated in upholding an abhorrent image of homosexuality, depicting it primarily as a vice of patricians or priests and using this argument to draw the working class into the SDAP.

THE JACOB ISRAËL DE HAAN SCANDAL

In 1904, Jacob Israël de Haan, a Jewish gay novelist and later a poet, provoked a scandal with his first novel *Pijpelijntjes*.[35] The book's protagonist was a promiscuous boy-lover and homosexual masochist. At the time, De Haan was responsible for the children's column in the socialist daily *Het Volk*, a position from which he was abruptly dismissed following the novel's publication; he was simultaneously fired as a schoolteacher. Clearly autobiographical in character, *Pijpelijntjes* discussed the lives and loves of two students named Joop and Sam–the actual nicknames of De Haan and Arnold Aletrino, who was a physician at that time. Aletrino, to whom the book was dedicated, had courageously and publicly defended homosexuality as a sexual preference (but not as a sexual practice) both in the leading Dutch psychiatric journal and at the Fifth Congress for Criminal Anthropology, which had drawn a learned audience–including Cesare Lombroso–to Amsterdam in 1901.[36] Aletrino had probably helped De Haan in his coming out as a homosexual, but De Haan went too far when he depicted him as a sadomasochistic bisexual (Aletrino was at the time in his second marriage; his first wife had committed suicide)–too far both for Aletrino and for his own financée. They bought up nearly the entire first edition of the novel and had it destroyed. Shortly afterward, De

Haan published a revised edition, without the dedication to Aletrino and with two new names for the leading characters; on the other hand, the second edition of the novel was even more homoerotic than the first.[37]

The SDAP was in a difficult situation. It was election time, and the Christian parties were using homosexual emancipation as championed by Aletrino and Von Römer to attack liberal and socialist institutions. The socialists were simultaneously engaged in a quarrel with the Christian parties over the issue of socialist teachers, arguing that there was a distinction between teachers' politics and their profession, and that socialists were entirely capable of teaching neutrally to non-socialist children. But with the publication of *Pijpelijntjes* by the children's columnist of their own daily, the socialists were not only embroiled in a homosexual scandal but snared in a contradiction: they were disregarding a journalist's professional capabilities and firing him because of his morality. For some time, letters were exchanged in *Het Volk* between De Haan and Pieter Lodewijk Tak, the editor and president of the SDAP, with many readers and party leaders commenting. In 1905, De Haan published an *Open brief aan P. L. Tak* (Open Letter to P. L. Tak), a verbose and rather ineffectual defense. He attacked the hypocrisy, stupidity, and cultural barbarism of the socialists but continued to hope for clemency from the socialist leadership. Tak–himself a bachelor–remained quite firm: male love could be discussed by scholars, but not in literature, for books such as De Haans' would incite readers to sexual perversions. He regarded it as out of the question to employ a children's columnist who had written such a harmful book.[38]

Despite this setback, De Haan went on writing homosexual novels and poetry, staunchly adhering to his uncompromising vision of justice. After a journey to Russia, he authored a pamphlet against the tsarist prison system[39] as well a second gay novel, *Pathologieën* (1908), with pronounced decadent and sadomasochistic thematics. A Zionist, De Haan moved to Palestine at the end of World War I but, angered by the unwillingness of the Zionists to cooperate with the Arabs, joined the anti-Zionist movement of orthodox Jews who had coexisted with the Arabs in Palestine for centuries. For this "betrayal," De Haan was slain in 1924 by Zionists who sought to pin the blame on the Arabs, suggesting that they had murdered De Haan because of his pederasty. De Haan died as an advocate of some of the twentieth century's losers: Palestinian Arabs, Russian prisoners, and Western European homosexuals.

HOMOSEXUAL EMANCIPATION AND DUTCH SOCIALISM

Lucien von Römer, a physician and scholarly collaborator of Hirschfeld, was the most outspoken advocate of homosexual emancipation in the Netherlands in the first decade of the twentieth century. He authored books, lengthy essays for Hirschfeld's *Jahrbuch für sexuelle Zwischenstufen* (Yearbook for Sexual Intermediates), a number of pamphlets against both the Christian political leader Abraham Kuyper and a university professor who had dared to declare the *Jahrbuch* tendentious, and some articles for the socialist press.

The debate sparked by Von Römer began with his lecture on homosexuality for the Reinlevenbeweging (Pure Life Movement), a Christian-socialist movement that promoted the sort of sexual mores favored by the abolitionists. They maintained that sexual relations were permissible only for heterosexual couples when procreation was possible and love was present. All other sexual practices, especially prostitution and masturbation, but also homosexuality and lustful heterosexuality, were considered impure. Arguing that homosexuality was a natural sexual variation, Von Römer tried to get homosexual love placed on an equal footing with idealized heterosexual love. Most leaders of the Reinleven movement condemned this standpoint, as did Aletrino, who was willing to defend homosexuality only as an orientation, not as a practice. The Christian leader Kuyper joked that Von Römer was defending the sins of Sodom in the name of pure life.[40]

In the November 1904 issue of the theoretical journal of the SDAP, *De Nieuwe Tijd* (The New Age), the socialist physician Louis Heijermans discussed Von Römer's and Hirschfeld's theories. If homosexuals were natural variations, he argued, then they were certainly biological zeroes ("non-valeurs"). Since it did not contribute to human propagation, homosexuality was characterized by Heijermans as a sick condition to be placed on a par with masturbation. The danger posed by homosexuality was the seduction of normal young men, and the state had to control such corruption. Interestingly, Heijermans stated that there was no socialist explanation for homosexuality.[41] Von Römer replied furiously, charging that his objectivity was being impugned because he was a homosexual–an inference which Heijermans denied. Von Römer reaffirmed his conviction that homosexuality was a natural variation.[42] He elided the sexual side of the homosexual experience, so that Heijermans in his reply again had the opportunity to reproach homosexuals for their sexual escapades.[42]

In 1905, Von Römer published "Letters to My Friend: Love Life" in the Flemish socialist monthly *Ontwaking* (Awakening). Here he stated: "A sexual act does not defile our lives and our souls, nor is the sexual in itself impure and vile, for it is high and holy when it flares up from men's ecstasy of soul at the approach of Beauty and Goodness, at being in a life that knows no misery. But impure and vile is the lewd desire for lust, only for lust itself."[44] With this spirited article, published outside the realm of Dutch debates, Von Römer concluded the discussion, for no one responded to him anymore.

The single most important contribution to the socialist discussion was a lecture entitled "Social Examination of Homosexuality" given by Frank van der Goes, the ideological leader of the SDAP, on November 7, 1907.[45] Van der Goes's position was clear: homosexuality as an orientation had to be acknowledged, but as a practice it had to be "eradicated" (an outlook that anticipated the position later taken by Wilhelm Reich and by many churches nowadays). In the ideal socialist state it would no longer exist as a sexual experience. He acknowledged the existence of an innate homosexuality but opined at the same time that homosexuality could be learned. Homosexuality had in some periods been a contagious or epidemic disease: during the Crusades, under certain kings such as Henry III of France, in the German military of his day (the lecture coincided with the Eulenburg scandal in Germany), in countries with sharp class differences such as classical Greece and Rome. It was very rare, Van der Goes maintained, among classless groups–students and workers, for example. Under capitalism and in slave societies, it was typically a manifestation of the abuse of power. Such abuses would cease to exist under socialism, when there would be no pleasure outside the realm of labor.[46]

PARLIAMENTARY DEBATES

Debauchery was made a political issue by the Christian parties that held political power in the Netherlands beginning in 1900. Dutch sex laws had already become more restrictive under nineteenth-century liberal regimes, but liberals lacked a political vocabulary to discuss sexuality because of their ideology of private and public spheres: sex was private and should thus be nonpolitical. Starting at the turn of the century, however, and continuing until 1911, Christian leaders hesitantly introduced such legislation into parliament. When new sex laws were first proposed by Minister of Justice Antonius Petrus Laurentius Nelissen, same-sex practices were not even mentioned. Nelissen retired soon afterwards and was succeeded by Edmond Hubert Robert Regout, who had long urged the passage of a special law against homosexual abuses.[47] As soon as he became minister, Regout proposed an amendment to the original draft (Article 248ter), which penalized the seduction of minors, irrespective of gender, by financial inducement; the amendment (Article 248bis) specifically called for the criminalization of "lewdness" with same-sex minors.[48]

In the parliamentary debates which ensued, three currents could be discerned. The first was supported by the Christian parties that followed Regout in all respects, if necessary quoting the Bible. A second, very active group was the socialists and progressive liberals. They favored defeating Regout's amendment on the homosexual seduction of minors and restoring the original Nelissen draft. A third group consisted of traditional liberals, who rejected both proposals because they interfered too much in private life. In the end, both Nelissen's original draft and Regout's amendment were introduced. Notwithstanding their differences of opinion on the criminalization of homosexuality, all the speakers in parliament–Christians, socialists and progressives, and traditional liberals–made it abundantly clear that they loathed homosexuals, or at best pitied them. The point of the second current, which included the socialists, was that sanctions had to be imposed for the seduction of young women as well as young men.[49] Moreover, some liberal members of parliament voiced concern that the specific criminalization of homosexual acts might result in the emergence of a homosexual emancipation movement like that in Germany.[50] Liberals and socialists wanted to punish seduction by financial inducement, not sexual acts per se. They reasoned that older men could be seduced by younger men or women of means, in which case it would be unjust to hold the senior party guilty; to do so would moreover be an invitation to blackmail. On the level of language, all groups spoke of "homosexuality"; one traditional liberal used the Latin term "crimen nefandum," and Regout also used the Greek term "pederasty."[51]

At one point in the debate, the leader of the Dutch socialists stated that the criminal law amendment he backed was inspired by the same feeling of morality shared by all other members of parliament.[52] He argued that he was nonetheless opposed to any special criminalization of homosexual acts, as were the liberals and even a respected old Christian leader, Alexander Frederik de Savornin Lohman. The proposal jointly sponsored by liberals and socialists was rejected by a vote of 61 to 22, and Regout's article 248bis concerning homosexual acts with minors passed by a vote of 50 to 34. Thirteen parliamentarians voted against both proposals, but none of them was a socialist.[53] The traditional liberals opposed state moral controls even more strongly than did the socialists, who actually took an active part in drafting the sex laws. The socialist amendment, in revised form, became part of the criminal law.

CONCLUSION

As Wilfried Eissler has found in the case of the German socialists of the Weimar years, Dutch socialists between 1890 and 1911 were quite ambivalent in their attitudes towards homosexuality.[54] Their critique of capitalism led to an anti-liberal outlook that enabled them to join with the Christian parties on many points concerning morality. This was clearly the case with prostitution and in some respects also with homosexuality. On the other hand, liberals never enunciated a consistent political perspective on sexuality, because they considered it a private affair. They relied strongly on the medical profession for a sexual ideology, but this alliance was weak.

While the liberals were in principle opposed to state intervention, in practice they allowed the medical profession to intervene forcibly in private affairs, as in the matter of prostitution. Liberals thus undermined their own position without developing a consistent new ethic. In the absence of a clear-cut ideology, they had to yield the terrain of sexuality to new political groups, such as the Christian parties, feminists, and socialists.

But the socialists likewise did not dare to elaborate an explicit sexual ideology. Moreover, they were too devoted to economic struggles and to an ideology of utility, labor, and rationality to conceive of the importance of moral debates. With both liberals and socialists yielding on this issue to other groups, the Christians found it easy to take the high moral ground. The interventions of the socialists in the parliamentary debate cannot be considered as in any sense liberatory for homosexuals; indeed, quite the contrary. Denunciations of pederasts and inverted lovers in the socialist-oriented yellow press were perhaps most indicative of the popular perspective on homosexuality in leftist circles.

The most explicit socialist text on homosexuality was the 1907 lecture by Frank van der Goes. He stated quite clearly that homosexuality had to be acknowledged as an inborn orientation; and on this point he concurred with homosexual emancipation. But he went on to say that homosexual practices had to be eliminated–if not in capitalist, then in socialist society. The progressiveness of socialists was thus quite limited on the matter of homosexuality. Their negative attitude toward homosexual practices notwithstanding, they opposed Article 248bis, and socialist leaders such as Van der Goes were later the first to sign a petition against this law.[55] The most positive thing we can say about the socialists is that in contrast to the Christian parties, they did not want to use the criminal law to campaign against homosexuals under the prevailing conditions of capitalism. Concerning the socialist state they envisioned for the future, their tactics were to be more in the realm of prevention, as in the case of prostitution: sex education, policies promoting better possibilities for marital life, and marriage itself. Centered on rationality, labor, and utility, traditional socialist ideologies were anti-hedonist and anti-libertarian. In the sphere of sexual practices, they condoned at most a restrained heterosexuality and were fundamentally homophobic.

AUTHOR NOTE

Gert Hekma is Codirector of Homostudies within the Sociologisch Instituut of the Universiteit van Amsterdam. He has published widely on the history and sociology of sexuality and homosexuality, and he was coeditor of *The Pursuit of Sodomy: Male Homosexuality in Renaissance and Enlightenment Europe* (co-published simultaneously as *Journal of Homosexuality*, 16(2)) (New York: Harrington Park Press, 1989). His most recent book deals with homosexuals in the world of sports.

NOTES

1. The main introduction to the history of homosexuality in this period for the Netherlands is Gert Hekma, *Homoseksualiteit, een medische reputatie: De uitdoktering van de homoseksueel in negentiende-eeuws Nederland* (Amsterdam: SUA, 1987).

2. The main defense of medical control of prostitutes is Alexandre Jean Baptiste Parent Duchatelêt, *De la prostitution dans la ville de Paris* (Paris: Baillière, 1836). See also Alain Corbin, *Les filles de noce: Misère sexuelle et prostitution, 19e siècle* (Paris: Aubier Montaigne, 1978), and Judith Walkowitz, *Prostitution and Victorian Society: Women, Class and the State* (Cambridge: Cambridge University Press, 1980).

3. See Hekma, pp. 149-64.

4. K. H., "Is ontucht noodzakelijk?" *Het Maandblad: Getuigen en Redden* 5.3 (March, 1883): 44-45.

5. Gillis van Overbeek de Meijer, "Boekbespreking," *Nederlandsch Tijdschrift voor Geneeskunde* 36, part 2 (1892): 421-22.

6. Pierre F. Spaink, "Bijdrage tot de casuïstiek der urningen," *Psychiatrische Bladen* 11 (1893): 143-65; reprinted in *Honderd jaar homoseksuelen: Documenten over de uitdoktering van homoseksualiteit*, ed. Gert Hekma (Amsterdam: Het Spinhuis, 1992), pp. 40-61.

7. Friedrich Engels, *The Origin of the Family, Private Property and the State* (1883), reprinted in Karl Marx and Frederick Engels, *Selected Works in One Volume* (New York: International Publishers, 1968), p. 511: "We are now approaching a social revolution in which the hitherto existing economic foundations of monogamy will disappear just as certainly as will those of its supplement–prostitution. . . . Since monogamy arose from economic causes, will it disappear when these causes disappear? One might not unjustly answer: far from disappearing, it will only begin to be completely realized. For with the conversion of the means of production into social property, wage labor, the proletariat, also disappears, and therewith, also, the necessity for a certain–statistically calculable–number of women to surrender themselves for money. Prostitution disappears; monogamy, instead of declining, finally becomes a reality–for the men as well."

8. Marc-André Raffalovich, *Uranisme et unisexualité* (Lyon: Storck; Paris: Masson, 1896) defended homosexual love and simultaneously advocated sexual abstinence for homosexuals, condemning the sexual escapades of Oscar Wilde. Raffalovich was a poet of Russian origin who wrote scholarly works on uranism in French and homoerotic poetry in English. See Timothy d'Arch Smith, *Love in Earnest: Some Notes on the Lives and Writings of English "Uranian" Poets from 1889 to 1930* (London: Routledge & Kegan Paul, 1970), pp. 29-34, and Hans Hafkamp, "Een katholieke apologeet van de kuise mannenliefde: Marc-André Raffalovich (1864-1934)," in *Pijlen van naamloze liefde: Pioniers van de homo-emancipatie*, ed. Hans Hafkamp and Maurice van Lieshout (Amsterdam: SUA, 1988), pp. 62-67.

9. On Ulrichs, see Hubert Kennedy, *Ulrichs: The Life and Works of Karl Heinrich Ulrichs, Pioneer of the Modern Gay Movement* (Boston: Aylson, 1988).

10. On Kloos and his relations, see Peter van Eeten, *Dichterlijk labirint* (Amsterdam: Polak & Van Gennep, 1963), and Peter Kralt, *De Dichter, zijn Geliefden en zijn Muze: Over de vroege poëzie van Willem Kloos* (Leiden: Dimensie, 1985).

11. See Harry G. M. Prick, *Jongenslief en jongensleed: Karel Alberdingk Thijm als leerling van de kostschool Rolduc; Lodewijk van Deysssel als auteur van De Kleine Republiek* (Nijmegen: Cadans, 1989).

12. See Arnold Aletrino, "Over uranisme en het laatste boek van Raffalovich (Marc André)," *Psychiatirsche en Neurologische Bladen* 1 (1897): 351-65, 452-83.

13. See Kees Joosse, *Arnold Aletrino: Pessimist met perspectief* (Amsterdam: Thomas Rap, 1986), and my review "De strijd van Arnold Aletrino tegen christelijke zedenmeesters," *De Groene* (November 16, 1986), p. 17.

14. The major, albeit homophobic, biography of De Haan is Jaap Meijer, *De zoon van de gazzen* (Amsterdam: Polak & Van Gennep, 1967). His major scandal is described in detail by Rob Delvigne and Leo Ross in their introduction to the reprint of J. I. de Haan, *Open brief aan P. L. Tak* (Amsterdam: Peter van Velden, 1982; 1st ed., Amsterdam: Van Cleef, 1905).

15. See Maurice van Lieshout, "Het ongekende leed van een tropendokter: Lucien von Römer (1873-1965)," in *Pijlen van naamloze liefde*, pp. 89-95.

16. L. E. J. Brouwer & C. S. Adama van Scheltema: *Droeve snaar, vriend van mij. Brieven*, ed. Dirk van Dalen (Amsterdam: Arbeiderspers, 1984). The diaries of Adama van Scheltema, which contain many passages on male love, are preserved in the Nederlands Letterkundig Museum, The Hague.

17. See, for example, the discussion of Oscar Wilde in *Het Maandblad: Getuigen en Redden* 17 (1895): 86-87.

18. See, for example, Louis Martineau, *De clandestiene prostitutie* (Amsterdam: A. van Klaveren, 1888; 1st French ed. 1885), and Edmond Dupouy, *De prostitutie bij de volken der oudheid* (Amsterdam: A. van Klaveren, 1889; 1st French ed. 1887). Jacobus Schoondermark was the principal Dutch translator of such books and pamphlets on public health, sexual perversion, and neo-Malthusianism. See Gert Hekma, "De windhandel met een hersenschim: J. Schoondermark (1849-1915)," in *Pijlen van naamloze liefde*, pp. 68-73.

19. *De Roode Duivel* 2.20 (December 11, 1893): 3, 4.

20. Ibid., 2.29 (February 12, 1894).

21. Ibid. 2.29 (April 23, 1894); 3.1 (August 6, 1894); 3.2 (August 13, 1894); and 3.3 (August 20, 1894).

22. Ibid. 2.3 (August 20, 1894).

23. Ibid. 5.1 (January 4, 1897).

24. Ibid. 5.8 (February 22, 1897).

25. Ibid. 5.9 (February 29, 1897).

26. Ibid. 5.34 (August 23, 1897).

27. Ibid. 5.50 (December 13, 1897).

28. "Ontmaskering! Geen genade! Onthullingen uit de Sodom-Sociëteit" (Amsterdam: no publisher, 1897); the leaflet is in the Gemeente Archief Amsterdam, B (1897) no. 1.

29. *De Amsterdamsche Lantaarn* 1.1 (September 17, 1897): 1.

30. Ibid., p. 3

31. Ibid. 1.3 (October 2, 1897): 1; 1.5 (October 16, 1897): 1.

32. Ibid. 1.5 (October 16, 1897): 1.

33. Ibid. 1.11 (November 27, 1897): 1. A few weeks earlier, mention had been made of a hairdresser who wanted to start an asylum in Italy or Spain "where men can love each other"; ibid. 1.8 (November 6, 1897): 2.

34. Ibid. 1.24 (February 26, 1898): 4; continued in the next issue 1.25 (March 5, 1898): 4. On the place of the implicated bar, there is nowadays a gay/lesbian restaurant "De Huyschkamer." The next issue of *De Amsterdamsche Lantaarn* again featured George Hermans, 1:26 (March 12, 1898): 4.

35. Jacob Israël de Haan, *Pijpelijntjes* (Amsterdam: Van Cleef, 1904); reprinted with an afterword by Wim J. Simons, "De geschiedenis van een onzedelijk boek" (The Hague: Kruseman, 1974).

36. Arnold Aletrino, "La situation sociale de l'uraniste," in *Actes du cinquième congrès international d'anthropologie criminelle* (Amsterdam), pp. 25-36; the lecture itself appears on pp. 473-94, along with the discussion in which Lombroso, among others, participated.

37. On the novel and the scandal it provoked, see Joosse, pp. 154-66.

38. The best account of the scandal is by Delvigne and Ross (see note 14).

39. Jacob Israël de Haan, *In Russische gevangenissen* (Amsterdam: Maatschappij voor Goede en Goedkoope Lectuur, 1913).

40. Lucien S. A. M. von Römer, "Boekbespreking," *Rein Leven* 2.9 (March, 1903): 63-66. A discussion follows in the issues 3.9-12 (March-June, 1904), ending with an official debate at the General Meeting of the Movement, which resolved to combat homosexual acts on principle; see 4.3 (September, 1904). The discussion is aptly summarized by Von Römer himself in *Ongekend leed* (Amsterdam: G. P. Tierrie, 1904), pp. 51-77; reprinted in *Honderd jaar homoseksuelen* (see note 6), pp. 152-78.

41. L. Heijermans, "Het derde geslacht," *De Nieuwe Tijd* 9 (1904): 774-79.

42. Lucien S. A. M. von Römer, "Nogmaals het derde geslacht," ibid., pp. 857-62.

43. L. Heijermans, "Antwoord aan den heer L. S. A. M. von Römer," ibid., pp. 863-66.

44. Lucien S. A. M. von Römer, "Brieven aan mijn vriend. I. Liefde-Leven," *Ontwaking* new series 5.1 (January, 1905): 25-31; quote on p. 31.

45. Van der Goes's lecture was part of a series on "Prostitution and Alcoholism." The notes for this lecture are preserved in the Van der Goes files of the International Institute of Social History in Amsterdam, and the debate on his lecture was reported in *Het Volk*.

46. Frank van der Goes, "Maatschappelijke beschouwing van de Homosexualiteit," reprinted in *Homoseksualiteit, een medische reputatie* (see note 1), pp. 234-35.

47. Regout's vehement proposals in parliament to criminalize "lewdness" with same-sex minors are reported in *Het Maandblad: Getuigen en Redden*, 28.1 (January, 1906): 12; 29.1 (January, 1907): 16; and 30.1 (January, 1908): 6.

48. *Handelingen der Staten-Generaal* (February 24, 1911), p. 1523. The debates continued on February 28 and March 1, and are published on pp. 1523-67.

49. Ibid., pp. 1525-27; with Troelstra's speech.

50. E.g., the liberal M. Tydeman, ibid., p. 1536.

51. Ibid., p. 1541.

52. Troelstra, ibid., p. 1561.

53. Ibid., p. 1567.

54. Wilfried U. Eissler, *Arbeiterparteien und Homosexuellenfrage: Zur Sexualpolitik von SPD und KPD in der Weimarer Republik* (Berlin: Rosa Winkel, 1980). See also other articles in this volume.

55. The list of signatures is appended to the tract *Wat iedereen behoort te weten omtrent Uranisme* (The Hague: Nederlandsche afdeeling van het "Wissenschaftlich-Humanitär-Komitee," 1912); reprinted in *Een groeiend zedelijk kwaad: Documenten over de criminalisering en emancipatie van homoseksuelen 1910-1916*, ed. Maurice van Lieshout (Amsterdam: Het Spinhuis, 1993), pp. 167-218. Based on Hirschfeld's *Was soll das Volk vom dritten Geschlecht wissen?* (Leipzig: Max Spohr, 1901), this brochure was translated and revised for the Dutch situation by Jacob Anton Schorer, the leader of the Dutch chapter of the Wissenschaftlich-humanitäres Komitee founded in 1912 as a reaction to the inclusion of article 248bis in the criminal law. The list of signatories included mostly progressive writers and doctors; even the leaders of the Reinleven movement signed it.

Anarchism and Homosexuality in Wilhelmine Germany: Senna Hoy, Erich Mühsam, John Henry Mackay

Walter Fähnders

Universität Osnabrück

SUMMARY. Homosexuality and its social and legal suppression were heatedly discussed in early twentieth-century Germany, including on the left. Among the anarchists, positions with markedly diverse forms of argument were espoused by such prominent advocates of individualist anarchism as John Henry Mackay and others coming from the Bakuninist tradition, such as Senna Hoy and Erich Mühsam. Their writings evidence that prior to World War I and into the 1920s, German anarchists–especially when compared with the Social Democrats–intervened consistently on behalf of individual self-determination extending into the sexual sphere, even though an undercurrent of hostility toward homosexuals persisted within the leftist movement as a whole.

At the turn of the century, Imperial Germany witnessed a profusion of scientific, political, and literary initiatives focused on dis-

Correspondence may be addressed: Bismarckstraße 25, D-49076 Osnabrück, Germany.

[Haworth co-indexing entry note]: "Anarchism and Homosexuality in Wilhelmine Germany: Senna Hoy, Erich Mühsam, John Henry Mackay." Fähnders, Walter. Co-published simultaneously in *Journal of Homosexuality* (The Haworth Press, Inc.) Vol. 29, No. 2/3, 1995, pp. 117-153; and: *Gay Men and the Sexual History of the Political Left* (ed: Gert Hekma, Harry Oosterhuis, and James Steakley) The Haworth Press, Inc., 1995, pp. 117-153; and *Gay Men and the Sexual History of the Political Left* (ed: Gert Hekma, Harry Oosterhuis, and James Steakley) Harrington Park Press, an imprint of The Haworth Press, Inc., 1995, pp. 117-153. Multiple copies of this article/chapter may be purchased from The Haworth Document Delivery Center. [1-800-342-9678 9:00 a.m. - 5:00 p.m. (EST)].

cussing homosexuality and combatting its criminalization and moral denigration, as well as efforts to create the first organized groups opposed to § 175.[1] Reaching a high point in the early years of the twentieth century, these activities came to an end before World War I and were not resumed until the Weimar Republic. As marginal as the role of the anarchist movement may have been, it too was involved in these discussions and struggles. In the following, anarchist positions on the issue of homosexuality will be exemplified by presenting the contributions of three prominent German anarchists of quite dissimilar biographies and divergent political views: Senna Hoy, Erich Mühsam, and John Henry Mackay. By way of background, some brief remarks concerning the historical standpoint of the socialist movement on homosexuality may be in order.

Even in its early years, the German workers' movement had to deal with the topic of homosexuality, albeit unwillingly. In 1862, Johann Baptist von Schweitzer, the cofounder and president of the Frankfurt Workingmen's Association and later Ferdinand Lassalle's successor as chair of the Universal German Workingmen's Association (Allgemeiner Deutscher Arbeiterverein, or ADAV), was hailed before court and pronounced guilty of homosexual intercourse; he was sentenced to prison for two weeks and also disbarred from the practice of law. As a result, his political career in this first German workers' organization was beset by difficulties. It took an energetic defense mounted by Lassalle to allay concerns about Schweitzer's "moral offense" (as it was still termed in the 1970 biographical lexicon of the standard history of the German workers' movement).[2] A full half century later, August Bebel would still recall Schweitzer's behavior disapprovingly,[3] and even Lassalle stated that he "would not permit [his] daughter" to marry "a man who had committed such an offense," although he otherwise dismissed Schweitzer's behavior as a "matter of taste" or at any rate "not a crime that would oblige us to dispense with his outstanding skills."[4]

To the extent that German workers' movement addressed the issue of homosexuality in the closing years of the nineteenth century, the Social Democratic party (Sozialdemokratische Partei Deutschlands, or SPD) declared itself opposed in principle to its criminalization. On the other hand, the SPD failed to develop any program to repeal § 175, which had been carried over into the newly founded German Empire in 1871 from the penal code of the North German Confederation–and ultimately from the Prussian penal code of 1851. The party's attitude toward homosexuality remained quite ambivalent. Ignoring the early research findings of Johann Ludwig Casper and especially of Karl Heinrich Ulrichs (who had been deeply involved in the 1862 Schweitzer case),[5] August Bebel wrote for example in his *Woman under Socialism* (1879), a work that influenced generations of workers:

> Yet another evil, frequently met, must also be shortly touched upon. Excessive sexual indulgence is infinitely more harmful than too little. . . . Hence the number of "young old men," in the higher walks of life especially. The number of young and old *roués* is enormous, and they require special stimuli, excess having deadened and surfeited them. Many, accordingly, lapse into the unnatural practices of Greek days. The crime against nature is today much more general than most of us dream of: upon that subject the secret archives of many a police bureau could publish frightful information. But not among men only, among women also have the unnatural practices of old Greece come up again with force. . . . Yet another unnatural gratification of the sexual instinct manifests itself in the violation of children. . . .[6]

Bebel's text combined a socialist critique of the parasitical lifestyle of the ruling "leisure class" (to invoke Thorsten Veblen's term) with a moral condemnation of "this perversity in higher social circles, especially widespread in military and court circles"–as Bebel added in a later note.[7] With its deplorable yoking of pseudoscholarship and a political standpoint oriented on class struggle, Bebel's argumentative strategy sought to "unmask" the class enemy by using individual sexual self-determination as a rebuke, even though homosexuals were a distinct minority within the aristocracy. This profoundly antiemancipatory approach would later be criticized by authors such as Kurt Tucholsky and Klaus Mann when, in the 1930s, the homosexuality of the SA leader Ernst Röhm was assailed in the antifascist press.

It was not until the sensational trials against Oscar Wilde in 1895 that a sophisticated position on homosexuality was enunciated by Eduard Bernstein, the influential theoretician of SPD revisionism. In two remarkable articles in the party's theoretical journal, *Die Neue Zeit*, Bernstein followed Bebel by drawing a parallel between cultural decline and the moral decay of the ruling class, particularly between the fin de siècle aesthetic of decadence–brilliantly exemplified by Wilde–and specific sexual practices:

> It is tempting to seek an inner link between Wilde's literary and sexual inclinations, and to a certain extent such a link can easily be proven. Wilde, as a literary person, is utterly "decadent." . . . It may be that Oscar Wilde and the fellows who supped with him . . . did nothing to violate the law, but his art, his writing–the *intellectual direction* which marks all his utterances, his *pose*–is pederastic.[8]

For Bernstein, however, this was no cause to condemn the "pose"; the entire case against Wilde seemed instead to reveal the "unprincipled nature of the very society which had most relished Wilde's art."[9]

Following established Social Democratic practice, Bernstein diagnosed bourgeois decline at every turn; but in his highly principled second essay, "Judgment of Abnormal Sexual Intercourse," he argued in favor of a historical understanding of moral concepts and went on to reject the customary classification of homosexuality (adopted even by Bebel) as "unnatural." Thus Bernstein was also able to historicize the rebuke of decadence, arguing that "on no account is male love always a sign of a corrupt disposition, dissolution, bestial pleasure-seeking, and the like. Anyone who immediately brings forward such epithets is accepting the standpoint of the most reactionary criminal laws. . . ."[10]

Referring to Krafft-Ebing, Bernstein also called into question explanations based purely on notions of pathology. But even more importantly, Bernstein urged his party to take a stand: "even within the German Social Democracy," he noted, there were "very far-reaching differences of opinion." In "sexual matters," the SPD lacked that "firm, modern, scientifically grounded point of view" routinely applied to "other questions of public life":

There is [within the SPD] more *pre*-judging than *judging*, and an extreme concept of liberty borrowed from philosophical radicalism alternates with an almost pharisaical, ultra-puritan moralism. As subordinate in importance as the issue of sexual behavior may be for the economic and political struggle of Social Democracy, that does not make it superfluous . . . to find a means of assessing this side of social life based on a scientific perspective and knowledge rather than employing more or less arbitrary moral concepts. The party is strong enough today to influence the shape of written law; both its speakers and its press influence public opinion beyond the circle of its affiliates, and the party thus bears a certain responsibility for what is already happening today.[11]

The party was soon to embark upon such activities in connection with the Scientific-Humanitarian Committee (Wissenschaftlich-humanitäres Komitee, or WhK), founded by Magnus Hirschfeld in 1897. It is well known that one of the chief goals of this Committee–the first organization anywhere representing the interests of homosexuals–was reform of § 175. August Bebel was among the first signatories of a Reichstag petition initiated by the WhK for this purpose and endorsed by some 1,000 prominent figures, and it was Bebel who argued the position of the SPD at the 1898 Reichstag debate on this issue. His remarks on this occasion showed a modification of his earlier decadence thesis: Bebel now emphasized the large number of homosexuals to be found "in all social circles, from the lowest to the highest," and he also criticized the police policy of enforcing the law selectively to avoid upper-class scandal.[12]

The Social Democrats thus adopted what was assuredly an advanced position, and in the following years the SPD remained the sole party that voted to repeal § 175. Their attitudes nonetheless remained contradictory and subject to dispute, fluctuating between a biological–and partially historical–view of homosexuality (based on the teachings of Magnus Hirschfeld and others) as a deviation from "normal" patterns on the one hand, and a militantly class-based interpretation of homosexuality as a manifestation of bourgeois decadence on the other. In 1902, for example, the SPD's leading periodical, the daily *Vorwärts*, exposed the homosexual practices of the industrialist Alfred Krupp. Commenting on the "richest man in Germany," the journal stated: "The time has come to discuss the case publicly and with all due caution, for this is *not just* a capitalist contradiction."[13] And in 1905, when the WhK resubmitted its petition and the Reichstag engaged in a second debate on § 175, the SPD delegate Adolf Thiele delivered a speech entirely in keeping with the WhK's standpoint and devoid of any pseudo-militant undertones. But even more telling than this well-reasoned address was the intervention of the SPD delegate Georg von Vollmar, an influential revisionist, who disavowed Thiele's speech as a purely personal statement.[14] A short time later, the anarchist Erich Mühsam would take this disparity as a starting point to question the SPD's overall sincerity when it came to repealing § 175.[15]

This preliminary survey of SPD statements was undertaken in order to suggest the level of consciousness on the German left as articulated by the majority Social Democracy. It is beyond the scope of this essay to explore the degree of overt or latent prejudice (as well as their possible overlap) within the left, of tensions between SPD leadership and the grassroots level, divergences between workers and socialist intellectuals of bourgeois origins, and so on. But the anarchist role in these discussions must certainly be viewed in the context of the SPD program.

Among German-speaking anarchists, it was probably Robert Reitzel (1849-98) who first spoke out in defense of homosexuality in certain literary and critical essays published in the early 1890s in the USA, where Reitzel had lived since the 1870s.[16] At the time of the Oscar Wilde trials, the American anarchist Emma Goldman (1869-1940) took a stand firmly in favor of homosexuals, in keeping with her concept of "free love."[17] Within organized German anarchism,[18] the Berlin anarchist weekly *Neues Leben* devoted an extended series of articles in 1902 to the first three volumes of Hirschfeld's *Jahrbuch für sexuelle Zwischenstufen* (Yearbook for Sexual Intermediates).[19] Presenting detailed summaries of the WhK's pertinent findings to a broader anarchist readership for the first time, this journal integrated a critique of the "absurdly restrictive morality" of "public opinion" with the principled anarchist attack on the state and its function of "systematically stultifying the people."[20]

In its rejection of "bigotry," the series made occasional use of the most common colloquialism for homosexuals, the pejorative "queers" (*warme Brüder*, literally warm brothers)[21]–probably with the intention of enlightening the journal's predominantly proletarian readership. In any case, an article appearing a short time later in *Der freie Arbeiter*, which subsumed *Neues Leben*, explicitly thematized what it termed "popular prejudice." Commenting on the guilty verdict handed down against Magnus Hirschfeld in a court case concerning his statistical survey on the prevalence of homosexuality among students, this article not only championed Hirschfeld and the WhK but directly addressed "intolerance" toward "queers":

> If intolerance of and by itself is unworthy of any worker striving toward a freer reordering of the social order, it is especially to be condemned in matters that are so patently, so self-evidently concerns of each individual as the nature of his sexdrive life. Since, however, ignorance is the cause of this intolerance, it is everyone's duty to educate himself as best he can about the nature of abnormal sexual feeling.

The article explicitly censured any "mockery and ridicule" or "coarseness and abuse" meted out to homosexuals, recalling in this context the 1902 scandal involving Alfred Krupp, who had been driven to take his own life: "It was possible for Krupp to live out his drives freely and unhindered on Capri. Yet even this Croesus ultimately collapsed under the terrible power of prejudice."[22]

What is remarkable about these articles–which may not have been entirely representative of that era's anarchist press, but were all the more striking for that–is first of all their agreement with the WhK; moreover, the place of publication–*Neues Leben* and *Der freie Arbeiter*–signals a certain interest in the subject precisely within the proletarian wing of German anarchism. Following the collapse of the project of "intellectual" anarchism associated with Gustav Landauer's journal *Der Sozialist* in the late 1890s, German anarchism had entered a phase of gradual consolidation with the founding of the journal *Neues Leben* (1897) and its successor, *Der freie Arbeiter* (beginning in 1904), a shift carried out less by intellectual than by working-class activists. The key role in these journalistic as well as organizational developments was played by the metal worker Paul Pawlowitsch (among others). It is certainly no coincidence that he spoke at a WhK meeting in 1904, where he proclaimed "to the thunderous applause of the conference attendees," as the chronicler Senna Hoy reported, "that the struggle for liberation of the homosexuals met with complete understanding and complete solidarity in *working-class circles.*"[23]

The extent to which this was really true of proletarian anarchism as a whole cannot be settled here, but available sources do make two things clear. While prejudice was still quite virulent, resolute efforts to eliminate it were being undertaken within the framework of anarchistic popular education. Secondly, the contribution of certain early twentieth-century intellectual anarchists is also well documented. We will be concerned in the following with three writers—anarchists as much as authors—who were deeply involved with the issue:

John Henry Mackay (1864-1933), the reclusive Stirnerian; a self-described boy-lover; active as a writer within the Naturalist movement beginning in the late 1880s;

Erich Mühsam (1878-1934), bohemian, writer, journalist, and politician; active in literary and political circles well beyond the opening years of the twentieth century; who emphatically declared that he was not a homosexual;

Senna Hoy (i.e., Johannes Holzmann, 1882-1914), the "romantic rowdy" among the militant anarchists; involved both politically and as a writer in the anarchistic movement beginning at the age of twenty; and who, as he expressly put it, cultivated relations with homosexuals.

The contribution of these intellectual anarchists to the cause of homosexual emancipation was concentrated at the highpoint of the debates occurring shortly after the turn of the century, and the following remarks will take them up in the chronological sequence of their involvement with this campaign rather than their involvement with anarchism.

SENNA HOY

Senna Hoy (a pseudonym created by his close friend, the poet Else Lasker-Schüler, by reversing his first name, Johannes) was descended from a bourgeois Jewish family, became a teacher of religion in Berlin, and beginning in 1902 devoted himself exclusively to journalistic, literary, and political activities in the realm of bohemianism and anarchism.[24] He edited a number of mostly fugitive weeklies in 1902-3, the booklet *Das dritte Geschlecht* (The Third Sex) in 1903, and the journal *Kampf* in Berlin in 1904-5. Due to an unending series of conflicts with Prussian censorship, he emigrated to Switzerland in 1905 and travelled on to postrevolutionary Russia in 1907 to agitate on behalf of militant anarcho-communism. That year he was arrested on a charge of "expropriations" and sentenced to a term of fifteen years. Imprisoned in Moscow, he died in misery in 1914.

Senna Hoy's vita is by no means atypical for the younger bourgeois intelligentsia around 1900, which felt a profound sense of discomfort with the restraints of Wilhelmine society. As shown by the biographies of numerous German Expressionists, these intellectuals tended to challenge repression at home, at school, and from the state by raising fundamental claims to humanity and the rights of liberty. Along these lines, Senna Hoy founded a League for Human Rights (Bund für Menschenrecht) in 1903, the very name of which was just as programmatic as the editorial stance of his journal *Kampf* (Struggle), which bore the subtitle *Zeitschrift für–gesunden Menschenverstand* (Journal for–Common Sense) and aimed to advance the "freedom struggle for the rights of human nature."[25] Given the oppositional intelligentsia's defiance of Wilhelmine repressiveness, it is scarcely surprising that it was concerned not just with censorship, the role of the church, or the justice system, but also with § 175. In the case of Senna Hoy, a radical anarchist perspective was an outcome of his commitment, not its starting point.

In his early journalistic work, Senna Hoy–who emphasized that he was "not homogenically oriented"[26]–devoted a remarkable amount of space to homosexuality, both as a general topic and as an issue in current events. His sixteen-page booklet *Das dritte Geschlecht*, self-published in February of 1903, was entirely devoted to this topic and intended, according to its subtitle, as a "Contribution to Popular Education." Here he decried the "ignorance of people of all classes and all professions, all levels of educational background," and held the church to be primarily responsible.[27] Carrying out its educational premise, the booklet opened with a chapter on evolutionary development, went on to deal with biological topics, and then turned to current issues involving homosexuality.[28] Two formulations pointing to the principle of individual self-determination are particularly noteworthy. Recalling "Hellenic culture with its enthusiasm for beauty and sensuality," Senna Hoy distinguished between "properties inherent to the being of the individual, given to him by nature, thus inborn properties, and perversity, inculcated by overstimulated 'culture.' "[29] This distinction by no means implied a view of homosexuality as an "aberration of the aristocracy,"[30] and he forthrightly demanded that "society as a whole draw from human passions whatever is of use."[31]

Senna Hoy's most important publishing platform was undoubtedly *Kampf*,[32] which appeared in twenty-five issues (eleven of which were banned) in 1904-5 under his editorship. Neither a homosexual journal nor the official publication of a particular anarchist organization, *Kampf* provided a forum for "libertarian strivings" and featured both literary contributions by bohemian writers (Else Lasker-Schüler, Peter Hille, Erich Mühsam, and many others) and political articles devoted to topical issues involving justice, censorship, school reform, and the church. The journal was increasingly concerned with anarchist thought and dealt continuously with homosexuality.

Senna Hoy's article "Die Homosexualität als Kulturbewegung" (Homosexuality as a Cultural Movement) may be read as a programmatic essay on this topic.[33] Invoking the "struggle for individual rights, intervention on behalf of human rights with which we are endowed by birth," he challenged the "hypocritical morality of society" with its "compulsory 'morality' far removed from human nature and natural feeling." Hoy argued that "no one has the right to intrude in the private matters of another, to meddle in another's personal views and orientations, and that ultimately it is no one's business what two freely consenting adults do in their homes."

Making an allusion to the emperor Constantine's legendary victory under the sign of the cross, Senna Hoy continued:

But it is precisely the obstinacy, the unbounded fury with which enemies of ethical progress, opponents of moral culture and freedom combat homosexuality, *and with it man's right to himself*, that makes homosexuality into a cultural factor and the struggle for the human rights of homosexuals into a struggle for the freedom of cultural development. So we will take up the gauntlet that is flung at our feet whenever it is cast at homosexuality, and we are willing to seek victory *under this sign*, to see humanity and moral rights triumph over "morality and decency" under the sign of homosexuality.

This standpoint included a broad social dimension by interpreting the struggle against § 175 as an utterly indispensable component of universal and all-encompassing emancipation. Hoy's outlook thus differed dramatically not just from the standpoint of the Social Democracy, which regarded the matter as an isolated, marginal issue, but also from that wing of the gay movement around Adolf Brand's journal *Der Eigene* (The Special) and organized in his Community of the Special (Gemeinschaft der Eigenen), which defined itself as a separate and separatist movement. Against this background, particular importance attaches to Senna Hoy's insistence that the women's movement "must also not cast aside its obligation to combat the prejudice against homosexuals."[34]

All this amounts to a postulate of all-inclusive emancipation and liberation, both for society as a whole and for marginal(ized) groups. What was needed, according to Hoy, was "systematic subversion" in particulars.[35] Based on this premise, he went on to exclude one concrete tactic that was heatedly discussed at the turn of the century, particularly within Social Democracy: outing. At issue was the creation of sensational "cases," i.e., revealing the names of prominent individuals in order to hasten the repeal of § 175. (The "Krupp case" should also be seen within this context.) Deliberations on this tactic can be traced back to August Bebel's 1898 Reichstag speech, in which he had pointed both to the enormous "number of unknown cases" and to the judicial practice of selective enforcement. Referring explicitly to Bebel's speech, Senna Hoy took a stand on the issue

> of forcing the repeal in this manner. It is self-evident that this is not a decent weapon. Anyone who knows the names of individuals who could be affected by the provisions of § 175 was informed of them discreetly. At stake is not just the affected parties' social position, but–as I have been credibly assured by half-desperate individuals on repeated occasions– their very lives! And for anyone who advocates individual rights and thus challenges the state's power to meddle in individual matters that do not injure the rights of third parties or the existing state order, this step is impermissible–unless he is willing to remove ground under his own feet by practicing the very injustice that he opposes.[36]

Since he thus declared the rights of the individual to be inviolable and exploitation of the individual for the emancipation movement's aims intolerable, the one alternative that remained was to bring "science and the will of the people" to bear. And "what's needed is a worldview."[37] In this context, "worldview" (*Weltanschauung*) connoted precisely the principle of unconditional self-determination and the negation of the prevailing state morality; but beyond that, it also had an aesthetic dimension extending beyond morality. In an earlier article on "Moralizing Clergy–Aestheticizing Priests" that offered a statement of principles, Hoy had declared:

> . . . if two people not of different sexes feel bound to one another, they are persecuted as criminals.
> Who actually wrote *this* law book? It was not the constitutionally instated legislators who established these and similar norms; it was the few, who wanted to reduce everyone to servitude and have now gained the majority as a following. . . . It was and is the moral clergy.
> And here no *revision* of principles will help; what will help is tearing down and reconstructing. And a *replacement* for morality. I believe it is aesthetics.
> Priests of the aesthetic–those who see not the wicked, not the evil, not the moral and immoral: but instead ugliness and

beauty. Those who feel disgust for animalized desire, but worship chaste naked beauty. . . .
And these priests of the aesthetic will initially have to be fighters. Fighters for the raped, fighters against the moralizing clergy for a new worldview. Or rather, for the primordial worldview, given by nature.
And they will be fighters against the laws born of "moral" views.[38]

This sort of sweeping "aestheticization" of life, anything but foreign to turn-of-the-century thought, here took on a distinctive quality by its assertive turn outward, into the political and social sphere; and here, too, Senna Hoy linked this concept of the "aesthetic" and homosexuality by locating both of them in art.

In 1905, he published in *Kampf* a short prose sketch entitled "Die Kleider hindern" (Clothes Hinder), which may be decoded as a homosexual encounter in "beauty." It appears here in full not because of its literary value, which is not at issue here, but rather because it affords insights into the connections between homosexuality and the primacy of the aesthetic:

A human couple entwined.
On their mother's breast they lie, suckled from her strength, – on the earth, the mossy forest floor.
In boundless belongingness body clings to body, just as their souls have long since found each other.
Beauty presses to beauty, – thirsts, – seeks union . . . kiss of the body, as souls wed.
In boundless belongingness . . .
Clothes hinder! –
Beauty seeks beauty, – the alien hinders, – the unbeautiful disturbs the pure beautiful union of togetherness, sameness, likeness . . .
Clothes hinder, – and beauty's longing becomes a disgrace, the search for pure unconscious joy an affront . . .
A conscious affront! . . .[39]

By invoking "beauty," the author seeks to legitimate the forbidden sensuality of the couple as "priests of the aesthetic." And in the upshot, it indeed appeared that the state aimed to bolster Senna

Hoy's theses about its "ugliness." Coinciding with the confiscation of nude drawings by the artist Fidus, who was highly regarded in anarchist circles, and the incrimination of Friedrich Schiller's classic poem "Die Freundschaft" ("Friendship") for "glorifying incitement to pederasty,"[40] Senna Hoy's ultimately rather harmless sketch also fell victim to Wilhelmine justice. The issue of *Kampf* in which it appeared was confiscated and Hoy sentenced to pay a fine (or face six days in prison)[41]–one of the reasons for his escape to Switzerland in the year 1905. Caught up in anarchist activities of a different sort, he was no longer active in homosexual matters in the following years.

ERICH MÜHSAM

When Senna Hoy founded his League for Human Rights in 1903, he initially offered the chairmanship to Erich Mühsam.[42] Mühsam declined, stating that he regarded "the struggle for human rights [as] identical with that of international anarchism."[43] By this time, Mühsam's anarchism had already been evidenced in numerous journalistic and literary activities, which had accorded some prominence to the discussion of homosexuality.

The Jewish son of a pharmacist, Mühsam had been expelled from secondary school for "socialist activities." Around 1900, he joined the anarchist-inspired commune project of the New Community (Neue Gemeinschaft) in Berlin, and he would later be involved in the similar "Monte Verità" project in Ascona, Switzerland. Influenced in particular by the anarchism of his mentor, Gustav Landauer, Mühsam was prominent in anarchist and bohemian circles at the beginning of the century, and he traversed half of Europe as a vagabond. In 1918-19, he would play a key role in Germany's November Revolution. A leader in the Bavarian Soviet Republic, Mühsam served five years in prison after the revolution was quelled. During the years of the Weimar Republic, he was untiringly involved in nondogmatic-anarchist politics. He was arrested by the Nazis immediately after the Reichstag fire in 1933 and interned in the Oranienburg concentration camp, where he was severely tortured and ultimately murdered in 1934.

From Mühsam's anarchist perspective, state suppression of homosexuality was flatly unacceptable, and he referred sporadically to the topic throughout his writings.[44] He was well known for his topical verse written in a tone at once satirical and lyrical, and in a poem entitled "Widernatürlichkeiten" (Unnaturalnesses) he mocked the state clampdown on Fidus's drawings and Schiller's "Die Freundschaft": "The state's attorney is considering / How he can preserve morality. / To art he turns his gaze, / To works written and painted. / . . . Schiller was a German poet, / One of the greatest intellectual lights. / 'Friendship' he called a poem / That made the attorney uneasy. / Its culpability results / Easily from one hundred seventy-five. . . ."[45] In 1919, Mühsam also published a gay poem entitled "Hubert"–the sole one of the sort in his entire œuvre–in Adolf Brand's journal *Der Eigene*: "I loved you when your shy boy-gaze / sucked the pearling spume of primal knowledge / from other-worldly, miraculously foreign Romans– / and my love was a hot happiness."[46] Indeed, Mühsam's first book-length publication, *Die Homosexualität: Ein Beitrag zur Sittengeschichte unserer Zeit* (Homosexuality: A Contribution to the History of Manners and Morals in Our Time), was entirely devoted to the subject. Published in 1903, this work offered a singular mixture of biographical experience with attention to theoretical issues then being debated; it made it plain that Mühsam was fairly well read in the pertinent scholarly literature, ranging from Ulrichs to Hirschfeld. Addressing the contested question: "Is same-sex love the product of an inborn orientation of particular individuals or a habit cultivated by upbringing, satiation, or perverse debauchery?" Mühsam affirmed "unconditionally and without reservations" the standpoint taken by Hirschfeld and others: "Anyone who is homosexual was homosexual from the very beginning. His homosexuality is inborn and is grounded and necessitated in that particular Uranian's *physical or psychic being*."[47] (In the language usage of the nineteenth century, "Uranian" was synonymous with "homosexual.") Turning to an overall assessment of homosexuality, however, Mühsam's standpoint became rather convoluted:

> Even though I firmly dispute the notion that the Uranian as such is in any way ethically inferior to the heterosexual, I nonetheless want to concede that from a purely biological viewpoint, homosexuality does indeed signal inferiority vis-à-

vis the normal orientation; it is inferior because that feeling of the most blissful bliss imaginable, based upon the bolt of lightning of highest pleasure that shoots through two individuals *simultaneously* during closest bodily and spiritual unification of two people loving each other, must remain foreign to the Uranian. I would therefore like to conceive of homosexuality as a *manifestation of biological decadence.* But the very word "decadence" implies a protest against the assumption that the Uranian as social being is situated at a lower level; he merits this lowering of status solely as a sexual being. For the decadent is generally regarded as nothing less than a second-class person. I assert to the contrary . . . that in the decadent individual the highest culture of his lineage comes into being.[48]

This statement was linked to Mühsam's exceptional privileging of the "fine aesthetic feeling" of many homosexuals. He arrived here at a completely different evaluation of the connections between art, homosexuality, and decadence than had Eduard Bernstein in his essay on Wilde, even though Mühsam by no means regarded decadent literature as a model for his own writing, which was oriented more on Naturalistic and Realistic principles. Mühsam continued:

This probably provides an explanation for the disproportionately large number of artists with a Uranian orientation, and one may observe that in all areas of art homosexuals provide the best formalists. Thus Oscar Wilde was supremely interested in the outer polish, pure aestheticism. Among Germans it is Stefan George–whose poems undoubtedly allow the deduction of his Uranianism–who cultivates "l'art pour l'art" in poetry, pursuing it to a point that renders his creations almost unintelligible in content. . . .

Formalism is encountered at every step in contacts with homosexuals. Exquisitely elegant clothing, the preference for beautiful flowers, fragrances, etc. provide clear testimony of a pleasure in sensual aesthetic impressions.[49]

He firmly rejected, however, any exploitation of prominent artists to advance the homosexual cause (a stance with clear implications for instances of outing à la Krupp). He condemned the fact that Uranian artists are claimed wholesale by homosexuals in a manner that is irresponsible. On a human level, it is quite understandable. Pariahs, minorities persecuted for whatever reason–let me cite here the Jews–always feel the need to propound the high value of their entire group on the basis of particular outstanding individuals among their number. But one ought to keep in mind that Oscar Wilde–even if his contrary sexual feelings constituted an essential component of his art–was first and foremost a writer, and only secondarily a homosexual. What made Michelangelo a genius, and what we love him for, was his artistry, not his Uranianism. It makes a disagreeable impression to hear the names of such geniuses mentioned in connection with their sexual orientation over and over again.[50]

Mühsam argued that there should be no legal or moral limitations whatsoever in sexual matters, "that it is not the least business of any moralist what two mutually consenting adults do with each other."[51] In his later writings as well–concerning marriage, for example–he would defend sexual freedom as a fundamental individual right. He wrote in an essay on "Frauenrecht" (Women's Rights) for Gustav Landauer's journal *Der Sozialist* (1910): "These matters are of a wholly personal nature, are dependent upon temperament and the feeling of individuals, and can be affected neither by the terms reprehensible and ugly, nor by the terms sick and decadent."[52]

Mühsam probably had various reasons for devoting his first book publication to homosexuality. Beyond the current interest in the topic and the insistent calls for individual self-determination in all aspects of life–a demand made not just by anarchists–Mühsam's focus during these early years on the social underclass and outcasts may also have sharpened his optic for those ostracized because of homosexuality. In a review of Magnus Hirschfeld's *Der urnische Mensch* (The Uranian) which he wrote in 1903 for the anarchist weekly *Der arme Teufel*, Mühsam spoke in terms that might just as well have appeared in *Kampf* or elsewhere: "Anyone who still has a trace of feeling for justice and the least spark of respect for fellow humans ought to rebel against this § 175."[53] Indeed, Mühsam regarded social pariahs as his fellows; taking issue with the stereotype of "regrettable people," he declared homosexuals "regrettable" not because of their orientation but "because they are persecuted, because a law created in medieval delusion has declared them pariahs, outcasts, criminals."[54]

It is well known that the Bakuninist tradition within anarchism singled out the so-called lumpenproletariat, the "flower of the proletariat" (Bakunin), as the agent of historical change. Prior to World War I, Mühsam repeatedly emphasized this evaluation of the underclass, writing in a key essay on bohemianism published in 1906: "Criminals, hobos, whores, and artists–these are the bohemians who point the way for a new culture."[55] And in an account of his experiences at the Monte Verità commune at Ascona, he reiterated the "insight voiced a thousand times" that the "best elements of all nations are rotting in jails and prisons." He continued:

> I know from my own observation that one encounters in the hostels along German highways and in Berlin's criminal dives individuals shunned and regarded with revulsion by the pillars of society; but they have a heart that will make that of anyone who gets to know them better beat higher.[56]

He recalled Friedrichstrasse, "the sole place in Berlin from which a writer can extract poesy if he makes the effort to ease up on morality and to see into the hearts of the whores, pimps, and hustlers."[57]

It is unclear to what extent Mühsam was really familiar with this milieu and whether his privileging of the underclass may have formed the basis of such experiences.[58] His interest in homosexuality may have resulted, however, from a broad ensemble of general and specific anarchistic considerations–involvement in current social discussions, theoretical considerations, and the realm of biographical experience. It was most probably the last-named which led to an astonishing retraction: in an "Open Letter" to Albert Weidner, the editor of *Der arme Teufel*, just a few months after publishing his book on homosexuality, Mühsam sought to distance himself from the theories of Magnus Hirschfeld, whom he now said he had followed "blindly." This rupture came with Mühsam's discovery of the erotic dimension of "friendship," and he stated that "the forthright criticism of dear friends" had convinced him "that people who cleave to one another in closest friendship raised to erotic love are being lumped into one category with others marked by their contrary-sexual orientation as biologically inferior individuals." He interpreted this conflation as a "profaning of the best feeling we have"–friendship; and even though he declared his intention to continue opposing § 175 on the basis not of scientific arguments but solely because of "elements of social ethics" and "self-evident human rights," he regretted having written his book altogether and warned against "buying it." Moreover, he declared his intention to coauthor with Johannes Nohl a work on "the Humanitarian-Scientific Committee–or Culture and Pederasty,"[59] a work which was apparently never put to paper.

Responding to this change of outlook, Magnus Hirschfeld (whose *Jahrbuch für sexuelle Zwischenstufen* had incidentally carried a positive review of Mühsam's book)[60] noted with regret Mühsam's harsh words on the "contrary-sexual orientation" and his reinterpretation of homosexuality as a "cultural" rather than a "natural phenomenon"–a standpoint propounded by Hirschfeld's rival, Adolf Brand. Hirschfeld pointed out that Mühsam was not only hedging on the arguments in favor of homosexual emancipation but even retracting certain specifically anarchistic elements. For the readership of *Der arme Teufel*, according to Hirschfeld, "the socio-ethical impulse, which Mühsam regards as *solely* of importance for the elimination of § 175, is certainly sufficient. . . . But the great educated and less-educated masses will only be able to arrive at a more balanced judgment on this matter when persuaded by scientific proof that the homosexual inclination is not a product of culture and artifice, but instead an inborn trait indissolubly bound up with the entire personality of many individuals."[61]

Mühsam's disavowal–which did not prevent his publication from going through two more printings–was obviously connected with his acquaintance with Johannes Nohl beginning in late 1903. In a 1910 diary entry, Mühsam described meeting Nohl (to whom he had dedicated his 1909 volume of poetry, *Der Krater* [The Crater]) as "the most powerful event of my life,"[62] and one may assume that Mühsam found with Nohl what he celebrated as "friendship heightened to erotic love." This does not mean that Mühsam was homosexual, even if he was regarded by the police as a "pederast . . . because he spent so much time in the company of homosexuals"[63]

(which, of course, says little, as the denunciation of political unde-
sirables often took the form of morally discrediting them). But the
claim that he was a pederast was also raised publicly, and the
"rumor," as Mühsam complained in a 1910 letter to Richard Dehmel, that "I am homosexual" sufficed for him to be excluded from
the circle of contributors to the prestigious Munich journal *Jugend*.
The letter continued:

> Disputing my homosexuality helps not at all; the rumor counts
> for more than my assertion. That the rumor could arise isn't
> exactly surprising. I've spoken out vehemently against Para-
> graph 175 on several public occasions; among my closest
> friends are several homosexuals, and I've never taken ac-
> quaintances' ironic joshing seriously enough to be, say, out-
> raged, especially since I simply cannot recognize the charac-
> teristic of homosexuality to be criminal. Now I know that the
> claim that someone is a pederast is not an insult to the person
> involved but certainly is a severe injury.[64]

The setback Mühsam experienced due to rumors of his homosexuality was compounded when he was arrested for political agitation among the lumpenproletariat of Munich and pronounced guilty
of "conspiratorial activities." These circumstances led a large part
of the German press to refuse to publish Mühsam's work, a boycott
to which he ultimately responded by founding his own journal,
Kain, in 1911. The entire matter evidenced the power of homophobic prejudice, aggravated in the wake of the momentous Eulenburg
Affair.

In 1906-7, the journalist Maximilian Harden, editor of *Die Zu-
kunft* and a firm opponent of Kaiser Wilhelm II's politics, had
charged two close advisors of the emperor, Prince Philipp zu Eulenburg and Count Kuno von Moltke, the Commandant of Berlin, with
psychosexual deviation.[65] Harden's bold outing of those aristocrats
resulted in a series of six libel and perjury trials, in the first of which
Magnus Hirschfeld presented expert testimony on Moltke's "unconscious orientation" toward homosexuality. Coming just a few
years after the great Reichstag debate of 1905, the scandal initiated
an unprecedented public preoccupation with homosexuality as a
symptom of national decadence. Contrary to the hopes of Hirsch-

feld and the WhK, a "general antihomosexual mood" was the outcome; a strengthening of the penal code was also threatened when the petition committee of the Reichstag unanimously prepared such a draft.

The SPD played a role in this affair by making public pronouncements that were clearly regressive when compared with the postulates of Bernstein, Bebel, and Thiele. The SPD daily *Vorwärts* wrote, for example:

> Eulenburg, Hohenau, Moltke belong to the intellectual lights of the Junker class, they were entrusted with high posts in the civilian and military hierarchy, they formed the entourage of the head of state, and it was not just Harden who fought against their political influence; he created difficulties for the chancellor and drove him to the risky maneuver of dissolving the Reichstag. And what does the Moltke vs. Harden trial say about the psychological make-up of these men? It shows us irreparable degeneracy. A flight from the mind into the mists of mysticism, a degeneration of feeling and of sexuality into the abnormal. . . . We are opponents of the punishment of homosexual love, because it indeed is an irresistible, natural drive in many cases. But that cannot close our eyes to the fact that beyond the in born there is also the acquired type, or let us say an artificial type, which is the product of decay.[66]

Social Democratic interventions in the affair were marked by a distinct restraint, and the WhK and the entire movement against § 175 were put on the defensive.

Mühsam voiced his views on the scandal in a 1908 book entitled *Die Jagd auf Harden* (The Hunt on Harden), which dealt both with Maximilian Harden's journalistic practices and the issue of homosexuality. In a modification of his earlier disavowal, Mühsam now held that there were homosexuals

> who confirm Hirschfeld's theory–sexual intermediates erroneously endowed with genitalia that do not match their nature. These womanly men or manly women in fact tend to love and sexually desire people equipped with the same sexual apparatus as themselves. But to deduce that everyone capable of

sensuously loving a member of the same sex in fact has a homosexual "orientation" would be to forge a vicious circle that fails to close.[67]

Mühsam was willing to concede a biological grounding in certain instances of homosexuality, but only by arguing that "this variation of sexual life occurs with such frequency precisely in aristocratic circles that are degenerate due to frequent in breeding."[68] Even so, he continued to insist on his friendship theory:

> Love or friendship: where can one draw the boundaries? – Does one have to try to explain everything physiologically? At most the very individuals involved can sense–and only in rare happy hours–nuances in the spiritual attraction from person to person.[69]

None of this led Mühsam to the shortsighted conclusion that Harden had drawn (and which was increasingly being voiced by the Social Democracy)–that the Wilhelmine political elite could be discredited more effectively by attacking its alleged homosexual tendencies than by challenging its reactionary policies. Despite (or precisely because of) his tortuous dealings with homosexuality, Mühsam was far more thoughtful. In defiance of all taboos, he both defended homosexuality and went on to analyze the virulent homophobia of Wilhelmine society. He was convinced, he wrote,

> that the capacity to direct one's drives in varied directions allows for the deduction not of "abnormalcy" but rather of differentiation, and that the moral outrage of the mob, to the extent that it does not spring from a condescending sense of pity, is little more than rage over being excluded from a source of pleasure that others enjoy.[70]

JOHN HENRY MACKAY

In contrast to Erich Mühsam and Senna Hoy, whose political and literary activities date to the turn of the century, John Henry Mackay,[71] half a generation older, was rooted in the literary movement of socially critical Naturalism dating to the 1880s. His involvement with anarchism also began at that time, whereas his first intervention in the debates on homosexuality came relatively late, in the year 1905.

Born in Scotland but raised in Germany, Mackay pursued university studies in Berlin and elsewhere after prematurely breaking off an apprenticeship in the book trade. He quickly developed contacts with the Naturalist movement around the Hart brothers and with the circle of writers in the bucolic Berlin suburb of Friedrichshagen, without firmly affiliating with them. During a one-year sojourn in London in 1887-88, he familiarized himself with that city's social revolutionary movement. In addition, he was strongly shaped by his knowledge of works by the American anarchist Benjamin Tucker and even more so by his study of the left Hegelian Max Stirner (i.e., Johann Caspar Schmidt, 1806-56), who was nearly forgotten after his death; Mackay certainly deserves credit for rediscovering Stirner and his major work of 1844, *Der Einzige und sein Eigentum* (The Individual and His Property). Mackay also won recognition for his own writings, such as the social revolutionary poems collected in the volume *Sturm* (Storm, 1888), which was warmly received by the workers' movement, and his influential "Portrait of a Culture" *Die Anarchisten* (The Anarchists, 1891), a novelistic work which manifested his turn to Stirnerism.

In the following years, Mackay advocated an "individualist anarchism" that repudiated socialism of Marxist provenance as well as the anarchism of Bakunin or Kropotkin. Mackay achieved fame and even international recognition during the 1890s with his repudiation of politics, the state, and violence and with his demand for an unrestricted egoism à la the Stirnerian "Self-Owner." Rediscovered thanks to Mackay's efforts, Max Stirner rose (alongside Nietzsche) to the status of a prophet whose pronouncements became slogans for large sectors of the bourgeois-oppositional intelligentsia up to the turn of the century.

From the 1890s on, Mackay lived in Berlin as something of a recluse whose life was largely devoted to writing and researching Stirner (although the scholarly value of his works on Stirner is disputed). He was increasingly isolated by the intransigence of his Stirner cult and his self-stylization as a "self-owner," and after

1900 he was never able to match his early literary successes. A substantial inheritance enabled him to live as a "self-supporting writer" for many years, but his wealth was wiped out by the hyper-inflation of the early 1920s, and his later publications were supported by a Mackay Society founded by people who shared his outlook. He no longer played a significant role in the literary life of the Weimar Republic, and his autobiographical *Abrechnung* (Settling of Accounts, 1932) documented deep bitterness.

The manner in which Mackay "closely guarded [his] personal activities," in the words of Mühsam, was repeatedly noted by contemporaries and clearly based in the "egocentricity of his worldview." According to Mühsam, who had met Mackay at the turn of the century in Berlin, there could be "no doubt that Mackay made a spectacle of his crotchety stiltedness with a certain intentionality. He wanted to keep his emotional life, insofar as it was not expressed in his writings, entirely to himself. He wanted no one to be able to see into his heart, which was allowed to beat only in the setting of the splendid library in his Charlottenburg bachelor's apartment."[72]

This self-containment certainly functioned as a shield against legal incrimination because of Mackay's pederastic inclinations, although an ideological argument for social withdrawal was provided by his individualism and Stirnerism carried to the level of egocentricity. Offering a purely psychological explanation of Mackay's "complete abandonment of political involvement"[73] would, however, be short-sighted, for this was a recurrent phenomenon within an entire generation of the oppositional intelligentsia. During the 1880s, adherents of the Naturalist movement (including, briefly, Mackay) had proclaimed their solidarity with the labor movement at a time when it was declared illegal by Bismarck's Anti-Socialist Laws. Only after the repeal of these laws in 1890 did the tenuousness of the intended alliance between Naturalism and labor (or the Social Democracy) become apparent. Intellectual, left-radical tendencies had no place in the party, as evidenced both by the SPD's expulsion of the Young Ones (*die Jungen*), a faction which had been supported by the Naturalists, and by the Naturalism debate at the SPD party congress in 1896. Clashes of this sort led in the 1890s to gaps in the intellectuals' identification with labor and to the rise of influential cults of Zarathustran Nietzscheanism and

Stirnerism. This trend offered intellectuals a rationale for regarding themselves as "aristocrats of the spirit" above mere politics–a development in which Mackay was directly involved because of his work on Stirner.[74] Interpreting Mackay's "incapacity for true social participation" solely as the outcome of an "unresolved psychic conflict" would be reductive, because it would overlook the extent to which his stance was shared by many contemporaries. It may, however, be true that Mackay's anarchism contributed to a "certain psychic stabilization" that later enabled him to address "directly" the issue of homosexuality.[75]

It would appear that Mackay became aware of his homosexuality only late, and certainly by the year 1886, when he read Richard von Krafft-Ebing's *Psychopathia sexualis*, which appeared in that year. An account of the impact of this book is to be found in his novelistic autobiography *Fenny Skaller* (1913):

> He *begins* to understand.
> He knows nothing as yet.
> But he now knows one thing:
> There are others like him! . . .
> But to himself he from this time on no longer kept silent about his love. . . .
> The book he did not open again.
> He had forgotten what he had read. He understood only this much: his love had been locked in a scientific wax museum of grotesqueries, of deformities and monstrosities of all sorts–therein he had been classified, too: among people with whom he had nothing in common and could have and wanted to have nothing in common.
> But this love *existed*.[76]

Although Mackay did sign the (first) WhK petition against § 175, it was not until the death of his mother in 1902, which initially plunged him into a long depression and creative crisis, that he was able to deal with his own homosexuality in a new way. Working on his own, he began a campaign for the legalization of homosexuality and pedophilia in 1905. Mackay's decision to carry this out in a completely individual manner was clearly based on the elitist self-elevation of the "self-owner" understood in a Stirnerian sense. But as in the cases of Senna Hoy and Erich Mühsam, Mackay saw his "struggle" for the "honor, truth, and beauty of this love"[77] not as an isolated issue but in a broader anarchistic-libertarian context: "For the question of this love is at its deepest base a social question: the struggle of the individual against oppression, whatever form it may take."[78] Mackay's rigorous individualism was also prompted by the WhK's standpoint that set an "age of consent" at sixteen years.[79]

Mackay carried out his activities under the pseudonym Sagitta ("arrow") and did not reveal his real name up to his death, even though Emil Szittya had already identified Mackay as Sagitta in his *Kuriositätenkabinett* (1923). By using a pseudonym, Mackay sought not just to protect himself (one need only recall the campaign against Erich Mühsam) but also to avoid denunciation of the anarchist cause. Mackay's Sagitta project comprised a series of six texts, of which some were published individually in 1906 and all of which were collected in 1913 under the shared title *Die Bücher der namenlosen Liebe* (The Books of the Nameless Love). Mackay chose the term "nameless love" in part because he rejected all scientific, medical, or legal terms (and thereby all scientific etiologies); but the phrase also points back to Oscar Wilde, who spoke repeatedly of the "love that dare not speak its name" during his second trial.[80] In the "History of a Struggle" which opened the 1913 Sagitta writings, Mackay outlined his campaign of "One against All"[81] with a touch of self-dramatization and vanity. He explained here that he had aimed first to reach "the natural allies" before taking the "path to a broad public" and beginning "the actual work for the ends of enlightenment."[82]

On August 1, 1905, the publishing house of Bernhard Zack sent out the first advance offer to subscribe to Sagitta's "books of the nameless love."[83] This publicity was by no means addressed to the public at large; subscribers could receive the books only after giving written assurance that they would not be offended by the works. The first two, *Die namenlose Liebe: Ein Bekenntniß* (The Nameless Love: A Confession) and *Wer sind wir? Eine Dichtung der namenlosen Liebe* (Who Are We? A Poem of the Nameless Love), were released in 1906. Even though the initial response was limited[84]–Mackay's "first, major disappointment"[85]–the subscription campaign continued on July 1, 1906, for the third and fourth books, the novelistic autobiography *Fenny Skaller* and the play *Über die Stufen von Marmor: Eine Szene der namenlosen Liebe* (Over the Steps of Marble: A Scene of the Nameless Love), works which did not actually appear until 1913. Mackay's activities during the intervening years could not escape the effects of the scandal initiated by Maximilian Harden, whose outing of Moltke and Eulenburg had such a profound impact on Wilhelmine attitudes toward homosexuality. Mackay was taken aback that "a matter which up to this time, for millennia, [had been] covered up and silenced with all the means of overt and covert oppression"[86] was now being discussed in public–all the way from the yellow press to scientific and political circles:

The goal was the destruction of a political enemy who exercised influence in the circles of power. In politics, however, where all concepts that otherwise have at least occasional validity in people's lives and are still conceded a certain justification–such concepts as honesty and chivalry, respect for private life and personal liberty, and the like: in politics, where all these concepts without exception become null and void, and where every weapon, even a poisoned one, is accepted and indeed expected–what was easier than to take up arms by referring to an opponent's "sexual orientation," so easy to wield and so sure to strike its goal, and thus to destroy him with one blow, no, with one word.[87]

Clearly misjudging his own effectiveness and at pains to distance himself from the on-going campaign against § 175, Mackay reiterated his disinterest in reform activities:

For those of us who love our younger friends with manly love, it is not as if the persons implicated in precisely these current cases in the political games of this winter [1907-8] could be of any particular interest. . . . Once again–as always–it was we who were most strongly harmed in our love. For even if individual voices were speaking out in support of the demand for the "decriminalization of intercourse between adults"–youth had to be "protected," and nowhere, absolutely nowhere, did anyone rise up who would dare to suggest that there is no better protection for youth than the individual who secures for them true friendship and genuine love.[88]

Here Mackay clearly formulated separate interests that were not within the goals of the on-going campaign against § 175.

Mackay decided to enter the fray by circulating *Gehör–nur ein Augenblick!* . . . *Ein Schrei* (Listen–for Just a Moment! . . . A Scream), a brochure initially published by Bernhard Zack in 1908 and later included within the 1913 Sagitta volume as Part 6. Financed by the independent homosexual scholar Benedict Friedländer (who had also subsidized Senna Hoy's *Kampf*),[89] this brochure was mailed to over 3,000 potentially interested individuals, including the superintendents of Evangelical Lutheran youth homes, Reichstag delegates, public and municipal libraries, as well as journals and newspapers. While the brochure argued for the decriminalization of boy-love, its cover letter referred to the Eulenburg Affair and once again set forth Mackay's vision of a group of like-minded individuals. "I know today," he wrote,

that there is a scattered band of those who cannot be disheartened by anything. I would like to get through to them with these words: not to be gathered for a purpose of any kind (nothing could be further from me), but to feel myself with them. The aim is to gather, but not *with* others, or *among* others, but to collect oneself in *oneself*–with the hope that not yet everything is lost . . . with the recognition that we can still be effective.[90]

The witch-hunt atmosphere of this era was evidenced by the March 3, 1908, confiscation of this brochure and the first two Sagitta works. Mackay's publisher, Bernhard Zack, was brought to court on two separate charges. In the first case, Zack was found guilty of "slandering" a Magdeburg clergyman by having sent him the brochure; on appeal, the penalty was reduced to payment of a fine. The second case was heard in Berlin, where nineteen (!) Protestant clergymen likewise pressed charges of slander and the state attorney demanded not just a fine but four months' imprisonment as well. The trial dragged on for nineteen months, and in October, 1909, Zack was fined 600 Marks for distributing the first two Sagitta texts, held to be "indecent" despite the fact that they were literary works.

In the meanwhile, Mackay had sent out a third invitation to subscribe to *Am Rande des Lebens: Die Gedichte der namenlosen Liebe* (At the Brink of Life: The Poems of the Nameless Love), which ultimately became Part 5 of the Sagitta volume. In the aftermath of the court judgment, he sent out a second (and final) circular to 1,200 individuals, a letter of farewell in which he resignedly noted that there were "no serious friends of *this* cause."[91] In the introduction to the 1913 Sagitta volume, he finally declared the end of his struggle. Because of the court's finding, the book itself appeared with Paris as a feigned place of publication and with a Dutch cover address for distribution. Here he pointed out two noteworthy mistakes that had been made in the struggle for homosexual liberation. One was that the "nameless love" had been declared to be "a special one . . . , a 'nobler and better' one. That it is not. This love is a love like any other love, not better, but also not worse."[92] The second error lay in having attempted "to demand liberty of the love of man at the expense of woman. . . . That too is a mistake. As completely different as the position of the opposite sex (in all classes) may still be today–to thwart its possibilities of development and to deny it is tantamount not to turning friends into enemies, but turning today's enemies into irreconcilable enemies for today and forever, and this is above all a complete misunderstanding of the great law of the future. This law is called liberty. Liberty, however, includes all and excludes no one."[93]

The linkage between anarchism and homosexuality was especially complex in the case of Mackay. Based on the principles of individualist anarchism, the "self-owner's" self-consciousness aimed to rise above everyone and everything; moreover, this standpoint was clearly correlated with the marginalized status of the boy-lover within the homosexual community. Repudiating any initiative like that of the WhK, which "acquits the one while condemning the other,"[94] Mackay was inspired to strike out on an individually oriented campaign of "one against all"–a program which was perhaps doomed in this form. Yet it should be kept in mind that the far more broadbased effort of Hirschfeld's WhK was likewise unable to reach its goal. Mackay's approach was also notable because he opposed any sort of scientific argumentation. Whereas Senna Hoy had rather optimistically expected to get beyond the level of moral denunciation by pinning his hopes on enlightenment, including public education on the findings of medical and sexological research, Mackay repeatedly polemicized against "so-called scientific research . . . which replaces absolute ignorance with twisted and half-truths, whose horrible confusion causes us to suffer more today than we did previously."[95] Because of Mackay's unrelenting focus on boy-love, it was clearly impossible to integrate his campaign within the broader homosexual rights movement. Despite his extremely abstract discourse about "liberty" in the sense of individualist anarchism, Mackay was nonetheless able to incorporate the issue of homosexuality within the prospect of freedom held out by anarchism–in the hope "that the entire well-being of the future lies in liberating the individual, *each* individual, in his progressive development toward himself, hindered by no social or communitarian compulsion whatsoever, as the highest happiness of his life, his outlook, and his goal."[96]

Translated from the German by James Steakley

AUTHOR NOTE

Walter Fähnders is Adjunct Professor of German Philology at the Universität Osnabrück. Recent publications include *Anarchismus und Literatur* (Stuttgart: Metzler, 1987); *Arbeit und Müßiggang 1789-1914: Dokumente und Analysen* (Frankfurt a.M.: Fischer, 1991), with W. Asholt; editor of Franz Jung, *Werke 3: Proletarier / Arbeiter Thomas / Hausierer* (Hamburg: Nautilus, 1992); *Fin de Siècle: Erzählungen, Gedichte, Essays* (Stuttgart: Reclam, 1993), with W. Asholt.

The author would like to thank James Steakley and Harry Oosterhuis for their assistance in assembling materials for this essay.

NOTES

1. Paragraph 175 of the Imperial Penal Code stated: "Unnatural vice committed between persons of the male sex or by people and animals is to be punished with prison; judgment may also include the loss of civil rights." In contrast, for example, to Austria, lesbian love between women was not incriminated.

2. Institut für Marxismus-Leninismus beim ZK der SED, *Geschichte der deutschen Arbeiterbewegung: Biographisches Lexikon* (Berlin/GDR: Dietz, 1970), p. 423.

3. See James D. Steakley, *The Homosexual Emancipation Movement in Germany* (New York: Arno, 1975), p. 2.

4. Cited in Magnus Hirschfeld, *Von einst bis jetzt: Geschichte einer homosexuellen Bewegung 1897-1922*, ed. Manfred Herzer and James Steakley (West Berlin: Rosa Winkel, 1986), p. 95.

5. See the contribution by Hubert Kennedy in this volume.

6. August Bebel, *Woman under Socialism*, trans. Daniel De Leon (New York: New York Labor News Press, 1904), pp. 164-65; see also pp. 37-38. The German original: A. Bebel, *Die Frau und der Sozialismus* (Stuttgart and Berlin: Dietz, 1922), pp. 296-97; see also p. 43. On Bebel and the homosexual movement, see Hirschfeld, pp. 104-7.

7. A. Bebel, *Die Frau und der Sozialismus*, p. 207, note 1.

8. British and Irish Communist Organisation, *Bernstein on Homosexuality: Articles from "Die Neue Zeit," 1895 and 1898*, trans. Angela Clifford (Belfast: Athol, 1977), pp. 12, 16; the wording has been slightly modified here. Bernstein's text first appeared as "Aus Anlaß eines Sensationsprozesses," *Die Neue Zeit* 13, part 2 (1895): 171-76; quotes on pp. 172, 175; emphasis in original.

9. Ibid., p. 176; English edition, p. 19.

10. E. Bernstein, "Die Beurtheilung des widernormalen Geschlechtsverkehrs," *Die Neue Zeit* 13, part 2 (1895): 228-33; quote on p. 233; English edition, p. 27.

11. Ibid., p. 20; German edition, pp. 228-29; emphasis in original.

12. *Stenographische Berichte über die Verhandlungen des Reichstags*, IX. Legislaturperiode, V. Session (1897/98), vol. 1, p. 410.

13. "Krupp auf Capri," *Vorwärts*, November 15, 1902, p. 3; emphasis added.

14. *Stenographische Berichte über die Verhandlungen des Reichstags*, XI. Legislaturperiode, I. Session (1903/05), vol. 8, p. 5839. Citing von Vollmar verbatim: "I recognize the great zeal that inspires this movement [against § 175], although on the other hand I must admit in all candor that the matters connected with the agitation have frequently assumed a form in the last while that make it extremely difficult to favor its petition." And he added: "My worthy colleague Thiele, like every other colleague, speaks in this matter without any regard to party membership and is simply taking a personal position, and the Social Democracy has as little to do with this matter as any other party."

15. Erich Mühsam, *Die Jagd auf Harden* (Berlin: Neuer Biographischer Verlag, 1908), in *Erich Mühsam Gesamtausgabe*, vol. 3: *Prosaschriften I*, ed. Günther Emig (West Berlin: Verlag europäische ideen, 1978), p. 248.

16. Ulrike Heider, *Der arme Teufel: Robert Reitzel–Vom Vormärz zum Haymarket* (Bühl-Moos: Elster, 1986), p. 79. Reitzel referred to Whitman, Shakespeare, Shelley, Platen, and Turgenev.

17. See Jonathan Katz, *Gay American History: Lesbians and Gay Men in the U.S.A.* (New York: Collier, 1976), pp. 376, 379.

18. See Ulrich Linse, *Organisierter Anarchismus im Deutschen Kaiserreich von 1871* (West Berlin: Duncker & Humblot, 1969).

19. Karl Friedrich H. Hartmann, "Ein Emanzipationswerk der Kulturbestrebungen," *Neues Leben* 6 (1902), no. 7, p. 26; no. 8, pp. 31-32; no. 10, p. 39; no. 12, p. 48; no. 13, p. 53. That the author of this series was later recruited as a police spy does nothing to diminish its importance; see Linse, pp. 101-2.

20. Hartmann, no. 7, p. 26. In the final article of the series, Hartmann wrote: "For us anarchists . . . great expectations are bound up with the demand for the repeal of § 175. One dogma after the other must fall. Day by day things are torn away from society that are regarded as an unassailable, holy norm, *until slowly but surely the mask must be cast aside, until the only thing standing upon the earth is the free man who can live free of every compulsion, every limitation and oppression for the single condition which is humanly true and brings happiness: feeling good.* He will be able to do and not do whatever he wants. His upbringing, his lifestyle will be constrained by no one. A purely instinctual man, he will feel only good, but in keeping with living out his instinct he will see that his well-being is dependent upon his fellow and vice versa" (ibid., no. 13, p. 53; emphasis in original).

21. Ibid., p. 31.

22. Albert Weidner, "Strafrecht und öffentliche Moral im Bunde gegen die Humanität," *Der freie Arbeiter* 1.20 (May 21, 1904): 77-79.

23. Catulus (i.e., Senna Hoy/Johannes Holzmann), "Homosexualität und Frauenbewegung," *Das neue Magazin für Litteratur* 73.8 (1904): 564; emphasis in original.

24. On Hoy/Holzmann, see Walter Fähnders, "Johannes Holzmann (Senna Hoy) und der 'Kampf,' " in *Kampf. Zeitschrift für–gesunden Menschenverstand* (Berlin, 1904-05; reprint, Vaduz, 1988), pp. xviii-xlv; a bibliography on Senna Hoy, ibid., pp. xlvi-l. See also Walter Fähnders, "Ein romantischer Rowdy. Hinweise auf Leben und Werk des Anarchisten Senna Hoy," *Die Aktion* (Hamburg) 9.47-49 (1989): 706-31.

25. Senna Hoy, "Politische und moralische Pfaffen," *Kampf* 1.1 (1904): 5.

26. Ibid., p. 159; see p. 402 on his contacts (*Verkehr*) with homosexual circles.

27. Senna Hoy, "Ein Wort im voraus," in *Das dritte Geschlecht: Ein Beitrag zur Volksaufklärung*, ed. Senna Hoy (Berlin: by the author, 1903), p. 2.

28. In addition to the introduction by Senna Hoy and two texts by Adolf Brand, the booklet contains the following: Hoy, "Das dritte Geschlecht," pp. 4-7; August Behnsen, "Homosexualität und Entwicklungslehre," pp. 8-10; Paul Enderling, "Die Homosexualität–eine Krankheit?" pp. 10-12; S[enna] H[oy], "Um der Gerechtigkeit willen," ibid., pp. 12-15.

29. Ibid., p. 2.

30. Ibid., p. 13.

31. Ibid., p. 7.

32. On this journal overall, see Fähnders, "Johannes Holzmann" (see note 24). Senna Hoy was quite controversial within anarchist circles. Max Nettlau, the historiographer of anarchism, wrote that "the Berlin publication *Der Kampf,*

which deals with the homosexuals, made an unpleasant impression"; see Nettlau, *Anarchisten und Syndikalisten*, part 1 (Vaduz: Topos, 1984), p. 306. According to Nettlau, Gustav Landauer was accustomed to pitch the "red issues" of *Kampf* into the wastepaper basket (ibid., p. 218, note 248).

Landauer was also concerned about Erich Mühsam's sexual libertinage or postulates of self-determination and feared "that Nohl's homosexuality might damage Mühsam's development"; see Lawrence Baron, "Mühsams individualistischer Anarchismus," in *Erich Mühsam: Scheinwerfer oder Färbt sich ein weißes Blütenblatt schwarz* (West Berlin: Klaus Guhl, 1978), p. 161.

33. *Kampf* 1.5 (1904): 151-58; all of the following quotations are from this essay; emphases in original.

34. Catalus, "Homosexualität" (see note 23), p. 566.

35. *Kampf* 1.4 (1904): 158.

36. Senna Hoy, "§ 175 R.-Str.-G.-B. und der Fall Hasse," *Kampf* 2.14 (1905): 403-4.

37. Ibid., p. 404; on the high respect accorded science and scientific education, see *Kampf*, pp. 153, 159, 187-88, 266-67.

38. Senna Hoy, "Moralische Pfaffen–ästhetische Priester," *Kampf* 1.3 (1904): 90-91. On the relevance of "aesthetics" for Senna Hoy, see Fähnders, "Ein romantischer Rowdy" (see note 24), pp. 718-27; samples of Senna Hoy's essayistic work also appear there (pp. 732-48). On his own literary efforts, see the listing in the Senna Hoy bibliography (note 24).

39. *Kampf* 1.5 (1904): 141.

40. Adolf Brand had printed the poem in his journal *Der Eigene*; see *Kampf* 1:5 (1904): 160.

41. According to Senna Hoy on the last page of the final issue of *Kampf* (p. 788).

42. On Erich Mühsam, see Heinz Hug and Gerd W. Jungblut, *Erich Mühsam (1878-1934): Bibliographie* (Vaduz: Topos, 1990); Heinz Hug, *Erich Mühsam* (Glashütten im Taunus: Detlev Auvermann, 1974); Walter Fähnders and Martin Rector, *Linksradikalismus und Literatur: Untersuchungen zur sozialistischen Literatur der Weimarer Republik*, 2 vols. (Reinbek: Rowohlt, 1974); Gerd W. Jungblut, *Erich Mühsam: Notizen eines politischen Werdeganges*, 2nd ed. (Schlitz: Verlag der Slitese, 1986); Rolf Kauffeldt, *Erich Mühsam: Literatur und Anarchie* (Munich: W. Fink, 1983); Walter Fähnders, *Anarchismus und Literatur: Ein vergessenes Kapitel deutscher Literaturgeschichte zwischen 1890 und 1910* (Stuttgart: J. B. Metzler, 1987). An important article appeared after completion of this essay: Thea A. Struchtmeier, "Erich Mühsams Auseinandersetzung mit 'Homosexualität' als Ausdruck einer Patriarchatsdebatte zwischen 1903 und 1930," in *Sich fügen heißt lügen*, ed. Erich-Mühsam-Kreis (Berlin: Erich-Mühsam-Kreis, 1993), pp. 51-90.

43. Erich Mühsam, "Bemerkungen," *Kain* 4.2 (1914): 29.

44. Mühsam dealt with homosexuality in the following texts from the 1920s: "Strafrecht," *Fanal* 3 (1929): 34-39; "Geschlechtsnot der Gefangenen," *Fanal* 3 (1929): 209-13; a review of the homosexual novel *Alf* by Bruno Vogel, in *Fanal* 4 (1930): 164; "Maximilian Harden," *Fanal* 3 (1927): 66-68. See also Mühsam's 1930

play *Alle Wetter*, ed. Gerd W. Jungblut (West Berlin: Klaus Guhl, 1977), pp. 43-44. I wish to thank James Steakley for these and the following two references to Mühsam's writings concerning homosexuality.

45. "Der Herr Staatsanwalt bedenkt, / Wie er die Moral erhalte. / Auf die Kunst den Blick er lenkt, / Die geschrieben und gemalte. / . . . Schiller war ein deutscher Dichter, / Eins der größten Geisteslichter. / 'Freundschaft' nannt' er ein Poem, / Das dem Anwalt unbequem. / Seine Strafbarkeit ergibt sich / Leicht aus hundertfünfundsiebzig. . . ." Erich Mühsam, "Widernatürlichkeiten," *Die Gemeinschaft der Eigenen. Bund für Freundschaft und Freiheit. Ein Nachrichten- und Werbeblatt*, nos. 5-6 (August 7, 1920): 7.

46. "Ich liebte dich, als scheu Dein Knabenblick / aus weltenfernen, wunder-fremden Römern / der Urerkenntnis Perlenschäumen sog,– / und meine Liebe war ein heißes Glück. . . ." Erich Mühsam, "Hubert," *Der Eigene* 7.5 (December 20, 1919): 7.

47. Erich Mühsam, *Die Homosexualität: Ein Beitrag zur Sittengeschichte unserer Zeit* (Berlin: Paul Singer, 1903), in *Prosaschriften I* (see note 15), p. 15; emphasis in original.

48. Ibid., pp. 18-19.

49. Ibid., p. 35.

50. Ibid., pp. 36-37.

51. Ibid., p. 35.

52. Erich Mühsam, "Frauenrecht," *Der Sozialist* 2 (1910): 143.

53. Erich Mühsam, "Bücherbesprechungen," *Der arme Teufel* 2.24 (November 7, 1903): 305.

54. Mühsam, *Die Homosexualität* (see note 47), p. 43.

55. Erich Mühsam, "Bohème," *Die Fackel* 8:202 (1906); quoted from idem, *Ausgewählte Werke*, 2 vols. (Berlin/GDR: Volk und Welt, 1978), 2: 31.

56. E. Mühsam, *Ascona: Eine Broschüre* (Locarno: Birger Carlson, 1905; reprint, West Berlin: Klaus Guhl, [1976]), p. 57.

57. Ibid., p. 7.

58. See Ulrich Linse, "Der Rebell und die 'Mutter Erde': Asconas 'Heiliger Berg' in der Deutung des anarchistischen Bohemien Erich Mühsam," in *Monte Verità. Berg der Wahrheit. Lokale Anthropologie als Beitrag zur Wiederent-deckung einer neuzeitlichen sakralen Topographie*, ed. Harald Szeemann (Milan: Electra Editrice, 1978), pp. 26-36, especially pp. 34-35.

59. E. Mühsam, "Offener Brief," *Der arme Teufel* 3.1-2 (January 9-16, 1904): 5.

60. *Jahrbuch für sexuelle Zwischenstufen* 6 (1904): 500-3.

61. Magnus Hirschfeld, "Offener Brief," *Der arme Teufel* 3.3 (July 7, 1904): 3.

62. Mühsam's diaries are still unpublished; quoted here from Baron (see note 32), p. 160.

63. Ibid.

64. Letter of October 24, 1910, to Richard Dehmel, in Erich Mühsam, *In meiner Posaune muß ein Sandkorn sein: Briefe 1900-1934*, ed. Gerd W. Jungblut (Vaduz: Topos, 1984), vol. 1, pp. 127-28.

65. See James D. Steakley, "Iconography of a Scandal: Political Cartoons and

the Eulenburg Affair," in *Hidden from History: Reclaiming the Gay and Lesbian Past*, ed. Martin Duberman, Martha Vicinus, and George Chauncey, Jr. (New York: New American Library, 1989), pp. 233-63.

66. *Vorwärts*, October 24, 1907.

67. Mühsam, *Die Jagd auf Harden* (see note 15), p. 245.

68. Ibid., p. 250.

69. Ibid., p. 246.

70. Ibid., p. 245.

71. On John Henry Mackay, see Thomas A. Riley, *Germany's Poet-Anarchist John Henry Mackay* (New York: Revisionist, 1972); K. H. Z. Solneman (i.e., Kurt Zube), *Der Bahnbrecher John Henry Mackay: Sein Leben und sein Werk* (Freiburg: Mackay-Gesellschaft, 1979); Walter Fähnders, *Anarchismus und Literatur* (see note 42); Hubert Kennedy, *Anarchist der Liebe: John Henry Mackay als Sagitta* (West Berlin: Jochen Knoblauch, 1988), which is a revised and expanded version of idem, *Anarchist of Love: The Secret Life of John Henry Mackay* (New York: Mackay Society, 1983).

72. Erich Mühsam, *Unpolitische Erinnerungen* (1931; Berlin/GDR: Volk und Welt, 1958), pp. 107-8.

73. Wolf Wucherpfennig, "John Henry Mackay: Dichter, Anarchist, Homosexueller," *Jahrbuch des Instituts für deutsche Geschichte* 12 (1983): 230.

74. See Fähnders, *Anarchismus und Literatur* (see note 41), pp. 1-22.

75. Wucherpfennig, p. 230.

76. Cited from the new edition: John Henry Mackay, *Die Bücher der namenlosen Liebe von Sagitta* (West Berlin: Rosa Winkel, 1979), vol. 1, pp. 213-15. The first volume of this two-volume set contains the texts discussed here. These texts are also in English in John Henry Mackay, *Fenny Skaller and Other Prose Writings from the Books of the Nameless Love*, trans. Hubert Kennedy (Amsterdam: Southernwood, 1988). The edition of 1913 was followed by a second (no place of publication given) in 1924. Volume 2 contains the novel *Der Puppenjunge: Die Geschichte einer namenlosen Liebe aus der Friedrichstraße* (1926), Mackay's final novel, which represents a remarkable contribution to the homosexual literature of the Weimar Republic; it has appeared in English as *The Hustler: The Story of a Nameless Love from Friedrich Street*, trans. Hubert Kennedy (Boston: Alyson, 1985). Mackay's collected epic, lyrical, and dramatic efforts on homosexual themes collected in volume 1 of the Sagitta edition cannot, unfortunately, be dealt with here. See the brief remarks in Kennedy (see note 71) and in *Andere Lieben: Homosexualität in der deutschen Literatur. Ein Lesebuch*, ed. Joachim Campe (Frankfurt a.M.: Suhrkamp, 1988), pp. 228-29.

77. Mackay, *Bücher der namenlosen Liebe*, vol. 1, p. 13.

78. Ibid., p. 61.

79. Ibid., p. 69; on Mackay's relationship to the WhK and to Hirschfeld, see Kennedy, pp. 16-19.

80. See the pertinent quotations in H. Montgomery Hyde, *The Trials of Oscar Wilde* (New York: Dover, 1962), pp. 200-1.

81. Mackay, *Bücher der namenlosen Liebe*, vol. 1, p. 13.

82. Ibid., pp. 17-18.

83. On Mackay's publisher, see Manfred Herzer, "Max Spohr, Adolf Brand, Bernhard Zack–drei Verleger schwuler Emanzipationsliteratur in der Kaiserzeit," *Capri: Zeitschrift für schwule Geschichte* 4.1 (1991): 15-30.

84. The reception was, however, not as limited as Mackay described it; see the references to reviews in Kennedy, pp. 14-19. In a remarkable short review, the Expressionist and later Dadaist Walter Serner commented in 1915 on the first volume of the Sagitta writings that the book "is incapable of drawing very much attention today from those for whom it struggles. The reason lies both in the depths and also on the surface. Male homosexuality, the contempt against which is here supposed to be shattered by an erotic-ideal work of literature, is certainly no more contemptible than sexuality altogether. But it is sexuality and, ideally constructed, more sentimental than all sentimentality, because precisely male desire for man is least untruthful: the hairdresser regards it coolly and conventionally, the thinker earnestly and disapprovingly. To both of them, a work that seeks to eliminate from society the disapproval of their humanity by elevating them to a self-deceiving gobbledy-gook ('Happiness Lost') is unimportant, if not ridiculous. Better to be unjustly kicked out than dishonestly embraced." W. Serner, "Sagitta: Die Bücher der namenlosen Liebe," *Sirius* 1 (1915-16): 32.

85. Mackay, *Bücher der namenlosen Liebe*, vol. 1, p. 22.

86. Ibid., p. 27.

87. Ibid., p. 26.

88. Ibid., pp. 27-28.

89. Benedict Friedländer (1866-1906) published *Die Renaissance des Eros Uranios* (Berlin: Verlag "Renaissance" Otto Lehmann, 1904; reprint New York: Arno, 1975) and initially cooperated with Magnus Hirschfeld in the WhK; this organization split over the question whether or not "current cases" ought to be created in order to accelerate the struggle against § 175. The opposition formed a "Secession" which held that "the path across corpses would lead more quickly and easily to the goal," whereas Hirschfeld wanted to continue the path as an expert witness in court cases, popular education, and so on. Together with Adolf Brand, the influential editor of the journal *Der Eigene* (vols. 1-13, 1896-1932; in addition *Wochenberichte*, leaflets, etc.–a complete bibliography in Herzer, pp. 25-27), Friedländer founded in 1903 the Community of the Special (Gemeinschaft der Eigenen). The journal and organization were strongly influenced by Stirnerian individualist anarchism. See Harry Oosterhuis and Hubert Kennedy, eds. *Homosexuality and Male Bonding in Pre-Nazi Germany: The Youth Movement, the Gay Movement, and Male Bonding Before Hitler's Rise* (reprinted simultaneously as *Journal of Homosexuality* 22.1-2) (New York: Harrington Park Press, 1991).

90. Mackay, *Bücher der namenlosen Liebe*, vol. 1, pp. 34-35.

91. Ibid., p. 53.

92. Ibid., p. 62.
93. Ibid.
94. Ibid., p. 63.
95. Ibid., p. 30. See Mackay's polemic against science, ibid., pp. 51, 59, 63-64; against Hirschfeld, pp. 68-69, 263, 457-58.
96. Ibid., p. 77.

Soviet Policy Toward Male Homosexuality: Its Origins and Historical Roots

Laura Engelstein

Princeton University

SUMMARY. Sodomy was a crime under tsarist criminal law. Having abrogated the tsarist legal codes in the name of socialist justice, the new Soviet regime did not at first impose criminal sanctions on sodomy. It was only in 1934, after Stalin had consolidated power, that an anti-sodomy statute was added to the Soviet criminal code. Although Russian radicals had never been friendly to variant sexual practices, which they viewed as the product of capitalist decadence, Soviet sexologists in the 1920s participated in the international movement for sexual reform and criminologists deplored the use of penal sanctions to censor private sexual conduct. The 1934 return to legal prosecution represented the recovery of two traditions: the radicals' disregard for issues of sexual freedom and tsarist legal custom. It was not, however, a clear reversal of the seemingly enlightened legal practice of the 1920s. This essay examines the trial of a group of homosexual men and the investigation of a lesbian couple, both from 1922, which show that Soviet courts tried to repress sexual variation even when homosexuality was not a crime. These cases and the status of homosexuality in general reflect on the murky status of the law and on the ambiguities of Soviet politics in the early years of the new regime.

Correspondence may be addressed: Department of History, 129 Dickinson Hall, Princeton University, Princeton, NJ 08544.

[Haworth co-indexing entry note]: "Soviet Policy Toward Male Homosexuality: Its Origins and Historical Roots." Engelstein, Laura. Co-published simultaneously in *Journal of Homosexuality* (The Haworth Press, Inc.) Vol. 29, No. 2/3, 1995, pp. 155-178; and: *Gay Men and the Sexual History of the Political Left* (ed: Gert Hekma, Harry Oosterhuis, and James Steakley) The Haworth Press, Inc., 1995, pp. 155-178; and *Gay Men and the Sexual History of the Political Left* (ed: Gert Hekma, Harry Oosterhuis, and James Steakley) Harrington Park Press, an imprint of The Haworth Press, Inc., 1995, pp. 155-178. Multiple copies of this article/chapter may be purchased from The Haworth Document Delivery Center. [1-800-342-9678 9:00 a.m. - 5:00 p.m. (EST)].

155

Marxist theorists, though primarily concerned with understanding social relations of production, have also considered the impact of social and economic relations on the organization and cultural categories of private and sexual life. Friedrich Engels examined the nature of the family under capitalism, and August Bebel described the emancipation of women under socialism. Before October 1917, Russian Marxists by and large considered such questions a diversion from the more central problem of mass political organization. The Bolshevik feminist Aleksandra Kollontai constitutes the outstanding exception to this rule, arguing forcibly from the early years of the twentieth century that the question of women's rights and civic equality must constitute an explicit element in the Marxist revolutionary program. In the 1920s she defended the value of free sexual expression as the vital emotional cement of a truly collective society. But even Kollontai's defense of "Winged Eros" was limited to an endorsement of freely chosen heterosexual contacts and emphasized the social importance of maternity as women's contribution to building the new socialist order.

Kollontai's later writings form part of a widespread discourse in the 1920s on the cultural reconstruction of Russian society, for once the Bolsheviks came to power they were faced with reshaping all manner of social relations, including the complexion of private and sexual life.[1] To understand how and with what justification they did so, it is not sufficient to consider the Bolsheviks only in light of the Marxist tradition, but also as part of the legacy of the Russian intelligentsia in the broad sense of the term and as heirs to the administrative and legal edifice of the tsarist regime. Therefore to evaluate the way in which the Soviet authorities handled the question of sexual diversity, one must place the record in historical context: first, in relation to the imperial precedent; and second, in relation to the broader field of sexual regulation in general.

In a path-breaking essay on "Russia's Gay Literature and Culture," Simon Karlinsky has argued that before 1917 both the regime's official posture and the prevalent social response were more tolerant of homosexuality than came to be the case under Soviet rule.[2] It is certainly true that the educated elite in late tsarist society had far greater latitude for cultural expression and personal idiosyncrasy (despite the regime's political heavy-handedness) than their

Soviet analogues later enjoyed, and that conservative Stalinist policies in regard to many aspects of intimate life (contraception and abortion, as well as male homosexuality) took a serious toll on the health and happiness of countless people. Two cautions are nevertheless in order. First, the vision of the tsarist period as a golden age of sexual toleration needs serious qualification; and second, the situation in the early 1920s needs more careful interpretation. This essay will confine itself to setting the historical context and to exploring—in a strictly preliminary fashion—the ambiguities of the brief interregnum between the Bolshevik seizure of power and the consolidation of Stalinist control.[3]

To begin with the imperial background. The tsarist criminal code drafted in 1845, modified in 1885, and still in effect in 1917 considered both bestiality and sodomy (defined as anal intercourse between men) criminal offenses. Article 995 penalized anyone convicted of "sodomy, the vice contrary to nature" (*protivoestestvennyi porok muzhelozhstva*) to loss of civil rights and a term of penal servitude of four to five years. Offenders of the Christian faith were in addition subject to religious penance imposed by the ecclesiastical authorities. Article 996 increased the penalty to loss of rights and exile at hard labor for nine to twelve years if the act were accompanied by the use of violence or performed with an underage or mentally defective man.[4] Lesbianism was not a crime in tsarist law.

In the 1880s the ministry of justice formed a committee to revise the criminal code. Its mandate was to bring the law into conformity with the progressive legal principles embodied in the judicial reforms of 1864 that had been enacted by Alexander II in connection with the liberation of the serfs. The committee consisted of high-ranking bureaucrats and eminent legal scholars. Its efforts resulted in a draft code, representing the latest principles of modern jurisprudence, which was officially approved in 1903 but never enacted in its entirety.[5] In line with the framers' modernizing intentions, the 1903 code removed certain outmoded provisions of the existing law in regard to sexual offenses. Rape was reclassified, from an insult to female honor to the cause of physical and psychic damage, and religious penalties (such as the penance imposed for sodomy) were no longer invoked. In other respects, the draft continued in the direction established by the 1845 text. It retained the penalties for statutory rape and went even further in protecting children from sexual intrusion and in penalizing a range of erotic behavior other than heterosexual vaginal intercourse previously ignored in the law.

In relation to sexual deviation, the code did not go as far as some members of the legal community might have liked. To the approval of almost all experts, it decriminalized bestiality and made the same distinctions in punishing anal rape between men as it did in the case of heterosexual rape (depending on the victim's age, state of mind, and relation to the offender). It did not, however, eliminate the statute against anal intercourse between consenting adult men, despite the objections of a number of legal commentators that the act injured no one's rights or interests and should therefore not be considered a crime.[6] The draft did, however, reduce the penalties for simple sodomy from the existing four to five years' penal servitude to a prison term of no less than three months, and it also eliminated the quasi-religious language (the vice contrary to nature) from the text.[7]

While it is true that few men were ever prosecuted in tsarist courts for the crime of consenting (homosexual) sodomy, it is not the case that imperial legislation, or even the dominant opinion among progressive legal scholars and lawmakers, exempted sodomy from repression. The tsarist regime was notorious both for ignoring the law (acting through imperial fiat or passing "emergency legislation" that superseded formal procedures and guarantees) and for its laxity in implementing the laws it did endorse. The relative neglect of sodomy in the courts may say more about the inefficiency of the legal system than about active tolerance for sexual diversity.

It may well be that Russians were less concerned with the menace of sexual deviation than contemporaries in the West, but such comparisons are risky. It is true that Russia produced no analogue to the Oscar Wilde scandal in England or the Eulenburg case in Germany, both known to the Russian reading public, and that certain highly placed figures pursued successful careers at court despite their widely known homosexual preferences. It also seems to be the case that Russian physicians and psychiatrists, though fully acquainted with the Western medical literature, did not focus on homosexuality as a problem of particularly acute social significance, although they faithfully echoed current scientific pronouncements on the biological origins and attributes of this sexual predilection.[8] Like their counterparts abroad, most Russian experts insisted that homosexuality was both pathological and morally repugnant.[9] It should be added in this context that nineteenth-century arguments for the organic origins of homosexual tastes (homosexuality as a disease rather than a vice) were understood as a progressive alternative to criminal prosecution, not the insidious pejoratives they are considered today.

If there is one figure in the prerevolutionary years who spoke out unambiguously for decriminalization (though on certain occasions his pronouncements were qualified by conventional phrases of moral distaste), it was the aristocratic anglophile liberal Vladimir Dmitrievich Nabokov, the father of the famous novelist and the son of the reforming minister of justice who had initiated the revision of the criminal code. A leading member of the Kadet (Constitutional Democratic) party who later held a post in the Provisional Government before emigrating to the West, Nabokov was a fierce proponent of individual rights and of the right to privacy. In this regard, he did not differ from the authors of the new code, although they did not follow the logic of their own juridical principles as ruthlessly as Nabokov did his. A product of this liberal, though privileged, professional and bureaucratic milieu, the 1903 code nevertheless testifies to the limits of the liberals' legal imagination. It also provides a baseline against which to evaluate the achievements of early Soviet justice, since it was the unimplemented 1903 draft that provided an important model for the first Soviet criminal code, enacted in 1922.[10]

But before they became legislators in their own right, Russian radicals expressed themselves as cultural critics and ideological watchdogs, often in dialogue with professionals and with representatives of the mainstream and avant-garde cultural establishment. Radicals and moderates joined in interpreting current events as a key to the public psyche, though they differed in their conclusions. While the experts (pedagogues and psychologists, for example) typically worried that the revolution of 1905 had unleashed a level of sexual passion damaging to the psychic well-being of enthusiastic youth, radical leaders saw 1905 as an exercise in sexual self-discipline. It was only in the postrevolutionary lull that radicals began to worry about the moral profile of their followers and the sexual temper of the times.[11] What political moderates and radicals shared was a fear of unbridled sexual expression; they differed only in the ideological coloration they gave to this fear.

In regard to sexual values, the Marxists did not differ from other intelligentsia radicals. Populists and Social Democrats alike were convinced that "sexual perversion" was the province of aristocratic roués and petty bourgeois degenerates. In their guise as cultural critics, some denounced the sexually explicit literature that appeared after 1905 (liberated by the relaxation of censorship rules and stimulated by increased public discourse about sex) as a product of "bourgeois" satiety and moral turpitude (according to the Marxist schema, 1905 was supposed to be the "bourgeois" revolution).[12] And while it is tempting to see in the splenetic denunciations of supposedly upper-class vice and the fervent defenses of folk purity and naturalness of genital desire the quirks of a peculiarly left-wing (or even Marxist) ideology, such attitudes were not confined to radical circles alone.

The conviction that vice was an upper-class affair, indeed a product of Western social and cultural development and of urban civilization in particular, pervaded educated Russian society. Archconservatives in the bureaucracy denounced "perversion" as a product of Western ways and, in Russia, of the cities.[13] Despite the concentration of prostitutes in rural market fairs and their presence in village taverns, physicians en masse refused to contemplate the possibility that peasant women might indulge in promiscuous sex, except under the compulsion of economic necessity and then only once having left the countryside behind.[14] They also preferred to think of male homosexuality as a practice largely confined to the Muslim areas of the Empire and to well-heeled gentlemen spoiled by idleness and rich food. In the face of evidence that both women and men sought sexual pleasure in the embrace of their own kind, among peasants and the urban poor as well as among their educated clients, most physicians and psychiatrists elected to think otherwise, at least until the revolution of 1905 finally unsettled their idealized image of the common folk.[15] It was only then that physicians, sociologists, psychologists, and criminologists began to admit that syphilis among children might be spread by precocious sexual and even homosexual play; or that prostitutes might indulge in lesbian as well as promiscuous heterosexual activities. Nor was there any suggestion in these disturbing reports that such behavior was anything but deplorable.

In short, on the eve of World War I, educated Russians had largely caught up with the cultural prejudices and advantages of the West. Physicians and psychiatrists described homosexuality as pathological; criminologists looked for sexual perversion among juvenile delinquents and found it; and commercial culture opened new possibilities for talk and images of sex. Dirty postcards were sold on the streets of the capitals; newspapers advertised pornographic images, sexual services, and sexual cures. Films translated erotic potboilers of domestic origin (Anastasiia Verbitskaia's *Keys to Happiness*) and literary texts of exotic appeal (Oscar Wilde's *Dorian Gray*) onto the screen for popular audiences. Cheap pamphlets warned against masturbation and birth control; others explained and advertised available forms of contraception. Some of the outstanding lights of the cultural avant-garde did not bother to disguise their homosexual affairs; others wrote openly of homosexual love–male and female–in poetry and prose.[16]

For all its (relative) openness to cultural expression in the last decade of rule, however, the tsarist regime never demonstrated the respect for individual rights that in the West has laid the foundation for sexual toleration. The reformed 1903 code was not adopted precisely because its principles (recognition of individual rights and equality before the law) were incompatible with existing legal institutions. And even this enlightened document retained a statute penalizing anal intercourse between consenting adult men, although commentators admitted that the act did not formally qualify as a crime. In this, of course, the code did not differ from some Western laws at the time–and to this day–that have penalized homosexuality, in deference to religious tradition and as an expression of other cultural prejudices.

The two revolutionary regimes of 1917, though signalling the demise of tsarism, also demonstrated certain continuities with the defunct order and with the reforming countercurrents that wove in and out of the imperial establishment. The Provisional Government, which hesitantly assumed responsibility for affairs of state after the fall of the monarchy in February 1917, represented the liberal impulse among the political elite. Cautious in regard to formal niceties, the new rulers refused to consider themselves the nation's legitimate successor government until the anticipated convocation of a constituent assembly. They nevertheless began piecemeal to dismantle the legal structure of the old regime. It was under the Provisional Government that women achieved civil rights, that religious and ethnic discrimination was abolished, along with the death penalty and deportation to Siberia, and that the possibility of divorce was enlarged.[17] The Provisional Government also formed commissions to revise the existing statutory law, including the criminal code.[18] It would be relevant to our argument to learn what these editorial commissions envisioned as the basis for the revised statutory corpus, and what opinions they expressed on the various sexual behaviors penalized in the existing and proposed codes, but these deliberations are not available to us.

By contrast, when the Bolsheviks came to power in October, they showed no timidity in overturning the legal basis of the old regime. Indeed, they immediately ordered the newly instituted "people's courts" to obey Soviet decrees and to reflect "revolutionary legal consciousness," while selectively applying only those existing laws that did not contradict socialist principles. By the end of 1918, the Soviet authorities had prohibited the application of any tsarist law. To fill the legislative gap, the new government issued numerous decrees imposing penal sanctions for specific transgressions but failed to introduce any clearly defined order or precise definitions on which the courts could rely. During 1920-21 the Commissariat of Justice authorized the production of a new criminal code, which went into effect on June 1, 1922, to be revised four years later.[19]

Thus, between 1917 and 1922, the acting courts could rely on no formal, organized directives defining the nature of criminal activity or regulating the imposition of sanctions. It is not surprising that in the turmoil of seizing and defending power a new government should delay before formalizing its official norms. Moreover, the definition of crime was itself in flux, as the violence of revolution and civil war created its own exceptional standards. It was not considered murder, for example, to kill in defense of the revolution or as a matter of "class justice." Such conduct was thought the stuff of heroism, not delinquency. Yet the absence of codified laws and the state of general uncertainty did not mean that all behavior formerly considered criminal was now officially sanctioned or left unpenalized.[20] On the one hand, individual decrees did single out particular criminal acts for punishment, although it was not until 1920 that murder and bodily injury were specifically enumerated.[21] On the other hand, even in the absence of specific decrees, the courts continued to prosecute conventional offenses.[22] Thus the omission of sodomy (along with other prerevolutionary offenses) from positive law in these confused early years did not imply official neutrality.

It was only with the publication of the 1922 criminal code that the omission of sodomy from the list of sexual crimes became a significant issue. As a matter of legal principle, this omission must have been deliberate and cannot be elided with the neglect of sexual crimes in the preceding five years.[23] But even after 1922, the legal situation was not simple. Although the code finally provided a systematic enumeration of punishable acts and appropriate penalties, its effect on the practice of justice must be qualified in two ways. First, it is difficult to ascertain to what extent the activity of the courts was guided by the precise content of the statutory law, and how far extrajudicial (administrative) jurisdictions, neither constrained by law nor responsible to the Commissariat of Justice, competed or interfered with the competence of the courts.[24] Second, the code itself allowed for the application of law by analogy, a principle rejected by liberal jurists in the old regime. Thus, an infraction not specifically mentioned in the code might nevertheless be prosecuted in court on the basis of its resemblance to a formally recognized crime.[25] In relation to sexual crime, both the positive content of the code and the uneasy relationship between written law and judicial practice gave rise to certain paradoxes in the 1920s.

In terms of the positive content of the 1922 statutes, it is clear that the code represented a break with tsarist justice, but it is less certain that the document as a whole did not in fact derive from the liberal tradition nascent within the old regime. Its place in Russian legal history is a matter of dispute. Soviet scholars boast that the 1922 code rejected the corrupt principles of bourgeois justice (including the long cherished notion of a rule-of-law state [*pravovoe gosudarstvo*]), which they condemn for its formalistic (and hypocritical) insistence on the impartiality and transcendent authority of the law. They claim that one of the early drafts rejected by the Commissariat for embodying precisely these suspect assumptions had been modeled by its Socialist Revolutionary authors on the self-consciously liberal 1903 text.[26] Orthodox Soviet commentators thus berate the Socialist Revolutionaries for their bourgeois attitudes, while praising the adopted code for its allegedly socialist principles. The émigré jurist Nikolai Timashev contends, by contrast, that the 1922 code itself drew heavily on the 1903 model, while delving even further back in time (and further to the right on the political spectrum) in relying on the last tsarist code for precedents in certain cases.[27] He takes pleasure in noting the contribution of liberal jurists like himself toward the establishment of a progressive national tradition, reflected in the constructive aspects of Soviet law. Conversely, he also takes pleasure in debunking Soviet claims to originality and to the transcendence of what was retrograde about tsarist law.

To add our oblique perspective to the larger question of continuity and change, and to try to fathom the juridical principles behind the omission of sodomy from the law, let us compare the 1922 and 1903 codes on the matter of sexual crime. On the level of classification the Soviet code represents an interesting–and juridically significant–compromise between the principles represented in the 1845/1885 and 1903 texts. As befitting a state that relied so heavily on police mechanisms of social control, the tsarist code included sexual misconduct, with the exception of rape, among other forms of disorderly behavior threatening to public decorum.[28] Its concern to bolster traditional notions of social hierarchy was reflected in the conception of rape as an insult to female honor.[29] The 1903 text, by contrast, separated the sexual crimes in a specifically designated section of the code and included rape among the other offenses to the sexual integrity of persons.[30] Critics of the reformed draft objected that this isolated category contradicted the framers' professed secular values. A strictly secular conception of sexual crime, they claimed, would have led the framers to integrate these transgressions into the broader corpus of the law on the basis of principles more general than those attached to conventional morality.[31] The decisions taken by the authors of the 1922 code seem to reflect this latter approach, since the new code classified the sexual crimes among those violating "the life, health, liberty, and dignity of the person." Thus, like the tsarist code it did not isolate the sexual crimes, but like the 1903 draft it conceived them as a species of personal injury, not an aspect of public discipline.

As to the content of the statutes on sexual crime, the Soviet lawmakers stripped sexual transgression down to the essentials. Their minimalism reflected the prevailing desire to limit the number of crimes in all specific categories.[32] Sex was covered by a mere six articles, which penalized: the knowing transmission of venereal disease; sexual relations with a sexually immature person (statutory rape, aggravated when involving defloration or perverted forms of contact); the sexual corruption of children under eighteen (defined as "indecent contact or bodily movements and various indecencies in oral, written, or symbolic form"); rape (aggravated by the victim being underage, lacking consciousness, or by the involvement of multiple perpetrators); compelling a woman in a position of dependency to have sexual intercourse or suffer other unwanted sexual advances (what we would call sexual abuse or harassment); and forcing or simply recruiting a woman to engage in prostitution, as well as pandering and running a brothel. The 1922 code thus followed the 1903 draft in offering special protection to children, dependents, and women subject to exploitation in commercial sex, and in decriminalizing bestiality. As in prerevolutionary law, prostitution was not in itself a crime.[33]

Where Soviet law now went beyond the 1903 code was in exempting from criminal punishment anal intercourse between consenting adult males. Incest was also eliminated. Given the articulate sexual conservatism of prerevolutionary Russian Marxists (indeed of the radical intelligentsia as a whole), this is a striking omission, which cannot be interpreted as an inadvertent product of juridical disarray but must be seen as a principled decision. The formal decriminalization of sodomy did not, however, mean that such conduct was invulnerable to prosecution. The prohibition against lewd behavior with minors presumably (though not explicitly) would have covered homosexual contacts. Though the rape statute did not specify the gender of the victim, it did use the term "sexual relations" (*polovoe snoshenie*), which in the tsarist code had referred only to the penetration of a woman's vagina by a man's penis.[34] Thus, anal rape would not have been covered by the strict language of the law. The absence of language did not, however, mean that crimes excluded from the statutes were not penalized in the courts. Legal experts concluded, for example, that incest should be juridically controlled even though it had formally been decriminalized. Although they insisted that "the proletarian state does not intrude into the intimate lives of individual persons and does not dictate the form of marriage and families," they also stressed that the state must combat "behavior that fosters biological degeneration," including marriage between close blood relations.[35] The principle of prosecution by analogy, anathema to prerevolutionary liberal jurists, allowed the courts to extend the range of penalized behavior beyond the strict limits of the written law. The justification was public welfare.

The absence of statutes against anal intercourse or lesbianism (which had not been penalized under tsarist law either) also did not stop practitioners from prosecuting homosexual behavior as a form of disorderly conduct.[36] Such creative application (or manipulation) of the law is exemplified in the account of two trials that occurred in 1922, after the publication of the code.[37] The first case arose when the local security police (Cheka) noticed that small groups of men, mostly sailors (*voenmory*), often congregated in a Petrograd apartment. Interrupting one such meeting, which they suspected of harboring a political agenda, the officers were surprised to discover a peaceful domestic scene apparently consisting of brides and grooms, gentlemen and ladies, decked out in appropriate attire. Upon closer inspection the participants all turned out to be men. They were not political conspirators, the press report indicated, but members of a "club" or "den" (*priton*) for "sexual perverts," who presented no less of a public danger. "Homosexual behavior," the report warned, "spreads not only among people obviously afflicted with organic abnormality, but also by attracting suggestible people, drawn to their example by curiosity, who accidentally succumb to perverted urges." The eminent psychiatrist Vladimir Bekhterev testified at the trial that although homosexual activity was not a criminal offense, "the public demonstration of such impulses might attract unstable people into the ambit of perversion. The introduction of homosexual tastes and activities to the broad public," he admonished, "is socially harmful and cannot be permitted. The creation of clubs or dens for such purposes must be punished under the criminal law."

Such an argument, of course, had nothing particularly Bolshevik, or Soviet, about it. Bekhterev himself had been an extremely distinguished representative of the imperial medical establishment and had written about the problem of male homosexuality in his prerevolutionary career.[38] The menace of public contagion that he invoked in 1922 had also served its rhetorical purposes under the old regime, as the opinions of the progressive tsarist judge Anatolii Koni demonstrate. During a 1902 debate with his colleague Vladimir Nabokov before the St. Petersburg Juridical Society, Koni defended the criminal prosecution of homosexuals as active propagandists for nonprocreative sex, a practice harmful to the national interest. He rejected Nabokov's contention that consenting relations between adults ought always to be considered a private affair, shielded from legal intervention.[39]

The other 1922 case concerning homosexuality evoked that same conflict between public interest and private right. It involved the conduct of a woman from a provincial town who changed her name from Evgeniia to Evgenii, adopted male attire, and settled down in marriage with another woman. Instructed by their employers to dissolve their "marriage," the two refused, claiming that "no one had the right to interfere in their intimate lives." "Unsuccessfully defined" as a "crime against nature," the press report noted, the case had bogged down in the courts as investigators tried–and failed–to find signs of abnormality in the defendants' behavior. A psychiatrist, it was suggested, might have been more successful in defining as deviant the pair's falsification of documents and stubborn refusal to part.

It is hard to see how either case supported the conclusion, offered by the commentator, that the public display of deviant sexual inclinations, supposedly constituting a menace to the welfare of young or "unstable" observers, should be punished under the law, since both involved essentially private (or at least discreet) behavior. Only the one female partner who dressed as a man actually had enacted any kind of public performance. If, moreover, as the report suggested, the statute against brothel-keeping might by some stretch of the imagination apply to the owners of the apartment in which the men had gathered, neither the participants themselves nor the female couple could be said to have violated any law. None had been detected in the commission of sexual acts which in any case were not illegal.

The account presented in the legal journal regretted the absence of available sanctions. The principle of protected privacy, which the female couple invoked in their own defense, seems to have been part of the ideological environment, since it was the same idea invoked by legal authorities to explain why the criminal code refrained from imposing incest barriers to marriage. But it was an idea as frequently violated as proclaimed. The same paragraph that explained the state's reluctance to intrude on the marriage relation defended the prohibition of incest on racial hygiene grounds, as a defense against degeneration. And while the argument for prosecuting homosexual conduct was carefully framed in terms of the public good, as a matter of display rather than morals or psychic injury, the practical implication of the argument was to narrow the bounds of privacy and enlarge the sphere of public intrusion.

Ominous as the interpretation of these two cases might sound, the men who framed the 1926 version of the criminal code ignored its implications.[40] Like the original decision to decriminalize sodomy, the statute's absence from the 1926 edition indicates yet again that the prosecution of homosexual conduct was not accepted as official policy during these years. During the 1920s Soviet delegations participated in international sexual reform congresses in Europe.[41] The entry under "homosexuality" (*gomoseksualizm*) in the 1930 edition of the Great Soviet Encyclopedia mentioned approvingly the theories of Sigmund Freud and of the German homosexual emancipationist Magnus Hirschfeld. It explained that homosexual inclinations resulted from psychological anomalies, which bore no implication of guilt or criminal responsibility. Prerevolutionary anti-sodomy legislation was denounced as "absurd," ineffective, and psychologically damaging to the homosexuals themselves. By contrast, the author lauded Soviet law for refusing to recognize "so-called crimes against morality." "Our legislation, based on the principle of social defense [*zashchita obshchestva*] imposes penalties only in those cases when the object of the homosexuals' sexual interest is underage." The entry concluded on a self-congratulatory utopian note, predicting that socialism would eventually alleviate the social distress of those suffering from this psychic "anomaly":

Along with prophylaxis and curative measures, our society will create those indispensable conditions under which the everyday interactions of homosexuals will be as normal [*bezboleznennye*] as possible and the sense of estrangement [*otchuzhdennost'*] they usually feel will be resorbed in the new collective.[42]

Such scientifically informed toleration ceased only at the end of 1933, when the Central Executive Committee of the Communist Party introduced a statute penalizing consenting homosexual relations between men. Appearing in 1934 as article 154-a, inserted after the first five sexual crimes and before the last, concerning prostitution, the sodomy statute "deprived of liberty" for three to five years any man convicted of performing anal intercourse with another, willing, man. Use of force or abuse of the partner's dependent position increased the penalty to a term of five to eight years' confinement.[43] These penalties, especially in the case of sodomous rape, were milder than those exacted by the last tsarist code (four to five years' penal servitude for simple sodomy, nine to twelve years' hard labor for aggravated forms) but potentially harsher than those in the 1903 draft, which indicated a minimum sentence of three months in prison for simple sodomy. The penalties for sodomous rape, by contrast, seem to have been more severe in the 1903 text: from three years' corrective incarceration to a maximum of eight years at hard labor.[44]

Why the government considered it necessary to recriminalize homosexual relations between adult men after a hiatus of sixteen years, during which popular attitudes may not have changed but when the law remained neutral, cannot be deduced from the available sources. The most one can assert is that the move occurred in the context of an altered juridical climate. Certainly the Stalinist turn introduced more repressive policies in relation to other aspects of intimate life (the recriminalization of abortion, for example) and even less respect for the protections of privacy than the fledgling regime in its confused early years had shown. Peter Solomon, in his study of Soviet penal policy, affirms that the "progressive" penal ideas current in the 1920s gave way to more draconian notions of justice as the Stalinist regime consolidated its hold. Thus, he notes that numerous new laws were added to the books in the early 1930s, imposing serious penalties for various political and economic crimes (theft, resistance to collectivization), and at the same time extrajudicial sanctions were more freely applied.[45] In other words, Stalinist "justice" was characterized by greater stringency in the application of the law and greater tendency to circumvent it.

More specific indications of the lawmakers' motives in regard to sodomy can be gleaned, however, from the language in which the legal turn was couched. Judging from statements by Maxim Gorky and justice commissar Nikolai Krylenko, as well as from the revised entry in the second edition of the Great Soviet Encyclopedia, the standard rhetoric associating privilege with perversion made a comeback at this time, displacing the preferred scientific discourse of the intervening years. In 1934, for example, Gorky identified homosexuality as a form of bourgeois "filth" linked to the emergence of fascism in Germany:

> In the land where the proletariat governs courageously [*muzhestvenno*; also translated as manfully] and successfully, homosexuality, with its corrupting effect on the young, is considered a social crime punishable under the law. By contrast, in the "cultivated land" of the great philosophers, scholars, and musicians, it is practiced freely and with impunity. There is already a sarcastic saying: "Destroy homosexuality and fascism will disappear."[46]

Reinforcing the new tone (or rather, reviving an old theme), Krylenko, in a related vein, asserted that homosexuality was a noxious remnant of the capitalist past:

> The laboring masses believe in normal relations between the sexes and are building their society on healthy principles. In this environment there is no place for such effete gentlemen

[*gospodchiki*]. Who provides our main clientele for such affairs? The laboring masses? No! The déclassé riff-raff, whether from the dregs of society or the remnants of the exploiting classes. With nowhere to turn, they take up pederasty. In their company, in foul secret dens, another kind of work also takes place, using this pretext–counterrevolutionary work. These are the people who destabilize [*dezorganizatory*] the new social relations we are trying to establish between people, between men and women, within the laboring masses. And therefore it is these gentlemen [*gospoda*] whom we prosecute in court and deprive of five years of freedom.[47]

These remarks were uttered in the context of a 1936 speech before the party's Central Executive Committee, concerning recent amendments to the criminal code.[48] Krylenko's rhetoric conveys the transformation in official attitudes toward the law and toward social conflict that coincided with the consolidation of Stalinism. Having earlier derided bourgeois legality as an instrument of class oppression, by December 1934, in the wake of Sergei Kirov's assassination, the commissar of justice had come to praise the application of criminal penalties for their "educative, political, and often frankly terroristic role."[49] The law, he now declaimed, was an instrument of warfare against the newly aggressive class enemy and also a means by which to "reconstruct" individual citizens and reshape the general tenor of social life. It was for this reason, he announced in early 1936, that a series of specific crimes had been added to the existing statutes.[50] The list included treason, terrorism, parasitism, hooliganism, juvenile crime, sodomy, pornography, workplace indiscipline, and failure to pay child support, in that order. The purpose of these laws, Krylenko affirmed, was to fight not only the "class enemy but also déclassé elements . . . and all those who destabilize our new social order [*obshchestvennyi byt*]." Numbered among the latter were incorrigible juvenile delinquents and homosexuals. The previous failure to penalize sodomy, the commissar explained, reflected the erroneous notion derived from "bourgeois Western schools of thought" that the practice was always a sign of illness. Medical experts might determine the cases in which sodomy indeed indicated a pathological state, but homosexuality, like alcoholism, could not in every instance constitute a sign of diminished responsibility.[51] On the contrary, such sexual habits signalled the perpetrators' underlying antisocial intentions (destabilization and even counterrevolution).

Krylenko's remarks on the legal and social status of sexual diversity thus constituted a sharp turnaround. It was the very liability of (male) persons engaged in homosexual activity to criminal prosecution that the 1930 edition of the Great Soviet Encyclopedia had associated with the cruel and irrational practices of bourgeois justice. The editors of the second edition, by contrast, denounced homosexuality as a feature of capitalist society, in which, they asserted, homosexuality was left "de facto unpenalized." "By the healthy standards of Soviet morality," they boasted, reversing the recent official line, "homosexuality, as a sexual perversion, is considered shameful and criminal [*pozornyi i prestupnyi*]. Soviet criminal law penalizes homosexuality, with the exception of those cases in which it is a symptom of psychological disturbance."[52] Gone was the utopian vision of a collective, humane and tolerant enough to encompass sexual diversity in its midst. The criminal courts were now to ensure that "communist discipline" replaced the "vestiges of capitalist psychology" among the working masses.[53]

In the end, what conclusions can be drawn about the attitudes of Russian Marxists, the Bolsheviks in particular, toward sexual alternatives? In relation to tsarist jurisprudence, Soviet law was distinguished by its secularism, also, if Peter Solomon is to be believed, by the relatively more lenient penalties it exacted for crimes across the board.[54] Both attributes are features of judicial modernism. But what might be considered progressive ideals were overridden in Soviet criminal practice by a very unmodern disregard for law itself. This disregard was not peculiar to the sexual domain. While it is true that the Stalinist state abused the laws on sexual crime to persecute troublesome people, it also abused the law in every case. The abuse was not merely practical or accidental, however. Soviet jurists prided themselves on a "flexible" approach to law and rejected the literal-mindedness of bourgeois jurisprudence.[55]

In recriminalizing sodomy, furthermore, the Soviet legal establishment did no more than restore tsarist legal precedent. In so doing, however, it was no less hesitant to break with tradition than the late imperial legal reformers, so resolute in their liberal principles, who had also recoiled before taking sodomy off the books and had justified their timidity in terms of the public welfare. This custodial rationale was compatible both with a medical discourse that favored therapy over repression and with an administrative approach to public morality that used the law as an instrument of social control. If the attitudes prevalent in the first years of Soviet rule favored the first combination, those that came to dominate after 1933 favored the last. In both cases the choice must have been political, but it is precisely this dimension that remains unexplored. Without taking my account into the recent Soviet past, I would like to close with the suggestion that the story of abuse is less interesting (because more predictable, though of course no less harrowing for that) than the story of the brief, exceptional moment in the Soviet record. Why did homosexuality escape the law between 1917 and 1934? That is the still obscure and intriguing tale.

AUTHOR NOTE

Laura Engelstein is Professor of History at Princeton University. She is the author of *The Keys to Happiness: Sex and the Search for Modernity in Fin-de-Siècle Russia.*

NOTES

1. For a scientific look into the matter of sexual behavior, see Sheila Fitzpatrick, "Sex and Revolution: An Examination of Literary and Statistical Data on the Mores of Soviet Students in the 1920s," *Journal of Modern History* 50 (June 1978): 252-78; on abortion policy, see Wendy Goldman, "Women, Abortion, and the State, 1917-36," in *Russia's Women: Accommodation. Resistance. Transformation*, ed. Barbara Evans Clements, Barbara Alpern Engel, and Christine D. Worobec (Berkeley, 1991); on the increased interest in sexuality in the mid-1920s, see Eric Naiman, "The Case of Chubarov Alley: Collective Rape, Utopian Desire, and the Mentality of NEP," *Russian History* 17.1 (1990): 7, 17.

2. Simon Karlinsky, "Russia's Gay Literature and Culture: The Impact of the October Revolution," in *Hidden from History: Reclaiming the Gay and Lesbian Past*, ed. Martin Bauml Duberman, Martha Vicinus, and George Chauncey, Jr. (New York, 1989), pp. 347-64. See also Karlinsky's earlier essay: "Russia's Gay Literature and History (llth-20th centuries)," *Gay Sunshine: A Journal of Gay Liberation*, no. 29-30 (Summer-Fall 1976): 1-7.

3. This question is intelligently addressed by Daniel Healey, "A Social History of Homosexuality in Soviet Russia, 1917-1934," unpublished master's thesis, School of Slavonic and East European Studies, University of London, 1991. I would like to thank Mr. Healey for sending me a copy of his work, which I read after my own essay was completed.

4. *Ulozhenie o nakazaniiakh ugolovnykh i ispravitel'nykh: Izdanie 1885 goda, so vkliucheniem statei po prodolzheniiam 1912, 1913 i 1914 godov* (Petrograd, 1916), pp. 212-13.

5. For a brief description of this background and of the fate of the draft, see N. S. Timasheff, "The Impact of the Penal Law of Imperial Russia on Soviet Penal Law," *The American Slavic and East European Review* 10.4 (1953): 443-44; for more on the sexual aspects of the reform, see Laura Engelstein, "Gender and the Juridical Subject: Prostitution and Rape in 19th-Century Russian Criminal Codes," *Journal of Modern History* 60.3 (1988): 458-95.

6. A minority in the Moscow Juridical Society favored decriminalization: "Proekt osobennoi chasti ugolovnogo ulozheniia v obsuzhdenii Moskovskogo iuridicheskogo obshchestva," *Iuridicheskii vestnik*, no. 10 (1886): 375. For another argument in favor of decriminalization, see the opinion of the Samara circuit court, cited in N. A. Nekliudov, ed., *Materialy dlia peresmotra nashego ugolovnogo zakonodatel'stva*, 7 vols. (St. Petersburg, 1880-1883), 3: 307-8; also V. D. Nabokov, *Elementarnyi uchebnik osobennoi chasti russkogo ugolovnogo prava*, vyp. 1 (St. Petersburg, 1903), p. 81, and idem, "Plotskie prestupleniia, po proektu ugolovnogo ulozheniia," *Vestnik prava*, no. 9-10 (1902), reprinted in V. D. Nabokov, *Sbornik statei po ugolovnomu pravu* (St. Petersburg, 1904), pp. 117, 119, 125. See also the argument of the St. Petersburg Juridical Society, cited in *Ugolovnoe ulozhenie: Proekt redaktsionnoi komissii i ob''iasneniia k nemu*, 8 vols. (St. Petersburg, 1895-97) [henceforth *UU*], 6 (1897): 591. For the strongest argument, see Nabokov's translation of his Russian article: Vladimir v. Nabokoff, "Die Homosexualität im russischen Strafgesetzbuch," *Jahrbuch für sexuelle Zwischenstufen* 5.2 (1903): 1159-71.

7. Article 516, *Ugolovnoe ulozhenie, Vysochaishe utverzhdennoe 22 marta 1903 goda* (St. Petersburg, 1903), pp. 181-82.

8. For a discussion of a medical text on lesbianism that manifests some of these features, see Laura Engelstein, "Lesbian Vignettes: A Russian Triptych from the 1890s," *Signs* 15 (1990): 813-31. The text in question is I. M. Tarnovskii, *Izvrashchenie polovogo chuvstva u zhenshchin* (St. Petersburg, 1895).

9. For example, V. M. Tarnovskii, *Izvrashchenie polovogo chuvstva: Sudebno-psikhiatricheskii ocherk dlia vrachei i iuristov* (St. Petersburg, 1885).

10. This argument is made in N. S. Timasheff, "Impact."

11. See Laura Engelstein, *The Keys to Happiness: Sex and the Search for Modernity in Fin-de-Siècle Russia* (Ithaca, 1992), chapter 6.

12. Among the Social Democrats, see, for example, Iu. M. Steklov, *Literaturnyi raspad: Kriticheskii sbornik*, 2 vols. (St. Petersburg, 1908-9), and G. S. Novopolin, *Pornograficheskii element v russkoi literature* (St. Petersburg, 1909). For Maxim Gorky's hostile comments about homosexuality, see Vladimir Kozlovskii,

Argo russkoi gomoseksual'noi subkul'tury: Materialy k izucheniiu (Benson, VT, 1986), p. 152. For similar sentiments expressed by a populist physician, see D. N. Zhbankov, "Polovaia vakkhanaliia i polovye nasiliia: Pir vo vremia chumy," *Prakticheskii vrach* (1908), no. 17, 308-10; no. 18, 321-23; no. 19, 340-42.

13. For example, the procurator of Archangel Province, R. K. Kraus, quoted in *UU* 6: 594-95.

14. See Laura Engelstein, "Morality and the Wooden Spoon: Russian Physicians View Syphilis, Social Class, and Sexual Behavior, 1890-1905," in *The Making of the Modern Body: Sexuality and Society in the Nineteenth Century*, ed. Catherine Gallagher and Thomas Laqueur (Berkeley, 1987), pp. 169-208.

15. On homosexuality among peasant and urban lower-class women, see I. M. Tarnovskii, *Izvrashchenie polovogo chuvstva u zhenshchin*, and the medical report from the Sakhalin penal colony by Dr. A. D. Davydov, *Ezhenedel'nik*, no. 1 (1895), cited ibid., p. 127; on homosexuality among urban lower-class men, see V. Merzheevskii, *Sudebnaia ginekologiia: Rukovodstvo dlia vrachei i iuristov* (St. Petersburg, 1878), p. 207-9; among the Muslim population, see Grigorii Iokhved, "Pederastiia, zhizn' i zakon," *Prakticheskii vrach*, no. 33 (1904): 871-73. For Russians' disregard of the evidence on class, see Engelstein, *The Keys to Happiness*, chapter 4.

16. See Karlinsky, "Russia's Gay Literature," pp. 351, 354-55; on film, N. M. Zorkaia, *Na rubezhe stoletii: U istokov massovogo iskusstva v Rossii, 1900-1910 godov* (Moscow, 1976). For an ambivalent but strikingly frank discussion of homosexuality, see the work of the Christian philosopher V. V. Rozanov, *Liudi lunnogo sveta: Metafizika khristianstva* (St. Petersburg, 1911; 2nd ed. 1913; reprint, Moscow, 1990).

17. H. J. White, "Civil Rights and the Provisional Government," in *Civil Rights in Imperial Russia*, ed. Olga Crisp and Linda Edmondson (Oxford, 1989), pp. 299-302; also Robert Paul Browder and Alexander F. Kerensky, eds., *The Russian Provisional Government 1917: Documents*, 3 vols. (Stanford, 1961), 1: 191-242.

18. Timasheff, "Impact," p. 444.

19. Ibid., pp. 444-47. A statement of guiding principles issued in 1918 suggested various punishments but failed to define particular offenses. On the legal situation immediately following the revolution, see John N. Hazard, "Soviet Law: The Bridge Years, 1917-1920," in *Russian Law: Historical and Political Perspectives*, ed. William E. Butler (Leyden, 1977), pp. 235-55.

20. This assertion is made in Karlinsky, "Russia's Gay Literature," p. 357, in refutation of claims made by John Lauritsen and David Thorstad that the absence of an antisodomy statute implied official endorsement of the practice; see *The Early Homosexual Rights Movement (1864-1935)* (New York, 1974), p. 63. Karlinsky's assertion (from his *Gay Sunshine* essay) is repeated in Kozlovskii, *Argo*, p. 152.

21. A. Gertsenzon, "Sotsialisticheskoe ugolovnoe zakonodatel'stvo v period do izdaniia pervogo sovetskogo ugolovnogo kodeksa [UK RSFSR 1922 g.]," *Sotsialisticheskaia zakonnost'*, no. 12 (1937): 83.

22. Thus D. I. Kurskii commented in 1919 that "active decrees have not established norms, even for the protection of the individual's physical inviolability or for the regulation of such actions as insulting behavior, bodily injury, or murder. However, data on the activity of the people's courts show that they react quickly and strictly against such actions." "Novoe ugolovnoe pravo," *Proletarskaia revoliutsiia i pravo*, no. 2-4 (1919): 28. Rape was among the specific crimes included in early Soviet decrees: ibid., p. 24.

23. This is precisely the elision made by those who read all of Stalinism's worst excesses back into the revolution's early years and wish to discredit any positive aspect of the new regime. It is the point intended by Karlinsky and reiterated by Kozlovskii, *Argo*, p. 152.

24. Peter H. Solomon, Jr., begins to answer both these questions, but not in relation to sexual crime: see his "Soviet Penal Policy, 1917-1934: A Reinterpretation," *Slavic Review* 39.2 (1980): 195-217; and "Criminalization and Decriminalization in Soviet Criminal Policy, 1917-1941," *Law and Society Review* 16.1 (1981-82): 9-41.

25. Timasheff, "Impact," p. 448.

26. G. V. Shvekov, *Pervyi sovetskii ugolovnyi kodeks* (Moscow, 1970), pp. 106-9. The agrarian socialist SRs were at first the Bolsheviks' allies but were later prosecuted by the Soviet state. Solomon agrees with Shvekov that the SR affinity for the classical penal principles represented by the 1903 draft did not reflect the so-called progressive penal ideas championed by the authors of the 1922 code. The two basic elements of "progressive" policy, according to Solomon, were leniency and differentiation: that is, lowering the severity of punishment and avoiding incarceration; and tailoring individual sentences to the perpetrators' character (based either on personality or class). See Solomon, "Criminalization," p. 197.

27. Timasheff, "Impact," pp. 447, 462.

28. Chapter 4, "O prestupleniiakh protiv obshchestvennoi nravstvennosti" (On Crimes against Public Morality), of which the sexual crimes formed the first subsection.

29. In Chapter 6, "O [sic] oskorbleniiakh chesti" (On Insults to Honor), section one, "O prestupleniiakh protiv chesti i tselomudriia zhenshchin" (On Crimes against the Honor and Chastity of Women).

30. Chapter 27, entitled "O nepotrebstve" (On Depravity).

31. See opinions cited in *UU* 6: 567-69; also, Nabokov, "Plotskie prestupleniia," p. 90, and idem, *Elementarnyi uchebnik*, pp. 74-75.

32. Some jurists went so far as to propose eliminating all specific crimes from the books, leaving both definition and sentencing up to the courts: see Robert Sharlet, "Pashukanis and the Withering Away of the Law in the USSR," in *Cultural Revolution in Russia, 1928-1931*, ed. Sheila Fitzpatrick (Bloomington, 1978), pp. 176-77.

33. For statutes, with commentary, see D. Karnitskii and G. Roginskii, eds., *Ugolovnvi kodeks RSFSR: Posobie dlia slushatelei pravovykh vuzov, shkol i iuridicheskikh kursov* (Moscow, 1935), pp. 208-16, and A. N. Trainin, V. D. Men'sha-

gin, and Z. A. Vyshinskaia, eds., *Ugolovnyi kodeks RSFSR: Kommentarii*, gen. ed. I. T. Goliakov (Moscow, 1941), pp. 188-92.

34. On application of the statute to "perverted" (*razvrashchennve*) forms of sexual contact, see commentary in "Diskussionnaia stranitsa po primeneniiu ugolovnogo kodeksa: Voprosy i otvety," *Ezhenedel'nik sovetskoi iustitsii*, no. 24-25 (1922): 20.

35. Ibid. This case is cited in Timasheff, "Impact," p. 458.

36. Timasheff, "Impact," p. 458.

37. G. R., "Protsessy gomoseksualistov," *Ezhenedel'nik sovetskoi iustitsii*, no. 33 (1922): 16-17.

38. For example, V. M. Bekhterev, "Lechenie vnusheniem prevratnykh polovykh vlechenii i onanizma," *Obozrenie psikhiatrii, nevrologii i eskperimental'noi psikhologii*, no. 8 (1898): 587-97.

39. Summary of Nabokov's presentation reported in the proceedings of the St. Petersburg Juridical Society, *Pravo*, no. 1 (1903): 50-56. Summary of Koni's reply, in "Khronika: Iz deiatel'nosti iuridicheskikh obshchestv. Ugolovnoe otdelenie S.-Peterburgskogo obshchestva, 7 dekabria 1902," *Zhurnal ministerstva iustitsii*, no. 1 (1903): 235. Koni was the judge who presided over the trial exonerating Vera Zasulich, the would-be assassin of St. Petersburg's municipal governor. Like Bekhterev, but unlike Nabokov, he remained in the Soviet Union after 1917.

40. Timasheff, "Impact," p. 458.

41. Kozlovskii, *Argo*, p. 151. On the Soviet role in these congresses, see Healey, "A Social History," pp. 12-14.

42. Entry quoted in full in Kozlovskii, *Argo*, pp. 171-75.

43. Trainin et al., *Ugolovnyi kodeks*, p. 191. The text of the amending decree (identical to the article), adopted December 17, 1933, announced March 7 and April 1, 1934, may be found in *Sobranie zakonov i rasporiazhenii raboche-krest'ianskogo pravitel'stva SSSR*, no. 1 (Jan. 5, 1934): 6; ibid., no. 15 (March 23, 1934): 209; and *Sobranie uzakonenii i rasporiazhenii raboche-krest'ianskogo pravitel'stva RSFSR*, no. 15 (April 25, 1934): 114. Karlinsky says the law prescribed a term at hard labor ("Russia's Gay Literature," p. 361), but the actual text mentions only "loss of liberty."

44. The reduction in severity probably does not indicate a more tolerant view of the crime, since penalties for all crimes in the 1922 code were lower than those in the tsarist (or 1903) codes: see Solomon, "Soviet Penal Policy," p. 198.

45. Ibid., pp. 208-10, 214-15; also idem, "Criminalization and Decriminalization in Soviet Criminal Policy," p. 35, on Stalin's return to the court system as an instrument of social control in the mid-1930s.

46. Quoted in Kozlovskii, *Argo*, p. 152.

47. Excerpt from 1936 speech, quoted ibid., p. 154.

48. For the entire text, see N. V. Krylenko, "Ob izmeneniiakh i dopolneniiakh kodeksov RSFSR," *Sovetskaia iustitsiia*, no. 7 (1936): 1-5.

49. N. V. Krylenko, "Proekt ugolovnogo kodeksa Soiuza SSR," *Sovetskaia iustitsiia*, no. 11 (1935): 2. The assassination of Kirov, the Leningrad party boss,

set off the wave of prosecutions within the party known as the great purges. On Krylenko's early attitudes toward law, see Sharlet, "Pashukanis," pp. 170-71.

50. Krylenko, "Ob izmeneniiakh," p. 1.

51. Ibid., p. 3.

52. Entry quoted in Kozlovskii, *Argo*, pp. 178-79.

53. Krylenko, "Ob izmeneniiakh," p. 5.

54. Solomon, "Soviet Penal Policy," p. 198.

55. For example, Krylenko's defense of the principle of analogy: Krylenko, "Proekt," p. 2.

Gide in the U.S.S.R.:
Some Observations on Comradeship

Patrick Pollard

Birkbeck College, University of London

SUMMARY. After 1914-18, Gide emphasized the value of the Comradeship of Mankind rather than the essentially individualistic ethos to which he had been previously committed. However, while believing in the social benefits of tolerating pederasty, he still saw a person's difference from the norm as the guarantee of authenticity. Political idealism and curiosity took him to the U.S.S.R. in 1936, and on his return he criticized the inertia, ignorance, and conformism which he considered were encouraged by the Soviet state's promotion of the family unit. This essay examines how his attitude towards sexuality led him to question alleged political freedoms and to see in the Soviet oppression of minorities, including homosexuals, the denial of the revolutionary spirit.

In his recent book, Rudolph Maurer writes of Gide's reaction to the change in the penal code of the U.S.S.R. in early 1934 whereby homosexual acts were recriminalized.[1] Gide's dreams of "a new Sparta" were to be disappointed, but he decided not to write a letter of protest to the Russian leadership, naively putting his faith in the

---

Correspondence may be addressed: 97 New Bond Street, London W1Y 9LF, United Kingdom.

[Haworth co-indexing entry note]: "Gide in the U.S.S.R.: Some Observations on Comradeship." Pollard, Patrick. Co-published simultaneously in *Journal of Homosexuality* (The Haworth Press, Inc.) Vol. 29, No. 2/3, 1995, pp. 179-195; and: *Gay Men and the Sexual History of the Political Left* (ed: Gert Hekma, Harry Oosterhuis, and James Steakley) The Haworth Press, Inc., 1995, pp. 179-195; and *Gay Men and the Sexual History of the Political Left* (ed: Gert Hekma, Harry Oosterhuis, and James Steakley) Harrington Park Press, an imprint of The Haworth Press, Inc., 1995, pp. 179-195. Multiple copies of this article/chapter may be purchased from The Haworth Document Delivery Center. [1-800-342-9678 9:00 a.m. - 5:00 p.m. (EST)].

belief that the law would not be enforced in all its rigor. Was it with hopes like this that he journeyed to the Soviet Union in 1936? It is certain that closer contact with the social and political realities of Stalin's regime, including widespread official sexual intolerance, fuelled the denunciations which he printed in *Retour de l'U.R.S.S.* (1936) and *Retouches à mon Retour de l'U.R.S.S.* (1937). But during his journey in the U.S.S.R. we must imagine him exploring, questioning, and discovering what lay behind the new political venture which he had so strongly supported from the ill-informed distance of Paris.

What may best explain his predisposition to welcome the new Soviet state can be located both in his awareness of social deprivation, which had only crystallized during World War I, and in his "comradely" Whitmanesque aspirations. We must therefore go back in time.

A moment of change is marked in his *Journal* on January 16, 1916, when he had come face to face with the suffering of Belgian refugees in the Foyer Franco-Belge for which he was working: "Confronted by this continuous procession of misery which deeply moved me, I became ashamed of all superiority, and repeated the words of Montesquieu's Marius to myself: 'The price of raising oneself above mankind is too great.' "[2] What is being rejected here is a Nietzschean ethic, previously articulated most notably in Gide's *Les Nourritures terrestres* (begun in 1893-94 and published in 1897) and in *L'Immoraliste* (begun in about 1899 and published in 1902). Ménalque is the spokesman for the doctrine in both these works; Michel, in the second, exemplifies the dangers inherent in the attempts of a weak man to live the life of such a Hero.

There is additionally the attitude toward the family which Gide expressed in his earlier period. It will reappear in his critique of the U.S.S.R. but with an ideological shift towards seeing in it new dangers arising from conformity. Given his Protestant background, we might have expected him from the outset to be fully in favor of upholding the values of the Christian institution of marriage. In a sense this was so: he did not condone adultery, but his stance was contradictory and paradoxical. The problem was how to avoid being stifled by the constrictions of bourgeois morality. He heeded what is said in Mark 10:29-30 on the need for followers of Christ to leave home and family, and he molded it to suit his ethic of salvation through adventure to show that only the *Übermensch* is capable of victory. Ménalque's outburst against families reveals how bourgeois habits shackle an individual's freedom: "I hated homes and families, those places where a man thinks he can find peace; and continuous affections and faithful loves"; and again: "Families, I hate you! homes closed in on themselves, doors firmly shut; happiness jealously possessed."[3] This is taken up in Gide's deployment of the symbol of the bastard, whose lack of family context is a guarantee of his natural authenticity. Thus two adolescent characters gain in significance: Lafcadio in *Les Caves du Vatican* (first conceived in 1893 and published in 1914) and his avatar Bernard in *Les Faux-monnayeurs* (originally conceived as a sequel to *Les Caves* and published in 1925). But this is the symbol of anarchy under another name, and the ethic being presented denies the value of corporate identity. The self-development of the individual is achieved at the expense of other people, even though it is presented as an example for disciples to imitate.

Gide had also wished to explore the theme of individualism in a play, *Le Roi Candaule* (1899), remarking in his *L'Évolution du théâtre* on March 25, 1904, that a "strong" hero should be put on stage.[4] Some critics have wanted to see in *Le Roi Candaule* an early form of Gide's communism. But, as I have argued elsewhere, I believe that the play is about possession, which strengthens selfhood and constitutes the power of the individual to resist what would otherwise destroy him.[5] It is not easy to square this with a communistic ethic of generosity and shared benevolence.

As for his political attitudes in the 1890s, Gide seems, for example, curiously ambivalent about the issues raised by the Dreyfus Affair. Claude Martin describes Gide's involvement thus: it appears that he was at first in favor of a letter of support for Zola, whose *J'accuse!* had provoked a hostile reaction from the anti-Dreyfusard authorities.[6] But a letter to Valéry on January 18, 1898, reveals that he was less keen to take a public stand. And he distanced himself again in a letter to another correspondent, Eugène Rouart, on January 24, 1898, disclosing his anti-Jewish feelings. Gide's argument, however, turned less on the demerits of the case against Dreyfus than on the idea that France would be undermined by attempts to deal dishonestly with such a scandal. A similar cry for truth is to be found at the end of *Retouches*. His position in 1898 was therefore a basically nationalistic one, with the additional observation that things had gone too far for free speech to be repressed.

A related nationalistic attitude can be perceived in a section of Dialogue IV of *Corydon* (1924) written before World War I: "Reprehensible or not, this behavior ['ces mœurs', i.e., pederasty (here: the love of a man for an adolescent boy), but also including male homosexuality in a more general sense] is so far from being a softening influence, and is so close to being soldierly, that I openly admit to you that on the occasion of those noteworthy trials in Germany [of Eulenburg, Moltke, and others in the years 1907-9] I trembled for us [French]. . . . Some people in France were naive enough to see these events as evidence of decadence! Whereas I thought to myself: let us beware of a nation whose very debauchery is warlike."[7] We see here a presentation of the link between pederasty and a warrior society, related to the image of Sparta by Gide's spokesman in these dialogues. Manly virtue equals power, and the political question is still formulated in nationalistic terms.

As for Sparta, although such a society did not produce the glorious flowering of artistic beauty that we rejoice to find in Periclean Athens, so goes Corydon's reasoning, the culmination of moral perfection may be seen in states which favor pederasty. Gide draws his examples from Plutarch's *Lives* of famous Spartan kings and warriors, choosing carefully for Corydon's argument evidence which supports his contention, but omitting contradictory stories. Ancient Thebes was another city-state which, by the institution there of the Sacred Band of warrior lovers, ensured moral nobility and martial success. But again Corydon's argument is specious, and counter-evidence is passed over in silence.

What is noticeable about these examples is that they are not expressly antitotalitarian, for they do not focus on the political structures of the states in question–democratic in the case of Athens, dual kingship in Sparta, oligarchic in Thebes, and imperial in Germany. Nor is the philosophical attitude underlying Gide's discourse dependent on a Marxist, or even on a Darwinian deterministic, construct. It rests rather on a view derived from his reading of Nietzsche and Schopenhauer. There is also a comment in his

Journal in 1933 that it was not Marx but the New Testament which had paved the way for his attachment to communism.[8]

But it is equally important to emphasize two connected strands in Gide's perception of social behavior. There is on the one hand his tendency to see certain socially beneficial aspects as being fostered by the toleration (and even more by the encouragement) of pederasty. And on the other there is his own personal search for the "Comrade." This last is in evidence in an early *Journal* entry (August 21, 1888: "A friend, a friend; my heart needs to share the affection which weighs it down") and in *Les Cahiers d'André Walter* (1891: a desire to join with Breton boys and with the vagabonds seen by the hero–a transposition of authorial material into the text). It continues throughout *Les Nourritures terrestres* and is found elsewhere in the recurring citation from Vergil's *Bucolic* X 35: "Would that I were one of you. . . ." A note appears in the *Journal* manuscripts, probably to be dated 1894, about two classical mythological figures, Castor and Pollux. These twin brothers, one mortal, the other divine, symbolize for Gide the quest that such a love entails: "Castor and Pollux do not flee from each other–on the contrary they seek each other out, in parallel. They find it impossible to meet because of the equal nature of their love."

This is the very expression of that sentimental need for male companionship which Gide recognized so well. But it includes within itself the recognition that such a union is impossible–a view of Gide's that depends on his interpretation of Schopenhauer's pessimism. In a later period, when he discovered Walt Whitman's poems,[9] the term "comrade" was to gain in significance for him, particularly when he was in contact with Henri Ghéon. Their sexual preferences were similar–they were both attracted to youths–and Ghéon is the "Franc Camarade" of the dedication to *L'Immoraliste*, a book whose undeniably homosexual subtext is nonetheless subordinated to the general issues about vice which are raised in it.

Since Gide thought of himself as a liberationist with a social conscience, it is instructive to contrast his attitudes with those of Magnus Hirschfeld, the German sexologist. The preface to *Corydon* (dated 1922, but referring back to the prewar period) features an attack on Hirschfeld's theories of a "third sex," for Gide wanted to distance his educational justification of the naturalness and desir-ability of pederasty from the physiological model which Hirschfeld was proposing. Gide was also protesting against a clinical construct which, in his view, implied degeneracy and illness. But in saying nothing about Hirschfeld's attempts to reform the antihomosexual § 175 of the German penal code he demonstrated the limits of his own concerns at this date. Nor did he mention anything about Hirschfeld's other socially supportive activities regarding transvestites, prostitutes, and marriage counselling. All in all, Gide emerges from these comments in the preface to *Corydon* as a moralist whose concern is more with the individual than with wider social and political questions. It is, however, true that elsewhere an awareness of social issues may be observed in his fascination with cases in the law courts,[10] but, with the exception of some homosexual examples referred to in *Corydon*, they provided a focus for his observations on the nature of crime (which is, he contended, misunderstood in a bourgeois culture) and on the victimization of people who do not conform to society's rules.

Gide made one important prerevolutionary contact with Russia, apart, that is, from his predilection for Dostoyevsky. When the Ballets Russes came to Paris in 1909 he became very excited, despite being essentially no great admirer of avant-garde music. He wrote enthusiastically to Ghéon about performances which he had attended. The attraction of Nijinsky, Diaghilev, and the troupe was in all probability not entirely artistic,[11] but no one would confuse their politics–and especially the politics of Stravinsky, whom Gide met in 1910–with those of the Revolution.

What then happened to realign the various strands in Gide's perception of society? Did the growing conflict between left- and right-wing forces in the 1930s oblige him to take up a politically committed position? Or did his attitude towards sexuality lead him naturally, in a more open society, to question related freedoms?

Geneviève, one of three novels in a trilogy including *L'École des Femmes* and *Robert*, provides an answer to the last question. In this work, composed over the period 1930-36, Gide intended to tackle "head on" the question of feminism.[12] He wrote in his *Journal* on January 2, 1932: "Yesterday morning I had the sudden revelation of what a future book on communism could and should be. Refutation of the usual arguments. Wrong to wish to give to Geneviève–to an imaginary hero–opinions which are today my own. My [*Geneviève*] must not include them and should remain of sentimental interest." In fact Gide had great difficulty in writing the novel, and what he eventually published in 1936 was technically unfinished and scarcely pleased him.

Geneviève is an adolescent girl on the threshold of "dangerous friendships." There is a strong suggestion of a lesbian attraction towards her classmate Sara and a consequent jealous possessiveness. She is also seeking to assert her feminine independence by becoming pregnant without being married. Geneviève, Sara, and Giselle invent a secret society, *La Ligue pour l'indépendance féminine*, which owes a great deal to feminist ideas Gide encountered in England from 1918 onwards when he frequented Enid McLeod, Ethel Whitehorn (both friends of Elisabeth van Rysselberghe), and members of the Bloomsbury Group, including Dorothy Bussy.[13] In a context of adolescent friendship, although the tone is sororal, it must be said that Gide was attempting a psychological rather than a political portrait. When the girls swear an oath of loyalty to each other, it is likened by one of them to the "Oath on the Grütli." This reference to Wilhelm Tell and the struggle for Swiss independence retains its connotations of liberty and solidarity in the context of the episode in the novel but has no political overtones. After the oath there is a long silence, described by Geneviève, the narrator, as being "like after Holy Communion." This suggestion of reverent awe is what seems to be most important to her.[14]

It may well be thought that the social concerns evident in *Geneviève* are in the last analysis rather parochial, especially when one remembers what was happening in Spain, Germany, and Russia at the same time. Social conscience also figures in an episode in *Les Faux-monnayeurs* where Bernard confronts an angel who takes him to visit the poor and destitute. This scene is reminiscent of the Ghost in *A Christmas Carol*, but Gide is no more a communist here than is Dickens.

Wanderlust and curiosity took Gide to the Congo and Chad in 1925-26. On his return he published a volume of travel notes that was also an indictment of the abuses perpetrated in those countries by the concessionary companies based in imperialist Europe.[15] He had not been able to ignore what he had observed. Similarly, but for slightly different reasons, he went to the U.S.S.R. In his *Journal* on July 19, 1932, he had written: "[Social questions] occupy my thoughts almost exclusively. I keep on returning to them and cannot keep my mind off them." And he remarked that during the Great War one's duty had been to obey and to repress one's indignation and one's urge to revolt. "Now . . . our duty is to speak out."

When he went to Moscow in 1936, he found that the attitude of the authorities towards homosexuality had indeed undergone a transformation since the early days of the Revolution. Simon Karlinsky, in a well-researched article,[16] traces the changes in toleration from the days of the provisional government (February to October 1917) through the seizure of power by Lenin and Trotsky in October 1917 to the promulgation of the new Soviet Criminal Code in 1922 (amended in 1926). "This Code," Karlinsky writes, "prohibited sex with minors under the age of sixteen. . . . It did not mention sexual contacts between consenting adults, which meant that adult male homosexuality was legal." In this regard the Code was very much like the French penal code as it stood then and with which Gide was familiar.[17]

But official attitudes were not benevolent: homosexuality was seen as an illness to be cured–an opinion which was at this date very widespread in the West as well–and, notes Karlinsky, "in the literary and intellectual spheres," namely those very people with whom Gide was to come in contact, "it was all but unmentionable by 1930." The reason for this hostile puritanism, Karlinsky believes, can be found in the opinions of such key revolutionary figures as Lenin, Trotsky, and Stalin. Lenin, who died in 1924, had regarded "*any* kind of sexual liberation as antisocial and non-Marxist."[18] Homosexual conduct was equated with what was seen as decadent bourgeois morality, and it is certainly an open question as to whether the oppression of homosexual authors had "as much to do with their class backgrounds (as perceived by the regime) as with their homosexuality."[19] From being a moral crime, homosexuality was turned into a crime against the state by Article 154-a (soon to become Article 121) of the Soviet penal code, which was made compulsory for all republics of the Soviet Union on March 7, 1934. Karlinsky writes: "[The article] outlawed sexual relations between men and prescribed five years of hard labor for voluntary sexual acts and eight years for using force or threats and for sex with a consenting minor."[20] Gide refers to the five-year penalty, describing it as "deportation," in a footnote to *Retour*,[21] and it is noteworthy that his preferred age range lay somewhere between fifteen and twenty-one. Karlinsky continues: "Maxim Gorky, true to form, hailed that decree on the pages of both *Pravda* and *Izvestiia* as a 'triumph of proletarian humanitarianism' and wrote that legalization of homosexuality had been the main cause of Fascism." If Gide misunderstood the position regarding homosexuals in the U.S.S.R. and thought that the Bolshevik leaders were more tolerant than the fascists, then he was no different from many Western intellectuals at the time, who believed that ' "the Soviet government, when it came to power in 1917, had declared that all forms of sexual intercourse between consenting adults are a private matter, outside the law.' "[22] When Gide arrived in Moscow, Gorky, whom he had admired as a writer, had just died. What thoughts, one wonders, went through his mind as he attended the funeral?

During the Stalinist age, however, it does appear that a tolerant blind eye was sometimes turned in the direction of homosexuals, provided that their attitudes and activities were discreet. They could also, of course, be usefully engaged in espionage and blackmail, and Maurer suggests, citing the testimony of Jef Last, one of Gide's travelling companions,[23] that if the authorities made it relatively easy for Gide to make sexual contacts it was partly at least in furtherance of a policy of entrapment. But at the time of Gide's visit there were certainly mass arrests of homosexuals in Moscow, Leningrad, Kharkov, and Odessa.[24]

Gide was accompanied by four other friends, in addition to Last: Pierre Herbart, Louis Guilloux, Jacques Schiffrin, and Eugène Dabit. Two of the group spoke Russian, at least two of them were homosexuals, and all were to the left. With them he could hope to make a meaningfully direct contact with the country in the brief time he was to be there despite the careful surveillance of the official guide. Maurer remarks that Gide did manage to "amuse himself" and clearly enjoyed meeting Soviet youths on the parade ground, in youth camps during specially organized events, and even in a prison for young offenders.[25] In Sotchi, a certain sentimental moment with political overtones occurred when Gide visited the writer Nicholas Ostrovsky, who was blind and paralyzed, and reverently kissed him on the forehead. Gide recorded the event in *Retour*,[26] describing how he felt "waves of quivering sympathy" emanating from the young man.

Retour contains the recantation of Gide's former naive enthusiasm, though he still remarks on the positive side of the Russian state; *Retouches* takes the offensive more sharply and constitutes a more detailed attack on Russia under Stalinist rule.

But when did Gide realize that Utopia was very far from having been achieved? And what did he think it was most important to note in his *Retour?* The *avant propos* of the *Retour* says: "Three years ago I declared my admiration and my love for the U.S.S.R. Out there an unprecedented experiment was taking place, which filled our hearts with hope and from which we expected very great progress–a leap forward capable of carrying with it the whole of humanity."[27] These are hardly the words with which to preface an outright denunciation! The documentation for *Retouches* was obtained after Gide's return,[28] and he prided himself on not taking official figures as a truthful representation of fact.[29] He learned as he travelled, and he says that when he first arrived in Moscow his dream was still intact. This may well have been so, for he seems previously to have given little credence to comment hostile to the U.S.S.R., setting it aside as mere propaganda. On June 20, 1936, he gave an official speech at Gorky's funeral, the tone of which was conventionally eulogistic. It could hardly have been otherwise. But when the text was published in *Retour* (p. 98) it did appear with a note marking Gide's recantation of what he had said.

So, during his visit Gide observed the good and the bad, aiming to set down the abuses in *Retour* precisely because he admired the U.S.S.R. He maintained his conviction that the best would triumph in the end. But the embarrassing, if honest, nature of some of his descriptions of the workers reveals a disarming sentimentality: "People of workers . . . I have been able to taste moments of profound joy. Among these new comrades I felt a sudden sympathy arise, I felt my heart dilate and blossom. And how often, out there, did tears come to my eyes through excessive happiness, tears of tenderness and love: for example in the miners' rest home in Bombas. . . ."[30]

There is another side to this sentimentality. Gide was sixty-six when he went to the U.S.S.R. It is therefore perhaps not surprising that he should put the accent on youth. However, his attraction to adolescents was not simply a function of his age. In *Les Nourritures terrestres* he had adopted as a narrative strategy the image of a youth, Nathanaël, to whom the book was addressed, and he had presented the work as an education towards future liberation and fulfillment. In *Corydon* a similar pedagogic role emerges as the explanation and justification of pederastic love. The image of the goddess Demeter and her son Triptolemus (Triptolème) was also used to symbolize the potential of youth and hope in the future as early as Gide's *Proserpine*, in a section of the text written probably in the 1890s and recast in *Perséphone* (composed in collaboration with Stravinsky 1933-34). It is repeated at the start of *Retour*: "I imagine the great goddess Demeter leaning over the radiant infant, as if over future generations of mankind."[31] The myth conveys a powerful message of hope once used by the ancients in the context of the Mysteries, and it is not surprisingly similar to symbols used by other modern writers in connection with the Russian Revolution and the birth of communism. Karlinsky cites Sergei Esenin, who equated Russia giving birth to worldwide revolution with nature yielding a harvest and the Virgin Mary giving birth to Christ.[32] What is absent from the version of the story in *Retour*, but to the fore in the description of the boy in *Perséphone*, is the child's attractive beauty.

The author's sensitivity in this regard is present in the portrayals of children and youths in *Retour* (they are of both sexes, but boys predominate): "A children's camp near Borjom, very modest–almost humble–but where the children, shining with happiness and health, seem to wish to offer me their joy."[33] The same sentimentality is here as before. There is another, more austere, picture which reveals a truly worthy puritanism: at the Culture Park in Moscow Gide cannot take his eyes off the gymnasts, but notes, "In this crowd of young men and women and older people, everywhere there is seriousness and decency. Not the slightest suspicion of stupid or vulgar joking, larking about, licentiousness, or even flirting." This view of sexual modesty corresponds well to the ideal set forth in *Corydon*, where it is applied to heterosexuals and homosexuals alike.

Admitting that he was less interested in describing the countryside than in observing mankind (and attributing this rather disingenuously to his age), Gide recorded a number of contacts he was able to make. He moves gradually from enthusiastic admiration of a group of "charming members of a Komsomol," whom he met on a train, to a criticism of monotonous social conformity. Of these boys and girls he noted how youth is prolonged in the U.S.S.R., in contrast to France where everything "congeals" at the age of fourteen.[34] The naive idealism of this statement reveals a great deal about the nature of his attraction to the U.S.S.R.

Gide has much to say about the undesirability of Russians only questioning adherence to a rule, not querying the rule itself. On their lack of individuality he makes an interesting set of observations, noting the dangers of inertia creating a new privileged bourgeois class within the state. He links this with the need for a "critical spirit" and proceeds to comment on the recent laws against abortion and homosexuality.

Indeed, the promised plebiscite on the abortion law had not been held, and so the "vast majority," who, Gide maintained, were "more or less openly, it is true," against the proposals, had not expressed their opinion. In the newspapers there had been unqualified praise for the new law, but in Gide's conversations with workers he had heard nothing but "timid recriminations and plaintive resignation."[35] Similarly, in the appendix to *Retouches*, he recorded the story of a student whom Jef Last had befriended and who was frightened by the legislation–contraceptives being unavailable, it was "best to abstain." This leads on to a remark that according to "certain doctors out there, the U.S.S.R. is the country where masturbation is most widespread"–but Gide's tone is clearly skeptical. Noting that the abortion law might possibly be justified because of the "most deplorable abuses" (not further specified) which had been taking place, Gide was all the more at a loss to explain why homosexuals should be criminalized. Not mentioning the eugenic or medical argument, he recognized that they were being conflated with the category of counter-revolutionaries and understood that it was nonconformity which was under attack.[36] Both measures represented a development towards reestablishing bourgeois values, in his opinion: "With the restoration of the family (as the social cell) and of inheritance, the taste for wealth and private possession becomes more important than the need for comradeship, sharing, and a life in common."[37] It is clear that, in making the distinction between family and comradeship in proximity to remarks on sexual conformity and homosexuality, Gide's perspective is a homosexual one.

Among the materials printed as an appendix to *Retour* are two contrasting pieces which bear witness to two concerns of Gide, criminality and childhood, which transcend the purely Soviet context. First: in "Bolchevo," he describes a visit to a new town, founded by Gorky, which is peaceably populated by former convicts. The official idea is that since criminals are victims and have gone astray they will respond to reeducation. Bolchevo proves this to be true, writes Gide–but then he adds ironically: "I do not know whether in other countries mankind is so malleable."[38] His earlier footnote about the laws against homosexuality is more critical. Second: in "Les Besprizornis," Gide writes about the abandoned children in Sebastopol. Some of them are less than ten years old, and, he notes, they have mostly left their homes because of poverty, though several are in quest of adventure. He seems here to be less willing than he was before World War I to emphasize the theme of youthful vagabondage. He describes in detail where they shelter and how one eight-year-old is lifted into a truck by a policeman: "Few things in Russia had moved me as much as the way this man behaved with this child: the persuasive softness of his voice (ah! how I would have wished to understand what he was saying to him), all the affection that he must have been putting into his smile, the caressing tenderness of his embrace when he lifted him in his arms."[39] The sensibility revealed here strikes one as a great deal truer than in the eulogies on the children's camps, though the tone is still sentimental.

In *Corydon* and elsewhere, Gide emphasized the special quality which an individual possesses by virtue of his "anomaly." Homosexuality is a privileged example of this difference from the norm. Here, his argument calls into question the inertia, the ignorance, and the conformism encouraged by the Soviet state. He writes that what the U.S.S.R. calls counter-revolutionary is that critical and disruptive spirit which caused the revolution in the first place: "One would like to be able to think that an overflowing love for mankind, or at the very least an urgent need for justice fills men's hearts. But once the Revolution has been achieved . . . we hear no more of that."[40] Those who still manifest a revolutionary spirit are therefore suppressed–and Gide was well positioned to observe this happening. The persons whom he had in mind were dissidents of several sorts (although he does not name them). It is open to us to conjecture that he perceived the link between his line of reasoning and the position of homosexuals in the U.S.S.R. It is therefore more than a little curious to read the anecdote in *Retouches* concerning the homosexual poet Sergei Esenin. Somewhat cautiously (disingenuously, perhaps?), Gide wrote: "Esenin killed himself. . . . A love affair, so people say. Perhaps. We are free to imagine some deeper reason for committing suicide."[41] And then Gide went on to tell how he heard an anti-clerical poem of Esenin's, which praised the beauty of Christ. The poem was circulating unofficially, and the poet was widely known as a dissident (hence the official guide's alarm at the mention of his name). The poem "revealed regions of secret tenderness" in the soul of the rough man who was reciting it, observes Gide–though whether he was hearing it in Russian or French he does not say. His eagerness to get to know more was aroused, but he was unable to find this particular poem later.[42]

Sergei Eisenstein is another homosexual whom Gide mentions, though this aspect of the filmmaker's life may well have been unknown to him. Of course, we have no record of private conversations Gide may have had about these matters. We can only note what is recorded in *Retouches*: Eisenstein had been required to suspend his activities on a new film "which does not meet the requirements of doctrine," and to recognize his ' "errors" ' (Gide's quotation marks).[43] As in the case of Esenin, this might well contain a covert reference to Eisenstein's sexual behavior.[44]

There are many other remarks, together with other examples, in Gide's two books (especially in *Retouches*) of denunciations, harassment, and, as time went on, of ways the Soviet state "had betrayed all our hopes."[45] The particular interest of the references to Esenin and Eisenstein lies in the way in which they illustrate in Gide's eyes a significant aspect of dissidence.

Nonconformity is the key to the link between sex and politics in Gide's critique of the Soviet system. A dissenting, inquiring mind was not welcome in Stalin's state, as Gide was quick to realize once he had been there to see for himself. Gide's definition of culture was one in which "anticonformism" played an essential part,[46] and, if he was looking towards the creation of a new culture in the U.S.S.R., he came to understand that, according to his own definitions, he was never going to find it. Truth and freedom were both victims of state oppression. While the communists called homosexuality "fascist decadence" and the fascists described it as "communist corruption," each political group was revealing the extent to which it feared the dissidents within its own ranks. "And I doubt whether in any other country today, even in Hitler's Germany, man's mind is less free, more bowed down, more fearful (terrorized), more placed in bondage."[47]

AUTHOR NOTE

Patrick Pollard is Senior Lecturer in French at Birkbeck College, University of London. He was a member of the Gay Liberation Front (GLF) shortly after it became established in England in 1970. He organized and published the proceedings of a colloquium entitled "Gide et l'Angleterre" held in London in 1985. He has also written *André Gide: Homosexual Moralist* (New Haven: Yale University Press, 1991).

NOTES

1. Rudolph Maurer, *André Gide et l'U.R.S.S.* (Berne: Editions Tillier, 1983), p. 84. See also Daniel Moutote, *André Gide: L'Engagement 1926-1939* (Paris: SEDES, 1991); Jef Last, *Mijn vriend André Gide* (Amsterdam: Van Ditmar, 1966); André Gide, *Littérature engagée. Textes réunis et présentés par Y. Davet* (Paris: Gallimard, 1950) (contains material published 1930-38); *André Gide et notre temps (Entretien tenu au siège de l'Union pour la Vérité le 23 janvier 1935)* (Paris: Gallimard, 1935).

2. Patrick Pollard, *André Gide: Homosexual Moralist* (New Haven: Yale University Press, 1991), p. 347.

3. André Gide, *Les Nourritures terrestres* (Paris: Gallimard, 1958), Book IV, pt. i.

4. André Gide, *Nouveaux Prétextes* (Paris: Mercure de France, 1951), pp. 11-27.

5. Pollard, pp. 338-46.

6. Claude Martin, *La Maturité d'André Gide. De Paludes à L'Immoraliste (1895-1902)* (Paris: Klincksieck, 1977), pp. 257-61.

7. André Gide, *Corydon* (Paris: Gallimard, 1924), p. 171. See also ibid., p. 37.

8. André Gide, *Journal* (Paris: Gallimard, 1951), p. 1176.

9. *H. Ghéon–A. Gide, Correspondance 1897-1944*, ed. Jean Tipy and Anne-Marie Moulènes (Paris: Gallimard, 1976)–see letter dated March 19, 1899, but the possibility of Gide's earlier knowledge of Whitman is not to be excluded.

10. André Gide, *Ne Jugez Pas* (Paris: Gallimard, 1969).

11. See *Correspondance Ghéon–Gide*, June 15, 1910.

12. *Journal*, March 9, 1930.

13. Emily S. Apter, "La Nouvelle 'Nouvelle Éloise' d'A. Gide: Geneviève et le féminisme anglais," in *Gide et l'Angleterre*, ed. P. Pollard (London: Colloque Gide, 1986), pp. 95-99.

14. André Gide, *Geneviève* (Paris: Gallimard, 1961), p. 1371.

15. André Gide, *Voyage au Congo et Retour du Tchad* (Paris: Gallimard, 1928), first published in the *Nouvelle Revue Française* 1926-27; Marc Allégret, *Carnets du Congo*, ed. Daniel Durosay and Claudia Rabel-Jullien (Paris: CNRS, 1987).

16. Simon Karlinsky, "Russia's Gay Literature and Culture: The Impact of the October Revolution," in *Hidden from History: Reclaiming the Gay and Lesbian Past*, ed. Martin Bauml Duberman, Martha Vicinus, and George Chauncey, Jr. (New York: New American Library, 1989), pp. 347-64. For further comment, see Laura Engelstein's article "Soviet Policy Toward Male Homosexuality: Its Origins and Historical Roots" in the present volume, especially pp. 169-73 and her note 43.

17. Pollard, pp. 439-40 (Articles 330-334).

18. Karlinsky, p. 353.

19. Ibid., p. 360.

20. See Engelstein's correction, n. 43.

21. André Gide, *Retour de l'U.R.S.S.* (Paris: Gallimard, 1936), p. 36.

22. Karlinsky, p. 357, citing Christopher Isherwood, *Christopher and His Kind* (New York: Farrar, Straus & Giroux, 1976), pp. 17-18.

23. Maurer, p. 107.

24. S. Karlinsky, "Russia's Gay Literature and Culture," p. 362 (citing Wilhelm Reich, *The Sexual Revolution*).

25. R. Maurer, *André Gide et l'U.R.S.S.*, p. 107.

26. *Retour*, pp. 113-15.

27. Ibid., p. 11.

28. André Gide, *Retouches à mon Retour de l'U.R.S.S.* (Paris: Gallimard, 1937), p. 53.

29. Ibid., p. 7.

30. *Retour*, p. 19.

31. Ibid., p. 9.

32. Karlinsky, p. 357.

33. *Retour*, p. 20. Cf. also "handsome," "well-cared for," "joyful" (p. 21), and "admirable" (p. 26) Russian youth.

34. Ibid., p. 31.

35. Ibid., p. 63.

36. Ibid.

37. Ibid., p. 64.

38. Ibid., p. 122.

39. Ibid., p. 125.

40. Ibid., p. 66.

41. *Retouches*, p. 89.

42. Ibid., p. 91. See Karlinsky, pp. 355 and 359.

43. *Retouches*, p. 22.

44. See Karlinsky, p. 361: "[Eisenstein] did yield to his gay desires when visiting Berlin and Paris and even more so during his 1930-1932 stay in Mexico . . . where he became openly gay and almost caused an international scandal"; with further references to M. Seton, *Sergei Eisenstein* (London: Dobson, 1978).

45. *Retouches*, p. 68.

46. *Retour*, p. 79.

47. Ibid., p. 67.

Communists, Social Democrats, and the Homosexual Movement in the Weimar Republic

Manfred Herzer

Berlin

SUMMARY. Two clichés of gay historiography concerning the relationship between homosexuals and the political parties of the Weimar Republic are here subjected to critical examination. The notion that the political left of that era was similar in its homophobia to the right-wing and centrist parties is challenged with a number of particulars showing that the goals of the homosexual movement were supported almost exclusively by the left, especially the Communist Party, and that leftist homophobia was an atypical exception. Attention is also devoted to the active involvement of homosexual men in the Nazi movement and the destruction of the Weimar Republic, which casts doubt on the notion that homosexuals were merely passive victims of Nazi homophobia and persecution. The possibility of a special affinity between homosexual men and the Nazi movement is explored using the example of the Nazi leader Ernst Röhm.

From its very beginnings, the current gay movement in Germany has been grappling with the issue of its relationship to the labor movement. In these deliberations, the events of the years 1918 to

Correspondence may be addressed: Blücherstraße 61, D-10961 Berlin, Germany.

[Haworth co-indexing entry note]: "Communists, Social Democrats, and the Homosexual Movement in the Weimar Republic." Herzer, Manfred. Co-published simultaneously in *Journal of Homosexuality* (The Haworth Press, Inc.) Vol. 29, No. 2/3, 1995, pp. 197-226; and: *Gay Men and the Sexual History of the Political Left* (ed: Gert Hekma, Harry Oosterhuis, and James Steakley) The Haworth Press, Inc., 1995, pp. 197-226; and *Gay Men and the Sexual History of the Political Left* (ed: Gert Hekma, Harry Oosterhuis, and James Steakley) Harrington Park Press, an imprint of The Haworth Press, Inc., 1995, pp. 197-226. Multiple copies of this article/chapter may be purchased from The Haworth Document Delivery Center. [1-800-342-9678 9:00 a.m. - 5:00 p.m. (EST)].

1933 have played a particularly important role. During the Weimar Republic, prior to the pivotal defeat of the labor movement as well as the homosexual movement at the hands of the Nazis, homosexuals as well as Communists and Social Democrats reached the greatest power they had ever achieved, and the relationship between the labor and homosexual movements took on an unprecedented complexity.

One key historiographical problem stands at the center of this essay. When researching and portraying the Weimar era, historians of the gay movement have repeatedly taken a particular stance, one to be challenged here on the basis of historical material. My investigation of the relationship between the political left and the homosexual movement in the Weimar Republic has led me to critique gay historiography to date. My standpoint can be summarized in the following theses:

- Previous presentations have consistently suffered from the deficiency of affirming, by turns indignantly and smugly, the "homophobia" of the political left during the Weimar era.[1]
- A methodological problem necessarily arises when the concept "homophobia"–a term not even coined until the 1970s–is applied to such a temporally remote epoch as the Weimar Republic.[2] Rather than passing over it in silence, we at least need to discuss it if we are to avoid falling into naive, ahistorical sociologism.
- "Homophobia" on the political left during the Weimar Republic needs to be analyzed and interpreted on the basis of the prevailing conditions at that time. A purely moralizing affirmation of the simple finding may be justified in terms of today's gay politics, but it cannot replace historical analysis and explanation.
- Any balanced investigation of leftist "homophobia" in the prefascist German Reich can ignore neither the overall propensity of Weimar society to persecute and suppress homosexuals nor the multifarious expressions of the hatred of homosexuality by political groupings of the right and center. If we neglect to contextualize the leftist outlook on the homosexual question, we will never get beyond a moralizing condemnation based on ahistorical standards.

- Among the homosexual men of the Weimar Republic, aggressive antisocialism and anticommunism–to the point of active support of the Nazi movement–was no less common than in the remainder of the population, which ultimately allowed the Nazis to take power by peaceful means. Any real grasp of the "homophobia" of the political left will elude us if we disregard this fact. As far as the scope of homosexual men's support of the Nazis is concerned, we face a self-imposed void in our knowledge that has nearly taken on the dimensions of an ideologically motivated taboo. Within gay historiography, even such a repugnant figure as the Nazi leader Ernst Röhm has repeatedly been consigned to the role of a victim, first of leftist and later of Nazi "homophobia," for only by doing so has it been possible to perpetuate a slanted account of history that persistently portrays homosexuals as persecuted martyrs and passive victims.

To begin with, an analysis of the pertinent conditions in prefascist Germany requires a reinterpretation of the established facts, and this will be attempted in the following.

None of the three major leftist parties of the Weimar Republic–not the Social Democratic Party (Sozialdemokratische Partei Deutschlands, SPD), nor the Communist Party (Kommunistische Partei Deutschlands, KPD), nor the Independent Social Democratic Party (Unabhängige Sozialdemokratische Partei Deutschlands, USPD), which was founded in 1917 and merged with the SPD in 1922–advanced a homosexual policy formulated in programmatic statements or by party decree. On this level, the leftist parties were no different than the political parties of the right or the liberal center. Decisions on homosexual matters were largely improvised spontaneously and by happenstance; they evidently sprang to a considerable extent from emotionally fraught situations and from the gut reactions of politicians, without much forethought. The visibility and voice of homosexuality had only attained a level that allowed the topic to enter the political arena on rare occasions initiated by external events. Prime instances were the case of the homosexual serial murderer Fritz Haarmann (1924), the Reichstag debate on penal law reform (1928-29), and the public disclosure of

Ernst Röhm's homosexuality (1931-32). On homosexual matters, the political culture of the first German republic scarcely represented an advance over the preceding regime under Kaiser Wilhelm II. The Haarmann and Röhm cases, for example, which led to extensive public discussions of homosexuality, had parallels in the Krupp (1902) and Eulenburg (1907-08) scandals during the final phase of the Wilhelmine empire.

Concerning the Röhm affair, which will be treated in some detail below, it should be emphasized at the outset that this was *not* an early "outing" campaign initiated and waged by the leftist press; rather, the public scandal had been preceded by a seething, monthslong dispute within the Nazi movement itself over the issue whether Röhm's homosexuality–widely known within the Nazi Party–rendered him unfit to be an SA leader. It was only three months later, in April 1931, that an SPD daily, the *Münchener Post*, responded to this internal party dispute by reporting publicly on Röhm's homosexuality. Another eleven months would elapse prior to the publication of Röhm's private letters, an event which was sensational but did not introduce any fundamentally new themes into the public discussion. This affair was not stirred up by the SPD, which instead was responding to the uproar within the Nazi Party itself. By contrast, when the Nazis had attacked the SPD in October 1929 for its pro-homosexual stance in the penal law reform debates, the SPD had maintained silence on Röhm.

Penal code reform and thereby the issue of the future of § 175, the anti-sodomy statute, was a topic of discussion at least sporadically during the entire first third of this century–and actually up through its various reforms in postwar Germany and its final repeal in March 1994. To be sure, the pre-World War I SPD lacked a unified opinion on the homosexual question, as did all three leftist parties after 1918; but it can easily be documented that none of Germany's other larger political formations was nearly as advanced in overcoming anti-homosexual sentiments as the Social Democrats and Communists. To describe the left's position as relatively "advanced," however, does not mean that it had completely overcome anti-homosexual feelings; we are confronted instead with a range of outlooks, extending on the one side to the views of that era's homosexual movement and on the other side to a sort of residual prejudice or tacit condoning of the legal status quo, i.e., continued social discrimination and homosexual vulnerability to blackmailers. By contrast, the dominant perspective among conservative and Christian parties as well as the Nazis demanded a more punitive approach toward homosexuals, who were perceived as a growing threat. This view was entirely lacking on the left–or at least not publicly articulated.

The ultimate goal envisioned by homosexuals themselves–in this instance, the circle around Magnus Hirschfeld–was the "liberation of homosexuals."[3] This rather abstract formulation, in essence a slogan, implied far more than the repeal of a particular law targeting homosexual men. Rather, liberation meant "elimination of the existing prejudices among the people." To back up this point, Hirschfeld pointed to his own "observations in France, Italy, Holland, and other countries, where prejudices continue to exist almost unchanged" despite the repeal or at least reform of anti-sodomy statutes in those countries.[4]

The most sophisticated and "modern" form of prejudice circulating at that time was no doubt the notion that homosexuality constituted a mental illness, a concept initially propounded by nineteenth-century forensic medicine and psychiatry. At the 1927 party congress of the SPD, when it established a majority consensus on the issue of homosexuality and the law, the resolution's final words articulated precisely this prejudice: the Social Democrats demanded "repeal of the legal penalization of . . . unnatural intercourse" because it was simply wrong-headed "to combat illnesses with the penal law."[5]

AMBIVALENCE OF THE GERMAN LEFT

The prehistory of this Social Democratic perspective can be traced back to the year 1895, when the Oscar Wilde trial led the authoritative theoretician of the SPD's right wing, Eduard Bernstein, to develop a quasi-binding standpoint on the homosexual question. His views received an official status not just because the text in question appeared in the party's theoretical journal, *Die Neue Zeit*: in the essays on the homosexual question which appeared in the following years in the SPD press, there was no contradiction of Bernstein's position, and thirty years later it continued to inform the party resolution just cited. Thus the outlook that Bernstein had taken over from the most progressive psychiatrist of his era, Richard von Krafft-Ebing, formulating it as the party standpoint, still held valid in 1927: homosexuality between adult men ought not to be punished under any circumstances, for it was not the proper role of the state and the law to be guardians of morality. Concerning the cause of male-male love, Bernstein held that it could result from either "dissolute licentiousness" or an endogenous pathology.[6]

By contrast, the pre-war SPD's left wing, from which the KPD emerged in 1918, never took any position at all on the subject of homosexuality. Leftist SPD members subjected Bernstein's revision of Marxism to radical and vehement critique, but they passed over in silence his statements on homosexuality and its penalization. This silence is quite ambiguous: it might be taken as tacit approval of Bernstein's views, but it could equally well have signalled censure and utter disdain for anyone who even dealt with such a minor and tangential topic, one which (from the leftist perspective) concerned only decadent members of the bourgeoisie and diverted attention away from core issues of the class struggle.

On October 4, 1920, right-wing radicals carried out an assassination attempt on Magnus Hirschfeld in Munich. This provided virtually the entire German press with an opportunity to speak out on the homosexual question and on Hirschfeld's liberation struggle, for it was patently obvious that the would-be assassins had been motivated not just by anti-Semitism but by hatred of homosexuals. Indeed, this was repeatedly trumpeted by articles in the radical-right press in late 1920, and seven months earlier, insurrectionists involved in the abortive Kapp Putsch had declared publicly that upon seizing power they intended to "terminate Dr. Hirschfeld" for "introducing Oriental mores into Germany."[7]

In their reports and comments on the Munich assassination attempt, Socialist and Communist newspapers emphasized the attackers' anti-Semitic motive while exercising a peculiar restraint concerning the homosexual aspect of the entire incident. The day after the attack, the SPD's official party daily *Vorwärts* carried a report headlined "A Deed of Anti-Semitic Heroism" that rather obliquely characterized the assailants' motive as "envy" for Hirschfeld's "scientific accomplishments."[8] Hirschfeld himself wrote a report for the largest SPD daily of Bavaria, the *Münchener Post* (the paper that would later make Röhm's homosexuality a public issue), and here at least he mentioned that one of his would-be killers had called out: "This man brought Eulenburgishness to Germany."[9] The *Berliner Volkszeitung*, a daily associated with the USPD, proved to be an exception in its comments on the incident by pointing–without naming names–to the presence of numerous homosexuals within "German *völkisch* circles" (as the radical rightists termed themselves).[10] But a direct position statement on the issue of homosexual rights is not to be found in the USPD press. It did manage to express general support for Hirschfeld's theory, deriving from it the conclusion that the homosexual orientation was equally represented among all political parties and, contra radical-rightist doctrine, had nothing to do with decadence, corruption, or seduction.

THE COMMUNISTS' PRO-HOMOSEXUAL STANCE

Concerning penal law, the position of the KPD toward homosexuality appears to have been what might be termed minimalistic: the rejection of punishment. The party apparently never voiced a concept of "homosexual liberation" going any farther.

The authoritative KPD outlook on this issue was expressed by the jurist Felix Halle in his 1931 volume *Geschlechtsleben und Strafrecht* (Sexual Life and Penal Law), to which Magnus Hirschfeld contributed a preface. Here Halle stated that while proletarians (and thereby presumably also their party) took a "tolerant" view of homosexuality, they by no means "cultivated" it (whatever that might mean):

> The working class, far removed from cultivating same-sex inclinations and activities, be they between men or between women, takes a tolerant approach toward such manifestations of sexual life–insofar as this activity does not transgress the boundaries likewise imposed for social reasons on intercourse between man and woman–because the proletariat feels itself fertile and confident of the future as a collective, as a class.[11]

Despite its arm's-length treatment of homosexuality and its compensatory gushing over proletarian fecundity, this position was vastly superior to that of the normal German National, Christian-conservative, let alone Nazi type of thought and feeling.

Of course, any such lining up of opposed political camps in the Weimar Republic in terms of favoring and opposing homosexual emancipation is only partially and broadly true, like all historical attempts at categorization. The half-heartedness of the left's support for homosexual rights (Halle's assurance that the proletariat by no means "cultivated" homosexuality or the SPD party congress resolution of 1927) introduces intermediate shadings that make the overall picture more nuanced and complex. The same can be said of the Reichstag delegate Wilhelm Kahl of the People's Party (Deutsche Volkspartei), the most liberal of the bourgeois parties. As chair of the Reichstag's Penal Law Reform Committee, Kahl voted in 1929 for the repeal of § 175, but largely because he hoped "by doing so to take the wind out of the sails of unrestrained agitation and propaganda for homosexual practices."[12] Even so, Kahl's position within his party was that of an isolated outsider: both of his fellow party members in the Penal Law Reform Committee, Richard Leutheusser and Johannes Wunderlich, acted entirely differently, voting to toughen § 175.

Prior to the Reichstag elections in September 1930, Hirschfeld's homosexual-rights organization, the Scientific-Humanitarian Committee (Wissenschaftlich-humanitäres Komitee, or WhK), conducted a survey of the political parties' views on § 175, just as it had prior to previous elections. The 1930 survey results led the WhK's co-chairman, the pundit Kurt Hiller (a political independent), to comment rather aptly on the breadth of the homophobia across the party spectrum:

> The parties of the right (Hitler, Hugenberg, Westarp, Bredt) and the center unquestionably have a hostile attitude toward our efforts. In the German People's Party it appears that Privy Councillor Kahl, with his relatively reasonable views, will continue to be just as isolated as he has been up to now. The State Party is an unreliable ally; on this issue there is no guarantee that the former Democrats, whose delegates in any case agreed with our views only partially, will win over their fellow fraction members from the Young German Order and the Christian unions. As far as the Social Democratic Party is

concerned, those of our members and supporters who do not regard an age of consent of twenty-one as unreasonably high can entrust themselves to this party. The sole party which has represented the Scientific-Humanitarian standpoint without any reservations and, so far as humanly possible, will again represent it in the new Reichstag, is the Communist Party of Germany. I note this because I acknowledge and honor the truth, and despite the fact that I don't belong to this party and am critical of it in various respects.[13]

The KPD was founded at the end of the year 1918 by men and women of whom almost all had previously belonged to the SPD's radical left wing. It is probably no coincidence that at the time they still belonged to the SPD, the members of this left minority had not participated in any way in the debates about the "emancipation struggle of homosexuals." Paragraph 175 and the injustice of discrimination in all its forms had been made into a public issue by members of the party's right wing, such as Eduard Bernstein and Adolf Thiele, and by politicians who sought to mediate between the wings, such as August Bebel and Karl Kautsky. Representatives of the left wing had kept silent; not a single prominent left Social Democrat ever signed Hirschfeld's petition against § 175.[14] Most of those within the KPD who later backed what Hiller called a "Scientific-Humanitarian standpoint without any reservations," such as Felix Halle (born 1884), Arthur Ewert (born 1890), Peter Maslowski (born 1893), and Richard Linsert (born 1899), were members of a later generation. The male and female party veterans who had left the old SPD to form the KPD continued to taboo the entire topic, no doubt because they harbored continuing reservations.

The only Communist delegate who held a Reichstag speech condemning § 175 and the government's plans to bolster it in a reformed penal code was Wilhelm Koenen (born 1886—and thus, incidentally, the same age as Ernst Thälmann, KPD chair beginning in 1925). Occasioned by the first reading of the "Official Penal Code Draft" on May 16, 1927, Koenen's speech fell short of offering any substantive critique of either the old or the new versions of the sodomy law. Rather, he merely termed § 175 "reactionary" several times, just as reactionary as the laws on abortion and adultery, and he called upon "the appropriate organizations" to "resist" them.[15] As early as 1924, the Communist Reichstag fraction, of which Koenen was a member, had introduced a motion to halt the enforcement of § 175–a step hailed by Magnus Hirschfeld as "the first time . . . in the history of our struggle" that any political party had advanced such a proposal.[16] The motion surely would have gone down to defeat, but in fact it was never brought up for a vote because of the impending elections of December 1924–which brought a steep decline in support for the KPD as the Weimar Republic entered a period of relative stabilization.

Yet the 1924 motion is just as characteristic for the KPD's position on male homosexuality as Koenen's 1927 Reichstag speech, the 1929 votes of Maslowski and Ewert in the Reichstag's Penal Law Committee, and Halle's 1931 statement. During the Weimar era, the KPD was the one political force which most consistently and unreservedly helped the homosexual movement in its "liberation struggle." Thus Kurt Hiller's 1930 assessment applies to pre-Hitler Germany in its entirety.

HOMOSEXUAL NAZIS

Any thorough investigation of the relationship between left parties and homosexuals during the Weimar years cannot ignore the other side of the coin: the political views of homosexual men themselves. As a group, however, homosexuals are widely divergent and anything but unified; shared desire for sex with other men is such an isolated characteristic and accommodates such a sweeping range of forms that it says little or nothing about political views or activities. One must also keep in mind that during the Weimar years, few homosexual men were open enough about their sexuality to seek any sort of involvement with the homosexual movement. This step was taken only by a minority, amounting to roughly a few thousand men throughout Germany, and among them there was anything but a shared outlook on the parties of the left–or the right.

The three sizeable homosexual organizations of that era–the WhK, the Community of the Select (Gemeinschaft der Eigenen, or GdE), and League for Human Rights (Bund für Menschenrecht, or BfM)–regularly took a shared approach to Reichstag elections by calling upon their members to vote only for parties that opposed § 175, i.e., primarily for the SPD and the KPD; and it may well be that the leading activists of these organizations actually did vote for them.

If one examines the political endorsements in the homosexual press somewhat more closely, however, it is noticeable that they were intended for a readership that was probably no less divergent in its political sympathies than the electorate as a whole. That meant: primarily tilted toward the right and, as 1933 approached, increasingly toward the radical right and the National Socialists. In 1921, Kurt Hiller speculated that seventy-five percent of the homosexuals voted for "the right-wing parties, the parties of monarchistic restoration and revanchism."[17] In 1927, Richard Linsert referred in passing to the "numerous members of the National Socialist German Workers Party and the German People's Freedom Party [Deutschvölkische Freiheitspartei]" who simultaneously belonged to the WhK.[18] In late 1932, the BfM all but bragged that the Nazi leader Ernst Röhm was to be counted among its members.[19] In exile in 1934, Magnus Hirschfeld remarked retrospectively on the homosexuals "who could not praise Hitler enough for his tolerance toward Röhm and his cronies and who therefore switched to his camp in droves."[20]

These scattered references do not allow any firm conclusions about the political views, voting patterns, or party affiliations of most homosexuals during the Weimar years. In no way do they warrant the conclusion that homosexuals were more oriented toward the political right than were heterosexuals. On the other hand, they do support the assumption that most German homosexuals were just as conservative and antidemocratic in outlook as heterosexual Germans, and their votes for the Nazi Party (or any of the right-wing parties allied with it) contributed to the peaceful revolution of January 30, 1933, and the defeat of the left.[21]

One might suppose that homosexuals would have disproportionately supported leftist parties because of their relatively pro-homosexual stance, and that the aggressive homophobia of the conservatives and radical right-wingers would have acted as a deterrent to homosexuals. But political and ideological outlook is not usually shaped by sexual considerations; such a complex matter as sexuality seldom allows a rational weighing of interests. In an essay entitled "The Homosexual and the Reichstag Election," Magnus Hirschfeld reacted to the phenomenon of homosexual support for anti-homosexual parties with equal measures of empathy and help-lessness:

> All the more difficult is the conflict of conscience that the Reichstag election causes for homosexual women and men who, by virtue of descent, upbringing, and worldview, find themselves in the camp of conservative or clerical parties that reject out of hand any reform in the prosecution of homosexu-als. . . . Every homosexual voter who leans toward the right, perhaps because he is a staunch monarchist or a militarist, must therefore grapple with his conscience and consider which issue appears most important to him; he must weigh the differ-ent interests that come into play for himself and others. . . . We fully recognize the difficult conflict that arises for a homo-sexual voter rooted in old, comfortable ideas and ideals; he will have to make a sacrifice on the one side or the other; there is no way around it. Just how many absurdities are concealed by the ballot is shown by a case reported from Munich. In the most recent state election held there a Jewish homosexual is said to have voted for the German People's Party, i.e., for anti-Semites and anti-homosexuals. The man must have been a masochist.[22]

The appeal of anti-homosexual institutions for homosexual men is a phenomenon that by no means first arose with the Nazis or other radical right-wing parties. Before and since, homosexuals with a particular outlook have been drawn "in droves" to the churches, the military, and other conservative groups. Along with a possible masochistic streak, which Hirschfeld (perhaps tongue in cheek) surmised in the case of the Jewish homosexual who voted for the German People's Party, he also pointed to "descent, up-bringing, and worldview" as causes for anti-homosexual voting behavior on the part of homosexuals.

Active participation by homosexuals in homophobic institutions and parties may seem paradoxical at first glance, yet anyone aston-ished by this apparent self-hatred or masochism ought to take into account that homophobia was woven into the entire social fabric of Germany in the 1920s. The difference in the level of homophobia between society as a whole and such institutions as the Nazi Party or a Christian church was by no means a qualitative one, but instead incremental. In both settings, the pressure to conceal and deny homosexuality was virtually overwhelming, and apart from a lucky few in minor niches of tolerance, revealing one's homosexuality entailed severe disadvantages and could easily destroy one's livelihood.

"ROUGH AND READY FIGHTERS" AND "A DECADENT AND COWARDLY PACK OF CINAEDI": MORAL PROBLEMS WITH THE HOMOSEXUAL NAZI LEADER ERNST RÖHM

The Nazis scored a stunning success in the September 1930 election, winning 107 Reichstag seats and thereby increasing their representation of twelve seats nearly ninefold.[23] They now figured as Germany's second-strongest party, trailing only the SPD. Their paramilitary terrorist organization, the Storm Troopers (Sturmabteilung or SA), had by now grown to about 60,000 members but was leaderless due to the resignation of its leader Franz von Pfeffer. After naming himself "Supreme Führer of the SA and the Party," Hitler appointed a certain Otto Wagener to the newly created post of "SA Chief of Staff" for a few months prior to promoting his old friend Ernst Röhm to the position in early January 1931. Röhm's accession to his new duties was preceded by a conversation between Hitler and Wagener about Röhm's homosexuality and the setback to be expected were Röhm's peculiarity to become public knowledge. Indeed, Hitler was urgently warned not just by Wagener but also by at least one other leading Nazi of that time, Gregor Strasser.[24]

In retrospect, the concerns of Wagener and Strasser appear to have been exaggerated, while Hitler proved to be the realist with his determination to stick with Röhm. A press campaign did erupt three months after Röhm's appointment and went on to reach its greatest fury in the spring of 1932 with the publication of some of Röhm's private letters, in which he related to a friend (the physician Karl-

Günther Heimsoth, active in the GdE) his support for the homosexual movement as well as details about his sex life. Yet even this
campaign of vilification ultimately posed no serious obstacle on the
Nazis' path to power,[25] and they even succeded in more than doub-
ling their Reichstag strength in the July 1932 elections, thus becoming by far the strongest party in Germany. The proximity of the
Röhm scandal and the Nazis' electoral victory might tempt one to
conclude that there was even a cause-and-effect relationship between the two; and while that deduction would certainly be prepos-
terous, the fact remains that the controversy over Röhm and the
Nazis because of their toleration of a homosexual leader failed to
thwart either the party or the individual.

It is more difficult to determine whether the leftist press campaign against Röhm resulted in a setback for homosexuals and their
movement; we lack any unambiguous historical data that would
resolve the question. The Röhm affair overlapped with the general
decline of the homosexual movement from about 1929 on, manifest
in its shrinking membership and the contraction of the homosexual
press, but this was primarily caused by the Great Depression. A
rigorous policy of anti-homosexual harassment was initiated in
Prussia in October 1932, but it can be attributed to Reich Chancellor
Franz von Papen (Center Party), a Nazi ally who swept aside the
government of Prussia in July 1932 in a putsch-like action and
appointed a new police directorate that launched "a comprehensive
campaign against Berlin's vice-ridden nightlife."[26]

Almost one year after the scandal broke, the homosexual activist
and KPD member Richard Linsert began publishing an extended
chronicle on "the Röhm case" in the newsletter of the WhK.[27] Here
he compiled and commented on various newspaper articles–probably
the most important ones–from both the leftist press and the Nazi
press.[28] The articles he culled from Social Democratic and Communist papers will be re-examined here in order to test the evaluation
which they have heretofore received in gay historiography.

On April 4, 1931, under the headline "175 Cronies," the Social
Democratic daily *Münchener Post* carried its first report on confidential remarks Hitler had made to party comrades concerning the
Nazi functionaries Ernst Röhm, Edmund Heines, and Karl Zentner,
whom he allegedly termed "175ers." Some days later, on April 23,

the same paper carried a short article with the mocking title "Racial Improvers."[29] It dealt with a hustler who had engaged in sex with a "passionate proclaimer of the Third 'Röhman' Reich" and subsequently quarreled with him over the price. The word play on the First, or Holy Roman Empire (Reich) of medieval Germany clearly identified Ernst Röhm. Both texts were reacting, albeit with a few months' delay, to intense disputes within the Nazi Party over the person of the new SA Chief of Staff. Apart from the aforementioned exchanges between Strasser, Wagener, and Hitler, there had apparently been numerous protests ("reports and charges") concerning the increasing presence of homosexuals in the party leadership.

This internal dissension had provided the context for Hitler's "Decree No. 1," circulated to all higher party functionaries on February 3, 1931. Without explicitly mentioning homosexuality, which was clearly at the heart of the matter, Hitler had here declared the "private" lives of Nazi leaders off limits.[30] Hitler's decree documents that by early 1931, the simple fact of Röhm's homosexuality was no longer subject to dispute within the Nazi Party–at issue was whether he, with his sexuality, was fit for the duties assigned to him. By implying that homosexuality need not hamper the party career of a leader, Hitler's fiat stood in conflict with the aggressive homophobia of Nazi propaganda–but only superficially so. In their repeated attacks on the SPD for supporting–however half-heartedly–the reform of § 175, Nazi Reichstag delegates and the Nazi press had made it abundantly clear that homosexuality was by no means a matter that ought to be accorded privacy.[31] On more than one occasion, the Nazis' anti-homosexual invective amounted to a verbal anticipation of their later policy of wholesale persecution and elimination.[32] The apparent contradiction is subsumed within the sort of demagogic opportunism so characteristic of the Nazis: they excelled, for example, in anti-capitalist phrasemongering while simultaneously drawing their financial backing precisely from capitalist entrepreneurs.

But word of the controversy had obviously leaked beyond party circles, for on June 22, 1931, the *Münchener Post* could directly quote from Decree No. 1 Hitler's risible reference to "rough and ready fighters":

We [the SPD] know that the carryings-on of Röhm and his disciples have triggered indignation and outrage in wide circles of the National Socialists. We know that letters of complaint to Adolf Hitler have been piling up sky-high. But despite all complaints, the Führer of the German "renewal party," the enthusiast for "rough and ready fighters," is keeping his Chief of Staff.[33]

The taboo on public discussion of any Nazi leader's "private life" was espoused not just by Hitler but also by the homosexual press when it objected to the *Münchener Post*'s stories on Röhm and later to the publication of his letters. The WhK, for example, hastened to "warn" against "making the private sexual matters of an opponent into an object of polemical debates,"[34] and Linsert reproached the SPD for "making use of the most wretched means, that of sexual denunciation."[35] But homosexual leaders were undoubtedly aware that Röhm's homosexuality was no secret first revealed by the *Münchener Post*; instead, it had simply made a broader readership aware of what had agitated the Nazi Party for months.

In their critique of the SPD campaign against Röhm, Linsert and most leaders of the homosexual movement of that time appear to have relied on a sort of unwritten law that one could not speak openly about the homosexuality of any living person. This quasi-moral standard was regarded as so self-evident and universally binding that it was unnecessary to offer any rationale for it; it simply went without saying. The SPD "ought to have had enough decency" to keep silent about what it knew. At issue were not just morality ("decency") but also aesthetics ("good taste"), according to the WhK:

With the discussion of their opponent's sexual peculiarities, not only have they transgressed the boundaries of good taste, but also [and here follows a third argument, that of expediency] they ought not to forget how quickly sexual denunciation can become an arrow that falls back on him who shoots it. Those who live in glass houses shouldn't cast stones.[36]

The argument of taste is both doctrinaire and hollow, for to ignore a quarrel about sexual mores being conducted within the camp of a political adversary would scarcely qualify as more tasteful. And the warning that the Nazis would unmask homosexual Communists or Social Democrats probably unnerved no one.[37] On the moral question, the matter of respect supposedly due private life, Kurt Hiller took a stand in 1928 that leaves nothing to be desired in terms of clarity and principle but which apparently was not accepted within the WhK. In an "Open Letter" to Richard Linsert concerning the question whether the name of a homosexual cabinet minister in the fascist government of Italy could be revealed, Hiller wrote some fundamental thoughts on denunciation in 1928:

> . . . we fighters against the outlawry of same-sex love have a whole range of tasks other than denouncing homosexuals in high places as homosexuals; but that applies only to innocent, to decent homosexuals, not to a decadent and cowardly pack of cinaedi ensconced in power who make themselves complicit in the persecution of their less comfortably situated fellows. A homosexual minister who watches silently and passively as the cabinet to which he belongs, in a state which has tolerated homosexuality for forty years now, drafts and releases penitentiary punishments for homosexuals deserves many things from our side, but not this: to be spared. That is my opinion, and I declare it openly before our movement because the tactical-moral question at issue here has significance not just for Italy but also for Germany. All indications point to the prospect that in the course of reforming our penal law, a sensible regulation of the homosexual issue will encounter the most heated opposition from the nationalist-conservative and clerical camps. . . . If we learn (reliably) that supporters of the movement opposed to our cultural action have every reason to wish the success of our action, then we ought to name their names, ruthlessly and with a clear conscience. Our solidarity with the homosexuals of all classes and political viewpoints extends very far; but it does not include traitors to their own cause. . . .[38]

"MARXIST SWINISHNESS"

Insofar as the articles in the leftist press attacked the Nazis for their hypocrisy–leading Nazis were homosexual, and at the same time the Nazi Party was demanding heightened criminalization of homosexuality to the point of the death penalty–they met with approval in the homosexual movement. Homosexual leaders did object, on the other hand, to language such as "hair-raising whorishness under the terms of § 175," "shameless carryings-on of unnatural vice," "perverse activities," "queers," "homosexual affairs," as well as the *Münchener Post's* demand that the district attorney "do what ought to be done" in light of the Nazis' homosexual affairs.[39] But the latter was not, as the WhK imagined, simply a call to apply § 175. Also at issue was the fact that in the private army of the Nazis, the SA, the rules were suspended which applied in state matters. No civil servant and no officer of the Reichswehr was allowed to be homosexual. If the homosexuality of such a person became known, dismissal and professional proscription followed, even if no direct violation of the terms of the law were proved.[40]

One may assume that the Social Democratic and Communist editors approved of this regulation–which incidentally is still in effect in today's German military.[41] The prospect of Röhm's exploiting his military authority over young Nazis for his "private" interests was the target of such headlines in the leftist press as "Captain Röhm Abuses Unemployed Young Workers,"[42] "Fox Guards Chicken Coop,"[43] or "Physical and Moral Health of German Youth at Stake."[44] It could scarcely go unremarked–least of all out of consideration for Röhm's "private life"–that regulations otherwise rigorously implemented were suspended precisely in the Nazis' private army, that the professional proscription of homosexuality that applied to every teacher, every officer, and every church functionary did not apply among the Nazis.

The press campaign against Röhm and his clique[45] was stepped up in March 1932, when four letters[46] of Röhm to his sometime friend Heimsoth as well as the transcript of a police interrogation were published in the Communist daily *Die Welt am Abend*. Röhm had deposed to the police that he was "bisexually oriented" and had masturbated with "guys" but had never engaged in "intercourse punishable under the terms of § 175."[47] These revelations led the leftist press to even more formulations of the sort already cited, and here outright homophobia undeniably surfaced in the journalistic treatment.

At first glance there is a striking similarity between a Communist headline such as "Captain Röhm Abuses Unemployed Young Workers" (*Die Welt am Abend*, April 1932) and a headline in the Nazi press such as "German Mothers, Workers' Wives! Do You Want to Hand Over Your Children to Homosexuals?" (*Völkischer Beobachter*, October 1928). But the conclusion drawn by gay historiography to date, namely that the leftist press aimed at "across-the-board harrassment of homosexuals"[48] or "the defamation of all homosexuals using the example of Röhm,"[49] disregards the different historical contexts in which these anti-homosexual formulations were made. The homophobic passages in leftist press reports unquestionably aimed to win votes by smearing the Nazis, but I would argue that they nonetheless had a totally different weight than homophobic formulations in conservative, Christian, or Nazi texts.

The Communist article about Röhm's abuse of unemployed young workers also included passages such as the following, which were entirely lacking in the right-wing, centrist, and SPD press; they cannot be disregarded if we are to arrive at a fuller understanding of the relative valence of homophobic discourses:

> We decisively reject, even vis-à-vis an opponent, deviating from our basic position in the struggle against § 175. We will never under any circumstances reproach anyone on the basis of his orientation, but we will not be hindered from revealing the abysmally deep hypocrisy of the corrupt circles which characterize the struggle against § 175 as "Marxist swinishness" but themselves seek to profit from this struggle. . . .[50]

Under the headline "Queerness in the Brown House [i.e., the Nazi Party headquarters]: Sex Life in the Third Reich," the *Münchener Post* quoted the *Völkischer Beobachter*'s attack on leftists who backed the repeal of § 175. In doing so, the SPD paper aimed not to rebut the Nazis' supposed reproach but to expose their "repulsive hypocrisy":

> "Together with Marxists of all shadings, from Dietrich to Thälmann, the great constitutional scholar Dr. Kahl of the

German People's Party is fighting with a giant's strength and no little success to wipe out § 175, so that unnatural vice will go scot-free, German freedom will finally be achieved, and beauty and dignity will finally be realized in fulfillment of the promise of a prominent man."–Gregor Strasser in the *Völkischer Beobachter* of June 21-22. Thus one of the leaders of the Nazi Party adopts an ironic tone, seeking to persuade people that the renewers under the swastika banner are waging a struggle against unnatural vice, homosexuality. . . .[51]

On May 29, 1932, the chairman of the WhK wrote a letter to the governing board of the SPD protesting against the homophobic language used in the SPD press. In addition to such terms as "queers" and "homosexual affair," this letter objected to a Social Democratic sticker with the (rhymed) slogan: "Down with Hitler, / the gendarme, / And with Captain Röhm, / the queer."[52] In the process, the moral issue raised by the presence of Nazis within the homosexual movement became clear, if only by indirection. The organizations in question did not regard it as a problem that members of the National Socialist Party, a militantly anti-homosexual formation, were involved in the WhK and that Röhm was the member of another homosexual group, the BfM,[53] which even falsely asserted in its periodical that Röhm had "always freely and openly acknowledged his homosexual orientation."[54] WhK chairman Heinrich Stabel interpreted the jingle attacking the queer Captain Röhm and the gendarme Hitler as an SPD demand for heightened persecution of homosexuals. Apparently it never occurred to him that the slogan called instead for opposition to the terrorist regime of the Nazis and could be addressed to homosexuals as well as straights. Instead, he evidently felt that he had to represent the interests of the Nazis within his own organization.

A close look at the political and moral arguments advanced by all those involved in making Röhm's homosexuality public ought to make it clear that the truly scandalous side of the entire affair was the homosexual movement's heated protests against any encroachment upon the "private life" of a sinister Nazi leader. We today may still feel a sense of dismay at sharing the same sexual orientation with such a brute as Ernst Röhm, and had it been felt at that time rather than repressed, homosexuals could have played quite a different role in the antifascist struggle. While German homosexuals who, in Hirschfeld's bitter formulation, shifted "in droves" to Hitler were acting no differently than the rest of the German populace, this scarcely lets them off the hook. And we must recall a fact that is often forgotten or played down nowadays: more than any other social group, it was the German left, "Marxists of all shadings," who embraced the demands of the homosexual liberation movement as their own.

AFTER 1933: EXILE, ILLEGALITY, CONFORMITY

The homosexual movement, already weakened by the Great Depression and police persecution beginning in the summer of 1932, effectively ceased to exist in the first half of 1933, after von Papen and Hitler had formed a "coalition government of national consolidation" on January 30. The GdE had already folded in early 1932 with the demise of its journal *Der Eigene*.[55] The WhK summoned its members to a final assembly on June 8, 1933, at 7 p.m. in the apartment of its secretary Peter Limann; the sole item on the agenda was "Dissolving the Scientific-Humanitarian Committee, Inc."[56] The BfM likewise disbanded in late 1934.[57]

After the left parties, first the KPD and then the SPD, were banned, their members went into exile, engaged in resistance, or were swept up in mass arrests following the Reichstag fire. The homosexual liberation struggle was a dead letter in Germany and virtually every other country, with just three modest exceptions. In Switzerland, a small circle of lesbians and homosexual men formed around the journal *Schweizerisches Freundschafts-Banner*; in the Netherlands, the Nederlandsch Wetenschappelijk Humanitair Komitee continued up to the invasion of the Nazi army; and in England, shrouded in total discretion, the tiny British Sexological Society persisted for a time. Apart from these frail organizations, homophobia ruled the world, and the conditions in the European democracies, in America, and in the Soviet Union were no different from those in Nazi Germany until the slaying of Röhm in July 1934.

Up to this point, the figure of the homosexual Nazi leader, who by late 1933 had risen to a ministerial post, was a frequent target of derision in the exile press[58] and within the illegal resistance circles inside the Nazi Reich. Erich Honecker, later head of state of the German Democratic Republic, recounted the following vignette in his memoirs:

> Although we illegals were constantly exposed to the gravest dangers, we wouldn't allow our courage to be taken away. Wherever it was possible we subjected the enemy to ridicule. I experienced an example of it at the Dortmund sports stadium in the summer of 1933. At that time it was an open secret that the Chief of Staff of the SA, Ernst Röhm, along with various other high SA leaders, was given to homosexual inclinations. In the night before a big SA march planned for Dortmund at which Captain Röhm was to inspect the ranks, the girls and boys of the Communist Youth Organization of Dortmund put a huge slogan on a wall of the stadium: "Attention, SA, pants down, Röhm is coming."[59]

In this and other such statements of German Communists and Socialists, there is unquestionably a good deal of homophobia. Such thoughtless acceptance of heterosexism was part and parcel of bourgeois culture and imitated in a diluted form by leftists, who at least had not invented it. Far from autonomous, the subcultures of the Social Democratic and Communist workers' movements existed in a subaltern relationship to the hegemonic culture of the ruling class.

That there is not a single Communist or Social Democratic statement on the homosexual liberation struggle in the period from 1933 until the victory over Hitler fascism must probably be taken as clear-cut evidence of leftist homophobia. When making such judgments, however, we ought to apply a standard of comparison from that era, and then we would surely find that the bourgeois opposition to Hitler, whether in emigration or in resistance, proved to be not a bit more civilized or enlightened than the leftists. Leftist homophobia is presumably only a variant of the universal homophobia that took on epidemic proportions in the 1930s and 1940s, permeating the cultural life of all European states and societies.

Likewise, this is the background against which the "regressions in the Soviet Union" under Stalin ought to be judged. Even though the level of our research on the situation there is lamentably inadequate, the Soviet persecution of homosexuals in the 1930s and 1940s must in all fairness be compared with the corresponding situation in Western countries of that era, when homophobic police terrorism was the order of the day in Great Britain, the United States, and most other Western democracies.

Soviet Russia had no anti-sodomy law from 1918 on, but there are virtually no indications of a self-aware homosexual life there. On March 7, 1934, a new "law on the penal culpability for pederasty" was promulgated which set a minimum punishment of three years for "sexual intercourse of a man with a man." Regrettably, we know all too little about the forms of homosexual persecution there in the years prior to the 1934 law, just as we have little data about the extent of persecutions since that time.[60] Within the German homosexual movement, only the WhK had occasionally pointed to the absence of an anti-sodomy statute in the Soviet Union as exemplary,[61] and it was also the erstwhile WhK co-chairman Kurt Hiller who strongly criticized this Soviet step backwards. In conversations with him, party-line Communists defended the new law by claiming that the Russian government sought in this way to combat a "hotbed of oppositional propaganda" within the Red Army.[62]

Soviet homophobia certainly had an effect on opinion formation among German Communists during World War II and the postwar years, just as the homophobia of Western democracies influenced German Social Democrats, but this topic would take us far beyond the focus on the positions of the KPD and the SPD between 1918 and 1933. Not until decades later would these two left parties return to their former positions: in 1969, the Social Democracy used its share in power to bring about a reform of § 175 in the Federal Republic of Germany; and almost simultaneously, in 1968, the Communists reformed § 175 in their sphere of power, the German Democratic Republic, finally fulfilling the demands advanced by the homosexual movement in the Weimar Republic.

Translated from the German by James Steakley

AUTHOR NOTE

Manfred Herzer, a librarian in Berlin, is a cofounder and staff member of the Gay Museum (Schwules Museum). He edited *Bibliographie zur Homosexualität* (Berlin: Rosa Winkel, 1982), a chronological bibliography of over 3,000 German non-fiction writings on homosexuality. The editor since 1987 of *Capri*, a journal of gay history, he has authored numerous essays as well as the monograph *Magnus Hirschfeld: Leben und Werk eines jüdischen, schwulen und sozialistischen Sexologen* (Frankfurt a.m.: Campus, 1992).

NOTES

1. See, for example, Wilfried U. Eissler, *Arbeiterparteien und Homosexuellenfrage: Zur Sexualpolitik von SPD und KPD in der Weimarer Republik* (Berlin: Rosa Winkel, 1980), and Hans-Georg Stümke, *Homosexuelle in Deutschland: Eine politische Geschichte* (Munich: C. H. Beck, 1989).

2. George Weinberg is credited with having first employed the term "homophobia" in his *Society and the Healthy Homosexual* (New York: St. Martin's Press, 1972); see also Gregory K. Lehne, "Homophobia in Men," in *The Forty-Nine Percent Majority: The Male Sex Role*, ed. Deborah S. David and Robert Brannon (Reading, MA: Addison-Wesley, 1976), pp. 66-88. The term appeared even earlier in Dutch, albeit with a different meaning: a heterosexual's fear that he may be taken to be a homosexual. See Frits E. Frenkel, "Homofilie en Homofobie," *Symbiose* (The Hague) 5.3 (1966): 130-44.

3. A very early formulation of the goal of homosexual "liberation" appeared, for example, in *Jahrbuch für sexuelle Zwischenstufen* 1 (1899): 281. In his magnum opus, *Die Homosexualität des Mannes und des Weibes* (Berlin: Louis Marcus, 1914), Magnus Hirschfeld spoke of a "liberation struggle" (p. 973 et passim). I have portrayed the relationship of Hirschfeld and his circle to the leftist parties in *Magnus Hirschfeld: Leben und Werk eines jüdischen, schwulen und sozialistischen Sexologen* (Frankfurt a.M.: Campus, 1992), pp. 27-50.

4. Magnus Hirschfeld, *Die Kenntnis der homosexuellen Natur, eine sittliche Forderung* (Charlottenburg: Fritz Stolt, 1907), p. 5.

5. Sozialdemokratische Partei Deutschlands, *Sozialdemokratischer Parteitag 1927 in Kiel* (Berlin: J. H. W. Dietz Nachfolger, 1927), pp. 264 and 153.

6. British and Irish Communist Organization, *Bernstein on Homosexuality: Articles from "Die Neue Zeit" 1895 and 1898*, trans. Angela Clifford (Belfast: Athol, 1977), p. 27. Bernstein's text first appeared as "Die Beurtheilung des widernormalen Geschlechtsverkehrs," *Die Neue Zeit* 13, part 2 (1895): 228-33; quote on p. 233.

7. [Magnus Hirschfeld], "Aus der Bewegung," *Jahrbuch für sexuelle Zwischenstufen* 19 (1919-20): 111-33; quote on p. 121.

8. "Ein antisemitisches Heldenstück," *Vorwärts*, October 5, 1920; cited in [Magnus Hirschfeld], "Aus der Bewegung," *Jahrbuch für sexuelle Zwischenstufen* 20 (1920-21): 107-42; quote on p. 131.

9. Magnus Hirschfeld, letter to the editor of the *Münchener Post*, reprinted ibid., pp. 124-26; quote on p. 125.

10. "Von Hirschfeld bis Hirschfeld," *Berliner Volkszeitung*, October 22, 1920; reprinted ibid., pp. 130-33; quote on p. 132.

11. The relevant chapter of Halle's book, entitled "Die Stellung des klassenbewußten Proletariats zur Homosexualität," was reprinted in *Mitteilungen des Wissenschaftlich-humanitären Komitees*, no. 30 (August 1931): 310-13; quote on p. 312.

12. The committee's deliberations on October 16, 1929, are reprinted in their entirety in "Die Verhandlungen des Strafrechtsausschusses des deutschen Reichstages über die Strafwürdigkeit der Homosexualität," *Mitteilungen des Wissenschaftlich-humanitären Komitees*, no. 24 (September-October 1929): 176-91; Kahl's speech on pp. 186-87; quote on p. 187.

13. Kurt Hiller, "Die Reichstagswahl," *Mitteilungen des Wissenschaftlich-humanitären Komitees*, no. 28 (April-August 1930): 278.

14. Eissler (see note 1), pp. 37-48, offers a good overview of Social Democratic statements on homosexuality in the Wilhelmine era; an English summary appears on pp. 127-30. It is entirely possible that the WhK did not even solicit signatories for its petition from the leftists within the SPD. Since no leftist ever made any statement whatsoever about the homosexual question prior to 1918, it is more likely that Karl Liebknecht, Rosa Luxemburg, Klara Zetkin, and the other leftists more or less spontaneously decided to ignore and taboo the matter.

15. An abridged version of Koenen's speech appears in Richard Linsert, "Erste Lesung des Strafgesetzentwurfs im Reichstage," *Mitteilungen des Wissenschaftlich-humanitären Komitees*, no. 8 (July-August 1927): 63-64.

16. Magnus Hirschfeld, "Antrag auf Abschaffung des § 175 im Deutschen Reichstag," *Die Freundschaft* (Berlin) 6.7 (October 1924): 145-46.

17. Kurt Hiller, *§ 175–Die Schmach des Jahrhunderts!* (Hanover: Paul Steegemann, 1921), p. 78.

18. Linsert, "Erste Lesung," p. 61.

19. *Blätter für Menschenrecht* 10.10-11 (October-November 1932): 13.

20. Magnus Hirschfeld, "Männerbünde. Sexualpsychologischer Beitrag zur Röhm-Katastrophe," *Pariser Tageblatt*, July 20, 1934, p. 2. See also Max Hodann's obituary for Magnus Hirschfeld: "There is a darker and more savage irony in the fact that the Nazis should have treated him as an archenemy; for the Nazi ranks are notoriously honeycombed with all degrees of homosexuality, and Hirschfeld is indisputably the man to whom it is mainly due that the right of these 2 per cent of sexual abnormals in the mass of European populations to exist and to function on their own lines is now a matter for public discussion and public agitation." M. Hodann, "Magnus Hirschfeld: In Memoriam," trans. F. W. Stella Browne, *Marriage Hygiene* (Bombay), 2 (November 1934): 123-26; quote on p. 123. This obituary originally appeared in *Internationales Ärztliches Bulletin* (Prague) 2.5-6 (May-June 1935): 73-76. Claudia Schoppmann has recently shown that prior to 1933, there were Nazi adherents among the leading lesbians in the homosexual emancipation movement. As an example she names the case of Elsbeth Killmer, a leading editor of the most important lesbian periodical of that time, *Die*

Freundin, who was active in the Nazi organization NS-Frauenschaft early on. See C. Schoppmann, *Nationalsozialistische Sexualpolitik und weibliche Homsexualität* (Pfaffenweiler: Centaurus, 1991), pp. 171-72.

21. The "coalition government of national consolidation" formed on January 30, 1933, after Reich President Hindenburg had appointed Hitler Reich Chancellor, consisted of ministers from the Nazi Party, the Center Party, the German National People's Party, and independents.

22. Hirschfeld, "Der Homosexuelle und die Reichstagswahl," *Die Freundschaft* 6.2 (May 1924): 28.

23. In this section I base my remarks on two key studies: Eissler (see note 1), pp. 106-14, and Burkhard Jellonnek, *Homosexuelle unter dem Hakenkreuz* (Paderborn: Ferdinand Schöningh, 1990), pp. 57-79. My disagreements with these two authors will be apparent in my treatment of the Röhm case.

24. Jellonnek, p. 58; listed there are the sources on Wagener and Strasser.

25. The homosexual writer Klaus Mann did not comment on the press campaign against Röhm until 1934, after the Nazis had achieved victory and murdered Röhm. He aptly remarked that the campaign "was ineffectual" and failed to "damage Captain Röhm"–an observation that can be applied to all anti-Nazi actions, which in January 1933 had all proved to be ineffective. As well, Mann's criticism remained on an aesthetic plane: the campaign was "very coarse," "out of place," "quite ridiculous and embarrassing," and the struggle against Röhm had been conducted "in an undignified manner." See K. Mann, "Die Linke und das 'Laster,' " *Europäische Hefte* (Prague) 1.36-37 (24 December 1934): 675-78.

26. On the 1932 police sweep, see Wolfgang Theis and Andreas Sternweiler, "Alltag im Kaiserreich und in der Weimarer Republik," in *Eldorado: Homosexuelle Frauen und Männer in Berlin 1850-1950: Geschichte, Alltag und Kultur,* ed. Michael Bollé (Berlin: Frölich & Kaufmann, 1984), p. 73.

27. That Richard Linsert (1899-1933) was homosexual is only probable, not certain. There is no statement by Linsert in which he declared his sexual orientation. He was, however, active in the WhK from 1923 until his death, as was his friend Peter Limann, with whom he shared a Charlottenburg apartment for a time. On Linsert, see Kurt Hiller, *Leben gegen die Zeit*, vol. 2: *Eros* (Reinbek bei Hamburg: Rowohlt, 1973), pp. 87-114.

28. Herbert Heinersdorf (i.e., Richard Linsert), "Akten zum Falle Röhm," *Mitteilungen des Wissenschaftlich-humanitären Komitees*, no. 32 (January-March 1932): 349-68; no. 33 (April-August 1932): 387-96; no. 34 (September 1932-February 1933): 419-28.

29. The headline ("*Rassehochzüchter*") was a play on the wording of a draft law just introduced in the Reichstag by the Nazis, who called for imprisoning anyone guilty of "racial treason (*Rassenverrat*)" by "limiting the natural fertility of the German people through artificial means" or by having sex "with members of the Jewish racial community or with colored races." The humor was obviously supposed to arise from the fact that homosexual practices certainly did nothing to advance "the natural fertility of the German people," and any homosexual Nazi was thus violating his own party's goals.

30. The wording of this peculiar memorandum, published by Heinrich Bennecke, *Hitler und die SA* (Munich: G. Olzog, 1962), p. 243, is here cited as it appears in Hans Peter Bleuel, *Sex and Society in Nazi Germany*, ed. Heinrich Fraenkel, trans. J. Maxwell Brownjohn (Philadelphia: J. B. Lippincott, 1973), pp. 97-98 (with the addition of the final sentence, deletion of paragraphing, and a revised translation of "rauhe Kämpfer"):
"Decree No. 1. The Supreme Command of the SA has considered a number of reports and charges levelled at SA officers and men, most of them embodying accusations in respect of their personal conduct. It emerges from an examination of these matters that most of them fall entirely outside the scope of SA service. In many cases, attacks by political or personal opponents have been taken on trust. Some people expect SA commanders of high and senior rank to take decisions on these matters, which belong purely to the private domain. I reject this presumption categorically and with all the force at my command. Quite apart from the waste of time which could be better employed in the fight for freedom, I am bound to state that the SA is a body of men formed for a specific political purpose. It is not an institute for the moral education of genteel young ladies, but a formation of rough and ready fighters (*rauhe Kämpfer*). The sole purpose of any inquiry must be to ascertain whether or not the SA officer or other rank is performing his official duties within the SA. His private life cannot be an object of scrutiny unless it conflicts with basic principles of National Socialist ideology. In the future, high SA leaders who receive such reports are required to check initially whether to call to responsibility the accusers who are sowing ill will and unrest in the SA and if necessary to apply for their expulsion from the SA or the movement. Adolf Hitler."
    31. Kurt Tucholsky, who formulated perhaps the most sophisticated critique of the campaign against Röhm, likewise missed this connection. He regarded the outing of Nazi leaders as morally defensible only if the Nazis attacked homosexuality as an "Oriental vice" introduced from abroad by the enemies of the German people; see Ignaz Wrobel (i.e., K. Tucholsky), "Röhm," *Die Weltbühne* 28.17 (April 26, 1932): 641. But this is precisely what the Nazis had been proclaiming from the very outset whenever they made pronouncements on the topic of homosexuality: it was a vice promoted by Jews and Marxists with the intent of damaging the German people.
    32. The *Völkischer Beobachter* reached a highpoint in this regard on August 2, 1930, when it concluded an article entitled "Die Koalition zum Schutz der Päderastie" attacking Jews, homosexuals, and Social Democrats as follows: "All the evil impulses of the Jewish soul to thwart the divine plan of creation by corporeal relations with animals, siblings, and members of the same sex we will soon designate by law as what they really are: as thoroughly revolting deviations of Syrians, most heinous *crimes to be prosecuted by the noose* or expulsion."
    33. "Warme Bruderschaft im Braunen Haus: Das Sexualleben im Dritten Reich," *Münchener Post*, June 22, 1931; here cited from *Mitteilungen des Wissenschaftlich-humanitären Komitees*, no. 32 (January-March 1932): 351.

34. Heinrich Stabel, Richard Linsert, Kurt Hiller, "Kundgebung des WHK an die deutsche Presse betr.: den Fall Röhm," *Mitteilungen des Wissenschaftlich-humanitären Komitees*, no. 31 (September-October 1931): 315-16.

35. Heinersdorf (i.e., Linsert), p. 357.

36. "Der Fall Röhm," *Mitteilungen des Wissenschaftlich-humanitären Komitees*, no. 32 (January-March 1932): 370.

37. Magnus Hirschfeld, a Social Democrat, was repeatedly exposed as a homosexual in the radical-right press. On October 31, 1928, the *Völkischer Beobachter* carried a story about Hirschfeld with the following headlines: "Homosexuals as Guest Speakers in Boys' Schools: Magnus Hirschfeld, the 'Veteran Campaigner' for the Repeal of § 175, Allowed to Speak in German High Schools."

38. Kurt Hiller, "Offener Brief," *Mitteilungen des Wissenschaftlich-humanitären Komitees*, no. 16 (June-July 1928): 126-27. With his idea of exposing the homosexuality of homosexual opportunists and beneficiaries of homophobia, Hiller was just as unsuccessful as are today's advocates of outing (such as the German filmmaker Rosa von Praunheim). "Average" homosexuals, today as in the past, hasten to invoke "good taste" and the right to privacy, forgetting all too easily that these aesthetic and legal criteria do not hold for victims of homophobia.

39. Letter of the WhK to the executive board of the SPD, dated May 29, 1932; reprinted in "Kundgebungen," *Mitteilungen des Wissenschaftlich-humanitären Komitees*, no. 33 (April-August 1932): 372-75; quotes on p. 374.

40. In his historical study of the topic, Günther Gollner notes: "At least from the turn of the century on, the German civil service code upheld the principle that no homosexual could remain in office, let alone enter one. Homosexuality seemed so dangerous that not just those convicted of homosexual practices were removed from office but even anyone indicted." See G. Gollner, "Disziplinarsanktionen gegenüber Homosexuellen im öffentlichen Dienst," in *Seminar: Gesellschaft und Homosexualität*, ed. Rüdiger Lautmann (Frankfurt a.M.: Suhrkamp, 1977), pp. 105-24; quote on p. 106.

41. "Homosexuelle Neigungen eines militärischen Vorgesetzten. Homosexuelle Neigungen schließen die Eignung eines Soldaten zum Vorgesetzten aus," *Neue Juristische Wochenschrift* 33 (1980): 1178-79.

42. This was a headline in the Communist *Welt am Abend*, as cited by Heinersdorf (i.e., Linsert), p. 423.

43. This was a headline in the Social Democratic *Welt am Montag* on March 14, 1932, where the article concluded: "Our position in the Röhm case has obviously nothing to do with a principled stand on the repeal of § 175; we are not criticizing Röhm's private live, we are denouncing the political immorality of the Brown House."

44. *Münchener Post*, June 22, 1931.

45. The following Nazi leaders, mostly friends of Röhm, were likewise suspected of homosexuality by the left press: Edmund Heines, Karl Ernst, Röhrbein, Karl Ze(h)ntner, Gauleiter Helmuth Brückner, Karl du Moulin-Eckart, Rossbach.

Only in the case of Röhm was there clear-cut evidence in the form of an admission.

46. According to Linsert, the *Welt am Montag* began printing Röhm letters from the years 1928 and 1929 on March 7, 1932; see Heinersdorf (i.e., Linsert), p. 425. The "entire left German press" then began reprinting them, at least in part, and the Social Democrat Helmut Klotz (a former Nazi) authored two brochures in which they appeared as facsimiles; see H. Klotz, *Euer Hochwohlgeboren!* (Berlin-Tempelhof: by the author, 1932), and idem, *Der Fall Röhm* (Berlin-Tempelhof: by the author, 1932).

47. Linsert reprinted this transcript "because it proves incontrovertibly that Captain Röhm has abused neither prepubertal children nor his power of office, charges that incredibly have been raised over and over again"; Heinersdorf (i.e., Linsert), p. 425. Linsert erred, however, for none of the leftist press articles cited by him claimed that Röhm had sex with children or abused his "power of office." Instead, they constantly invoked the possibility that "large segments of German youth" could be led to homosexuality through abuse of military authority by SA members, most of whom were teenagers. When Klotz wrote about "the homosexual infection of German youth" by the Nazis (*Der Fall Röhm*, p. 4), he was simply turning around a Nazi argument used against "Marxists of all shadings" and applying it against the originators themselves.

48. Jellonnek (see note 23), p. 62.

49. Eissler (see note 1), p. 112.

50. *Welt am Abend*, quoted by Heinersdorf (i.e., Linsert), p. 423.

51. "Warme Brüderschaft im Braunen Haus: Das Sexualleben im Dritten Reich," *Münchener Post*, June 22, 1931, quoted by Heinersdorf (i.e., Linsert), p. 351.

52. The German text is: "Fort mit Hitler, / dem Gendarmen, / und mit Hauptmann Röhm, / dem Warmen." Quoted in "Kundgebungen" (see note 39), p. 374.

53. See Klotz, *Euer Hochwohlgeboren!*, p. 7.

54. Anonymous, "Kleine Unterschlagungen," *Blätter für Menschenrecht* 10.10-11 (October-November 1932): 13. The article continues: "The Committee [i.e., the WhK] reproduces the original text of the Röhm letters but tampers with it by simply omitting a certain passage that relates to the League [i.e., the BfM] and apparently doesn't suit the Committee. I therefore declare that Lieutenant Colonel Röhm's letter of December 3, 1928, states correctly: 'By the way, I work together with Mr. Radszuweit and am of course a member of his League.' No comment needed."

55. On November 29, 1933, GdE chairman Adolf Brand wrote an account to the British Sexological Society in London in which he reported on a total of five police searches and seizures in his house. He also commented on measures taken in 1933: "Immediately after seizing power, the government of Reich Chancellor Adolf Hitler immediately began to suppress the homosexual movement with all sorts of strict measures. For the most part, however, these persecutions were directed only against ugly excesses of the movement. At that time they were still limited to closing the prostitution establishments, which had always damaged the movement greatly in the eyes of all decent people, and to withdrawing the liquor

licenses of bars that had sought to turn a profit on the seduction of male youths. These police actions were to be welcomed in the interest of cleanliness and in the interest of the movement's image. . . ." Copy in the author's possession.

56. A copy of the letter of invitation to this final meeting is included in the facsimilie reprint of the *Mitteilungen des Wissenschaftlich-humanitären Komitees 1926-1933* (Hamburg: C. Bell, 1985), p. xxxi.

57. According to Claudia Schoppmann (see note 20 above), p. 165, the Landesarchiv Berlin contains a letter of BfM chairman Paul Weber to the district court dated November 9, 1934, in which he notifies the authorities in the bureaucratically correct manner that the organization has dissolved. She offers no sources, however, for her assertion that the BfM co-chairman Martin Radszuweit was murdered in a concentration camp and that a BfM publishing house somewhere in Potsdam was "plundered." The concentration camp death of Martin Radszuweit, at least, is a fiction: he died in the 1980s in his house in Berlin-Köpenick.

58. Two widely distributed *Brown Books* issued by Communist émigrés in Paris contained totally invented stories about the role of homosexuality in the Reichstag fire. See *Braunbuch über Reichstagsbrand und Hitler-Terror* (Basel: Universum-Bücherei, 1933), available in an abridged English version as *Brown Book of the Hitler Terror and the Burning of the Reichstag*, prepared by the World Committee for the Victims of German Fascism (New York: Alfred A. Knopf, 1933), and *Braunbuch II: Dimitroff contra Göring: Enthüllungen über die wahren Brandstifter* (Paris: Éditions du Carrefour, 1934).

59. Erich Honecker, *Aus meinem Leben* (Berlin: Dietz, 1980), p. 69.

60. See Simon Karlinsky, "Schwule Literatur und Kultur in Rußland: Die Folgen der Oktoberrevolution," *Capri*, no. 8 (1990): 3-26, a translation of idem, "Russia's Gay Literature and Culture: The Impact of the October Revolution," in *Hidden from History: Reclaiming the Lesbian and Gay Past*, ed. Martin Duberman, Martha Vicinus, and George Chauncey, Jr. (New York: New American Library, 1989), pp. 347-64; and Siegfried Tornow, "Männliche Homosexualität und Politik in Sowjet-Rußland," in *Homosexualität und Wissenschaft II*, ed. Schwulenreferat im Allgemeinen Studentenausschuß der Freien Universität Berlin (Berlin: Rosa Winkel, 1992), pp. 267-84, also published as "Homosexuality and Politics in Soviet Russia," in *Sexual Minorities and Society: The Changing Attitudes toward Homosexuality in the 20th Century Europe*, ed. Udo Parikas and Teet Veispak (Tallinn: Institute of History, 1991), pp. 78-93.

61. See "Zur Bestrafung der Homosexualität in Sowjet-Rußland," *Mitteilungen des Wissenschaftlich-humanitären Komitees*, no. 18 (October-December 1928): 146-47.

62. Kurt Hiller, "Rückschritte der Sowjet-Union," *Sozialistische Warte*, no. 14 (1936): 326-31.

The "Jews" of the Antifascist Left: Homosexuality and Socialist Resistance to Nazism

Harry Oosterhuis

Rijksuniversiteit Limburg

SUMMARY. In the early 1930s, German Social Democrats and Communists seized upon the homosexual orientation of some Nazi leaders, especially Ernst Röhm, with the aim of discrediting the entire National Socialist movement. In Western Europe as well as the Soviet Union, there was a general tendency among socialists in the 1930s to identify homosexuality with Nazism. Antifascist leftists created the impression that homosexuality was widespread in Nazi organizations. Such socialist theorists as Wilhelm Reich tended to view homosexuality sociologically and psychologically as a typical rightist, nationalist, and above all fascist aberration. Leftist aversion to homosexuality was not only an expression of political opportunism. Prejudices against homosexuality were part and parcel of socialist thinking and became even more deep-rooted among leftists as a consequence of the ideological and moral confrontation with National Socialism. Against the presumed immorality and perversion of the Nazis, the antifascists stressed their own rationality and purity.

Correspondence may be addressed: Vakgroep Geschiedenis, Rijksuniversiteit Limburg, Postbus 616, 6200 MD Maastricht, Netherlands. E-mail: harry.oosterhuis@history.rulimburg.nl

[Haworth co-indexing entry note]: "The "Jews" of the Antifascist Left: Homosexuality and Socialist Resistance to Nazism." Oosterhuis, Harry. Co-published simultaneously in *Journal of Homosexuality* (The Haworth Press, Inc.) Vol. 29, No. 2/3, 1995, pp. 227-257; and: *Gay Men and the Sexual History of the Political Left* (ed: Gert Hekma, Harry Oosterhuis, and James Steakley) The Haworth Press, Inc., 1995, pp. 227-257; and *Gay Men and the Sexual History of the Political Left* (ed: Gert Hekma, Harry Oosterhuis, and James Steakley) Harrington Park Press, an imprint of The Haworth Press, Inc., 1995, pp. 227-257. Multiple copies of this article/chapter may be purchased from The Haworth Document Delivery Center. [1-800-342-9678 9:00 a.m. - 5:00 p.m. (EST)].

Prior to World War II, the attitudes of German Social Democrats and Communists toward (male) homosexuality were at best ambivalent.[1] This vacillation was particularly pronounced in the thirties, the decade in which the Nazi regime came to power and consolidated its hold in Germany. On the one hand, both the Social Democratic Party (Sozialdemokratische Partei Deutschlands, SPD) and Communist Party (Kommunistische Partei Deutschlands, KPD) maintained their nominal support of the German homosexual-rights movement's campaign to repeal § 175 of the penal code, which punished "unnatural vice" with imprisonment. On the other hand, some party spokesmen and publicists constructed a highly pejorative stereotype of homosexuality by linking it with Nazism.

How can this Janus-faced outlook of the left be explained? How was it possible for leftist activists and intellectuals to compromise their parties' platforms in the domain of sexual politics? This essay will argue that political pragmatism in the struggle against Nazism as well as a more deep-seated sense of anxiety and aversion toward homosexual desire were responsible for the contradictory attitudes on the German left.

THE RÖHM AFFAIR

In the turbulent years 1930-34, which witnessed the Nazis' rise to power, Germany's Social Democrats and Communists displayed a general tendency to link homosexuality with National Socialism. The stereotype of homosexuality as a characteristic not just of individual Nazis but of the Nazi system as a whole was firmly established during three episodes: (1) the Röhm affair in 1931-32; (2) the Reichstag fire in 1933, when the destruction of the parliament building was followed by mass arrests of the Nazi regime's political opponents; and (3) the so-called "Night of the Long Knives" or "Röhm putsch" in 1934, when a large number of the leaders of the SA (Sturmabteilung), the paramilitary troops of the Nazi party, were liquidated for political reasons.

When Adolf Hitler appointed Ernst Röhm commander in chief of the SA in 1931, various left-wing politicians and journalists sought to discredit the National Socialist movement by seizing upon the homosexual preferences of Röhm and other SA leaders alleged to be homosexual.[2] In the spring of 1931, the *Münchner Post*, a Social Democratic daily, began publishing a series of articles that portrayed a clique of homosexual leaders playing key roles in an internal power struggle within the SA. The exposés in the *Münchner Post* were based on private correspondence bought from a disgruntled Nazi–letters later revealed to be forgeries. The *Münchner Post* further alleged that Röhm had been blackmailed by a male prostitute (which may well have been true) and had been prosecuted on charges of violating § 175. This campaign of calumny failed, however, to bring about Röhm's removal from a leadership position in the Nazi party. Indeed, he demonstrated considerable self-assurance when defending himself in public, and the Nazi daily *Völkischer Beobachter* rose to his defense.[3]

The campaign against Röhm was renewed when the SPD press agency released some of Röhm's authentic private correspondence surreptitiously acquired by Helmut Klotz, a renegade Nazi and former Reichstag delegate who had gone over to the side of the Social Democrats. Röhm had written these letters in Bolivia, where he had worked as a military adviser, to a Nazi friend in Germany, the homosexual physician Karl Günther Heimsoth; and they described in frank terms Röhm's sexual interest in young men. The letters also revealed Röhm to be a rather forthright and even militant homosexual, one who favored the repeal of § 175 and was a member of the largest homosexual organization of the Weimar Republic, the League for Human Rights (Bund für Menschenrecht). Röhm had written that he was not at all unhappy about his orientation and that his comrades in the Nazi movement should get used to it.[4]

Röhm's correspondence was published just a few days before elections were to take place in Germany. Clearly, the SPD's intention was to discredit the Nazi movement, although the letters neither established any connection between Röhm's sexual orientation and his political outlook nor documented any recruitment of sexual partners among SA subordinates. Röhm's utterances were characterized by the leftist journalist Kurt Tucholsky as "not even unsympathetic,"[5] and one spokesman of the homosexual-rights movement averred that they conveyed a more positive than negative image of Röhm.[6] The SPD's decision to publish these revelations on Röhm's private life might conceivably have been defensible if the party had simply intended to prove that the Nazis were hypocrites, guilty of maintaining a double standard. For, at least publicly, Nazi spokesmen had vehemently demanded that homosexuality be severely punished because of the danger it posed for the German people. The *Völkischer Beobachter* characterized homosexuality as one of the "evil propensities of the Jewish soul," the "typically inferior aberrations of Syrians."[7] Yet at this very time homosexual men were affiliated with the Nazi party, especially the SA and the Hitler Youth (Hitlerjugend),[8] and even though Hitler knew of Röhm's homosexual propensities, he continued to protect him. Prior to 1934, Nazi policy toward homosexuality was indeed characterized by inconsistency, probably due to a lack of consensus among the Nazi leadership.[9]

Homosexual activists such as Adolf Brand, the leader of the Community of the Special (Gemeinschaft der Eigenen), and Kurt Hiller and Richard Linsert, officers of the Scientific-Humanitarian Committee (Wissenschaftlich-humanitäres Komitee), tried to expose this double standard, characterized by Hiller as "hypocrisy that stinks to high heaven."[10] But articles in the socialist press made it abundantly clear that this was not the central issue for the Social Democrats. Instead, the *Münchner Post* shrilly declared that "the most appalling harlotry in the sense of § 175 is making itself at home in the organizations of the Hitler party,"[11] while devoting scant attention to the Nazis' homophobic pronouncements. The Social Democrats attempted and to some extent succeeded in creating the impression that homosexuality was accepted and widespread in Nazi organisations. "This fish stinks from its head. Decay reaches deep into the ranks of the NSDAP," wrote the Social Democratic Reichstag delegate Helmut Klotz. If strong action were not taken, he warned, the German people would fall prey to a "poisoning of national life" and "the demoralization of ethical and moral powers."[12] Such all-male organizations as the SA and the Hitler Youth, he maintained, were exploited by homosexual leaders who abused their powers by forming coteries and practicing favoritism. Any boys and young men thinking of joining the Hitler Youth and the SA were urgently warned that they might become victims of the lusts of Röhm and other SA leaders. This picture of the Nazi movement–clearly a distortion of reality–led one journalist at the *Münchner Post* to conclude that "the moral and physical health of German youth is at risk." The goings-on in the SA, in which youths were at the mercy of the voluptuary Röhm, ought to concern the entire German people, he continued, and it was the duty of the government to take legal steps.[13] The editors of the *Münchner Post* justified their methods by pointing to the dangers "to which the Hitler Youth is exposed, given such an abnormally oriented top leader as Herr Röhm. For youth must be protected from being delivered over to the lusts of such an abnormally oriented person. It is patently the duty of the press to point this out and to warn the public."[14]

The leading Social Democratic daily, *Vorwärts*, appealed to the "healthy sensibility of the people," thus invoking precisely the same terminology utilized by the Nazis. In a blatant ploy to heighten the anxiety of parents whose sons had joined the Nazi movement, the Social Democrats claimed that membership in the SA and the Hitler Youth implied compulsory homosexuality. *Vorwärts* reproached Hitler for extending his protection to "lustful perverts" such as Röhm; this proved "how closely interrelated the Nazi bureaucracy is." And in a thinly veiled reference to the decline of the "decadent" Roman Empire, the commentary continued: "Their system has been unmasked once again. It is the Röhman system that shrinks at nothing and is disgusted by nothing."[15] In another issue of *Vorwärts*, homosexuality was again labelled as an intrinsic part of the Nazi movement. "The conclusion is: Röhm, who lauds the youth of the Black Reichswehr as his sexual delicacy, can and is allowed with his orientation to remain Highest Leader of the similarly oriented Hitler army."[16]

The most important homosexual rights organization in Germany, the Scientific-Humanitarian Committee, which had always relied on the political support of the SPD, had good reason to protest the press campaign against Röhm. "The statements in the *Münchner Post,* hearkening back to the Apostle Paul and employing the entire vocabulary of our conservative-clerical persecutors, could have been printed without changing a word by the most strictly Catholic press."[17] The Committee even felt obliged to send a letter to the SPD executive, inquiring whether the party still supported the campaign against § 175.[18] The party answered in the affirmative but chose not to issue a public statement, because openly supporting homosexual rights would clash with the current tactics of the anti-Nazi campaign of the Social Democrats. For the moment, the party preferred posturing as the guardian of respectability and appealing to widespread prejudice against homosexuality. In fact, it had long since become clear that Social Democratic support for the homosexual movement was by no means inspired by any genuine tolerance toward homosexuality. As one member of parliament had explained at the end of the twenties, most Social Democratic politicians were of the opinion that § 175 should be abolished because punishment was not the proper way to deal with sick men suffering from a "constitutional abnormity."[19] Despite the party leadership's renewed pledge that it did not despise homosexuals, several SPD newspapers persisted in denouncing the fascist movement by exploiting the stereotyped image of Nazi leaders who molested young, innocent boys.[20] As a political tactic in the 1932 electoral struggle, however, the Social Democratic campaign against Röhm proved to be no guarantee of success: the NSDAP gained more votes that year than ever before. In the short term, the only result was that antagonism toward homosexuality was intensified within the Nazi party.[21]

Communist papers commented on the Röhm affair in a similar vein. In the Communist *Antifaschistische Aktion*, one could read that young "SA proletarians" were being victimized by the unnatural lusts of Röhm and other SA leaders.[22] Headlines in the Communist daily *Welt am Abend* accused Röhm of abusing and corrupting unemployed, young workers. The paper flatly maintained that the Nazi party was founded on homosexuality and hypocrisy.[23] By characterizing the Nazis as hypocrites, it should be noted, the Communists were being somewhat more faithful to their principles than the Social Democrats. Although Communist journalists (writing, for example, in the daily *Die rote Fahne*) described homosexuality as fundamentally "unproletarian," they made some effort to clarify that their purpose was not to harm homosexuals but to expose the disparity between the Nazis' policies and practices.

A short time later, however, following the Reichstag fire and the imposition of Nazi dictatorship with the imprisonment of political opponents, the Communists adopted the same course of action as the Social Democrats. This is clearly evidenced by the *Braunbuch über Reichstagsbrand und Hitler-Terror* (Brown Book on the Reichstag Fire and Hitler Terrorism), written by a collective of leading German Communists in exile and published in 1933 by the Comintern's propaganda section in Paris. Translated into twenty languages and distributed on a large scale (some 500,000 copies in 26 countries), the *Braunbuch* aimed to refute Nazi accusations that the Reichstag had been torched by an international communist conspiracy. The arrested arsonist, the Dutchman Marinus van der Lubbe, was in fact a former member of the Dutch Communist Party, but he now called himself an anarchist and had single-handedly started the fire with the intention of motivating German workers to fight the Nazi regime.[24] The *Braunbuch* authors therefore rightly held that there had been no communist conspiracy. At the same time, however, they created a new myth, namely that there had been a conspiracy of homosexual Nazis.

The *Braunbuch* collective distanced itself from Van der Lubbe in a striking manner, focusing on his homosexuality to claim that he had never been a loyal communist–more, that as a Trotskyist and anarchist he was even a traitor to the communist cause. "The task set this book demands that Van der Lubbe's life be illuminated to the final detail. Along with his drive to achieve fame, Van der Lubbe's homosexuality influenced his life decisively. This question is therefore more than a private matter."[25] Van der Lubbe's upbringing in his Dutch hometown Leiden was recounted to show that he had been extremely vulnerable to corrupting, bourgeois influences and that his homosexuality was therefore "unproletarian." The *Braunbuch* collective invented the story that he had developed contacts with Nazi circles while roaming about in Germany, had associated with homosexual SA leaders in Berlin, and had even been Röhm's sexual partner. Van der Lubbe had thereby become a pliable instrument in the hands of certain homosexual conspirators who, with the knowledge of the Nazi leadership, plotted to burn down the Reichstag in order to create a pretext for the arrest of leftist politicians. With this widely publicized account, linking a homosexual orientation with unreliability, betrayal, and violence, the KPD jettisoned even the half-hearted support for homosexual rights that had set it apart from the SPD during the Röhm scandal.[26]

The Communists continued on this course in 1934, when Hitler, with the support of the army, had Röhm and several other SA leaders liquidated–an operation followed by intensified persecution of homosexuals throughout the Third Reich. Hitler and other party bosses covered up their true reasons for eliminating the SA leadership by accusing Röhm and his supporters of engaging in a "homosexual conspiracy."[27] The same Hitler who had once protected Röhm against homophobic attacks from the left was now posturing as a resolute opponent of immoral behavior. Two weeks after the so-called "Night of the Long Knives," Hitler solemnly proclaimed before the Reichstag that any leader in the Nazi Party, the SA, the SS, and the Hitler Youth guilty of homosexual practices would face severe punishment.[28] Röhm's position was assumed by SS Chief Heinrich Himmler, who emerged as the driving force behind the persecution of homosexuals in the Third Reich.

Although the Nazis now revealed their homophobic outlook unambiguously, this by no means led antifascists to discard the stereotype of homosexual fascism. Instead, in a rather self-congratulatory tone, they maintained that everything they had asserted about the sexual aberrations of Röhm and other SA leaders had simply been validated. In an introduction to Röhm's memoirs, published posthumously in France in 1934 to remind readers of his sexual orientation, one of these antifascists wrote: "Blame falls solely on those who knew everything, approved of it, covered it up, tolerated it. . . ."[29] And the author of the *Weißbuch über die Erschießungen des 30. Juni* (White Book on the Shootings of June 30th) on the Röhm putsch paid no attention at all to the persecution of homosexuals. Instead, he was at pains to explain that the NSDAP leadership had decided to eliminate Röhm and his coterie because it wanted to wipe out the homosexual perpetrators of and witnesses to the Reichstag fire.[30]

HOMOSEXUALITY IN THE SOVIET UNION

The homophobia of German Communists was bolstered by developments in the Soviet Union, where "pederasty" (defined as anal intercourse between males) was criminalized in a new law, introduced in December 1933 and promulgated as penal code article 154-a in all Soviet republics in 1934–just a few months before the German "Night of the Long Knives." During the twenties, following the abolition of the tsarist moral laws, homosexual acts between consenting adults had been free of legal sanctions. This recriminalization was part of the Stalinist regime's broad revocation of sexual reforms carried out by the Bolsheviks after the Revolution. Beyond homosexual men, all women were also affected: in 1936, abortion was recriminalized, and during World War II legal obstacles to divorce were introduced.

It remains open to question whether the Soviet government embraced a policy of genuine sexual liberation in the twenties. Sexual reforms affected mainly the social and legal emancipation of women, but it is unclear whether–as some Soviet officials stated– the absence of legal sanctions against homosexuality in the Soviet penal codes of 1922 and 1928 reflected a bona fide state policy of non-interference in sexual matters so long as no minors were involved, nobody was injured, and no one's interests were encroached upon.[31] Several pronouncements of leading communists militate against such an interpretation. Lenin, for example, condemned free love (including homosexuality) as bourgeois and antisocial. In a 1920 conversation with the German Communist Clara Zetkin, Lenin said: "The absence of self-control in one's sexual life is a bourgeois phenomenon. The revolution requires the concentration of all one's forces, and wild sexual excesses are symptomatic of a reactionary outlook. We need minds that are healthy."[32] For Lenin, sexuality was not merely a private affair: "More important than everything, however, is the social side. . . . Love requires two, and a third, a new life can arise. In this fact there is a social interest, a duty toward the collective."[33] Alexandra Kollontai, the leader of the women's section of the Communist Party, also contrasted individualistic, bourgeois morality with the collectivist virtues of a communist utopia. "Love is an important factor of the collective. Love is also part of a full person in a laboring society. But youth must be taught that the joy and sorrow of love can never be the chief content of life. . . . Bourgeois morality demanded: everything for one's beloved; communist morality proclaims: everything for the laboring collective."[34] This approach was shared by the renowned psychologist Aaron Borisovich Zalkind, who wrote in 1925: "If a particular sexual practice has the result of *isolating* an individual in relation to his own class, makes him less efficient in his work or less active in the struggle, it will become necessary to put an end to it. The only kind of sexual activity which can be tolerated is that which will contribute to the full flowering of the collectivist spirit."[35]

While homosexual acts were not punishable in the Soviet Union between 1917 and 1934, this does not mean that they were accepted and tolerated. To begin with, most communist ideologues and politicians were simply indifferent, for they regarded economic issues as more urgent than sexual matters; furthermore, several medical and educational experts viewed homosexuality as a perversion and illness that should be cured. Some of them even advocated legal measures. Finally, whereas homosexuality played an important role in the literature and fine arts of tsarist Russia, it was increasingly suppressed as an artistic theme in the Soviet Union.[36]

The Soviet law against homosexual intercourse was even more severe than the one that had prevailed in tsarist Russia: according to the penal code drafted in 1903, "pederasty" between consulting adults was to be punished with a prison sentence of at least three months; article 154-a of the Stalinist penal code entailed a prison sentence of three to five years.[37] This measure was accompanied by a press campaign decrying homosexuality as a symptom of the "degeneracy of the fascist bourgeoisie" and of "sexual orgies in fascist countries"; one journalist spoke of the "fairies of Goebbels's propaganda ministry."[38] The renowned Soviet writer Maxim Gorky placed homosexual activities on a par with alcoholism, hysteria, and veneral diseases–all typical expressions of bourgeois decadence and fascist perversion. In an article entitled "Against Fascism, for Proletarian Humanism," which appeared not just in the Soviet newspapers *Pravda* and *Isvestiia* but also in the leftist journal *Rundschau über Politik, Wirtschaft und Arbeiterbewegung* published in Basel, Gorky contrasted the purity and healthiness of socialist ethics with the moral corruption of Nazi Germany. While proletarian youths were protected against homosexual seduction in the Soviet Union, according to Gorky, this degenerate capitalist vice was hardly punished in Nazi Germany, where–far from being supressed–it was thriving within the fascist movement itself. And therefore, Gorky added, a new slogan was appropriate: "Exterminate all homosexuals, and fascism will vanish."[39]

By linking counterrevolutionary activities, sabotage, and espionage with homosexuality, it was made into a grave political offense against the Soviet state and society. As the People's Commissar of Justice Krylenko explained in a 1936 speech, homosexuals did not belong to the working class: "Are they working men? Of course not–they are either the dregs of society or remnants of the exploiting classes. [Applause] They don't know what to do with themselves, so they take to pederasty. [Laughter] And besides them, there is another kind of work that goes on in filthy little dens and hiding places, and that is the work of counterrevolution. That is why we take these disorganizers of our new social system, the system we are creating for men and women and working people–we put these gentlemen on trial and we give them sentences of up to five years."[40]

By exploiting the issue of homosexuality for political ends, Communists and other antifascist leftists implemented the same tactic as the Nazis. Both left and right aimed to mobilize public opinion against political adversaries by tarring them with the brush of sexual deviance–rhetoric that was in fact initiated by German Social Democrats and Communists. Later, after coming to power, the Nazis would adopt it on several occasions. Hitler primarily used this charge as a means of eliminating political opponents, both within the party and without: after the SA leadership had been removed, the regime also leveled accusations of homosexuality against Catholic clerics as well as military officers who would not comply with Nazi policies. The leftist stereotype resembled the Nazi image of homosexuality: it was yoked with seduction, clique-formation, intrigue, sabotage, and conspiracy. Rightists and leftists alike attributed the spread of homosexuality to contagion and unfavorable social conditions. The Nazis claimed that homosexuality throve in the "decadent" democracy of the Weimar Republic, when it was protected by Jews as well as Marxists,[41] while the mouthpieces of the Soviet regime maintained that it was a widespread vice in capitalist and fascist countries.[42]

MALE BONDING AND HOMOSEXUALITY

The examples of Social Democratic and Communist aversion to homosexuality in the thirties cited above might lead one to argue that leftist homophobic utterances were perhaps only careless, impulsive statements prompted by political opportunism. This thesis is at best dubious. I would submit that prejudice against homosexuality was part and parcel of socialist thinking on sexuality. Prior to the thirties, the socialists had frequently associated homosexuality with aristocratic and bourgeois decadence and with capitalist exploitation and abuse of power. They tended to regard homosexuality as something belonging to the antisocial domain of the unproductive, uncontrollable, and irrational; as such it had no future. The legal adviser of the KPD, Felix Halle, who advocated sexual reforms in his *Geschlechtsleben und Strafrecht* (Sexual Life and the Penal Law, 1931), exhibited a half-heartedness characteristic of both Communists and Social Democrats. According to Halle, the working class would free itself of bourgeois and Christian prejudices while keeping an open mind in sexual matters. But referring to the fecundity of the proletariat, Halle simultaneously suggested that homosexuality was foreign to its nature. "The working class, far removed . . . from cultivating same-sex inclinations and activities, takes a tolerant approach toward such manifestations of sexual life–insofar as this activity does not transgress the boundaries likewise imposed for social reasons on intercourse between man and woman–because the proletariat feels itself fertile and confident of the future as a collective, as a class. The class struggle of the proletariat includes the effort to fight for and build a new and better world for the offspring slumbering in the gonads of the living generation."[43]

Uneasiness about homosexuality became even more deep-rooted among Social Democrats and Communists in the course of their ideological and moral clash with National Socialism. Some prominent socialist theorists tended to view homosexuality as a sociological and psychological aberration typical of right-wing, nationalistic, and above all fascist circles. The tone was set by the Marxist psychoanalyst and sexual reformer Wilhelm Reich, who, before he was expelled from the KPD in 1933 because of his sexual radicalism, headed the German Reich Association for Proletarian Sexual Politics (Deutscher Reichsverband für proletarische Sexualpolitik) or Sexpol in 1931-32. Reich's influential *Massenpsychologie des Faschismus* (The Mass Psychology of Fascism) appeared in 1933. Here Reich argued that because fascism was authoritarian and patriarchal, it was largely caused by a distortion of "natural" sexuality. According to Reich, bourgeois morality dammed up sexual energy, which would eventually break through in the form of neuroses and sexual aberrations. In fascism, which was only an extension of capitalism, such distortions were exploited for political purposes. For Reich, natural sexuality could only be heterosexual: homosexuality was put on a pathological par with sadism, masochism, and misogyny.

Reich linked homosexuality with Nazism in two ways: he regarded homosexuality as an outcome as well as the breeding ground of fascism. To begin with, he maintained that fascist male bonding was a revival of Greek patriarchalism, which had reduced women to breeding stock and domestic drudges. This male supremacy, he emphasized, was entirely homosexual, and he added: "The same principle governs unconsciously the fascist ideology of the male stratum of leaders. . . ."[44] For Reich, the fascist state was unquestionably a male state founded on homosexuality. In the typically German *Männerbund* (all-male association), which combined male chauvinism, militarism, and contempt for women, homosexual perversion was inevitable. In Reich's view, Nazism clearly resulted in an increase of homosexuality, but he added that fascism was compatible with bourgeois society. Thus he went on to assert in *Massenpsychologie des Faschismus* that the prudish suppression of heterosexuality in bourgeois society was responsible for the appeal of Nazism. Reich argued that in Germany, "natural sexual strivings toward the opposite sex, which seek gratification from childhood on, were replaced in the main by distorted and diverted homosexual feelings. . . ." And commenting on the sex life of youths in Nazi Labor Conscription Camps, he added: "*Sadism originates from ungratified orgastic yearnings.* The facade is inscribed with such names as 'comradeship,' 'honor,' 'voluntary discipline.'" But behind this facade one could discern, according to Reich, a "development of homosexual tendencies and the forming of relationships between boys who had never thought of such things, severe annoyances from homosexual comrades," and an "increase of nervousness, irritability, physical complaints, and various psychic disturbances."[45] One of the most important causes of the spread of homosexuality in Germany, Reich claimed, was the authoritarian, sex-segregated upbringing of boys and girls both before and after 1933. Only socialist sex education could guarantee healthy, genital-oriented heterosexuality, he maintained, and it therefore would have prevented the growth of Nazism. Reich repeatedly linked homosexuality with right-wing political sympathies, and he emphasized that healthy heterosexuality was a necessary condition for openness to socialist ideas.[46]

Even prior to his *Massenpsychologie des Faschismus,* Reich had voiced in a rather simplistic way the Freudian notion that homosexuality was a symptom of "sexual misidentification,"[47] of a psychological disorder and developmental disturbance pathological in nature.[48] In a 1932 brochure on sex education written for the KPD, Reich wrote that homosexual intercourse, which could never be as satisfying as heterosexual coitus, was often the result of unfavorable social conditions in sex-segregated institutions and could be prevented by introducing coeducation.[49] On the other hand, Reich did criticize the contempt and prejudices under which homosexuals suffered, and he opposed the penalization of homosexual acts, including in the Soviet Union.[50] Thus he described in a critical tone the mass arrests of homosexual men in some cities of the Soviet Union and the introduction of article 154-a. But he quickly explained this change in communist policy, maintaining that it was a reaction to a dramatic increase in homosexuality, especially within the army and the navy, which in turn had been caused by the increasing suppression of heterosexuality under the Stalinist regime. According to Reich, the negative attitudes and repressive policies concerning homosexuality in the Soviet Union were also connected to developments in Germany, especially the Röhm affair. "People failed to distinguish the *Männerbund* homosexuality, which, in fact, was at the basis of Röhm's as well as other organizations', from the emergency homosexuality among soldiers, sailors, and prisoners which was due to the lack of heterosexual opportunities." Although the latter form of homosexuality was more easily excused than the former, Reich held both to be undesirable and suggested that they could be reduced "by establishing all necessary prerequisites for a natural love life among the masses."[51] The best way to deal with homosexuality was through social policies that would preclude such disturbances altogether.

Reich viewed homosexuality as a contagious social disease fostered by political and social evils: Christian ascetic morality, capitalism, bourgeois morality, and nationalism, including fascism. In doing so, he presupposed a pure, natural sexuality that was heterosexual and genitally oriented. Referring to the anthropological findings of Malinowski, who had written about the sexual life of the Trobianders on New Guinea, Reich asserted that there was no "unnatural sexual activity" among these unspoiled people. "Such manifestations as sodomy, homosexuality, fetishism, exhibitionism, and masturbation are to the natives only miserable substitutes for the natural genital embrace and therefore bad and worthy only of a fool. The idea that he could be incapable of satisfying his drives pleasurably in a natural way would be particularly offensive to a Trobiander's pride. He despises perversions as he despises one who eats inferior or impure things instead of good clean food."[52] Reich added that any homosexual behavior that might occur among the Trobianders would be attributable solely to the impact of Western Christian and capitalist civilization.[53]

Socialist thinking about sexuality appears to have been influenced more by Freud's psychological approach than by the biological approach of the sexologist Magnus Hirschfeld, the most prominent leader of the homosexual-rights movement in Wilhelminian and Weimar Germany.[54] Hirschfeld's activities as a sexual reformer were disparaged as bourgeois and apolitical in the *Zeitschrift für politische Psychologie und Sexualökonomie*, the journal of Reich's Sexpol movement. Based on a fusion of psychoanalysis and Marxism, Sexpol claimed not only to connect sexual reform with social revolution but also to hold out greater promise of curing and preventing homosexuality. Whereas Hirschfeld's biological theory implied a conciliatory acceptance of sexual perversions as natural variations, truly revolutionary sexual politics would shape the sexual education of children and youths in such a way that homosexuality would diminish and eventually disappear altogether.[55]

Reich's Sexpol movement spurned homosexuality even more vehemently than did Freud, who refused to characterize it as a disease per se. "We are opposed to homosexuality," Sexpol adherents declared, "because (1) homosexual intercourse is never as satisfying and blissful as heterosexual intercourse; (2) the homosexual, without his '*Männerbund*,' is extraordinarily handicapped in modern society, and (3) because psychologically, homosexuality is deeply rooted in fascist ideology." And they emphasized that any such organization as the SA would produce homosexuality: "Strict discipline and subordination under a 'Führer' along with the glorification of unconditional loyalty and devotion to him had to activate the unconscious stirrings toward homosexuality that many boys raised in a bourgeois manner have during puberty and postpuberty. Normally, this time of enthusiastic friendships among boys soon gives way to attraction to a girl. But if purely in terms of time this is encumbered by constant tours of duty, drilling, etc., the boys will be ideologically deformed by an ideology of chastity, by emphasis on the value of 'comradeship'–it therefore comes as no surprise if and when their natural drive takes the wrong direction for lack of a healthy outlet. It comes as no surprise when people who are homosexually oriented from the outset seek to exploit such an institution as the SA by attaining leadership positions and then abusing them for their inclinations. For it is an abuse whenever people capable of a healthy development are artificially pushed into homosexuality. It is even reported that the wives of married men complain about the bad influence coming from the other men."[56]

Reich's views were echoed by several leftist intellectuals in Germany and beyond. Although the editors of the journal of the International Association of Socialist Physicians endorsed Hirschfeld's view that homosexuality was inborn and that § 175 should be repealed, these socialist émigrés simultaneously stressed that homosexual men posed a danger to society because they tend to organize *Männerbünde* in which they exploited their leadership positions to seduce youths.[57] In the sociological *Studien über Autorität und Familie* (Studies on Authority and the Family) published by the renowned Institute for Social Research (Institut für Sozialforschung) in 1936, Erich Fromm linked homosexuality with the sadomasochistic character. And homosexuality among youths was explained not only by referring to unemployment and boredom, but also by analyzing the "nonrevolutionary romanticism" of the bourgeois youth movement. Homoeroticism, widespread among the sons of the bourgeoisie according to these leftist social scientists, was rooted in unresolved conflicts between fathers and sons.[58]

Whereas the independent leftist journal *Die Weltbühne* had criticized the Social Democratic and Communist course of action in the Röhm affair, its successor in exile, the Communist-controlled *Die neue Weltbühne*, published a defense of the criminalization of homosexual acts in the Soviet Union. Justifying the rejection of same-sex behavior by the Russian people and Maxim Gorky, one author, Alexander Bessmerntny, argued that biological or psychological etiologies of homosexuality were totally irrelevant from a political viewpoint. "It is simply a fact that adult homosexuals have formed cliques, which became breeding grounds of active counterrevolution. . . . Whether it is inborn or acquired: homosexuality spawns the *Männerbund*, antisocial in its specific separatism and claim to preeminence, and the *Männerbund* spawns the *Männerbund* intrigue."[59] This reasoning can scarcely be distinguished from the way Hitler commented on the Röhm putsch.

In 1937, a top leader of the Nazi movement of the Sudeten Germans in Czechoslovakia was arrested for a homosexual offense, once again embroiling the party in a scandal that resembled the Röhm affair. *Die neue Weltbühne* carried a series of articles claiming that this episode furnished evidence of the homosexual roots of Nazism. The author, Walther Bartz, referred extensively to the male-bonding theories of the right-winger Hans Blüher. Influenced by Freud, Blüher had caused a sensation in 1912 by publishing a history of the German youth movement, the *Wandervogel*, in which he asserted that homoerotic friendships, fostered by sex-segregated education in Wilhelmine Germany, were essential for the cohesion and popularity of the *Wandervogel*. In Weimar Germany, Blüher turned out to be one of the most important conservative ideologues of the *Männerbund*, propagating a purification of German society under the guidance of all-male brotherhoods, in which members would be bound to one another by homoeroticism and charismatic leadership.[60] Blüher's nationalist ideal of the *Männerbund* was both sexually and politically pathological, Bartz argued, and would inevitably result in a homosexual dictatorship; the Nazi movement provided the final proof.[61] An irony of no little poignance attaches to the coincidence that at the very time when leftists were citing

Blüher to argue that the Nazi movement was homosexual to the core, Heinrich Himmler was also referring to Blüher's theories in a speech before SS officers. Warning that homosexuality could corrupt the National Socialist movement from the inside out, Himmler proposed severe countermeasures.[62]

Another very telling example of the impact of Reich on leftist thinkers is offered by the Dutch liberal anarchist Anton Constandse, renowned because of his radical calls for sexual freedom. During the thirties he authored two books on political aspects of sexuality, describing homosexuality as an unhealthy consequence of sexual segregation in schools, religious institutions, and above all the army. Constandse claimed that "because most National Socialist organizations are typically all-male societies, homosexuality was inevitable. . . . Everybody knows that the sexual abuse of youths was quite common in Röhm's SA."[63] From this he inferred that "the great danger of male bonding, especially in the military, is indeed homosexuality."[64] The antifascist journal *Het Fundament*, published in Holland, also characterized homosexuality as typical of fascism, although in a different way than Constandse: it was claimed that homosexuals' strong narcissistic and antisocial propensities made them especially susceptibile to Nazism.[65]

This sort of argument did not end with the 1930s; it handily survived World War II. In 1945, a Jewish émigré in England, Samuel Igra, published a book on "Germany's national vice" in which male bonding in German history was associated with homosexual vice and cruelty. Similar interpretations had been offered earlier by antifascist leftists, but Igra introduced a new element by positing a causal link between the Nazi persecution of Jews and the strong homosexual tendencies of the National Socialist movement. Igra argued that because Jewish religion and culture, like Christianity, had always denounced homosexuality uncompromisingly, the Jews were the natural enemies of homosexual Nazi leaders such as Hitler and Röhm. "I think it is reasonable," Igra concluded, ". . . to hold that the psychological forces that let loose the sadistic orgies of the concentration camps, the mass murders in Germany, . . . and the subsequent atrocities in the occupied countries may be attributed mainly to one source and that this source is the moral perversion which was rampant among the Nazi leaders and which had its typical embodiment in Hitler himself."[66]

Far from chronicling the persecution of homosexuals in the Third Reich and analyzing Nazi homophobia, several postwar historians of fascism preferred to speculate on the homosexual tendencies of Hitler and other Nazi leaders.[67] Translated into English, Reich's book on fascism was widely read in the sixties. Although Reich made some revisions, his statements on homosexuality remained unaltered, and this was also the case for reprints of his other books. The views of Reich and Fromm were also echoed in the sixties by Theodor W. Adorno, representing the Frankfurt School of critical theory, and by the German sociologist Reimut Reiche, an activist critical of the Frankfurt School's ivory-tower academicism, both of whom suggested that homosexuality entailed a penchant for law and order, as well as for sadomasochism and misogyny.[68] Even more remarkably, the association of fascism and male homosexuality was still alive in the seventies and espoused by writers inspired by Reich. It is abundantly evident, for example, in a frequently cited book on women and fascism authored by the Italian Communist and feminist Maria Antonietta Macciocchi. Her book bears the stamp of Reich's views, and more than once she recounts the supression of women in fascism and in the same breath speaks of homosexuality. The subordination of women in the "capitalist-patriarchal" society, according to Macciocchi, reached a high point in the extreme misogyny of "the brotherhood of male chauvinist fascists and homosexual Nazis."[69] Writing on the erotic aestheticism of Nazism, Susan Sontag explained the popularity of sadomasochism in the gay subculture of the seventies simply as an "eroticizing of Nazism." According to her, "there is a natural link" between homosexual sadomasochism and fascism.[70] The stereotype was also made visible in such films as Luchino Visconti's *The Damned* (1969), Bernardo Bertolucci's *The Conformist* (1971), Pier Paolo Pasolini's *Salò or the 120 Days of Sodom* (1975), and Volker Schlöndorff's *The Tin Drum* (1978, based on the 1959 novel by Günter Grass). Pasolini in particular used clichés borrowed from psychoanalysis to connect masculinity, sadism, and homosexuality.[71]

LEFTIST MORALS

To prevent misunderstandings, it must be emphasized that critical comments on these leftist authors are by no means a denial of the importance of the phenomenon of the *Männerbund* in any analysis of fascism and homosexuality. But the leftist arguments are one-sided and simplistic. The Nazi movement, especially before 1934, may have held an attraction for gay men because of its supposedly anti-bourgeois doctrines, the male comradeship in such organizations as the army, the SA, the SS, and the Hitler Youth, and the glorification of youth, masculinity, physical prowess, and beauty.[72] But this does not necessarily mean that the fascist *Männerbund* was founded on homosexual bonds: although they can overlap, the concepts of the "homosocial" and the "homosexual" cannot simply be conflated. Instead, one should argue the other way around: the homophobia of the Nazi regime and its persecution of homosexual men can largely be explained by the alarm over homosexual practices in all-male organizations felt by some important Nazi leaders, especially SS Chief Heinrich Himmler. After the liquidation of Röhm, § 175 was tightened in 1935, the number of convictions rose sharply, a Central Reich Office to Combat Homosexuality and Abortion (Reichszentrale zur Bekämpfung der Homosexualität und Abtreibung) was established, and several measures designed to prevent homosexual contacts were introduced, especially in the army and Nazi organizations. Alongside a range of medical remedies, a variety of severe penalties (including concentration-camp detention) was introduced, mainly because the Nazis believed that homosexuality was a contagious social disease which could easily spread in all-male groups.[73] In light of these measures, the standpoint of leftist antifascist intellectuals in the thirties is disturbing, for they largely played down the persecution of homosexuals—or even ignored it completely.

Apart from the spokesmen of the Scientific-Humanitarian Committee,[74] only a few individuals raised their voices against the political use of homosexuality in the antifascist camp: deserving of mention are the journalist Kurt Tucholsky and some of his collegues at *Die Weltbühne*,[75] the Dutch writer Jef Last,[76] and the German writer Klaus Mann. A 1934 essay by Klaus Mann entitled "Die Linke und das 'Laster' " (" 'Vice' and the Left") is particularly noteworthy.[77] Here Mann criticized the leftist ploy of automatically equating the fascist *Männerbund* with homosexuality. While acknowledging that male bonding played a significant role in the Nazi movement, Mann argued that it was not unique to fascism: the example of the American poet Walt Whitman provided evidence that the ideals of male bonding and friendship could also have a democratic character. He also referred to the German poet Stefan George, whose glorification of the *Männerbund* was aristocratic but definitely not fascist. Curiously, Mann did not refer to Blüher, although he had praised his work on the *Männerbund* in the twenties. Mann did not elaborate further on this issue, but I think he raised an important point, one that might further explain the negative opinions on male homosexuality in leftist circles.

It is significant that Klaus Mann's polemical essay, in which he characterized homosexuals as the "Jews of the antifascists," was ignored by the German exile community and sank into oblivion until the manuscript was rediscovered and reprinted, first under the title "Homosexuality and Fascism" in a 1969 collection of essays and again in the seventies as a pamphlet.[78] At the time of this article's 1934 publication, Klaus Mann–the openly homosexual son of Thomas Mann–was about to emerge as one of the leading intellectuals of the German antifascist exiles in Europe. His essay on homosexuality and Nazism bears testimony to his courage. Broadly speaking, homosexuals were tolerated in the antifascist camp only if they remained in the closet. For most of them, criticizing the prejudices of their heterosexual comrades in the struggle against Nazism was inconceivable, which makes Klaus Mann's essay exceptional. Although by no means a profound analysis, Mann's article is important both as a document testifying to the homophobic atmosphere in leftist circles at that time and also because of Mann's attempt, however tentative, to critique it.

The leftist aversion to homosexuality (and in fact to all sexuality that was not conventional, i.e., monogamous and heterosexual) had dire consequences for those antifascist activists who were homosexuals themselves. Their only choices were to go back into the closet with a negative self-image or, even worse, to pay lip service to leftist morals. Studies by Jörn Meve and Manfred Herzer of literary works written by German writers in exile reveal that far from being restricted to heterosexuals, the stereotype of Nazi homosexuality was current even among some homosexual antifascists.[79] Such semidocumentary literary works as Ludwig Renn's *Vor grossen Wandlungen* (Before Great Transformations, 1936) and Hans Siemsen's *Hitler Youth* (1940), for example, depicted perfidious homosexual Nazis who take advantage of their leadership positions to seduce innocent boys.[80] These homosexuals were polymorphously perverse and as such also violent, promiscuous, and hypersexual. Good homosexuals were ascetic or at least monogamous, were discreet about their sexual orientation, and were ready to sacrifice any personal life to the antifascist cause. Even Klaus Mann, who was courageous enough to expose the homophobia of his fellow antifascists, could not escape tormenting doubts about his own sexual proclivities. In his second autobiography, *Der Wendepunkt* (The Turning Point, 1949), he wrote rather guiltily about his sexual experiences in the Turkish baths during a 1937 visit to fascist Hungary: "To be sure, I know–and was not so frivolous as to forget it in frivolous Budapest–: it's not very far from the animalistic, which I like, to the bestial, which I abhor. Even if it's true that satisfying one's urges deflects from destructive impulses or transforms them into positive and libidinous ones, it cannot be denied that unfettered sexuality has a grievous tendency to degenerate into the sadistic and destructive. The mass orgy I enjoy in my half ironic-bitter, half sweet-vulgar way contains the seed of mass murder; every frenzy is a potential blood lust, a fact with which I would like not to revoke my paean to lust but at least to modify it a seemly way."[81]

As a homosexual and one of the leading intellectuals among the exiles, Klaus Mann knew how it felt to face moral pressure from his fellow antifascists. One of his political friends, for example, the writer Hermann Kesten, who gave him the idea for his famous novel *Mephisto* (1936), proposed to him that it should be a novel about "a homosexual careerist in the Third Reich, . . . a satire of certain homosexual figures."[82] Although the protagonist in *Mephisto* was modelled on the homosexual actor Gustaf Gründgens, Mann transformed him into a heterosexual masochist. As far as his own lifestyle was concerned, Klaus Mann was forced to go on the defensive. In the twenties, he had lightheartedly celebrated homoeroticism, decadence, and hedonism. In his first autobiography, *Kind dieser Zeit* (Child of These Times, 1930), he wrote that he preferred "extravagance and eccentricity to moderation, soberness, and temperance; irrational intoxication to rational control and restraint."[83] When he turned to political activism after leaving Germany in 1933, his advocacy of hedonism was supplanted by a far more reticent, cautious attitude, as can been seen in the novels written in exile, such as *Symphonie pathétique* (1935) and *Der Vulkan* (The Volcano, 1939), as well as his essay on the Röhm affair.

It is striking, firstly, that he chose not to publish this essay in *Die Sammlung* (The Collection), the journal he himself edited in Amsterdam, but instead in a rather obscure Prague journal. According to Mann, *Die Sammlung* was to be a broad-based forum for antifascists, which also meant that prejudice against sexual orientation would not constitute grounds for refusing any article. However, he appears to have expressed to a German Communist his willingness not to stir up any disputes about this subject.[84] Secondly, in his essay he described homosexuality only as an innate phenomenon, not as an overtly practiced lifestyle. And by describing socialist humanism as an alternative to fascism, he defended homosexuality only in abstract political terms, emphasizing that it could be useful to the community and should therefore be integrated into a future socialist society. He had little to say, however, on how this integration could be implemented. Like other homosexual antifascist activists, he was ostracized on the grounds that he was predisposed to place a higher priority on his personal interests as a member of a sexual minority than on the resistance to Nazism.[85] In leftist circles, homosexual rights were scarcely acknowledged to be a valid political issue.

CONCLUSION

Homophobia was as deeply ingrained among leftist antifascists as it was in Social Democratic and Communist policy. There was no place for homosexual emancipation in socialist politics of the thirties, for, on the whole, Social Democratic and Communist parties emphasized their moral superiority, i.e., conventionality. In the struggle against Nazism they did not hesitate to appeal to widely held prejudices against homosexuality. A few exceptions aside, a sound political analysis of sexuality was lacking in Marxist and Social Democratic thought. Socialists generally considered sexuality a minor issue subordinate to economic considerations, and if it was discussed at all, current ideas about natural and healthy sexuality were the norm; they did not break with bourgeois respectability. From a socialist perspective, the body was primarily a tool for labor and production; lust was suspect as an antisocial force, and sexual liberation as a cause in itself could only be viewed as a symptom of bourgeois decadence and selfish individualism. For mainstream communism, even Reich and his Sexpol movement were on the wrong track, because they held sexual revolution to be fully as important as economic revolution. To the extent that Communists and, to a lesser degree, Social Democrats criticized the liberal public/private dichotomy, their critique was counterproductive. Despite the good intentions of some individual Communists, rejection of the "bourgeois'" separation of the personal from the political did not result in sexual liberation, but, on the contrary, as the Soviet Union demonstrated, in a total subordination of sexuality to collectivist politics. This leftist politicizing of sexuality was detrimental to the social position of homosexuals.

Especially during the struggle against Nazism, homosexual practices increasingly rankled many leftists. In their view, fascism proved how easily sexual instincts could be distorted, manipulated, and employed for atrocious political ends. Using clichéd labels and simplistic explanations borrowed from psychiatry and especially from psychoanalysis, they sought to expose Nazism as a pathological and irrational political system, in which barbaric passions reigned and brutish lusts were satisfied by violence and destruction. For Reich and many other antifascists, it seemed easy to prove that fascism was a sign of perversion, sadism, and masochism, from which it was only a small step to homosexual vice. To counter the presumed sexual immorality of the Nazis, the antifascist left stressed its own enlightened rationality and moral purity, constructing an ethical system that rigorously excluded homosexuality.

AUTHOR NOTE

Harry Oosterhuis is Assistant Professor of History at the Rijksuniversiteit Limburg in Maastricht. He has published books on the history of Catholicism and homosexuality in the Netherlands and on the early homosexual movement and male bonding in pre-Nazi Germany. At present he is researching the work of the German-Austrian psychiatrist Richard von Krafft-Ebing (1840-1902).

The author is indebted to James Steakley for helpful comments on earlier drafts of this essay and bibliographical information.

NOTES

1. See Wilfried U. Eissler, *Arbeiterparteien und Homosexuellenfrage: Zur Sexualpolitik von SPD und KPD in der Weimarer Republik* (Berlin: Rosa Winkel, 1980).

2. Two years earlier, Wilhelm Hillebrand's brochure *Herunter mit der Maske! Erlebnisse hinter den Kulissen der NSDAP* (Berlin: by the author, 1929) revealing the homosexual orientation of a number of prominent Nazis had already been circulated in Berlin. See *Mitteilungen des Wissenschaftlich-humanitären Komitees*, no. 19 (1929): 161.

3. Herbert Heinersdorf (i.e., Richard Linsert), "Akten zum Falle Röhm (I. Teil)," *Mitteilungen des Wissenschaftlich-humanitären Komitees*, no. 31 (1931): 349-68.

4. Paraphrased from Röhm's memoirs which were published posthumously in 1934: Ernst Röhm, *Die Memoiren des Stabschef Röhm* (Saarbrücken: Uranus-Verlag, 1934), pp. 163, 196, 200. Two years earlier, Röhm's letters were published in the Social Democratic newspaper *Welt am Montag* (March 7, 1932) and other periodicals as well as in a brochure widely distributed in Germany; see Helmut Klotz, *Der Fall Röhm* (Berlin-Tempelhof: by the author, 1932).

5. Ignaz Wrobel [i.e., Kurt Tucholsky], "Bemerkungen: Röhm," *Die Weltbühne*, no. 17 (1932): 641.

6. Herbert Heinersdorf (i.e., Richard Linsert), "Akten zum Falle Röhm (II. Teil)," *Mitteilungen des Wissenschaftlich-humanitären Komitees*, no. 33 (1932): 395.

7. *Mitteilungen des Wissenschaftlich-humanitären Komitees*, no. 28 (1930): 272, and Burkhard Jellonek, *Homosexuelle unter dem Hakenkreuz: Die Verfolgung von Homosexuellen im Dritten Reich* (Paderborn: Ferdinand Schöningh, 1990), pp. 51-56.

8. ***, "Nationalsozialismus und Inversion," *Mitteilungen des Wissenschaftlich-humanitären Komitees*, no. 32 (1932): 340-45; Adolf Brand, "Abwehr und Angriff," *Eros*, no. 3 (1930): 20-21; SS-Standartenführer X, "Warnung," *Die neue Weltbühne*, no. 9 (1936): 578-81; Manfred Herzer, "Hinweise auf das schwule Berlin in der Nazizeit," in *Eldorado: Homosexuelle Frauen und Männer in Berlin 1800-1950: Geschichte, Alltag und Kultur*, ed. Michael Bollé (Berlin: Frölich & Kaufmann, 1984), pp. 44-47; Jellonnek, pp. 85-94.

9. Jellonnek, pp. 68-72. In 1932, for example, NSDAP Reichstag delegates wrote to the League for Human Rights that they were unable at the moment to

formulate their views on homosexuality and that they had to wait for directives of the party leadership; see Hans-Georg Stümke and Rudi Finkler, *Rosa Winkel, Rosa Listen: Homosexuelle und "Gesundes Volksempfinden" von Auschwitz bis heute* (Reinbek bei Hamburg: Rowohlt, 1981), p. 141. Later that year, the NSDAP did publish its views on moral law but without broaching the issue of homosexuality; see Erhard Vismar, "Perversion und Verfolgung unter dem deutschen Faschismus," in *Seminar: Gesellschaft und Homosexualität*, ed. Rüdiger Lautmann (Frankfurt a.M.: Suhrkamp, 1977), p. 309. Homosexual cafés closed early in 1933 once Hitler was appointed chancellor were reopened that summer, probably at the instigation of Röhm; see Rudolf Diels, *Lucifer ante portas . . . es spricht der erste Chef der Gestapo* (Stuttgart: Deutsche Verlagsanstalt, 1950), p. 129. Although the library of Magnus Hirschfeld's Institut für Sexualwissenschaft (Institute for Sexology) was publicly burned and Hirschfeld himself escaped arrest only because he was abroad, such well-known advocates of same-sex love as Adolf Brand and Hans Blüher were not arrested (although their writings were suppressed). Brand's publishing house was raided by SA storm troopers, his journals, books, and photos confiscated. Even after 1934, some homosexual artists, among them the famous actor Gustaf Gründgens, enjoyed the protection of Nazi functionaries; see Herzer, pp. 44-47.

10. Kurt Hiller, "Antwort an ∗∗∗," *Mitteilungen des Wissenschaftlich-humanitären Komitees*, no. 32 (1932): 348. See also Adolf Brand, "Politische Galgenvögel. Ein Wort zum Falle Röhm," *Eros*, no. 2 (1931): 1-3; "Homosexualität und Nationalsozialismus," *Mitteilungen des Wissenschaftlich-humanitären Komitees*, no. 20 (1929): 161; and Kurt Hiller, "Ein anonymer Brief," *Die neue Weltbühne*, no. 19 (1936): 581-86.

11. Cited in *Mitteilungen des Wissenschaftlich-humanitären Komitees*, no. 31 (1931): 351.

12. Quoted by Jellonnek, p. 67.

13. Cited in *Mitteilungen des Wissenschaftlich-humanitären Komitees*, no. 32 (1932): 351, 355.

14. *Mitteilungen des Wissenschaftlich-humanitären Komitees*, no. 34 (1934): 419.

15. "Röhm bestätigt," *Vorwärts* 49.117 (March 10, 1932): 2.

16. "Die Röhm-Briefe echt!" *Vorwärts* 49.157 (April 4, 1932): 1-2.

17. "Kundgebung des Vorstandes des WHK an die deutsche Presse betr.: den Fall Röhm," *Mitteilungen des Wissenschaftlich-humanitären Komitees*, no. 31 (1931): 316. See also "Der Fall Röhm," *Mitteilungen des Wissenschaftlich-humanitären Komitees*, no. 32 (1932): 369-70.

18. *Mitteilungen des Wissenschaftlich-humanitären Komitees*, no. 33 (1932): 372-75.

19. Eissler (see note 1), p. 75.

20. *Mitteilungen des Wissenschaftlich-humanitären Komitees*, no. 33 (1932): 376-80.

21. Jellonnek, pp. 68-72.

22. Ibid., p. 113.

23. Quoted in *Mitteilungen des Wissenschaftlich-humanitären Komitees*, no. 34 (1933): 423.

24. See Martin Schouten, *Rinus van der Lubbe 1909-1934* (Amsterdam: De Bezige Bij, 1986).

25. *Braunbuch über Reichstagsbrand und Hitler-Terror* (Basel: Universum-Bücherei, 1933), p. 53. The English-language edition of this book toned down the language considerably: "Enquiries in Leyden have definitely established the fact that he [Van der Lubbe] was homosexual. This is of great importance for his later history. . . . Van der Lubbe's homosexual connections with the National Socialist leaders and his material dependence on them made him obedient and willing to carry out the incendiary's part." *Brown Book of the Hitler Terror and the Burning of the Reichstag*, prepared by the World Committee for the Victims of German Fascism (New York: Alfred A. Knopf, 1933), pp. 46, 52.

26. Ibid., pp. 44-56. A second *Braunbuch* appeared the following year: *Braunbuch II: Dimitroff contra Göring: Enthüllungen über die wahren Brandstifter* (Paris: Éditions du Carrefour, 1934). Leftist political friends of Van der Lubbe founded an "International Van der Lubbe Commitee" to defend him as a fighter for the socialist cause and published the *Roodboek Van der Lubbe en de Rijksdagbrand* (Amsterdam: Internationaal Uitgeversbedrijf, [1933]). Here Van der Lubbe's homosexuality as well as his involvement in "the muggy, pestilential atmosphere among Nazi homosexuals" (p. 69) were denied, but this did not dispel the image created by the first *Braunbuch*. See Martin Schouten, *Rinus van der Lubbe 1909-1934*. The *Roodboek* has also appeared in German as *Marinus van der Lubbe und der Reichstagsbrand*, trans. and ed. Josh van Soer (Hamburg: Edition Nautilus, 1983).

27. [Otto Strasser], *Weißbuch über die Erschießungen des 30. Juni* (Paris: Éditions du Carrefour, 1934), p. 9.

28. Franz Seidler, *Prostitution, Homosexualität, Selbstverstümmelung: Probleme der deutschen Sanitätsführung 1939-1945* (Neckargemünd: Kurt Vowinkel, 1977), p. 204.

29. *Die Memoiren des Stabschefs Röhms*, p. 18.

30. *Weißbuch über die Erschießungen des 30. Juni*, p. 105.

31. See *Mitteilungen des Wissenschaftlich-humanitären Komitees*, no. 18 (1928): 146-47; John Lauritsen and David Thorstad, *The Early Homosexual Rights Movement, 1864-1935* (New York: Times Change, 1974), pp. 62-64. Following Wilhelm Reich, *The Sexual Revolution: Toward a Self-Governing Character Structure*, trans. Therese Pol (New York: Farrar, Straus & Giroux, 1957), pp. 208-11, various authors have argued that toleration and even emancipation of homosexuality was part of Soviet sexual policy in the twenties. For example, see Joachim S. Hohmann, "Zum rechtlichen und sozialen Problem der Homosexualität," in *Sexualforschung und -politik in der Sowjetunion seit 1917*, ed. J. S. Hohmann (Frankfurt a.M.: Peter Lang, 1990), pp. 270-86; Gudrun Hauer, "Homosexualität in der Sowjetunion—Eine historische Analyse," *Rosa Liebe unterm roten Stern: Zur Lage der Lesben und Schwulen in Osteuropa*, ed. HOSI Wien/Auslandsgruppe (Vienna: Homosexuelle Initiative; Hamburg: Frühlings Erwachen, 1984),

pp. 49-68; and David Greenberg, *The Construction of Homosexuality* (Chicago: University of Chicago Press, 1988), p. 440.

32. Quoted by Mikhail Stern and August Stern, *Sex in the USSR* (New York: Times Books, 1980), pp. 32-33.

33. Clara Zetkin, *Erinnerungen an Lenin* (1924-25), in C. Zetkin, *Ausgewählte Reden und Schriften*, vol. 3: *Auswahl aus den Jahren 1924 bis 1933* (Berlin: Dietz, 1960), p. 140.

34. Cited by Richard Linsert, *Marxismus und freie Liebe* (1931; reprint Hamburg: Libertäre Assoziation, 1982), p. 14.

35. Quoted by Stern and Stern, p. 34.

36. Charlotte Wolff, *Magnus Hirschfeld: A Portrait of a Pioneer in Sexology* (London: Hutchinson, 1986), p. 261; Hauer, p. 65; Simon Karlinsky, "Russia's Gay Literature and Culture: The Impact of the October Revolution," in *Hidden from History: Reclaiming the Gay and Lesbian Past*, ed. Martin Bauml Duberman, Martha Vicinus, and George Chauncey, Jr. (New York: New American Library, 1989), pp. 347-64.

37. Hohmann, pp. 271, 278.

38. Wilhelm Reich, *The Sexual Revolution*, p. 210.

39. Maxim Gorki, "Gegen den Faschismus: Proletarischer Humanismus," *Rundschau über Politik, Wirtschaft und Arbeiterbewegung*, no. 34 (1934): 1298.

40. Quoted by Ben de Jong, "'An Intolerable Kind of Moral Degeneration': Homosexuality in the Soviet Union," *Review of Socialist Law*, no. 4 (1982): 342.

41. Cited in *Mitteilungen des Wissenschaftlich-humanitären Komitees*, no. 20 (1929): 161.

42. The second edition of the *Great Soviet Encyclopedia*, published in 1952, maintained that the occurrence of homosexuality was related to social conditions. "In capitalist society homosexuality is a widely spread phenomenon. . . . Drunkenness and also sexual impressions from early childhood are of great significance in the development of homosexuality. . . . The large majority of the people who practice homosexuality cease this perversion as soon as they find themselves in an environment which is socially beneficial. . . . In Soviet society, with its healthy moral climate, homosexuality is considered a shameful and criminal perversion. . . . In bourgeois countries where homosexuality is a symptom of the moral dissolution of the ruling classes, it is in practice not punishable." Quoted by de Jong, p. 343.

43. *Mitteilungen des Wissenschaftlich-humanitären Komitees*, no. 30 (1931): 310-13.

44. Wilhelm Reich, *Massenpsychologie des Faschismus* (Copenhagen: Verlag für Sexualpolitik, 1933), p. 139.

45. Cited in the English translation: *The Mass Psychology of Fascism* (New York: Farrar Straus & Giroux, 1971), pp. 192, 194; in the German edition of 1933, pp. 259-60, 262.

46. For example, see Wilhelm Reich, "What is Class Consciousness?" in idem, *Sex-Pol: Essays, 1929-1934*, ed. Lee Baxandall (New York: Vintage, 1972), p. 297.

47. Wilhelm Reich, *Der triebhafte Charakter* (Leipzig: Internationaler Psychoanalytischer Verlag, 1925), new edition 1975, p. 21. The German is "geschlechtliche Fehlidentifizierung."

48. Wilhelm Reich, *Der sexuelle Kampf der Jugend* (Copenhagen: Verlag für Sexualpolitik, 1932), p. 74.

49. Ibid., p. 75.

50. Ibid., p. 76. See also Julius Epstein, "Das neue Homosexuellen-Gesetz Sowjet-Rußlands," *Zeitschrift für politische Psychologie und Sexualökonomie* 2.1 (1935): 50-51. A critique of Soviet sexual policy in the thirties was offered by Wilhelm Reich, "Der Kampf um die neue Moral: Die Bremsung der Sexualrevolution in der USSR," *Zeitschrift für politische Psychologie und Sexualökonomie* 2.6 (1935): 145-59.

51. Reich, *The Sexual Revolution*, pp. 210-11; German-language edition of 1936: *Die Sexualität im Kulturkampf: Zur sozialistischen Umstrukturierung des Menschen* (Copenhagen: Verlag für Sexualpolitik, 1936), pp. 189-90.

52. Wilhelm Reich, *The Invasion of Compulsory Sex-Morality* (New York: Farrar, Straus & Giroux, 1971), pp. 31-32; German-language edition: *Der Einbruch der Sexualmoral* (Copenhagen: Verlag für Sexualpolitik, 1935), p. 21.

53. Ibid.

54. Manfred Herzer, "Wilhelm Reich und Magnus Hirschfeld–gescheiterte Konzepte sozialistischer Sexualpolitik und Faschismus," *Mitteilungen der Magnus-Hirschfeld-Gesellschaft*, no. 2 (1983): 9-16.

55. J[onathan] H[øegh] Leunbach, "Von der bürgerlichen Sexualreform zur revolutionären Sexualpolitik," *Zeitschrift für politische Psychologie und Sexualökonomie* 2.1 (1935): 14-25. See also Ernst Parell, "Unterschiede zwischen liberalischer Sexualreform und revolutionärer Sexualpolitik," *Zeitschrift für politische Psychologie und Sexualökonomie* 2.6 (1936): 99-103.

56. "Sex-Pol-Praxis: Wie sollen wir zur Frage der Homosexualität in der SA Stellung nehmen?" *Zeitschrift für politische Psychologie und Sexualökonomie* 1.3-4 (1934): 271-72. See also Julius Epstein, "Das Dritte Reich und die Homosexuellen," *Zeitschrift für politische Psychologie und Sexualökonomie* 2.3 (1935): 178-81.

57. See "Zum Problem der Homosexualität," *Internationales Ärztliches Bulletin: Zentralorgan der Internationalen Vereinigung Sozialistischer Ärzte* 4.9-10 (1937): 114-16.

58. *Studien über Autorität und Familie*, ed. Institut für Sozialforschung (Paris: Félix Alcan, 1936), pp. 125-27, 429, 669-705.

59. Alexander Bessmerntny, "Sexualität im Kulturkampf," *Die neue Weltbühne*, no. 31 (1937): 970-73.

60. Hans Blüher, *Die deutsche Wandervogelbewegung als erotisches Phänomen: Ein Beitrag zur Erkenntnis der sexuellen Inversion* (Berlin: Weise, 1912); idem, *Die Rolle der Erotik in der männlichen Gesellschaft: Eine Theorie der menschlichen Staatsbildung nach Wesen und Wert*, 2 vols. (Jena: Diederichs, 1917-18).

61. Walther Bartz, "Mann-männliche Politik," *Die neue Weltbühne*, no. 44 (1937): 1375-80. See also *Die neue Weltbühne*, no. 18 (1937): 544-48; no. 42,

pp. 1310-16; no. 46, pp. 1447-49. In Holland this affair was discussed in a similar way in a leftist journal: J. Pront, "De rol der homo-sexualiteit in de nationalismen," *Vrede. Orgaan van de Stichting Vredes Studie Bureau*, nos. 7-8 (1938): 106-8.

62. Heinrich Himmler, "Bevölkerungspolitische Rede vor SS-Gruppenführern über die 'Frage der Homosexualität' und ein 'natürliches Verhältnis der Geschlechter zueinander'" (1937), in *Heinrich Himmler: Geheimreden 1933-1945 und andere Ansprachen*, ed. Bradley F. Smith (Frankfurt a.M.: Propyläen, 1974), pp. 93-104.

63. Anton L. Constandse, *Sexuele nood en fascisme* (The Hague: De Albatros, 1935), pp. 7-8.

64. Anton L. Constandse, *Sexualiteit en levensleer: de sexuele en politieke psychologie van Dr. W. Reich* (Amsterdam: De ploeger, 1939), p. 33.

65. Editorial, "Soma-Paradijs of Socialisme," *Het Fundament* 10 (1935): 5.

66. Samuel Igra, *Germany's National Vice* (London: Quality Press, 1945), p. 71.

67. For examples, see Richard Plant, *The Pink Triangle: The Nazi War against Homosexuals* (New York: Henry Holt, 1986), pp. 13-19; Frank Rector, *The Nazi Extermination of Homosexuals* (New York: Stein and Day, 1981). After the war, even some well-known German homosexuals fostered the myth that many leading Nazis were homosexual. See Manfred Herzer, "Die schwarze Maria und der Männerbund: Ein Nazimärchen," *Capri: Zeitschrift für schwule Geschichte*, no. 2 (1987): 2-5; Hans Blüher, *Die Rede des Aristophanes: Prolegomena zu einer Soziologie des Menschgeschlechts* (Hamburg: Kala-Verlag, 1966), pp. 64-71.

68. See Theodor W. Adorno, "Sexualtabus und Recht heute," in *Sexualität und Verbrechen: Beiträge zur Strafrechtsreform*, ed. Fritz Bauer et al. (Frankfurt a.M.: Fischer, 1963), pp. 307-9; this essay also appeared in Adorno's *Eingriffe* (Frankfurt a.M.: Suhrkamp, 1963). See also Reimut Reiche, *Sexuality and Class Struggle*, trans. Susan Bennett (New York: Prager, 1971), p. 118; Reiche's book appeared originally as *Sexualität und Klassenkampf: Zur Abwehr repressiver Entsublimierung* (Frankfurt a.M.: Neue Kritik, 1968).

69. Maria Antonietta Macciocchi, *Vrouwen en fascisme* (Amsterdam: Feministische Uitgeverij Sara, 1977), pp. 29, 71, 119. This work appeared originally as *La donna "nera": "Consenso" femminile e fascismo* (Milan: Feltrinelli Economica, 1976).

70. Susan Sontag, "Fascinating Fascism," *Under the Sign of Saturn* (New York: Vintage, 1981), p. 103.

71. See Gert Hekma, "De Sade in Salò of Pasoloni's laatste reis," in *Tegenlicht op Pasolini*, ed. Leo Dullaart et al. (Amsterdam: De Woelrat, 1984), pp. 41-54.

72. George L. Mosse, "Homosexualität und Faschismus in Frankreich," *Capri: Zeitschrift für schwule Geschichte*, no. 2 (1987): 15-21.

73. I have argued this in greater detail in "Male Bonding and the Persecution of Homosexual Men in Nazi Germany," *Amsterdams Sociologisch Tijdschrift*, no. 4 (1991): 27-45, and in *Homosexuality and Male Bonding in Pre-Nazi Germany: The Youth Movement, the Gay Movement, and Male Bonding Before Hitler's Rise* (New York: Harrington Park Press, 1991) (published simultaneously as *Journal of Homosexuality* 22.1-2), pp. 247-58.

74. *Mitteilungen des Wissenschaftlich-humanitären Komitees*, no. 20 (1929): 161; no. 31 (1931): 315-16; Kurt Hiller, "Rückschritte der Sowjet-Union," *Sozialistische Warte*, no. 14 (1936): 326-31.

75. "Antworten: Mucker," *Die Weltbühne*, no. 29 (1931): 117; Tucholsky (see note 5), p. 641; Hermann Britt, "Bemerkungen: Ernst Röhm," *Die neue Weltbühne*, no. 27 (1934): 855-57.

76. Jef Last, "Een zonde tegen het bloed," *Het Fundament: Onafhankelijk Tijdschrift voor Politiek, Economie, Cultuur en Literatuur*, no. 3 (1935): 35-39; see also the Dutch sexologist Coen van Emde Boas, "Het probleem der verdringing," *Het Fundament*, no. 10 (1935): 35-47.

77. Klaus Mann, "Die Linke und das 'Laster,' " *Europäische Hefte*, nos. 36-37 (1934): 675-78.

78. Klaus Mann, "Homosexualität und Fascismus," *Heute und morgen: Schriften zur Zeit*, ed. Martin Gregor-Dellin (Munich: Nymphenburger Verlagsbuchhandlung, 1969), pp. 130-37; reprinted in Klaus Mann and Kurt Tucholsky, *Homosexualität und Faschismus*, 3rd. rev. ed. (Hamburg: Frühlings Erwachen, 1990), pp. 5-13.

79. See Jörn Meve, *"Homosexuelle Nazis." Ein Stereotyp in Politik und Literatur des Exils* (Hamburg: by the author, 1990), pp. 46-82; and Manfred Herzer, "Schwule Widerständskämpfer gegen die Nazis 1933-1945," *Dokumentation der Vortragsreihe "Homosexualität und Wissenschaft,"* ed. Schwulenreferat im Allgemeinen Studentenauschuß der FU Berlin (Berlin: Rosa Winkel, 1985) pp. 221-40. See also M. Herzer, "Gay Resistance against the Nazis, 1933-1945," *Among Men, among Women: Sociological and Historical Recognition of Homosocial Arrangements*, ed. Mattias Duyves et al. (Amsterdam: Universiteit van Amsterdam, 1983), pp. 322-23.

80. See Manfred Herzer, "Ludwig Renn. Ein schwuler kommunistischer Schriftsteller im Zeitalter des Hochstalinismus," in *Erkenntniswunsch und Diskretion: Erotik in biographischer und autobiographischer Literatur*, ed. Gerhard Härle, Maria Kalveram, and Wolfgang Popp (Berlin: Rosa Winkel, 1992), pp. 365-74, and Hans Siemsen, *Die Geschichte des Hitlerjungen Adolf Goers* (Berlin: Litpol, 1981); the latter is a German edition of the English-language version first published in 1940.

81. Klaus Mann, *Der Wendepunkt* (Berlin: G. B. Fischer, 1958), p. 390. Like other statements referring explicitly to Mann's homosexuality, this passage did not appear in the original English version, *The Turning Point* (New York: L. B. Fischer, 1942), published when he was both involved in the antifascist struggle and seeking U.S. citizenship.

82. Quoted by Eberhard Spangenberg, *Karriere eines Romans: Mephisto, Klaus Mann und Gustaf Gründgens* (Munich: Heinrich Ellermann, 1982), p. 67.

83. Klaus Mann, *Kind dieser Zeit* (Reinbek bei Hamburg: Rowohlt, 1982), pp. 179-80.

84. See Uwe Naumann, *Klaus Mann* (Reinbek bei Hamburg: Rowohlt, 1984), p. 72.

85. See Gert Mattenklott, "Homosexualität und Politik bei Klaus Mann," *Sammlung: Jahrbuch für antifaschistische Literatur und Kunst* 2 (1979): 29-38.

Male Inverts and Homosexuals: Sex Discourse in the Anarchist *Revista Blanca*

Richard Cleminson

University of Bradford

SUMMARY. Historically, the anarchist movement has placed great emphasis on the personal and the political and the desire to liberate sexual expression. This was no less the case in the Spanish anarchist movement during the first decades of this century. By analyzing one influential anarchist journal of the time, the *Revista Blanca*, this essay examines the treatment of same-sex eroticism by some Spanish anarchists and attempts to place their understanding and treatment of this in the context of the time. This essay can be viewed as a point of departure for further necessary work on Spanish anarchist views of same-sex sexuality.

THE REVISTA BLANCA *AS A THEORETICAL JOURNAL*

According to George Woodcock, the *Revista Blanca* was "the most important anarchist theoretical journal in Spain."[1] Created in 1898 as a response to the changing political situation in Spanish

Correspondence may be addressed: Department of Modern Languages, University of Bradford, West Yorkshire BD7 1DP, United Kingdom.

[Haworth co-indexing entry note]: "Male Inverts and Homosexuals: Sex Discourse in the Anarchist *Revista Blanca*." Cleminson, Richard. Co-published simultaneously in *Journal of Homosexuality* (The Haworth Press, Inc.) Vol. 29, No. 2/3, 1995, pp. 259-272; and: *Gay Men and the Sexual History of the Political Left* (ed: Gert Hekma, Harry Oosterhuis, and James Steakley) The Haworth Press, Inc., 1995, pp. 259-272; and *Gay Men and the Sexual History of the Political Left* (ed: Gert Hekma, Harry Oosterhuis, and James Steakley) Harrington Park Press, an imprint of The Haworth Press, Inc., 1995, pp. 259-272. Multiple copies of this article/chapter may be purchased from The Haworth Document Delivery Center. [1-800-342-9678 9:00 a.m. - 5:00 p.m. (EST)].

259

society and within the Spanish anarchist movement itself, the *Revista Blanca*, based on the Parisian *Revue Blanche*,[2] was to pass through two major editorial periods: 1898-1904, with a copy run of 8,000,[3] and 1924-36, with a maximum copy run of 12,000.[4] In its first period the journal was run by Joan Montseny and Teresa Mañé, and in the latter period principally by their daughter Federica Montseny i Mañé. In both cases, however, it seems that there was no clear or particularly strict editorial policy, but the esteem in which the journal was held in the circles of the National Confederation of Labor (Confederación Nacional del Trabajo, or CNT), the anarcho-syndicalist union, is indisputable.

The times of conception and birth of the *Revista Blanca* were not accidental. The Spanish ruling class had just suffered one of its worst historic defeats in its loss of the remnants of a once powerful and rich seaborne empire, as Cuba and the Philippines were finally wrenched from Hispanic hands. Demoralization and disillusion were rife in Spain. In itself, the fact that the colonial remnants of the Spanish state were crumbling probably little worried Spanish anarchists, but the creation of the *Revista Blanca* reflected changes that were taking place within Spanish anarchism (as indeed worldwide, especially in the French and Russian anarchist movements) and an increased urgency to state the anarchist case.

Since the anarchist idea as a political ideology had begun to take root in Spain towards the end of the 1860s, the Spanish anarchist movement had witnessed impressive bursts of energy interspersed by rapid declines. Organizations such as the Regional Workers' Federation (Federación Regional Española) and the Workers' Federation of the Spanish Region (Federación de Trabajadores de la Región Española) were established, both being affiliated to the International Working Men's Association. Organizations collapsed and mutated, to be resuscitated at a later date with altered physiognomy and nomenclature.[5]

The *Revista Blanca* also reflected the debate on, or perhaps the reaction to, the "terrorist" deeds of Russian, French, and Spanish individual "anarchists." As a result of the bomb attack on the Corpus Christi procession carried out in Canvis Nous Street, Barcelona, in 1896, a vicious wave of repression against anarchists ensued. Following the Corpus Christi bombing were the Montjuïc trials of 1897 in which many anarchists were imprisoned or executed. The *Revista Blanca*, reflecting and pre-empting the ideological change sweeping over anarchism (not only in Spain) as the "terrorist period" declined, saw itself as having a threefold mission: "the defense of prisoners involved in the last great 'attentats' of the terrorist period, scientific and political education of the people, as well as the spreading and development of the anarchist ideal."[6] In fact, even though the readers of the *Revista Blanca* at the outset were mainly from the elite of the proletariat,[7] for "that generation . . . traumatised by the loss of the Spanish colonial Empire" it is true to say that those men and women who had created the *Revista Blanca* "were like a ray of light, a little fresh air" for the Spanish working class.[8]

THE REVISTA BLANCA AND SEX

The *Revista Blanca* made no attempt to hide the fact that it was one of the most advanced cultural-sociological journals in Spain of the time, with correspondents in many countries. In this way it reflected intellectual debate on a wide range of areas. We can therefore consider the *Revista Blanca* a kind of barometer for the anarchist movement in Spain and to some extent internationally for two principal reasons: firstly, because of its advanced cultural and intellectual nature in that contemporary debates were reflected in the journal; secondly, because of the very fact that it was a journal that survived a crucial period of European progressive thought before World War II in the revolutionary and social domain, 1924-36. It passed through the vital period of analysis and reappraisal of the Russian and Soviet revolutionary experiment, the analysis of anarchist and syndicalist tactics in the light of that revolution, the concretization of the perceived necessity of an "anti-authoritarian" revolutionary movement, the degeneration of the Bolshevik state, and the rise of Nazism in Germany and fascism in Italy. As a reflector of the above issues, the *Revista Blanca* is an excellent, unrivalled indicator of debate in Spanish anarchism.

As such, and as an intellectual current within the Spanish libertarian movement, it would come as a surprise to us if the *Revista Blanca* did not reflect the debate that was emerging, primarily in

Germany, on sex and sex-related areas. The *Revista Blanca* can be used as a gauge for the discussion of such matters in the Spanish anarchist movement and especially as an indicator of the extent to which foreign ideas penetrated Spain, either through the anarchist movement or outside of it. Indeed, the *Revista Blanca* can provide an insight into the nature and level of debate on these issues which were becoming vital areas of discussion in German and other working-class movements.

Nevertheless, despite the fact that the *Revista Blanca* did reflect and initiate debate on these areas, it cannot be held that the publication was an attempt to create an anarchist manifesto on sexual politics in the 1920s and 1930s.[9]

SPANISH SOCIETY, ATTITUDES, AND SEXUAL CULTURE

It is clear that Spain in the 1920s and 1930s had little in common with the "permissiveness" of the Weimar Republic. Spain did not enjoy the thirty homophile publications that existed in Germany,[10] propounding various aims and reflecting various views. Spain had little or none of this. There was no conscious, active urban homosexual minority demanding recognition. It must be understood that in the 1930s Spain possessed many characteristics of a pre-industrial society (forty percent of the population worked on the land)[11] with industry concentrated in two main regions, Catalonia and the Basque Country. The power of the Catholic Church as ideological factory of the ruling class and patriarchal society was still uncurbed. The power and influence of such ideas were all-pervasive, and it is not coincidental that much Catholic morality reemerged in the Spanish anarchist and anarchosyndicalist movements as moral puritanism, sexual abstinence, and other manifestations of frugality. The stigma of same-sex acts was still strong in nearly all sectors of Spanish society, including the progressive ideologies. In Barcelona, for example, most activity of this type was carefully locked away in the Chinese Quarter of the city and was frequently the butt of satire and overt criticism.[12]

It must also be acknowledged that the level of knowledge on sex was very low in Spain. This can be seen by the nature of some of the questions that appeared in the "Consultorio General" section of the

Revista Blanca. Here, the level of mystification on body and sexual matters is clearly evident. For example, when a reader asks, "Which side should I lie on for my heart to work best?"[13] the reply comes back fairly and squarely that the right-hand side is best. On masturbation, for example, J. Alván asks whether such a practice can affect one's intelligence. The reply is: "Yes, it usually reduces it."[14]

MALE SAME-SEX EROTICISM AND THE REVISTA BLANCA

This essay attempts to document the treatment of male same-sex eroticism by the anarchist *Revista Blanca*.[15] The journal, in its references to same-sex sexuality, either implicitly or explicitly concentrated on male experience and reflected the male-oriented bias of the anarchist movement of the time. "Homosexuality" generally seemed to signify male-male experience, and while there are a few references to lesbianism in the journal I have not attempted to analyze them in this essay. Therefore, it is clear that the history of lesbianism both as discussed by anarchists and lived by anarchists still has to be written.[16]

The *Revista Blanca* was not yet in production at the time of Oscar Wilde's trial in England in 1895.[17] Thirty years later, however, it was to make its standpoint known in the words of Hugo Treni, one of the foreign correspondents. In an article entitled "Oscar Wilde y el anarquismo," the following remark is made on Wilde's inability to live life correctly:

> . . . above all his inability to free himself from pernicious influences, which made him drift without purpose, to the extent of becoming hardly a man but instead a shadowy replica. Proof of this is his material and above all moral poverty, and the fact that his whole existence was truly wretched. Although his life was bathed in splendor and glory, it was also deeply immersed in a mire of filth.[18]

One of the most interesting aspects of this commentary is that Hugo Treni does not mention here, or anywhere else in the article, what

Wilde was actually guilty of. We are not told why "his whole existence was truly wretched" or what were the "pernicious influences" under which he had fallen.

We may compare this commentary to one which appeared in the London *Evening News* on May 25, 1895:

> Never has the lesson of a wasted life come home to us more dramatically and opportunely. England has tolerated the man Wilde and others of his kind for too long. Before he broke the law of this country and outraged human decency he was a social pest, a centre of intellectual corruption. He was one of the high priests of a school which attacks all the wholesome, manly, simple ideals of English life, and sets up false gods of decadent culture and intellectual debauchery.

And further in the same newspaper:

> We venture to hope that the conviction of Wilde for these abominable vices, which were the natural outcome of his diseased intellectual condition, will be a salutary warning to the unhealthy boys who posed as sharers of his culture.[19]

Clearly, in the *Revista Blanca*, Oscar Wilde was vilified for his moral corruption, i.e., his inability to live "correctly." A similar line of reasoning is advanced by Camillo Berneri, the Italian anarchist, who in his article "La degeneración sexual en las escuelas" states that:

> Most information on the corrupting influence of schools has been provided by those who study psychopathic sexual disorders. All these experts agree that schools foster the development of abnormal tendencies, and may even stimulate inverted passions.[20]

Here what is important is that Berneri believed that a certain kind of environment could provoke an individual to commit same-sex genital acts. In other words, anyone was capable of doing so if he or she had the appropriate (immoral) conditions and the physical and mental weaknesses leading him or her to indulge in such practices.

In a subsequent article ("El contagio moral en el ambiente escolar"),[21] Berneri quotes from *La Contagion mentale* by Vigouroux and Juquelier: "Contagion of solitary or mutual onanism is *certain* in all those places where sexual satisfaction is impossible."[22] Berneri then states that "Onanistic practices are usually learned from study or games partners and are usually mutual from the outset."[23] The author later quotes from Nicéforo's *Le psicopatie sessuali acquisite ed i reati sessuali* in order to show the inevitable consequences of such activities: "From mutual masturbation [the school children] moved on to oral masturbation and even indulged in far stranger practices, such as licking each other's anus."[24] What becomes clear in this analysis of the conceptualization of same-sex eroticism is that Berneri and others who had written in the *Revista Blanca* on male-male sexual acts did not view the individuals involved as a separate category, who had an identity of their own. They were individuals like any others, but ones who had been diverted, "inverted" from their usual and correct gender roles. In other words, they were individuals with same-sex practices, directed against nature, "inverts" perhaps, but certainly not "homosexuals."[25]

As George Chauncey, Jr., has pointed out:

> Sexual inversion, the term used most commonly in the nineteenth century, did not denote the same conceptual phenomenon as homosexuality. "Sexual inversion" referred to a broad range of deviant gender behavior, of which homosexual desire was only a logical but indistinct aspect, while "homosexuality" focused on the narrower issue of sexual object choice. The differentiation of homosexual desire from "deviant" gender behavior at the turn of the century reflects a major reconceptualization of the nature of human sexuality, its relation to gender, and its role in one's social definition.[26]

Clearly, though, this reconceptualization had not achieved widespread acceptance in Spain by the end of the 1920s, and, as we shall see, only began to be discussed in the *Revista Blanca* in the mid-1930s.

Thus, in 1935, seven years on from Berneri's remarks on "inverted passions," there is talk of "homosexuality" in the *Revista*

Blanca. Eugenio Villacampa attempts to "explain" the incidence of homosexuality in the light of an ever-prevailing morally corruptive religion. The practicing of same-sex sex acts is now seen to be due not to environmental conditions but to ideological ones:

> Religion, until recently, has exerted execrable tyranny over the consummation of the sexual act . . . so causing many examples of individual aberration, which morality has sanctioned in an inexorable way. Religion sees no contradiction in portraying examples of people in the Bible as assiduous practitioners of homosexuality, incest, rape, and other abnormalities which it later attempts to combat. . . .
>
> Prejudice, which results in so many innocent victims, is created by religious beliefs as a means of believers reserving their place in the next world. . . . Virginity and chastity, which are surrounded by prejudice in most countries and therefore integrated into people's morality, condemns youth to almost complete sexual abstinence, which in turn results in serious physical consequences, if not those aberrations mentioned above.[27]

And if it is not the Church it is a lack of heterosexuality:

> There is sexual hunger for males and females! Yearning and hunger! Life slips between scepticism, chlorosis, and hysteria, between masturbation and homosexuality. Between a long procession of crooked youth.[28]

SHIFTING CONCEPTS OF SEXUALITY

It seems that from the early 1930s onwards, writers of articles published in the Spanish anarchist press show a shift in terms of opinions on various points of importance in attitudes towards sexuality. Not only do we find increased use of the term "homosexuality" but also, at least on a theoretical level in some quarters, a marked softening of approach to the phenomenon itself. Thus we see a series of articles published in the anarchist review *Iniciales* written by the French individualist anarchist Lorulot,[29] associated with E. Armand, known at the time for his radical views on sex.[30] These articles began to explore "sexual perversions" in a more scientific light and were not openly condemnatory.

Three years later Félix Martí Ibáñez, a young doctor who was a member of the CNT, was to write an article which probably stands as the most complete and reasoned analysis of homosexuality written by a Spanish anarchist of those times.[31] The article opened with the statement that in spite of repressive moralists, more and more scientists were making headway with the question of homosexuality. By analyzing acceptance and repression of homosexuality in history, outlining contemporary theses on the subject, Martí Ibáñez closed the article by calling on those of "normal sexuality" to help eliminate the cross that those of "deviated sexuality" bore. He also made a plea that "congenital inverts" should be allowed to enjoy the "freedom of sexuality"[32] that Magnus Hirschfeld had struggled for in Germany before the rise of Hitler, who "thrust the sword of his barbarous regime into the banner of Science."[33]

Shifts were also occurring in other areas of the organization of sexuality. On masturbation, for example, there is considerable difference between some of the articles on the subject in the 1920s, which were almost entirely critical and drastic in their warnings of dire peril due to the practice of onanism. For example, in *Generación Consciente* the doctor Franz Keller considers onanism one of the causes of impotence.[34] In 1931, the doctor Isaac Puente, a member of the CNT, was prepared to accept masturbation as a childhood disorder but not to justify it.[35] However, in 1935, A. G. Llauradó, in his article "The Rehabilitation of Onanism,"[36] after an exposition of the history of ideas on masturbation, arrived at the conclusion that onanism was not an illness or vice but "clean and hygienic" and far more moral than paying for sex in a brothel.[37]

On another level, that of debate around issues of sterilization, current at the time, there was also a shift away from the acceptance of sterilization of "degenerates"[38] to a much more careful analysis of its pros and cons in the light of Nazi policies on the subject.[39]

These shifts may well have been responses to several changes in Spanish society and Spanish anarchism of the 1930s. It is difficult at this stage of research to state categorically the reasons for such shifts. However, they may have reflected an increased openness of anarchism to revising old ideas, an intensification of the revolutionary process, or a realization that some aspects of eugenics were unacceptable.

In the journal that we are considering here, nevertheless, even though there was mention of same-sex sexuality in its pages, we cannot say that the subject received a particularly favorable appreciation. A handful of articles or allusions in articles hardly provides us with a clear picture of same-sex sexual activity and its perception both by protagonists and onlookers. That the *Revista Blanca* was still able in 1935 to refer to inverts as not "real men" and to enjoin anarchists not to associate with them does not suggest that the publication was liberal in its stance towards homosexuality.[40]

Let it be said, though, that concern over sexual matters was increasing and discourse on certain aspects of sexuality was becoming more intricate and intense in the build-up towards the revolutionary events of July 17, 1936. That this discourse was extant is illustrated by the following data on the occurrence of sex-related questions in the "Consultorio" sections of the *Revista Blanca*. On March 20, 1936, eight out of twenty questions were on sex and sex-related issues;[41] on April 24, 1936, there were five out of twenty;[42] on June 15, 1936, three out of nineteen;[43] and on July 15, 1936, two days before the generals' uprising, five out of nineteen.[44] However, two weeks after the uprising and the establishment of a revolutionary order in some parts of Spain, in tandem with profound economic, political, and social changes, questions on sex represented nine out of fourteen questions, that is more than fifty percent.[45]

This means little in itself though. Just because more questions on sex appeared in the pages of this particular journal does not mean that anarchists were necessarily closer to solving what the anarchist women's organization Free Women (Mujeres Libres) stated was the principal problem of revolutions:

> It is only by means of the social revolution that the collective solution to the economic problem, the political problem, and the sexual problem can be found–an exasperating triangle of problems that has bemused all previous generations.[46]

It is only by means of further and more detailed research into the journals and ideology of the Spanish anarchist movement that we

will be able to evaluate the anarchist contribution to sexual liberation in the 1930s. This will necessitate deeper comprehension of
attitudes current in Spanish society in the 1930s and of the spread of
ideas from the focal points of sexology into the Spanish left. It is
only then that we will be able to situate the contribution of the
anarchists to the change effected in the revolution of 1936 and
understand the ideas, efforts, and failures of the movement in the
context of the wider sexological movements.

AUTHOR NOTE

Richard Cleminson is a doctoral candidate at the University of The West of
England, Bristol, and lecturer in Spanish and Portuguese language and history at
the University of Bradford. His research centers on the Spanish anarchist sex
reform movement of the 1930s and, in particular, on anarchist attitudes toward
homosexuality. He is the editor of *Anarquismo y Homosexualidad: Antología de
Artículos de la Revista Blanca, Generación Consciente, Estudios e Iniciales* (Madrid: Ediciones Libertarias, 1995), an anthology of Spanish anarchist articles on
same-sex sexuality.
All translations from the Spanish and Catalan are by the author, who would
like to thank Gert Hekma and James Steakley for their helpful advice and encouragement in the preparation of this essay.

NOTES

1. George Woodcock, *Anarchism* (London: Penguin, 1970), p. 348.
2. The *Revue Blanche* was directed by Alexandre Natason and "had paid particular attention to some aspects of Spanish intellectual thought and had cordially
received and cared for those political exiles who left Spain for its neighboring
country." S. Tavera García, *Revista Blanca: Análisis histórico de una publicación
anarquista, 1931-1936* (Dissertation, Universidad de Barcelona, 1973), p. 3.
3. Various authors, *Els Anarquistes. Educadors del Poble. La "Revista Blanca" (1895-1905)* (Barcelona: Curial, 1977), p. 11.
4. Ibid. According to Federica Montseny herself, one of the later directors of
the *Revista Blanca*, the print run was not so high: "In order to give an idea of the
volume of publications that *Revista Blanca* [i.e., the publishing house] produced,
I can point out that of the *Novela Ideal* 50,000 copies were produced weekly, as
well as 20,000 of the *Novela Libre*. The profits from these publications, of a popular character, allowed us to continue producing the *Revista Blanca*, which was
never to have more than 6,000 copies printed per isssue." F. Montseny, *Mis pri-
meros cuarenta años* (Barcelona: Plaza y Janés, 1987), p. 56. The *Novela*

Ideal, "according to the Francoists, poisoned three generations of Spaniards."
Ibid., p. 41. The publications were anti-religious, and focused on anarchist morality, sex, and women.

    5. See Anselmo Lorenzo, *El proletariado militante*, 2 vols. (Barcelona, 1902
and 1925; rpt. Madrid: Alianza Editorial, 1974); Clara E. Lida, *Anarquismo y revolución en la España del siglo XIX* (Madrid: Siglo XXI, 1972); George Richard
Esenwein, *Anarchist Ideology and the Working Class Movement in Spain,
1868-1898* (Berkeley: University of California Press, 1989).

    6. *Educadors*, p. 20.

    7. Ibid., p. 12.

    8. Ibid., p. 13.

    9. While referring to General Primo de Rivera's 1923-29 dictatorship, F.
Montseny states: "We carried on publishing the *Revista Blanca*, which was, along
with *Generación Consciente* from Valencia, later named *Estudios* . . . , the only
publication which expressed and publicized anarchist ideas during those seven
years" (Montseny, p. 42). *Generación Consciente* and *Estudios* were two publications that also treated sex-related matters in great detail. Both were produced in
Valencia, and the latter is the continuation of the former.

    10. James Steakley, *The Homosexual Emancipation Movement in Germany*
(New York: Arno, 1975), p. 78. Here Steakley refers to the thirty publications
available during the years of the Weimar Republic.

    11. Illiteracy was also high. According to Ramírez Jiménez, in 1920, 34.82
percent of the population aged ten or over was illiterate, and in 1930 the figure
was 25.91 percent. See M. Ramírez Jiménez, *Los grupos de presión en la Segunda
República Española* (Madrid: Tecnos, 1969), p. 81.

    12. The flavor of the Chinese Quarter in Barcelona may be deduced from the
following excerpt: "Some shoeshiners can be seen selling cocaine, and inverts appear in the middle of the street showing off their parts." "Los bajos fondos de
Barcelona," *El Escándalo* 1:1 (October 22, 1925): 4.

    13. "Consultorio General," *Revista Blanca*, no. 275 (April 26, 1934).

    14. "Consultorio General," *Revista Blanca*, no. 297 (September 28, 1934):
748.

    15. I have chosen the term "male same-sex eroticism" as a general way of de-
scribing same-sex genital acts, without alluding to the labels of "invert" or "homosexual," social constructs which relate to certain groups of "male same-sex
eroticists."

    16. Some references to female same-sex eroticism in the context of anarchism
can be found in Martha A. Ackelsberg, *Free Women of Spain: Anarchism and the
Struggle for the Emancipation of Women* (Bloomington: Indiana University Press,
1991), and in my *Anarquismo y Homosexualidad: Antología de Artículos de la
Revista Blanca, Generación Consciente, Estudios e Iniciales* (Madria: Ediciones
Libertarias, 1994). On Emma Goldman, see Jonathan Katz, *Gay American History: Lesbians and Gay Men in the U.S.A.* (New York: Thomas Y. Crowell, 1976):
376-80, 523-30.

17. The Oscar Wilde trials, according to some commentators, contributed in a major way to a homosexual "public image" that was to reinforce demands for fairer treatment and help shape modern homosexual, and subsequently gay, identities. See Jeffrey Weeks, *Coming Out: Homosexual Politics in Britain, from the Nineteenth Century to the Present* (London: Quartet, 1977): 22.

18. Hugo Treni, "Oscar Wilde y el anarquismo," *Revista Blanca*, no. 127 (September 1, 1928): 176.

19. Quoted in John Marshall, "Pansies, Perverts and Macho Men: Changing Conceptions of Male Homosexuality," in *The Making of the Modern Homosexual*, ed. Kenneth Plummer (London: Hutchinson, 1981): 140-41.

20. Camillo Berneri, "La degeneración sexual en las escuelas," *Revista Blanca*, no. 118 (April 15, 1928): 696.

21. Camillo Berneri, "El contagio moral en el ambiente escolar," *Revista Blanca*, no. 122 (June 15, 1928): 10-15.

22. A. Vigouroux and P. Juqueliers, *La Contagion mentale* (Paris: O. Doin, 1905), p. 206.

23. Camillo Berneri, "El contagio moral en el ambiente escolar," *Revista Blanca*, no. 122 (June 15, 1928): 11.

24. Alfredo Nicéforo, *Le psicopatie sessuali acquisite ed i reati sessuali* (Rome: Fratelli Capaccini, 1897), pp. 35-36.

25. Note the following, for example: in *Revista Blanca*, no. 352 (October 18, 1935): 1007, "an anarchist woman" writes in to ask: "How would the editorial group of the *Revista Blanca* view a woman who claimed to be madly in love with another woman?" The reply comes back: "We would consider her as someone who is ill, who should be submitted to treatment so as to make her sex organs function properly and so that her feelings were not directed against nature."

26. Quoted in David Halperin, *One Hundred Years of Homosexuality* (New York and London: Routledge, 1990): 15.

27. Eugenio Villacampa, "Educación sexual de la Juventud," *Revista Blanca*, no. 340 (July 26, 1935): 707. Villacampa was a member of the Iberian Federation of Libertarian Youth (F.I.J.L.).

28. Santana Calero, "La Tragedia de los Sexos," *Revista Blanca*, no. 384 (May 29, 1936): 438.

29. Lorulot, "Perversiones y desviaciones del instinto genital," series of articles beginning *Iniciales*, no. 1 (January 1932), and finishing *Iniciales*, no. 9 (September 1932).

30. See Jean Maitron, *Le Mouvement anarchiste en France* (Paris: François Maspero, 1983).

31. Félix Martí Ibáñez, "Consideraciones sobre el homosexualismo," *Estudios*, no. 145 (September 1935): 3-6.

32. Ibid., p. 5.

33. Ibid., p. 6.

34. Franz Keller, "Estudio de la impotencia," *Generación Consciente*, no. 7 (February 1924): 114-15.

35. Un Médico Rural (Isaac Puente), "Necesidad de la iniciación sexual," *Estudios*, no. 18 (October 1931): 7. See also idem, "La masturbación," *Estudios*, no. 110 (October 1932): 17-18.

36. A. G. Llauradó, "Rehabilitación del onanismo," *Estudios*, no. 148 (December 1935): 20-23.

37. Ibid., p. 22.

38. Isaac Puente, "Eugénica preventiva," *Generación Consciente*, no. 20 (March 1925): 298.

39. Here see F. de Campollano, "La esterilización eugénica y los legófilos," *Estudios*, no. 129 (May 1934): 30-32, and Hem Day, "La esterilización sexual," *Estudios*, no. 139 (March 1935): 14-16. Both articles voice opposition to the sterilization of homosexuals.

40. See the question in the "Consultorio General" section of the *Revista Blanca*, no. 30 (July 26, 1935): 720: "What is there to be said about those comrades who themselves are anarchists and who associate with inverts?" The answer is: "They cannot be viewed as men if that 'associate' means anything apart from speaking to or saluting sexual degenerates. If you are an anarchist, that means that you are more morally upright and physically strong than the average man. And he who likes inverts is no real man, and is therefore no real anarchist."

41. "Consultorio General," *Revista Blanca*, no. 374 (March 20, 1936): 237-39.

42. Ibid., no. 379 (April 24, 1936): 337-38. Here we consider the first two pages only of the "Consultorio," as the last page was devoted to questions of an ideological nature.

43. "Consultorio Médico," *Revista Blanca*, no. 385 (June 15, 1936): 33-34. Here we consider the "Consultorio Médico" only and not the "General." The Medical Consultancy section appeared for the first time in *Revista Blanca*, no. 381 (May 8, 1936).

44. "Consultorio Médico," *Revista Blanca*, no. 387 (July 15, 1936): 105-6.

45. Ibid., no. 388 (July 30, 1936): 144-45.

46. *Mujeres Libres*, 10° Mes de la Revolución, no page number.

Anthony Blunt and Guy Burgess, Gay Spies

Fred Sommer

University of Nevada at Las Vegas

SUMMARY. Anthony Blunt and Guy Burgess were prominent figures in the Cambridge spy ring operating on behalf of the USSR
from the 1930s into the 1960s. The essay describes the complex personalities of Blunt and Burgess, whose homosexuality and communism were related aspects of a rebellious, antibourgeois culture in
1930s leftist Britain. The focus is on male homosexuality, and the
question is put whether, and in what sense, Blunt and Burgess served
the left, and whether they can be role models for gays at the end of
this century.

I

Anthony Blunt and Guy Burgess were two gay Englishmen who
worked as spies for the Soviet Union. They attained notoriety when
the British government named them, in separate revelations, as
spies; important aspects of their careers, however, remain obscure.
Both probably began their espionage during the 1930s, when they

---

Correspondence may be addressed: Department of History, University of Nevada at Las Vegas, Las Vegas, NV 89154.

[Haworth co-indexing entry note]: "Anthony Blunt and Guy Burgess, Gay Spies." Sommer, Fred.
Co-published simultaneously in *Journal of Homosexuality* (The Haworth Press, Inc.) Vol. 29, No. 4,
1995, pp. 273-293; and: *Gay Men and the Sexual History of the Political Left* (ed: Gert Hekma, Harry
Oosterhuis, and James Steakley) The Haworth Press, Inc., 1995, pp. 273-293; and *Gay Men and the
Sexual History of the Political Left* (ed: Gert Hekma, Harry Oosterhuis, and James Steakley) Harrington
Park Press, an imprint of The Haworth Press, Inc., 1995, pp. 273-293. Multiple copies of this article/
chapter may be purchased from The Haworth Document Delivery Center. [1-800-342-9678 9:00 a.m. -
5:00 p.m. (EST)].

273

were students and close friends at Cambridge University (Blunt also taught there for a time), and the spy ring they belonged to included at least two other students, Kim Philby and Donald Maclean. Blunt, Burgess, Philby, and Maclean all later held high-ranking, sensitive positions within British security agencies and the Foreign Office. Burgess and Maclean defected to the Soviet Union in 1951; Philby did the same in 1963. In 1964, Blunt, who was working as an art historian in London, admitted to British agents after lengthy interrogation that he had spied for the Soviet Union, and he pledged to cooperate with British authorities in return for their silence and immunity from prosecution. Rumors continued to swirl around Blunt, however, and the imminent publication of Andrew Boyle's *The Climate of Treason* late in 1979–in which Blunt figured under the rather transparent code name "Maurice"–finally forced the government to reveal at least part of what it knew.

On November 15, 1979, Prime Minister Thatcher announced before Parliament that Blunt, who had been knighted in 1956, was a confessed Soviet spy. Within minutes of Thatcher's statement, a crown official issued to the outraged citizenry a decree from Buckingham Palace divesting Blunt of his knighthood: He was no longer "Sir Anthony," merely "Professor Blunt." It was already widely known that Blunt, like the flamboyant Burgess, who had died in Moscow in 1963, was a homosexual, and within a week (November 22) the authoritative *Times* printed an editorial on the link between communist subversion and a certain kind of 1930s British male bonding that had flourished at Cambridge University. The *Times* asserted:

> Theirs was largely a homosexual culture, with necessary dependence on ties of friendship rather than on the functional ties of family, and a defiance of conventional sexual morality, leading to a broader moral relativism. . . . The rejection of ideal standards, the cult of personal standards, supported by an arrogant cult of the intellect, was the common foundation of the Cambridge school.

The *Times* was right, at least in pointing to the gay context, and it would be naive for anyone to write about Blunt and Burgess without discussing their homosexuality and its relation to the choices they made in the 1930s and thereafter. As the Austrian-born critic George Steiner has noted, "the homoerotic ethos may have persuaded men such as Blunt and Burgess that the official society around them, whatever prizes it might bestow on their talents, was in essence hostile and hypocritical."[1] This essay will examine certain aspects of Blunt and Burgess's espionage, exploring the links between their sexual and political identities. Only male homosexuality will be discussed, not out of misogyny but rather because Blunt and Burgess were gay men operating within an almost exclusively male power structure.

II

Blunt and Burgess were physically attractive men. The poet Louis MacNeice, a close friend and classmate of Blunt's in the 1920s at the prestigious Marlborough public school (i.e., private all-male boarding school), wrote in 1940 of the "wave of soft brown hair falling over his eyes . . . a pre-Raphaelite beauty."[2] The appeal of Burgess is much more amply documented; he was sexier, flashier than the scholarly Blunt. To John Costello, whose minutely researched account of the spy ring is suspicious of much that was Establishment or gay—or both—in Britain, Burgess was "a larger than life character . . . a shameless exploiter of his boyish good looks . . . the most notorious *homme fatal* of his generation."[3] Interviewed in the 1980s, Burgess's erstwhile working-class lover Jack Hewitt recalled the spy as a "fantastic, rather gorgeous creature . . . utterly charming, wildly good-looking and totally untidy."[4] A far more intimate assessment of Burgess has survived in Harold Acton's *More Memoirs of an Aesthete*: "Brian [Howard] confided to me that his equipment was gargantuan–'What is known as a whopper, my dear,'–which might account for his success in certain ambiguous quarters."[5] Clearly, the two gay spies were impressive physical specimens, as photos bear out.

Neither Blunt nor Burgess was the shadowy, blurred-image type of spy whose success could be attributed to invisibility. On the contrary, they were both aggressive, self-confident manipulators. Burgess in particular made a vivid impression on contemporaries; while some of their testimony has the ring of authenticity, some seems influenced by the Burgess legend. The headmaster at Eton, the prestigious school he attended, judged him favorably in 1929:

> The great thing is that he really thinks for himself. . . . It is refreshing to find one who is really well-read and who can become enthusiastic or have something to say about most things from Vermeer to Meredith. He is also a lively and amusing person, generous, I think, and very good-natured.[6]

The Cambridge student Leo Long, possibly in later years a fellow spy, also responded to Burgess's appeal:

> Burgess was fascinating just to look at. In a sense he was revolting, a sort of Dylan Thomas figure, who was larger than life, always drunk. He was a creature from a different world. Loud and camp, although that word didn't exist then.[7]

Perhaps most graphic is the view of Michael Straight, an American at Cambridge and a member of the Apostles, a secret Cambridge society to which both Blunt and Burgess belonged:

> He craved the companionship and the physical love of other men. . . . With his curly hair, his sensual mouth, his cherubic air, he seemed at first sight to embody in himself the ideal of male beauty that the Apostles revered. Then, on a closer look, you noticed the details: the black-rimmed fingernails, the stained forefinger in which he gripped his perpetual cigarette stub; the dark, uneven teeth; the slouch; the open fly.[8]

After impressing many at Cambridge, Burgess went on to the BBC and the Foreign Office. The Cambridge historian Noel Annan knew him for many years:

> At Cambridge he was a liberator—one of those students who appear to their contemporaries to be more assured, more able to liberate them from the conventions of family, school or class. . . . He could get a trade unionist to give a talk on the BBC worth listening to—and persuade his superiors that it was time the BBC did so. Churchill gave him a copy of his

speeches and wrote on the flyleaf praise for his 'admirable sentiments.' . . . And yet he was a spy.[9]

The critic Malcolm Muggeridge's famous passage on Burgess, written in the early 1970s, captures the spy's distinctive, effusive aura; the scene is a party in London in 1940:

It was the only time I ever met Burgess; and he gave me a feeling, such as I have never had from anyone else, of being morally afflicted in some way. His very physical presence was, to me, malodorous and sinister; as though he had some consuming illness. . . . There was not so much a conspiracy gathered round him as just decay and dissolution. It was the end of a class, of a way of life; something that would be written about in history books, like Gibbon on Heliogabalus, with wonder and perhaps hilarity, but still tinged with sadness, as all endings are.[10]

Equally revealing is the assessment of Goronwy Rees, a Welsh academic who knew Burgess at Cambridge:

Guy regarded sex as a useful machine for the manufacture of pleasure . . . and at one time or another he went to bed with most of his friends and in so doing released them from many of their inhibitions. . . . Long after the affair was over he continued to assist friends in their sexual lives[,] . . . to listen to their emotional difficulties and when necessary to find suitable partners for them. To such people he was a combination of father confessor and pimp.[11]

There is probably much truth in Blunt's own portrait of Burgess, the last in the special gallery presented here:

Those people who now write saying that they felt physically sick in his presence . . . are throwing back to his early years things that may have been true about Guy in his later years in this country. He was a terrific intellectual stimulus.[12]

An improbable figure, detestable to many; a role model for gays? Burgess's character was very gay, and many assertive gays, some of them leftist, will admire him and imitate him either by design or by second nature. Some may see an emancipatory, liberating moment for gays in his masterly role as the *éminence grise* of subversion. And history will find terms and categories for the fecundity of nature, time, and event that his life undoubtedly displayed. Burgess served as model for the central character of Julian Mitchell's play *Another Country* (1981; filmed three years later), in which a gay youth at an exclusive all-male school turns to communism after being punished for sex with a younger pupil. *Another Country* is not a documentary, but the thesis that Burgess may, even prior to his Cambridge years, have been a proto-communist, perhaps a proto-spy, is interesting.

Blunt, too, was a very gay type: the hard, disciplined, but still swishy academic. Costello perceived this and wrote of the

> deferential hush that overtook the corridors of the institute whenever the footfalls on the magnificent marble spiral staircase announced the descent of the director, his academic gown billowing out over a formal gray-flannel suit.[13]

Annan, who knew him, was also in awe:

> He fascinated people with his quick, engaging, cool and assured talk. He baited his conversation with gossip, inside gossip, gossip to which only he had access. When he had gone, it dawned on you with what skill he had faintly denigrated those about whom he talked. They would be humbled by a flick of the whip here and a twist of the knife there.[14]

Blunt was an expert on European painting and drawing from the Renaissance to Picasso; his book *Artistic Theory in Italy, 1450-1600*, which appeared in 1940, included a dedication to Guy Burgess for "the stimulus of constant discussion."[15] After serving in the British MI5 security agency during World War II, he advanced steadily in academia and became Director of the Courtauld Institute in London, which trained art historians, and Surveyor of the Queen's Pictures. He worked with the Queen,[16] and the *Times* editorial cited above registered in this connection a "hateful and unrepented personal treason to the monarch."

Blunt and Burgess were promiscuous and performed sexual acts in public toilets, an illegal practice known in England as "cottaging." Blunt used alcohol as a prop for these encounters. A longtime acquaintance of Blunt's recalled:

> If Anthony was with a young man he wouldn't be with him for more than ten minutes without trying to take the trousers off him. . . . It was said that he could talk the trousers off anyone when he was young. . . . I knew all about cottaging. . . . It was dangerous but Blunt did it because he loved danger. Everyone knows the toilet he used at Hyde Park, the big one near Speaker's Corner. . . . As the ancients would put it, Anthony never got ape-drunk (when men makes fools of themselves in their cups) but he did get goat drunk (when men become amorous in their cups). Or perhaps it would be better to say that he could face cottaging better after a stiff drink.[17]

Blunt was never caught by the police while "cottaging," but Burgess was and had to appear in court in 1938. Though the charge was thrown out, the episode cannot have endeared Burgess to the conservative British state, and it was around this time–the exact date is unknown–that he began his activity as a Soviet agent. "Cottaging," which continues in Britain and elsewhere under different names, is a controversial practice, though perhaps only slightly more controversial than homosexuality. Blunt and Burgess had learned from their gay peers to see sex in a cloacal context, and this is a legitimate, by no means exclusively gay perspective. MacNeice writes of the toilets at the school he and Blunt attended:

> "Please, Sir, may I cross court?" Crossing court was a euphemism for going to the lavatory. The school lavatories–or the rears, as they were called–consisted of a large shed with brick walls and a corrugated iron roof, open at each end to the wind and rain. The centre of this shed was occupied by two long rows of cells, set back to back and without doors, and each containing a fixed seat with a round hole in it; underneath was a channel which was flushed from end to end automatically every quarter of an hour; the time to excrete was of course immediately after this flushing. As it was one of the few places

where a boy could speak to a boy two or three years younger than himself without being observed by the masters, you would often see older boys prowling up and down there in the morning, looking for their favourites on the stools.[18]

This was their schooling, and in their adulthood sex in toilets was one of the range of forbidden acts which together comprised homosexual life. Sex between men was a crime and would remain so in Britain until 1967. The gays had not invented that situation, but they had to live with it, and only the dreamers (the Marxists?) among them dared believe that the state of affairs would change for the better. Blunt and Burgess were, as gays, pariahs if exposed; their sexuality inculcated a secrecy and deceptiveness which served them well as spies.

III

Britain in the 1920s, its adversary Germany and old rival Russia in temporary eclipse, could boast the primacy of an empire comprising thirteen million square miles of territory (including substantial holdings in Africa and the Middle East gained in the peace settlements) and close to five hundred million subjects. But the massive crisis which began around 1930 dimmed this glory, and the thirties were a time of jarring contrasts between wealth and poverty which, to many, raised the specter of revolution. Dining in 1936 at Sir Arthur Bailey's, the diarist Tom Jones noted the superb "waiters six feet high" attending to the "table loaded with gold plate" and shortly thereafter wrote to Sir Harold Wernher, chairman of Electrolux, about the hiring of servants:

What we have found in some of the more remote mining villages is this: Girls of 17-20 who have never slept alone in a room, who have never known what it is to have ordinary bedclothes, and some who are unfamiliar with knives and forks, all of which seems incredible today.[19]

In terms reminiscent of Marx almost a century earlier, the conservative historian Robert Sencourt recorded in *The Reign of Edward*

VIII the "hideous conditions of industrial poverty, with its desolate streets, its fetid mines, its noisy factories, the squalor of the masses of Great Britain"; and he remembered, too, a hedonistic, not-so-confident 1930s, an "age which lived in an uneasy pose between its dope and its stimulation, its cocktails, its cigarettes and its cinema."[20]

Political leadership in Britain was lackluster between the downfall of Lloyd George in 1922 and the coming of Churchill in 1940. When Labor, after governing weakly for two years, discarded its radical reformist program and formed a coalition national government with the Conservatives in 1931, and especially after Hitler's triumph in 1933, growing numbers of British intellectuals began to despair of their nation's capacity for change and to idealize the Soviet Union, both as a dynamic and just socialist order and as an international guarantor of humane values against fascism. The Communist Party of Great Britain–an electoral and agitational organization under intense government surveillance, and not generally the vehicle for recruiting Soviet spies–saw its membership rise steadily from 3,000 in 1929 and 1930 to 5,800 in 1934, and 12,250 in 1937.[21] Cambridge University, traditionally more radical than Oxford, became a center of sympathy for Soviet communism. At the beginning of 1934, the *Cambridge Review* noted that the "Russian experiment has roused very great interest within the universities. It is felt to be bold and constructive."[22] Countess Kàrolyi, a left-leaning aristocrat who visited Cambridge that year, found it "odd to see students of such a famous university, obviously upper-class and with well-bred accents, speak about Soviet Russia as a land of promise."[23]

To appeal to these young men of privilege, the Soviet Union dispatched select, formidable agents, the "illegals"–so called because they entered Britain using false papers and identities, concealing their link with the Soviet embassy and consulates. These "illegals" were largely Central European polyglot cosmopolitans of educated background born around 1900, urbane communist zealots who knew their history, literature, and–just as important–their manners. In a decade of brilliant leftists, the more adept "illegals" shone both as facile salon causeurs and as tireless organizers. Three of them, Otto Katz, Theodore Maly, and Arnold Deutsch, played a key role–though accounts are contradictory–in the recruitment of the gay spies.

Maly had been a Catholic chaplain in the Austro-Hungarian army, was taken captive by the Russians in the Carpathians, and joined the revolution: "I broke with my past completely. I was no longer a Hungarian, a priest, a Christian, even anyone's son. . . . I became a Communist and have always remained one." A Soviet colleague recalled Maly's "strong, manly face and large, almost childlike, blue eyes."[24] Upon arrival in London in 1932, Maly assumed the role of a businessman by establishing an East End rag business that entailed travelling widely in search of waste linen. His "passionate pride and his intellect and charm" enabled this secret agent "to pass himself off as a cultivated European intellectual."[25] He recruited Burgess, Philby, and Maclean and, according to Costello, must have also recruited Blunt "if Blunt was recruited anytime between 1934 and 1937."[26] Recalled to Moscow in July, 1937, Maly was executed there late that year. Before departing from London he had told a friend: "I know that as a former priest I haven't got a chance. But I have decided to go there so that nobody can say: 'That priest might have been a spy after all.' "[27]

No less compelling was another "illegal" with links to the gay spies, Otto Katz. Born in Prague and acquainted with Franz Kafka, this "dark and handsome man[,] . . . a fixer and contact man in European capitals," possessed great personal charm and "literary skills and facility with half a dozen languages."[28] And Katz crossed oceans, too. A contemporary recalled: "In Hollywood he charmed German émigré actors, directors and writers. Katz had an extraordinary fascination for women, a quality which greatly helped him in organizing committees and campaigns."[29] Arthur Koestler, who fled the continent for England in 1938, found Katz "a very likeable human being. He had the generosity of the adventurer and he could be warmhearted, spontaneous and helpful–so long as it did not conflict with his interests."[30] Katz made two visits to Britain in 1934; he served international communism until he was executed in Prague late in 1952 in one of the last waves of paranoid Stalinist terror. Costello asserts that Katz was Blunt's controller.[31]

The "illegals" were desperate visionaries whose bluff, panache, and charisma appealed to the young idealists Burgess and Blunt, an appeal akin to the special power exercised over the two gays by the legendary John Cornford, a handsome communist student at Cambridge, scion of a family of scholars, and a great-grandson of Charles Darwin. The historian Steven Runciman has claimed that Blunt and Burgess were "totally glamorized" by Cornford and spent a great deal of time "sighing in vain" for the unresponsive heterosexual. Blunt saw a certain beauty in Cornford's death at age twenty-one in the Spanish Civil War: "appropriate, though tragic, that he should have gone to Spain and been killed; he was the stuff martyrs are made of."[32] Service to international communism, to the historic struggle against fascism, necessarily involved sacrifice, risk, and danger; it was serious work.

A third "illegal" linked to Blunt and Burgess was Arnold Deutsch. Born in 1904 in Vienna, Deutsch, who like Katz was Jewish, entered the University of Vienna in 1923 and in less than five years was awarded a doctorate in chemistry. For several years beginning around 1928, Deutsch was active in Wilhelm Reich's Sexpol movement. Reich, a Viennese psychologist, sought "to integrate Freudianism with Marxism. Political and sexual repression, he argued, went together and paved the way for fascism."[33] In 1930, Deutsch left Vienna for Berlin, where he joined the Communist Party. Trained as an "illegal" in Moscow in 1933, he arrived the following year in London, where he posed as a university lecturer and arranged for Burgess to visit Moscow in 1934. He left England in 1938 for Moscow, where he served as a handwriting and forgery expert, and died in 1942, either in Austria, having been captured there when he parachuted in to organize resistance, or on the Atlantic, when his ship was sunk en route to the USA.[34]

Blunt and Burgess greatly admired the "illegals" and took them as role models. The gay spies knew what they wanted to be and the end to which their decision might lead them, but as things turned out neither Blunt nor Burgess died violently or heroically. Toward the end of his life in Moscow, Burgess–who had never learned much Russian and continued to hope that a "deal" would be struck enabling him to return to Britain–felt isolated and unhappy. At a party at the Chinese embassy, he was upbraided for urinating while quite drunk into a fireplace. Burgess complained of his loneliness to a visiting English friend, Tom Driberg, who quickly proved more adept at making the appropriate gay-life contacts. In the upshot, a blond electrician named Tolya moved into Burgess's Moscow flat and became the last of the spy's many lovers. Burgess was only fifty-two when he died in August, 1963, of liver and cardiovascular ailments. A band played the communist anthem, "The International," at his Moscow funeral,[35] and Maclean read a brief eulogy.

Blunt spent the last thirty years of his life living with a handsome ex-guardsman of working-class origin, a decade his junior. A steadying influence on the historian's work and a good cook to boot, he was deeply hurt when he learned of Blunt's espionage, about which he had known nothing. Photos of Blunt taken in 1979 and 1980, at the time of his public exposure, show a distinguished man with abundant silver hair. Blunt's lover was with him in March, 1983, when, at the age of seventy-five, he suffered a massive heart attack, dying in the couple's London apartment within hours.

IV

A passage in the 1848 *Communist Manifesto* of Marx and Engels asserts:

> Finally, when the class war is about to be fought to a finish, disintegration of the ruling class and the old order of society becomes so active, so acute, that a small part of the ruling class breaks away to make common cause with the revolutionary class.[36]

In turning against traditional Britain and allying themselves with international communism, Blunt and Burgess positioned themselves in this Marxist tradition, and it is significant that the background of the gay spies stood a degree apart from the nineteenth-century commercial middle classes. Both men hailed from an older, pre-industrial public service elite.

This was especially true of Blunt, son of an Anglican priest, the Reverend Arthur Stanley Vaughan Blunt, whose own father had been bishop of Hull. Blunt's mother (to whom he remained very attached until her death in 1969), born Hilda Violet Masters, and her sister Mabel were close friends from childhood of Queen Mary, the wife of George V (reigned 1910-36); she was also a second cousin of the Earl of Strathmore, whose daughter, Lady Elizabeth Bowes-Lyon, is the present Queen Mother. *Burke's Landed Gentry*, a guide to England's leading families, listed the Rev. Arthur Blunt and his heirs until 1922.[37] Of Blunt, one colleague reminisced in 1985: "One assumed that he was a sort of aristocrat. He was really a Whig, not a conservative. He was a patrician, that's the word."[38]

As for Burgess, his father, who died when Guy was thirteen, was a Royal Navy commander; his mother later married a retired Army colonel who showered his stepson with gifts in an unsuccessful effort to win his favor. Thus the parents of both spies were arbiters, commanders, gentleman officials of the crown; not middle-class businessmen, manufacturers, or professionals.

These distinctions mattered and probably conditioned the gay spies to a certain anti-bourgeois slant. Blunt saw himself as the guardian of Old World, European humanist art and values against the crass assaults of the nouveau-riche Americans. In a 1935 article in the *Spectator*, he lamented "American wealth and lack of discretion" in the art market. After World War II Blunt realized "to our great surprise–and to our slight horror–that Paris was no longer the centre of the art world, but that New York was." In 1971 Blunt again criticized, in the *Times*, American purchases of artworks from major British collections as a "sign of cultural barbarism."[39] Burgess for his part found the Americans shallow, lacking any sense of history, irony, or nuance. Warned by British Foreign Office colleagues that he should not discuss American racial segregation, Marxism, or homosexuality while in the USA, Burgess responded: "What you're trying to say . . . is: 'Guy, for God's sake don't make a pass at Paul Robeson'"[40]–a reference to the famous African-American singer whose communist activities provoked a professional boycott.

Burgess was ill at ease during his brief Foreign Office assignment in Washington, D.C., in 1950-51. His behavior, documented exhaustively in Verne W. Newton's study, included numerous visits to exclusive clubs and old-family country homes, drunken driving, and indiscreet criticism of General Douglas MacArthur, commander of US forces in Korea and popular hero of the political right who favored use of the atomic bomb against the Communist Chinese.

American culture was caught up in one of the first tense phases of what came to be known as the Cold War. Goronwy Rees noted the difficulties of his friend Burgess in adjusting to 1950s America:

> Senator Joe McCarthy's anti-communist crusade was in full swing, and Guy had come to the conclusion that he was both the most powerful and the most representative politician in the United States. . . . What aroused Guy almost to hysteria was McCarthy's identification of communism with homosexuality. . . .[41]

The unmasking of Burgess took place in the context of this 1950s wave of anti-communism, that of Blunt in a later, similar wave of the 1980s, but with a difference: what was simply old in the 1950s had, by the 1980s, taken on a fascination, an allure. A very sophisticated level of inquiry focused now on the 1930s, on the epicene "pinko-pansies" of the red decade. This fed a certain voyeuristic, confessional, or elegiac nostalgia not necessarily without sympathy for the spies, but it also made their guilt something apart from the lives of normal people, something unnatural, possibly monstrous.

When the gay spies were at Cambridge sixty years ago, tradition–though not unchallenged–was firm, and the union of throne and altar, the conservative state buttressed by respectable religion and its doctrine of sin, was central to English life, a centrality under-lined–to choose but one contemporary example–by the Abdication Crisis of 1936, when the Archbishop of Canterbury, speaking on the BBC, blasted the ex-king's "craving for private happiness . . . in a manner inconsistent with the Christian principles of marriage, and within a social circle whose standards and ways of life are alien to all the best instincts and traditions of his people."[42] If that much could be pronounced against illicit heterosexuality's threat to the conservative order, surely the objection to homosexuality did not require public explicitness; it was simply understood that Christian-ity opposed homosexuality. One may argue this point theologically, and there are assertive gay Christians in gay congregations, but the biblical passages–Genesis, Leviticus, Romans–are exceedingly clear, and there is no doubt that in the 1930s the vast preponderance of Christian believers in England considered homosexuality detest-able, a sin designated by God Himself as singularly abominable and highly punishable. Blunt, Burgess, and their gay peers knew that their sexuality had a limited appeal; according to the poet Robert Graves, homosexuality was "almost unknown among working people" (not the image given in Peter Parker's *Ackerley* [1989], about a gay writer), but by the 1920s it "had been on the increase among the upper classes for a couple of generations," and he attributed this to "the upper-class boarding school system of keeping boy and girl away from any contact with each other." Graves, a sensitive contemporary (born 1895) whose testimony has value, also noted that in postwar university circles Oscar Wilde was considered a "martyr to the spirit of intolerance."[43]

There is an interesting parallel between Blunt and Burgess and the two central figures of Martin Green's *Children of the Sun* (1975), a study of 1920s British aestheticism with special attention to Oxford. Brian Howard and Harold Acton, both gay and upperclass, both just three years older than Blunt, may be seen with the two gay spies to form an instructive four-paneled tableau: in the middle are the self-destructive, substance-dependent, garrulous, and flamboyant Burgess on the left and Howard on the right. At either end are Blunt and Acton, slender, disciplined, scholarly, enigmatic, and narcissistic. Blunt and Burgess on the left are Cambridge, 1930s politicization; Howard and Acton are on the right, Oxford, 1920s hedonism. All four men were born within a decade of the death of Victoria and between nine and sixteen years after the fall of Oscar Wilde. The shadow of Wilde–this is the central thesis of *Children of the Sun*–fell heavily on England after the poet's conviction for buggery and resultant disgrace in 1895.

Homosexuality and aestheticism, publicly censured in the Christlike figure of Wilde, went underground for a generation, as a triumphant Victorian respectability, and with it a bully, hearty, bluff manliness, reasserted itself. In a sense the mid-century treason of Blunt and Burgess was an act of revenge for the persecution and destruction of Wilde; a deliberate, historically conscious besmirching of the shining edifice by two gays who well knew how that edifice could twist and crush its victims. One need only ponder again Steiner's words, which say all: "the homoerotic ethos may have persuaded . . . Blunt and Burgess that the official society around them . . . was in essence hostile and hypocritical. It was, consequently, ripe for just overthrow, and espionage was one of the necessary means to this good end."[44]

It is impossible to assess precisely the damage the Cambridge spies did to British security. As Thatcher pointed out in her address denouncing Blunt in 1979, the government might not know what information a spy passes on, only what he has access to. But even this was not quite true: Blunt, a very good spy, was a master at stretching access, and he once identified a British informer to the Soviets after simply reading an intelligence report that had been left on a colleague's desk at lunchtime.[45] Blunt was ingratiating, amiable; this is how he approached the chief of British security:

> He made a general assault on key people to see that they liked him. I was interested in art and he always used to sit down next to me in the canteen and chat. And he betrayed us all. He was a very nice and civilised man and I enjoyed talking to him.[46]

The British government, empowered by the Official Secrets Act (which almost all writers on these matters have denounced as an infringement on free inquiry), has restricted access to many pertinent documents relating to the spy ring, and Steiner, citing no less than "a senior Oxford philosopher of impeccable shrewdness," doubted that any coherent, truthful account of Blunt's spying would ever emerge: the forces pressing for a discreet and gentlemanly silence were simply too powerful.

Faced with enigma, Steiner carefully hedges: Blunt "seems to have" handed information to the Soviets in the early 1940s, when he was monitoring neutral London embassies for the Secret Intelligence Service (SIS); and he "may well have" sent, by this action, many East European anticommunists to their deaths at Stalin's hands.[47] Truth is elusive here; this does not mean that the spies are not guilty, but no court of law–and Britain prides itself on being a culture of law, a *Rechtsstaat*–ever pronounced them guilty of a crime. The KGB defector Oleg Gordievsky and the near-omniscient Phillip Knightley considered Kim Philby the most important of the Cambridge spies, particularly at the beginning of the Cold War in 1947-49, when Philby was SIS station commander in Turkey.[48] As for Burgess and Maclean, it is even more difficult to pin a particular leak on them. A 1951 US Joint Chiefs of Staff damage assessment drawn up shortly after Burgess and Maclean defected stated that they, together with other spies, had delivered all pertinent "US/UK/ Canadian planning on atomic energy, US/UK post-war planning and policy in Europe" to the Soviets. Gordievsky has cited one F. V. Kislitsyn, also formerly of the KGB, as the agent to whom Burgess regularly handed over "briefcases full of Foreign Office documents which were photographed in the Soviet embassy and returned."[49]

Testimony involving espionage can be dubious, and juries have often been reluctant to believe double-agents and defectors. Malcolm Muggeridge, after parting from intelligence work, observed categorically that he had "never met anyone professionally engaged in it whom I should care to trust in any capacity."[50] And Graham Greene wrote that "moral judgments are singularly out of place in espionage."[51] As for Blunt, he remained an enigma till his death in 1983, perhaps "a classic double agent, 'turned' by both sides but loyal only to one."[52]

V

There is indeed something enigmatic and unsettling, but some justice, too, in the abrupt "Damn the man" with which Steiner concludes his sensitive 1980 essay "The Cleric of Treason"–an essay in part sympathetic to Blunt.[53] Damnation, once summoned, may engulf unfavorably placed individuals whom the damner would rather see spared. Blunt is guilty; is Britain's governing class innocent? Noel Annan, writing in 1989, noted that informed wrath, which circa 1980 focused on Blunt and the spy ring, had since turned to the cover-up and other, wider targets:

The prime target now is the British establishment and the upper classes. Both they and the security and intelligence services (MI5 and MI6) are represented as more corrupt than the spies. Do they not conceal the guilt of their contemporaries regardless of the damage the spies might still be doing? . . . Hardly surprising. For this was an upper class that had grown effete but maintained its power through the strength of the public-school network, the Oxbridge network, and the homosexual network. At the first sign of trouble they drew up the drawbridge and retreated within their castle, manning the walls of secrecy and disinformation. . . .[54]

Annan leaves no doubt that he thinks there is a degree of truth in the theses he paraphrases. And it is very significant that the change of focus away from the specific guilt of the spies by no means lessens the negative focus on homosexuality. It is seen as part of a corrupt, limp-wristed old-boy network. Implicit here is the contrast between working-class, nationalist-patriotic machismo and upper-class effeminacy, the "people" versus the jaded aristocrats. The gay spies are being made to pay, one senses, for long-festering inequities and resentments: fertile ground for cultural and/or religious fundamentalism. Blunt and Burgess would not have been so reviled in the eighties if they had been working-class and heterosexual. (They would not have been Blunt and Burgess either!) Certainly there have been, and are, corrupt old-boy networks where homosexuality is a shared value separating ins from outs; but other old-boy networks are anti-gay. Blunt and other 1930s Marxists may have believed that the revolution would sweep away such privileged enclaves. Perhaps in the 1990s there is in many countries a higher self-esteem among gay men and a greater openness about sexuality in general. The need for secrecy and deception may be vanishing, and perhaps the fearful and ghettoized quality of affinity-group networking will someday be supplanted by confidence and mutual support.

Coming to conclusions on Blunt and Burgess, from either a gay perspective or otherwise, is difficult. It is really a question of assessing not individual acts–which despite years of inquiry are still largely unspecified–but of measuring entire lives. A few observations may nonetheless be hazarded. The gay spies and their associates have been proclaimed guilty for helping the Stalinist apparatus consolidate itself against the peoples of Eastern Europe and the West in the 1940s and 1950s. But the aid furnished by Britain and the USA to the Soviet Union in the crucial period 1941-45 was vastly more substantial and long-term in its consequences than what the Cambridge spies furnished in their much longer careers. A sober understanding of this fact reduces the two spies' guilt by half, perhaps by ninety percent.

Interest in the gay spies is likely to continue to inform a kind of cult which, with its piquant interplay of personality and history, offers authentic period-piece flavor alluring on a purely atmospheric level. Though some will find this aesthetic approach morally callous or simply stupid, individual gay men may well pick up a mannerism or two from their preoccupation with Blunt and Burgess, just as some gays have gravitated into the orbit of Marlene Dietrich or Oscar Wilde. Blunt and Burgess, celebrated and attractive men, have the potential for becoming gay icons, though not necessarily role models. But the political lesson to be drawn from their lives–Blunt and Burgess would disagree strongly here–is one of caution and skepticism toward utopian political causes, particularly if they espouse violence or hatred, as Marxist "class struggle" more or less has to. Aiding a brutal system, Blunt and Burgess deceived and ultimately disappointed their friends. Though the revulsion directed against them was out of proportion and in many instances bigoted, they could derive scant comfort from this, and they both ended their lives unhappily.

AUTHOR NOTE

Fred Sommer was born in the United States in 1953 and was awarded a doctorate in German from the University of Wisconsin in 1983. He has taught English in Latin America and German in Europe. Interested in nineteenth- and twentieth-century European culture, he edited *Karl Emil Franzos: Kritik und Dichtung* (Frankfurt am Main: Peter Lang, 1991), a collection of prose by the nineteenth-century Austrian author.

NOTES

1. George Steiner, "The Cleric of Treason," *New Yorker* 56.42 (December 8, 1980): 183.

2. Louis MacNeice, *The Strings Are False: An Unfinished Autobiography* (London: Faber and Faber, 1965), p. 95.

3. John Costello, *Mask of Treachery* (New York: W. Morrow, 1990), pp. 189, 195.

4. Simon Freeman and Barrie Penrose, *Conspiracy of Silence: The Secret Life of Anthony Blunt* (New York, 1988), p. 203. This is by far the best book on the gay spies.

5. Harold Acton, *More Memoirs of an Aesthete* (London: Methuen, 1970), p. 87.

6. Freeman and Penrose, p. 79.

7. Ibid., p. 119.

8. Ibid., p. 121.

9. Noel Annan, *Our Age: Portrait of a Generation* (London: Weidenfeld and Nicolson, 1990), p. 226-27.

10. Malcolm Muggeridge, *Chronicles of Wasted Time*, vol. 2: *The Infernal Grove* (London: Collins, 1973), p. 107.

11. Goronwy Rees, *A Chapter of Accidents* (London: Chatto & Windus, 1972), p. 113.

12. Freeman and Penrose, p. 135. Burgess's code name within Soviet intelligence was "Mädchen"–German for "girl." See also John Costello and Oleg Tsarev, *Deadly Illusions* (New York: Crown, 1993), passim.

13. Costello, p. 467.

14. Annan, p. 230.

15. Freeman and Penrose, p. 156.

16. Two sources assert that George VI, father of the present Queen, sent Blunt to Friedrichshof castle at Kronberg, near Frankfurt am Main, Germany, in late April or early May, 1945, to retrieve early-1940s correspondence of the ex-King Edward VIII with German government officials. Publicity in the 1980s on Blunt's services to the royal family probably weakened the monarchy, a weakness which reached a crisis stage in the 1990s. See Costello, pp. 404-24, and Peter Wright, *Spycatcher: The Candid Autobiography of a Senior Intelligence Officer* (New York: Viking, 1987), p. 223. See also Sean Callery, *Scandals: Gripping Accounts of the Exposed and Deposed* (London: Apple, 1992), pp. 40-45.

17. Freeman and Penrose, p. 311.

18. MacNeice, p. 85.

19. Noreen Branson and Margot Heinemann, *Britain in the Nineteen Thirties* (London: Weidenfeld and Nicolson, 1971), p. 159.

20. Robert Sencourt, *The Reign of Edward VIII* (London: Gibbs and Phillips, 1962), pp. 31, 32.

21. Henry Pelling, *The British Communist Party: A Historical Profile* (London: A. and C. Black, 1958), p. 192.

22. Christopher Andrew and Oleg Gordievsky, *KGB: The Inside Story* (London: Hodder and Stoughton, 1990), p. 145.

23. Ibid., p. 151.

24. Ibid., p. 157.

25. Costello, p. 262.

26. Ibid., p. 263.

27. Andrew and Gordievsky, p. 178.

28. Costello, p. 280.

29. Andrew and Gordievsky, p. 148.

30. Arthur Koestler, *The Invisible Writing* (London: Hutchinson, 1969), p. 254.

31. Costello, p. 281.

32. Freeman and Penrose, pp. 88, 90.

33. Andrew and Gordievsky, p. 160. The carnal, worldly appeal wielded by Arnold Deutsch on the heterosexual spy Kim Philby has been described in these terms: "His name was Arnold Deutsch and, 50 years later, Philby seems still under the spell of Deutsch's magnetism, an almost sexual seduction. . . . Deutsch was a charismatic former sexologist, originally a follower of Wilhelm Reich, the Freudian Marxist schismatic who made healthy orgasms the key to personal as well as societal revolu-

tion. The lingering influence of this doctrine on Philby may be glimpsed in a not entirely facetious inscription in a book that turned up in the Sotheby's consignment . . . : 'An orgasm a day keeps the doctor away.'" Ron Rosenbaum, "Kim Philby and the Age of Paranoia," *New York Times Magazine,* July 10, 1994, p. 35.

34. Nigel West, *Seven Spies Who Changed the World* (London: Secker and Warburg, 1991), pp. 113, 223; Andrew and Gordievsky, pp. 159-61.

35. Phillip Knightley, *Philby: The Life and Views of the KGB Masterspy* (London: A. Deutsch, 1988), p. 222.

36. Friedrich Engels and Karl Marx, *The Communist Manifesto,* ed. David Ryazanoff (New York: Russell and Russell, 1963), p. 38.

37. Costello, pp. 32-34.

38. Freeman and Penrose, p. 307.

39. Ibid., p. 304; Costello, p. 228.

40. Freeman and Penrose, p. 328.

41. Rees, pp. 190-91.

42. James Laver, *Between the Wars* (London: Vista, 1961), p. 213.

43. Robert Graves and Alan Hodge, *The Long Week-End: A Social History of Great Britain, 1918-1939* (London: Faber and Faber, 1971), p. 97.

44. Steiner (see note 1), p. 183. In a passage written in 1952 that has considerable bearing on the psychology of Blunt and Burgess, the Italian writer Curzio Malaparte commented on a connection between European communism and (male) homosexuality: "In homosexual communism one sees above all an antibourgeois reaction against the conformity of upper-class society. The homosexuals who turned to communism acted out of stubbornness and spite, and spite played the more important part in this matter. I have known various homosexual communists, and what struck me in all of them was the attitude of confrontation directed against bourgeois society and against imperialist, bellicose America." Curzio Malaparte, *Mamma Marcia* (Florence: Vallecchi, 1959), pp. 321-22; my translation.

45. West, p. 100.

46. Andrew and Gordievsky, p. 243.

47. Steiner, pp. 172-76.

48. Andrew and Gordievsky, p. 175, and Knightley (see note 35).

49. Andrew and Gordievsky, p. 323.

50. Muggeridge, p. 157.

51. Graham Greene, *Collected Essays* (London: Penguin, 1970), p. 311.

52. Steiner, p. 175.

53. Ibid., p. 195.

54. Noel Annan, "The Upper Class and the Underworld," *New York Review of Books* 36.6 (April 13, 1989): 24.

Between Marxism and Psychoanalysis: Antifascism and Antihomosexuality in the Frankfurt School

Randall Halle

Cambridge, Massachusetts

SUMMARY. In their efforts to utilize individualist psychoanalysis as a tool for understanding mass behavior, the social theorists associated with the Frankfurt School increasingly came to rely on a static, essentializing construction of sexuality which ultimately led to an equation of fascism and homosexuality. Heretofore unexamined in studies of the Frankfurt School, this equation will here serve as the starting point for a fundamental critique of the concept of sexuality developed by this influential circle of Marxist thinkers. While directed at the concept of sexuality, such a critique more importantly opens up the underlying understanding of the social and psychological realms advanced by Critical Theory. Attending to the equation of homosexuality and fascism as the central point of concern, this essay will first trace the introduction of psychoanalysis into Critical Theory through Erich Fromm and then investigate the extent of Fromm's influence on the concept of sexuality propounded by his colleagues, especially Max Horkheimer and Theodor W. Adorno. Finally, it will take up a frequently overlooked essay by Herbert Marcuse which promoted a vision of sexuality radically different from that of his associates.

Correspondence may be addressed: 31 Rice St., Cambridge, MA 02140.

[Haworth co-indexing entry note]: "Between Marxism and Psychoanalysis: Antifascism and Antihomosexuality in the Frankfurt School." Halle, Randall. Co-published simultaneously in *Journal of Homosexuality* (The Haworth Press, Inc.) Vol. 29, No. 4, 1995, pp. 295-317; and: *Gay Men and the Sexual History of the Political Left* (ed: Gert Hekma, Harry Oosterhuis, and James Steakley) The Haworth Press, Inc., 1995, pp. 295-317; and *Gay Men and the Sexual History of the Political Left* (ed: Gert Hekma, Harry Oosterhuis, and James Steakley) Harrington Park Press, an imprint of The Haworth Press, Inc., 1995, pp. 295-317. Multiple copies of this article/chapter may be purchased from The Haworth Document Delivery Center. [1-800-342-9678, 9:00 a.m. - 5:00 p.m. (EST)].

295

I

With the end of the Cold War, the work of the Frankfurt School deserves increased attention. From the beginning, the social theorists associated with the Institute for Social Research occupied a difficult ideological position. Critical of the effects of capitalism on modernity and apprehensive about the increasing power of authoritarian structures throughout the world, they embarked on a series of studies which separated them from contemporary left and liberal positions. Their efforts to unite Marxist dialectics and psychoanalysis placed them outside traditional party lines. Their interdisciplinary research established paradigms applicable to current studies of culture. These paradigms have added significance, for the Critical Theory of the Frankfurt School was developed in the West, separate from the "scientific socialism" of the East Bloc, and continues to maintain its critical edge. It is beyond the scope of this essay to act as an introduction to the œuvre of the Frankfurt School, especially since historical studies by a number of scholars have extensively chronicled its development and described its place within the Freudian left.[1] Instead, in the spirit of Critical Theory itself, this essay will focus on and seek to critique one of its major tenets: precisely the union of Marxist dialectics and psychoanalysis. This essay will examine how, in their efforts to utilize individualist psychoanalysis as a tool for understanding mass behavior, the social theorists associated with the Frankfurt School increasingly came to rely on a static, essentializing construction of sexuality which ultimately led to an equation of fascism and homosexuality. In examining this untenable equation at length, this essay seeks both to historicize the Frankfurt School and to liberate its legacy for even more productive forms of critical analysis.

The introduction of the homosexual into Critical Theory can be traced to Erich Fromm. Born in 1900, Fromm remained in his hometown Frankfurt am Main until 1919. After studying law for two years, he transferred to the university of Heidelberg, where his interests turned to sociology, philosophy, and psychology. Fromm's exposure to psychoanalysis also began during this period. In 1927, he was invited to deliver his first lectures on psychoanalysis at the Berlin Institute for Psychoanalysis, whose membership formed an impressive list: Hans Sachs, Sandor Radó, Siegfried Bernfeld, Karen

Horney, Wilhelm Reich, and Ernst Simmel. It was not simply a matter of chance that the Institute, which had steadily grown in reputation until it finally came to rival Vienna, championed a rather unorthodox approach. Its location in Berlin, while still within German-speaking territory, allowed for some distance from Freud.

In 1929, one year prior to completing his training as an analyst, Fromm accepted a position at the newly founded Frankfurt Psychoanalytic Institute (Frankfurter Psychoanalytisches Institut), a branch of the Institute for Social Research (Institut für Sozialforschung). Max Horkheimer, recently elected head of the Institute for Social Research, was responsible for establishing this branch with the specific intent of drawing the psychoanalytic method into the working practice of the Frankfurt School with the hope that it would aid the Institute in its efforts at social criticism. For the next three years, Fromm travelled back and forth regularly between Berlin, where he had established a private practice, and Frankfurt, in order to hold lectures. This came to an end in 1933, when Fromm left Germany for a guest lectureship at the University of Chicago–a trip that turned into an extended period of exile.

Developing the foundation for a social-psychological method was not easy for Fromm, who found it necessary to overcome what he saw as the psychoanalytic concentration on individual psychology. The application of psychoanalysis on a social level required that Fromm make many modifications to orthodox Freudianism. Paradoxically, it was these modifications which would later force him to leave the Frankfurt School.

In his first essay for the Frankfurt School's journal, Fromm laid the foundation for his later theoretical developments. He admitted that psychoanalysis was deficient because of Freud's personal (pre)occupation with individual psychology. This (pre)occupation, combined with the psychoanalytic community's concentration on "sick and healthy members of modern society and largely of the middle class," meant turning "bourgeois-capitalist society into an absolute."[2] Such a generalization resulted in the exclusion of questions of class and economy, i.e., "the material living conditions of the group under study."[3] Fromm refrained from criticizing the psychoanalytic apparatus itself, critiquing just its class-specific deployment.

Dismissing the notion of the Oedipus complex as a product of this deployment, Fromm went on to define the proper object of a new social-psychological method: "to explain the shared, socially relevant, psychic attitudes and ideologies–and their unconscious roots in particular–in terms of the influence of economic conditions on libido strivings."[4] Fromm thus replaced the Oedipus complex with a drive-based concept of human behavior. In positing the existence of essential universal human drives, Fromm was asserting the fundamental psychological equality of all men. He was also able to explain the diversity of human desire as a result of social inequality. Class positions, he maintained, were responsible for variously limiting and deforming the expression of the drives, resulting in different forms of desire. He did not, however, support a heterogeneity of desire. Retaining a psychoanalytic base, Fromm gave coitus a privileged position as the telos of essential drives. Other forms of desire were thus positioned as deviant, as expressions of social deformation, and these desires were seen as forming character.

II

Social psychology found rapid acceptance at the Institute for Social Research. Max Horkheimer (1895-1973), a former analysand himself, was open to the psychoanalytic method and especially to Fromm's application of it. Born and raised in Stuttgart, Horkheimer delved into Gestalt psychology as a student, although he eventually turned his attention from Gestalt psychology to psychoanalysis. His university studies in Frankfurt soon led to a position as lecturer, an affiliation that helped him in establishing the Institute for Social Research, whose directorship he eventually assumed.

The influence of psychoanalysis on Horkheimer, and particularly Fromm's developing social-psychological model, can be discerned very clearly in an essay on "History and Psychology" that Horkheimer wrote for the first issue of the Institute's journal in 1932. Here Horkheimer pursued the understanding of social psychology set forth by Fromm in the same issue. History, Horkheimer asserted, could not remain theoretically unaffected by psychology. Following Fromm, he stated that as helpmate to history, psychology "is no longer concerned with man in the general sense":

Instead, for each epoch the totality of psychical forces which
can unfold in individuals, the strivings which underlie their
manual and intellectual accomplishments, and further the psychical factors which enrich social and individual life processes
must be differentiated from the relatively static psychological
constitution of individuals, groups, classes, races, nations that
are determined by the overall social structures in each
instance–in short, from their characters.[5]

Without such assistance from psychology, historiography was impossible.

With the introduction of psychoanalysis into Critical Theory, a
split occurred between what we can recognize as the social and the
psychic. Up to the point of Fromm's entry into the Frankfurt
School, dialectical materialism as adumbrated in the writings of the
young Marx had served as the main theoretical apparatus. Now
dialectical materialism became a theoretical tool with a specific
object: it was used to explain the social. This object was separate
from that of psychoanalysis, which was used to explain the psychic.
Before the work on social psychology, both theories had existed in a
state of competition as a result of their claims to be absolute epis-
temological systems. Fromm sought to undo this competition by
making them into cooperating theories within a unifying system of
social psychology. Through his rejection of the Oedipus complex, he
defined social psychology in such a way as to make both the social
and the psychic its objects of study. The psychic, as embodied by the
natural drives, was held to be immutable and static, whereas the
social was understood as alterable and dynamic. The psychic was the
moment of universality, and the social was the moment of limitation.
Individual character formed at the intersection of these two moments. Yet the social-psychological interest in character did not sub-
limate the difference between social and psychic.

Character was like a thin membrane between the social and the
psychological located on the individual. It grew out of the interaction of natural, universal human drives and a predetermined social
setting. Fromm posited certain types of character resulting from the
method of production of a particular society. Character was supra-
individual, and character typology (characterology) provided the

theoretical means to move between individual and mass. Fromm saw healthy character as the result of a balance between a healthy society and a healthy psyche.

As the means to bring about healthy social organization, Fromm devoted himself not to mass organizing but rather to understanding the interaction between society and the psyche. He regarded libidinal energy as a constant force towards genitality, an ever-present psychic drive whose redirection required that society expend a certain amount of oppositional energy. Society was always confronted with the demands of these drives, whose persistence led to a constant restructuring of society, resulting at times in a decrease, at times in an increase in the amount of social energy expended to direct libidinal demands. Neither revolutionary nor reformist, Fromm's understanding remained primarily a critical project directed at describing existing conditions.

In a second 1932 essay, "Psychoanalytic Characterology and Its Relevance for Social Psychology," Fromm sought to delineate the power dynamic of society and the psyche as constructed under capitalism.[6] He described how capitalism gave rise to anal character and went on to suggest that inasmuch as certain forms of social organization gave rise to types of character, these forms of organization could in turn be described as having their own social character. The essay ends rather abruptly, having relied heavily on a tautological argument.

Fromm nevertheless continued this type of analysis in his next major work, the "Social-Psychological Section" of *Studien über Autorität und Familie* (Studies on Authority and the Family). Published in Paris in 1936, when the Frankfurt School was already in exile, this volume was a collective work comprising contributions by various members writing from their own disciplinary perspectives. As a theoretical work, it can be read as a precursor to the Frankfurt School's later study of the authoritarian personality. Continuing his earlier work in his contribution, Fromm now responded directly to the fascization of the Western world market by positing an authoritarian character which existed in authoritarian social structures. In particular, he proposed a connection between authoritarian submissiveness and the homosexual. The homosexual character, like the anal character in Fromm's previous study, was both an agent and expression of an authoritarian society.

Confronted with the *Gleichschaltung* (thoroughgoing Nazification) of German society and the apparent willingness of the populace to submit to an authoritarian social organization, Fromm used the homosexual to interpret mass support for fascism. Here it was by no means a sexual act which signified the homosexual–or at least not a homosexual act. The submissive individual was "homosexual" by virtue of his character: "From a physiological perspective, the average authoritarian man is heterosexual. From a psychical perspective, however, he is homosexual."[7] Fromm did open up the possibility that this homosexual might engage in homosexual acts: "In a number of individuals, this component of homosexuality will also transform itself rather frequently into manifest homosexuality in the more narrow sense."[8] But the question of latent or manifest had little significance in this argument.

In Fromm's essay, the homosexual 'in the broader sense' was linked to authoritarian submissiveness through a discussion of sadomasochism. Understood as a form of sexual power dynamic, sadomasochism was used metaphorically to sexualize the power dynamic of fascism. Fromm equated the sadomasochist and the homosexual in terms of misogyny: the sadist beat women, the homosexual rejected them. Bearing in mind that for Fromm the "homosexual" in a broad sense was heterosexual and only in a narrow sense homosexual, it is clear how this linkage could occur. The heterosexual who hated women was the homosexual, provided of course that hetero-coital practices were accepted as the natural telos of sexual development and every other type of sexual practice was seen as deviating from this position. According to Fromm's paradigm, sex between men deviated because it placed the phallus elsewhere, not in the woman. Men who rejected the natural role of women as the 'phallic receptacle' were rejecting woman; they were misogynists.

This conflation of all that deviated from a constructed norm allowed for the simple identification of an anti-utopic force. It should be emphasized that homosexuality was not presented here as the negative in a dialectic process, the moment leading to new synthesis on the journey to utopia. Fascism itself occupied this antithetical position in Fromm's social psychology, while homosexuality was construed as a braking mechanism that slowed the dialectical process. Regarded as the result of adverse economic conditions, deviant (homo)sexuality was described by Fromm as acting as a conserving mechanism of those economic conditions. Clearly the goal of his antifascist struggle was not to liberate a heterogeneity of sexualities, but rather to establish a homogeneous sexuality. This notion of "homosexuality" became one of the underlying postulates of Critical Theory.

Having been established as a quintessential component of the social-psychological critique of fascism, the nexus of the homosexual and the fascist would reappear in Adorno and Horkheimer's work. Here, however, it was functionalized differently as a result of diverging understandings of the relation of society to the psyche. In exile in the United States, Fromm broke off his connections with his former colleagues because his work was taking him in other directions.

III

During this period, Theodor W. Adorno (1903-69) came to have increasing influence on Horkheimer. Born and raised in Frankfurt am Main, Adorno had maintained loose connections with the Institute for Social Research during his student years in the early thirties. It was not until 1938, when he was in New York exile, that Adorno actually became a full member. In their collaborations, Adorno and Horkheimer committed Critical Theory to an ultra-orthodox Freudianism, a position which resulted in growing tension with Fromm. Horkheimer accused Fromm of creating a psychology of mere "common sense" with his work on characterology.[9] On the surface, it would appear that the main source of the divergence was Fromm's rejection of the Oedipus complex. Yet beneath this superficial explanation lay a more fundamental difference in the understanding of the relation of society to the psyche. This can be elaborated most clearly by analyzing the appearances of the "homosexual"–the result of a specific theorizing of the social and the psychic–in the work of Adorno and Horkheimer.

Because of their refusal to view fascism as an isolated phenomenon, Adorno and Horkheimer were opposed to any direct discussion of fascism: "Anyone who does not want to discuss capitalism should also keep silent about fascism," Horkheimer would say.[10] Instead, they embedded their discussions of fascism in research on areas such as anti-Semitism and authoritarianism. "Anyone who wants to explain anti-Semitism must examine National Socialism. Without an understanding of what has happened in Germany, speaking about anti-Semitism in Siam or Africa remains meaningless. This new anti-Semitism is the emissary of the totalitarian order into which the liberalistic has developed."[11]

If we enter into the work of Adorno and Horkheimer through the homosexual, where do we find ourselves? Sprinkled throughout *The Authoritarian Personality* (1950) and mentioned only in a single reference in *Dialectic of Enlightenment* (1947), homosexuality was treated as a side issue, on the margins; even so, it was tied intimately to the study of anti-Semitism and authoritarianism. The homosexual is instrumentalized differently in these two works. Most blatantly and yet most overlooked in the contributions of Adorno and Horkheimer to the Frankfurt School, the homosexual stood at the borders at the very place where enlightenment, in its dialectic, flipped over into its negative. The homosexual here was an anti-Semite.

Dialectic of Enlightenment was written in two stages, the major studies having been ended, if not entirely completed, in 1944.[12] Since the book was never polished or refined, it retained a certain notebook quality, setting forth diverse theses and leaving them as such. Prior to publication in 1947, a final section was added to the chapter "Elements of Anti-Semitism: Limits of Enlightenment." The book was written during World War II and was a response to the war, but also to more than the war. Direct discussions of fascism, albeit numerous, were limited, because the book strove in its critique to go beyond the phenomena of war and fascism, taking as its object the metaphenomena which underlay these others.

The Holocaust was most directly addressed in the chapter on anti-Semitism. This chapter sought to analyze the conditions which could lead to the Holocaust or, more specifically, the mechanisms under which "individuals are branded as Jews and sent to the gas chamber."[13] This distinction, which focused on a "Jew brand," was an important one. Whether conscious or unconscious, intended or unintended, it excluded from study all the others who were victims of the Holocaust, focusing solely on the Jewish experience. The object of this chapter then was not the Holocaust in its entirety but the Jews as victims of the Holocaust. It made no pretensions to be a total explanation of the entire mosaic of victims of the Holocaust, all the lives stamped unworthy of life. This distinction alone made it possible for the homosexual to appear here as he did, not as victim but as victimizer.

Of the seven sections of the chapter on anti-Semitism, with the final one being a later addition, the section on the homosexual nature of anti-Semitism appeared as the sixth–the original concluding cause in 1944. The first five sections dealt with the sociohistorical sources of anti-Semitism in terms of its volkish religious foundation. The sixth turned to the psychological sources of anti-Semitism. Here Horkheimer and Adorno explained that their analysis followed "the psychoanalytical theory of morbid projection."[14] This theory led them beneath the surface of the individual subject to the construction of his unconscious. The use of this theory marked a break with Fromm's work on characterology by asserting more orthodox psychoanalytic theory. It further served to substantiate their assertion that "the forbidden action which is converted into aggression is generally homosexual in nature."[15]

The idea of morbid projection returned to the psychoanalytic notion of essential drives, yet it diverged from the understanding of these drives set forth by Fromm. For Adorno and Horkheimer, drives lay in the unconscious, waiting impatiently for their expression. In certain subjects, however, the superego prohibited direct expression of these desires, forcing the ego to discharge the drives of the energetic id through aggressive projection. The psychoanalytic map employed by Adorno and Horkheimer took them to the source of this abnormal prohibition: the "homosexual" character.[16] In this understanding, homosexual desire appeared as inherently repressible–the desire which cannot be named. There was no discussion of the social component of repression. It was presumed that the id of the homosexual, naturally unable to express homosexual desire, found release elsewhere–in anti-Semitism.

Within the Oedipal framework to which Adorno and Horkheimer subscribed, psychoanalysis explained homosexuality as originating in castration anxiety. Fear of castration at the hands of the father as a result of desiring the mother resulted in the child shifting desire onto the father. The heterosexual child repressed its desire until the time when it found a surrogate for its mother. The homosexual child continued to desire, yet that desire was left inexpressible, resulting in morbid projection.

Given the divergence between Adorno/Horkheimer and Fromm, it is important to point out common ground: once again the homosexual was not an identity whose signification relied on certain homosexual acts. The homosexual here remained a personality-constituting, essential trait, a character. Adorno and Horkheimer were interested in the homosexual as a source of acts, not in homosexuality as an act. In seeking to explain the psychological background to a mass act–the Holocaust–they posited a mass character–the homosexual–as source.

In 1950, the study *The Authoritarian Personality* was published. Here the homosexual functioned as he had in *Dialectic of Enlightenment*, albeit with more frequent references. He appeared directly in the discussion of the interview apparatus, yet not openly. Nowhere was any interviewee asked, nor was any interviewer instructed to ask, whether the interviewee was a homosexual. The most direct question which touched on the matter was: "Have you met many homosexuals in your travels?"[17] Yet in her description of the interviewing process, Else Frenkel-Brunswik stated clearly that along with "attention to the 'orality' and 'anality' of the subject . . . the problem of homosexual tendencies, their degree, and the subject's acceptance or rejection of them was also given consideration."[18] This was because "the problem of homosexuality relates to the different ways of failure in resolving the Oedipal conflict and the resultant regression to earlier [oral and anal] phases."[19]

With this conception of the homosexual, the study took a different tack than its approach, for example, to the role of childhood disciplining. For the analysts, discipline was a learning experience, a question of socialization, whereas homosexuality was regarded as an inherent trait, essentially immature, which prevented a "mature" relationship to authority. The notion of the homosexual personality was evidenced when R. Nevitt Sanford analyzed Mack in the section entitled "Submission, Passivity, and Homosexuality." Sanford in no way required homosexual acts to make a diagnosis of homosexuality in Mack's case. He hypothesized Mack's homosexuality on the basis of perceived personality traits. Sanford stated:

> Even without this piece of evidence [that Mack was afraid of a picture of a hypnotist] we would be led to hypothesize repressed homosexuality in order to explain some of the outstanding features of Mack's personality development. The material is replete with manifestations of authoritarian submission.[20]

Sanford plainly regarded authoritarian submission as a consequence of homosexuality. He illustrated this idea in a diagram tracing the impact of Mack's homosexuality on his personality construction. This elaborate diagram featured homosexuality as one of its main points. Not only was Mack's homosexuality directly responsible for his "authoritarian submission," but the diagram charted how it was also directly or indirectly linked with his "fear of weakness," "self-pity," "assertions of strength and independence," "glorification of powerful ingroup figures," "striving for power and status," "concealment of softness," "rejection of women," and more.[21] In this study the homosexual, Mack, ceased to function as an individual. He represented here the masses of A-type personalities.

A post-Stonewall episteme might lead one to ask: If only poor Mack could have come to terms with his true nature, would he have been so authoritarian? In the Frankfurt paradigm, however, Mack was a homosexual, albeit a repressed one. The goal of the analysis was hardly to cure Mack, and certainly not by helping to remove his 'repression.' Whether a source of anti-Semitism or a source of authoritarian submission, the homosexual functioned within these psychological critiques as the origin of pathological behavior. The homosexual was inherently pathological and had to be overcome, not liberated.

It is important to note that Horkheimer and Adorno's understanding of the homosexual and his relation to either anti-Semitism or authority maintained a strict theoretical division between the social and the psychic. In doing so they rejected the social-psychological attempts to bridge psychoanalysis and dialectical materialism, a rejection with the added consequence of breaking any causal relationships between the two moments. In *Dialectic of Enlightenment*, the homosexual character of the anti-Semite arose independently of society, determined by a purely psychological reason: fear of castration. To explain this development, Adorno and Horkheimer employed psychoanalysis as a purely psychological method. Society was likewise described as developing according to its own material laws that could be explained through dialectical materialism. And these developments were separate from the psyche. In the seventh section of the chapter "Elements of Anti-Semitism," they furthered the separation of the social and the psychic. The section's opening statement, "But there are no more anti-Semites,"[22] dramatically attested to Horkheimer and Adorno's belief in a spectacular alteration of the postwar world. In this thesis they went on to analyze how anti-Semitism had been sublimated into a different form in the postwar period, leaving the homosexual behind.

For Adorno and Horkheimer, the homosexual character found expression in authoritarian society. The homosexual as pathological deviant manifested itself in a pathological and deviant society. The Third Reich was a social structure in which "the pressure of pent-up homosexual aggression" found release in anti-Semitic projection.[23] The pathological homosexual preceded the anti-Semite, however, just as homosexual pathology preceded fascism. This understanding of the social and the psychic was highly deterministic and rejected Fromm's assertion of the fundamental equality of all men. For Adorno and Horkheimer, just as there was social inequality, there was also psychological inequality. Thus in the relation of the social and the psychic as set forth by Adorno and Horkheimer, the homosexual figured as an ever-present potential. The absence of authoritarian society would not mean that the authoritarian personality had disappeared as well, as the study on the authoritarian personality was meant to show. A tension was established in Critical Theory by Horkheimer and Adorno in relation to the homosexual. As much as Critical Theory did (or did not) act to change existing society, it left no provision for changing the psyche, unless it would be a declaration of war on heterogeneity. *The Authoritarian Personality* offered only descriptions, no solutions. Pushed back into the dark due to a shift in material conditions, repressed homosexuality lay waiting for a society which would allow it expression.

In all these instances, the ability to constitute a homosexual origin for anti-Semitism and authoritarian submissiveness resulted from an overinflation of the sexual. By committing themselves to psychoanalysis as the theoretical apparatus used to explain the psyche, Fromm, Adorno, and Horkheimer accepted a sex-based understanding of the subject. All of the individual's desires could only be understood as sexual. This was further compounded in the case of Horkheimer and Adorno by their insistence on the strict distinction between the psychic and the social. Critical Theory was forced into seeking explanations for subjective behavior without any social context. These explanations limited the heterogeneity of subjective desire to two homogeneous sexual sources, one of which was the pathological. The choice of the homosexual to represent the pathological in these explanations was not purely gratuitous. An already established Other to the privileged heterosexual of psychoanalysis, the homosexual had long since been functionalized in dialectical materialism's critique of capitalism.[24]

A superficial reading of Adorno's "Sexualtabus und Recht heute" (Sexual Taboos and Justice Today), published in 1963, might suggest that he later moderated his attitude towards homosexuality. Closer examination reveals, however, that although he seemed to express a spirit of tolerance here, he still had found no way out of the impasse of Frankfurt School social psychology. This essay initially appeared in an anthology entitled *Sexualität und Verbrechen* (Sexuality and Crime), intended by its editors as a response to the new penal code draft under discussion in the West German parliament. The proposed penal code basically brought back into effect pre-Nazi era standards and laws and, of particular concern to the editors, continued to criminalize abortion and homosexuality. The volume aimed to promote a discussion of these issues within the idea of tolerance, hoping that such a discussion might influence the parliamentary debates.

Adorno's contribution opened with a scathing critique of the very possibility of sexual liberation in an "unfree" society.[25] However, to represent where the possibilities of liberation lay, he again invoked the Freudian model of sexuality. At this point there seemed to be a fundamental revision of his attitude toward homosexuality. He wrote of the hegemony of genitality over the partial drives of the libido.[26] Carrying this critique further could not have undone the opposition of homo- and heterosexual in the Freudian paradigm, yet it could potentially have placed homosexuality on the same discursive level as heterosexuality. This potential remained unrealized. Adorno devoted only one single page to actual discussion of the homosexual. Using arguments already developed in the previous century, he disparaged the new penal code as a gift to blackmailers. He followed this "argument" with a further "defense": If homosexuality is caused by a neurotic inhibition of the normal resolution of the Oedipus complex, added social and legal pressures would only make it even more neurotic.[27] Adorno's brief discussion concluded with the assertion (perhaps a result of his work in exile with Thomas Mann) that many homosexuals are very good artists and thus useful to society.

Adorno dropped the discussion of homosexuality at this point. In all fairness, it should be noted that, contrary to the stated goals of the anthology, he did not even touch upon the issue of abortion. Instead he discussed at length prostitution and the age of consent, suggesting that under the hegemony of genitality two groups–prostitutes and minors–came to bear the burden of society's taboos. Individual social suffering, Adorno argued, was transferred onto sexuality and then projected outward.[28] But the essay offered neither an analysis of social suffering nor any suggestion on alleviating it. Adorno remained on the psychoanalytic level, excluding all questions of social power; for example, while focusing on the reason why people hate prostitutes, he entirely ignored the conditions which give rise to prostitution and passed over in silence the actual situation of prostitutes. He also viewed child abuse as a sexual act. While the overt homosexual had apparently become socially acceptable in this essay, the dangerous realm of latent sexuality remained intact. Such a discussion was only possible through the continued overinflation of the sexual, mediating all social actions through sexuality.

IV

The means to deflate this discursive sphere of the sexual, to prevent this conflation of the homosexual and the fascist, had already been mooted within the journal of the Institute for Social Research itself. Marcuse's 1936 essay "On Hedonism" marked an opening in Critical Theory which would later be shut down. Born in Berlin, Herbert Marcuse (1898-1979) had joined the Institute in 1932 after studying in Freiburg, where he had been heavily influenced by Martin Heidegger. The essay was written at a time when Marcuse was working most intently on Hegel and before he was heavily influenced by psychoanalysis, and it was published in the midst of a series of collaborations between Marcuse and Horkheimer. These collaborations figured as the initial manifestos of Critical Theory, committing it to dialectical analysis. This analysis, which provided the central theoretical framework for the historical development portrayed in Marcuse's essay, offered the means within the tradition of the Frankfurt School to obviate the division of the social and the psychic discussed above. Marcuse himself did not maintain this analysis, for his further work resulted in his acceptance of the psychoanalytic framework. After Fromm's departure from the Frankfurt School, Marcuse joined Adorno and Horkheimer as the most vocal defenders of Freudian orthodoxy as well as critics of Fromm's conception of social psychology.

In his 1936 essay, Marcuse returned to the classical philosophical debates on hedonism, situating them as the framework for the debates of the modern period. Marcuse pointed to a dialectical tension between happiness and reason in modern philosophy inherited from the Greek tradition, a tension primarily expressed in conceptions of the desiring individual and the state. In developing this argument, Marcuse promoted a structural relationship between the economic and the ideational world. Productive forces affected and were affected by the conceptual world, as expressed here in philosophy.

Marcuse constantly correlated developments in philosophy with developments in the means of production, identifying two types of hedonism within the philosophical tradition. The hedonism of the cynics stemmed from the more originary stance of an anarchic period of society. It was succeeded by the hedonism of the Epicurean tradition, which stemmed from a time after the development of a slave economy.[29] Epicurean hedonism responded to and resulted from the development of rational philosophy as part of a concurrent development out of anarchy. The desiring individual of the cynics, whose sole purpose in life had been the achievement of happiness, was opposed by rational philosophy which sought "the free rational shaping of the conditions of life, the domination of nature, and the critical autonomy of the associated individuals."[30] Epicurean philosophy extended the cynical critique to this new stage. The tension between rational and Epicurean philosophy, the result of the move out of economic anarchy, was then carried through all subsequent changes in the economic and ideational world, because at no point in time was the master/slave relationship ever completely undone. Marcuse pointed to the condition of the proletariat as the continuation of this relationship.

In the cynical concept of hedonism, the individual was understood as the locus of heterogeneous desires not primarily sexual. Marcuse accepted this conception of the desiring individual, yet sought through the category of truth to differentiate between the real and false desires of the individual. He turned first to Epicurean hedonism as the failed result of such a project and discussed how it made happiness a dependent subcategory of reason. Accepting reason as the highest human pursuit, the individual was doomed to accept present unhappiness for greater future happiness. Epicurean hedonism established a tenuous system whereby suffering, or the repression of pleasure, was accepted as necessary for the attainment of future pleasure. In response, the rational philosophy of Plato resulted in a further differentiation of real and false desires by defining real pleasure as a form of reasoning which supported the social order. "Only those wants may be satisfied which make the individual a good citizen."[31]

In order to differentiate between real and false desires, Marcuse established a form of analysis which, by taking the various constructions of desire as its object, broke with all previous critiques. Marcuse presented neither inscriptions of desire into various acts like coitus, as in Freud's work, nor moral modalities of sex-love, as in the work of Friedrich Engels or August Bebel.[32] He accomplished this through a double maneuver: proceeding in his analysis from the desiring individual, and analyzing the history of desire as the history of social limitations and constructions. Engels had begun such a process in the analysis of family structures, but he had assumed that desire itself was static, sexual, and limited to a specific choice of object. Marcuse, on the other hand, simply separated desire from reproduction, which had the added effect of liberating his analysis from viewing women as reproductive vessels. Marcuse's desiring individual was limited neither by sex nor by gender. Such limitations were understood as stemming from socioeconomic conditions, not as inherent and essential traits. In opposition to the work of Fromm, or the later developments of Critical Theory (which he himself would participate in), Marcuse did not separate the social from the psychic. If he assumed an individual who was essentially desiring, he did not follow the psychoanalytic model that resulted in essential forms of desire or character.

Marcuse traced the development of desire through the modern period, discussing the continued and growing alienation of individuals from their real desires. In the modern period, desire was constructed as external and damaging to the state. Desire, constructed as the "pursuit of happiness," excluded a pursuit of pleasure. The liberal understanding of the "pursuit of happiness," never available to the proletariat, became further limited in commodity capitalism to a pursuit of enjoyment. During this phase the false desire of commodities replaced real desire. According to Marcuse, enjoyment became bound to market commodities as consumption of expensive goods and entertainment. The proletarian masses, having no access to such goods, were excluded from enjoyment. The proletariat was left with the constant repression of pleasure without even the outlet of the hope of future pleasure. At this point in Marcuse's analysis, sexuality returned as the moment of revolutionary awakening.

Marcuse recognized a revolutionary moment in sexuality itself. Sexual pleasure had long since been excluded from the "pursuit of happiness," yet it remained the one sphere open to the masses which could disrupt the system. "The unpurified, unrationalized release of sexual relationships would be the strongest release of enjoyment as such and the total devaluation of labor for its own sake."[33] The moral prohibitions of the bourgeoisie, according to Marcuse, stemmed precisely from the need to close off the sexual sphere. Yet this could never be fully accomplished without the establishment of a reproductive prohibition. The admission of reproduction as a beneficial act to society allowed for (at least the

potential of) the individual to experience sexual intercourse as pleasure. In that one remaining moment of pleasure left to the proletariat
lay the potential for individuals to recognize the extent of their
exclusion from pleasure. And–as Marcuse pointed out–if the individual were then to liberate sexual pleasure from the reproductive
imperative, it would have extensive ramifications for the socio-eco-
nomic sphere:

> Augmented pleasure would represent immediately increased
> liberation of the individual, for it would demand freedom in
> the choice of the object, in the knowledge and in the realiza-
> tion of his potentialities, and freedom of time and of place.[34]

For Marcuse, sexual pleasure was not an end in itself, but rather
an act which referred the individual to the utopic demands of a
society reuniting reason and pleasure in all its forms. Although
clearly speaking here of coitus, the act of reproduction, the essay
remained open to a realm of sexual pleasure separate from reproduction. In this system, however, sexual pleasure was only one of
the forms of pleasure open to the heterogeneity of the desiring
individual, and the only limits imposed on this heterogeneity were
due to the choices which reasoning individuals made for themselves. No separation of the social and the psychic was envisioned;
individual consciousness was inseparable from lived social experience. And although the essay did not directly address fascism and
authoritarianism, it left no room for an intrinsic character giving
rise to these social forms.

Regrettably, this line of analysis remained an isolated foray within
the opus of the Frankfurt School.[35] Its abandonment was no doubt
due to the inadequacy of Marcuse's standpoint in meeting the needs
of the historical moment. His historically grounded argumentation
offered no remedy for the major shortcoming of dialectical materialism as promoted during the period, the very shortcoming which
social psychology and Critical Theory were better able to address.
Taking capitalism as its object, the historically descriptive method of
dialectical materialism formulated a nonexistent system; the cogency
of its analysis and description notwithstanding, this method could not
sufficiently account for the unrealizability of that system.

Marcuse's essay clearly evidenced this shortcoming through a break in the text. In the final section, he moved from historical analysis to an appeal for a superior form of ethics, the analysis alone proving incapable of altering the existent system. The system of ethics Marcuse called for could indeed only exist outside of the capitalist system, thus presuming a revolution of the existing system; yet it lacked the ability to enact such a revolution itself. Only an attentive mass audience would be capable of supplementing the appellative nature of Marcuse's work with the power necessary to establish the ethical system it envisioned, but such an audience was unresponsive. The mass following Marcuse could only hope for was in fact won by the fascist parties, which increased in power dramatically. Because Marcuse–and so many others–interpreted this support as contrary to the masses' own best interests, psychoanalysis as a form of behavior analysis proved to be a productive analytic addition to dialectical materialism.

The choice of psychoanalysis may have resulted in an overinflation of the sexual, but it did provide a means to account for behavior that could not be accommodated by the logic of dialectical materialism. Instead of seeking to prescribe what the masses should desire, the new social psychology sought to describe exactly what they did desire–fascism–and why they desired it. Yet as we have seen, this led the Frankfurt School to create a new logic that resulted in even more untenable positions.

What developments could have liberated Critical Theory from its fixation on the homosexual? Distinguishing rigidly between the social and the psychic, these thinkers were left fearing both the repressed masses and the removal of that repression. Critical Theory was forced to support exactly that which it purported to oppose. If the best that could be hoped for was to prevent the authoritarian personality of the psyche from expressing itself in the social realm, then an authoritarian system was not only justified–such a system was indeed indispensable to implement the essential repression of the psyche.

It was not, however, the sexual which caused the Holocaust, and least of all the homosexual. Individual consciousness is comprised of more than sexual desire. We must question how that desire in its entirety is directed to form identity. By attending to the social mechanisms which direct desire, we accept a commitment to ever-increas-

ing complexities of analysis. A shift in analysis to the social mechanisms directing desire also situates the individual subject at the
nexus of complex systems of determination which render any notion of homogenous masses hopelessly simplistic. Class, gender,
sex, and race only begin the list of determining moments that im-
pinge on the individual subject. This move requires rejecting the
psychoanalytic definition of the psyche as static, as well as breaking
the monopoly of the sexual discourse over the psyche. In accepting
the commitment to ever-increasing complexity, we gain the understanding of consciousness presented in Marcuse's essay. No longer
static, the psyche reveals itself to be quite as alterable as the social,
which allows for both terms to be sublimated into an understanding
of consciousness as socially constructed. Viewing consciousness in
this manner entails a change from the latent to the overt, shifting the
object of pathology from the dark and hidden to the realm of signi-
fying acts. Rather than locating the pathology of the system in a
latent homosexuality, it recognizes the system as operating through
an overt homosociality, allowing social power and privilege to ac-
crue to that which is defined as like. Far from eliminating the
conflict between descriptive and prescriptive moments, this move
sustains the question of what and why something is desired as the
object of study. Yet it redirects the question of 'what should be
desired' back onto the critic functioning as a subject in the political
sphere.

AUTHOR NOTE

Randall Halle received his doctorate from the University of Wisconsin-Madison with a dissertation project entitled "Containing Desire: Hegemony, Homosociality, and German Nationalism, 1780-1956." A related essay on "Homosexuality and Alterity: Wilhelm Reich's Response to Fascism" is forthcoming in
Homosexuality and Psychoanalysis, ed. Tim Dean (New York: Routledge).

NOTES

1. See Martin Jay, *The Dialectical Imagination: A History of the Frankfurt
School* (Boston: Brown, 1973); Susan Buck-Morss, *The Origin of Negative Dialectics: Theodor W. Adorno's Debt to Walter Benjamin* (New York: Free Press,
1977); Judith Marcus and Zoltan Tar, *Foundations of the Frankfurt School of So-*

cial Research (New Brunswick: Transaction, 1984); Helmut Dahmer, Libido und Gesellschaft: Studien über Freud und die Freudsche Linke (Frankfurt a.m.: Suhrkamp, 1973); and Paul A. Robinson, The Freudian Left: Wilhelm Reich, Geza Roheim, Herbert Marcuse (New York: Harper & Row, 1969). A study that may also be of interest is Andrew Hewitt, "A Feminine Dialectic of the Enlightenment? Horkheimer and Adorno Revisited," New German Critique, no. 56 (1992): 143-70.

2. Erich Fromm, "The Method and Function of an Analytic Social Psychology," in idem, The Crisis of Psychoanalysis (New York: Holt, Rinehart, and Winston, 1970), pp. 117-18. This essay originally appeared as "Über Methode und Aufgabe einer analytischen Sozialpsychologie," Zeitschrift für Sozialforschung 1 (1932): 28-55; quote on p. 36.

3. Ibid., p. 119; German version, p. 38.

4. Ibid., p. 121; German version, p. 40.

5. Max Horkheimer, "Geschichte und Psychologie," in idem, Gesammelte Schriften, vol. 3: Schriften 1931-1936, ed. Alfred Schmidt (Frankfurt a.m.: Fischer, 1988), p. 57. This essay originally appeared in Zeitschrift für Sozialforschung 1 (1932): 125-43; quote on p. 133.

6. Erich Fromm, "Psychoanalytic Characterology and Its Relevance for Social Psychology," in The Crisis of Psychoanalysis, pp. 135-58. This essay originally appeared as "Die psychoanalytische Charakterologie und ihre Bedeutung für die Sozialpsychologie," Zeitschrift für Sozialforschung 3 (1932): 253-78.

7. Erich Fromm, "Sozialpsychologischer Teil," in Studien über Autorität und Familie: Forschungsberichte aus dem Institut für Sozialforschung, ed. Max Horkheimer (Paris: Félix Alcan, 1936), pp. 77-135; quote on p. 126.

8. Ibid.

9. Rainer Funk, Erich Fromm (Reinbek bei Hamburg: Rowohlt, 1983), p. 98.

10. Max Horkheimer, "Die Juden und Europa," in idem, Gesammelte Schriften, vol. 4: Schriften 1936-1941, ed. Alfred Schmidt (Frankfurt a.m.: Fischer, 1988), pp. 308-9. This essay originally appeared in Zeitschrift für Sozialforschung 8 (1939): 115-43; quote on p. 115.

11. Ibid., p. 308; German version, p. 115.

12. Max Horkheimer and Theodor W. Adorno, Philosophische Fragmente (New York: Institute of Social Research, 1944). This preliminary version appeared in mimeographed form.

13. Max Horkheimer and Theodor W. Adorno, Dialectic of Enlightenment, trans. John Cumming (New York: Herder and Herder, 1944), p. 202. For the German version, see Dialektik der Aufklärung: Philosophische Fragmente (Amsterdam: Querido, 1947), p. 238.

14. Ibid., p. 192; German version, p. 226.

15. Ibid.

16. Ibid.

17. Theodor W. Adorno et al., The Authoritarian Personality (New York: Harper & Row, 1950), p. 319.

18. Ibid., p. 316.

19. Ibid.

20. Ibid., p. 798.

21. Ibid., p. 801.

22. Adorno and Horkheimer, *Dialectic of Enlightenment*, p. 200; German version, p. 235.

23. Ibid., p. 193; German version, p. 227.

24. See Friedrich Engels, *The Origin of the Family, Private Property, and the State* (1884), in Karl Marx and Friedrich Engels, *Selected Works* (New York: International, 1984), especially p. 302; and Heinz-Dieter Schilling, *Schwule und Faschismus* (Berlin: Elefanten Press, 1983).

25. Theodor W. Adorno, "Sexualtabus und Recht heute," in *Sexualität und Verbrechen*, ed. Fritz Bauer et al. (Frankfurt a.M.: Fischer, 1963), p. 301. This essay also appeared in a collection of Adorno's essays: *Eingriffe: Neun kritische Modelle* (Frankfurt a.M.: Suhrkamp, 1963), pp. 99-124.

26. Adorno, "Sexualtabus," p. 303.

27. Ibid., p. 308.

28. Ibid., p. 305.

29. Herbert Marcuse, "On Hedonism," in idem, *Negations: Essays in Critical Theory*, trans. Jeremy J. Shapiro (Boston: Beacon, 1968), p. 172. The essay originally appeared as "Zur Kritik des Hedonismus," *Zeitschrift für Sozialforschung* 7 (1938): 55-89; quote on p. 64.

30. Ibid., p. 167; German version, p. 61.

31. Ibid., p. 175; German version, p. 67.

32. For a discussion of sex-love, see Engels, *The Origin of the Family, Private Property, and the State*, and August Bebel, *Woman under Socialism* (1883; New York: New York Labor Press News, 1904).

33. Marcuse, p. 187; German version, p. 77.

34. Ibid., p. 189; German version, p. 79.

35. The next proponent of such a critique would not emerge until fifty years later and from outside the Frankfurt School. It was Michel Foucault's work which returned to this form of analysis, describing sexuality as being constructed by specific economic forms. See especially Foucault's *The History of Sexuality*, vol. 2: *The Use of Pleasure*, trans. Robert Hurley (New York: Random House, 1985), where he discussed the sexual economy of ancient Greece.

Homosexuality and the American Left: The Impact of Stonewall

David Thorstad

St. Paul, Minnesota

SUMMARY. Following the Stonewall Riots in New York City in June 1969, the left had to reassess negative appraisals of homosexuality that prevailed among virtually all leftist currents. Pressure for change came from within and from without. By the mid-1970s, three approaches had emerged: (1) radical support for sexual liberation and acceptance of same-sex love as being on a par with heterosexuality; (2) liberal support for the civil rights of homosexuals but without challenging heterosupremacy; and (3) continued adherence to the (Stalinist) view that homosexuality is a form of "bourgeois decadence" alien to the working class. This essay assesses the ways in which the left adapted to the new challenges that confronted it, with particular focus on attitudes toward the nature of homosexuality and its relation to the broader goals of the left.

The June 1969 Stonewall Riots at a gay bar in New York City's Greenwich Village caught most of the left unprepared. Sex-negative baggage inherited from Stalinism and bourgeois psychology would have to be scuttled before the left could relate to the new move-

Correspondence may be addressed: c/o NAMBLA, P.O. Box 174 Midtown Station, New York, NY 10018.

[Haworth co-indexing entry note]: "Homosexuality and the American Left: The Impact of Stonewall." Thorstad, David. Co-published simultaneously in *Journal of Homosexuality* (The Haworth Press, Inc.) Vol. 29, No. 4, 1995, pp. 319-349; and: *Gay Men and the Sexual History of the Political Left* (ed: Gert Hekma, Harry Oosterhuis, and James Steakley) The Haworth Press, Inc., 1995, pp. 319-349; and *Gay Men and the Sexual History of the Political Left* (ed: Gert Hekma, Harry Oosterhuis, and James Steakley) Harrington Park Press, an imprint of The Haworth Press, Inc., 1995, pp. 319-349. Multiple copies of this article/chapter may be purchased from The Haworth Document Delivery Center. [1-800-342-9678 9:00 a.m. - 5:00 p.m. (EST)].

ment–let alone have any influence on its course. From Stalinism came quasi-religious incantations labeling homosexuality a "product of bourgeois decadence," the "fascist perversion," something destined to "wither away," along with the state, under socialism. Homosexuals were too narcissistic and unstable to make "good revolutionaries." From bourgeois (neo-Freudian) psychology came the classification of homosexuality as a mental illness. Same-sexers were considered "security risks" and barred from both government employment and membership in most leftist groups.

The rebirth of a militant women's movement in the late sixties prompted a reassessment of sexual roles and of homosexuality. Women's reaffirmation of their sexuality proved contagious and–together with the civil-rights struggle, the anti-Vietnam War movement, and the hippie counterculture–inspired the gay rebels of the Stonewall generation. The women's and gay movements were movements of youth. Consequently, they spread quickly on the campuses. It was there that left-wing groups–"new" as well as "old"–first encountered challenges to the male chauvinist and heterosexist thinking that prevailed in their ranks. These external challenges, together with those by growing numbers of uncloseted homosexual leftists, discredited heterosupremacy. Prevailing positions became anachronistic and untenable.

What follows is a summary of this process as manifested in a variety of U.S. groups, with particular attention to those that formed part of the "old left"–especially Trotskyism, since it is there that the most extensive efforts to confront hetero dogma took place.

REACTION IN THE "VANGUARD"

The sex-negative, family-oriented outlook of Stalinism in the 1930s came to infect virtually every left-wing current: Stalinist, Trotskyist, Maoist, social democratic, even anarchist. By the 1960s, past support by leftists for homosexual rights–even a rationalistic or scientific understanding of sexual behavior–had vanished from collective memory.

"I am suspicious of those who always stare only at the question of sex the way an Indian holy man stares at his navel," Lenin told Clara Zetkin.[1] Taking its cues from Lenin, the left tended to trivialize personal questions and problems of daily life. Instead, it sought to concentrate on gaining support among the organized working class (seen as uniformly heterosexual) in hopes of eventually making a revolution—a sexually dysfunctional but "normal" worker would make a better revolutionary than one who led a deviant sex life.

Questions of sexuality and sexual oppression under capitalism were relegated to the far-off future of socialist utopia—the leftist equivalent of the Christian paradise derided by the Wobblies as "pie in the sky by and by when you die." Fighting against sexual oppression in the here and now was disparaged as petty-bourgeois self-indulgence, a diversion from more urgent goals, such as overthrowing capitalism. For the left, the personal was not political; communist society would not have room for same-sex love.[2]

Stalinism brought the annihilation of tens of thousands of revolutionaries, including the entire Bolshevik leadership, as well as the triumph of bourgeois family values, the outlawing of abortion, and repression of homosexuality. At the same time, Nazism destroyed the growing homosexual movement in Germany. Two decades later, in the United States, the McCarthyite witch-hunt made both communists and homosexuals into pariahs; support for homosexual rights receded even farther from the left's agenda. Change came only when homosexuals themselves rocked the boat.

Stonewall helped homosexuals to rediscover their history. They found that in the late nineteenth century their movement had met with tolerance, even support, in some (not all) German Social Democratic quarters—in particular with such leading figures as Ferdinand Lassalle, Eduard Bernstein, and August Bebel—as well as from the American anarchist Emma Goldman. Prior to Stonewall, historical awareness of the opinions of leftist thinkers on homosexuality was limited to the condemnation of pederasty by the socialist/anarchist Pierre Joseph Proudhon and Friedrich Engels's absurd belief that the ancient Greeks had fallen into "the abominable practice of sodomy and degraded alike their gods and themselves with the myth of Ganymede," and that the Germanic peoples had acquired a taste for "gross, unnatural vices" from their encounters with nomads around the Black Sea.[3]

The new ferment around sex provoked unprecedented discussions on the left. In some cases, these were more extensive than any that have occurred to date inside ruling-class organizations (except, possibly, Christian churches). The turbulent interfacing between gay liberation and the left that took place after Stonewall merits attention despite–perhaps also because of–the waning of interest in revolutionary ideologies in the wake of the collapse of Stalinism, not to mention the eclipse of a radical vision by bland assimilationism in the gay movement.

Stonewall fostered optimism, discovery of self, disdain for received prejudice, and solidarity between oppressed peoples, social underdogs, sexual outcasts. The streets were the preferred arena of struggle. Happiness lay in confronting conformity and in discovering sexual variety: "Love is a many-gendered thing," gay banners proclaimed. Faith in assimilation and career advancement–through electoral politics or appointment to lower levels of government bureaucracy–were faint glimmers on the horizon. The medicalization of homosexuality that had occurred in the late nineteenth century became a target, in particular the sickness theories of the neo-Freudians. Could anyone have imagined that within a few years not only would psychiatrists be advertising in gay magazines, but AIDS would have contributed to a remedicalization of homosexuality?

Following Stonewall, radical homosexuals saw themselves on a path leading toward a world free of exploitation and racial and sexual oppression. They were determined to secure for homosexuality its rightful place in the socialist society of the future. After years of struggling for other people's causes, their time had come: "No revolution without us!"

The Gay Liberation Front (GLF), the first group to emerge from Stonewall, was a radical countercultural collection. A number of explicitly left-wing gay groups also sprouted over the next few years, among them the Red Butterfly, a group of revolutionary socialists inside the GLF; Gay Revolution and Gay Flames; the Gay Left in England; the Lavender & Red Union in Los Angeles; a group of radicals inside New York's Gay Academic Union, which gave rise to the Committee of Lesbian and Gay Male Socialists; the Lavender Left. Such groups influenced the debates within the left, but will be dealt with only tangentially in this essay.

Before examining some of the positions that evolved out of this ferment, it should be noted that on the whole the left *reacted* to these historic events rather than actively influencing them. Self-described "vanguards" scurried to catch up and adjust decades-old positions.

STALINISM

Some saw no reason to change. This was true of groups generally described as "Stalinist"–Communist parties and most Maoist groups, which banned homosexuals from membership. Typical was the position adopted in 1973 by the Maoist Revolutionary Union (RU):

1. Homosexuality in the USA today is an individual response to the intensification of the contradictions brought about by decaying imperialism; in particular it is a response to the contradiction between men and women which is rooted in male supremacist institutions and male chauvinist ideology. Because homosexuality is rooted in individualism it is a feature of petty bourgeois ideology which puts forth the idea that there are individual solutions to social problems.
2. Because homosexuality is based on petty bourgeois ideology and deals with the contradiction between men and women by turning its back to it (at least in intimate personal relationships), homosexuals cannot be Communists, that is, belong to communist organizations where people are committed to struggle against *all* forms of individualism, in *all* aspects of their lives.
3. Gay Liberation in its putting forth of gayness as a strategy for revolution in this country is a reactionary ideology and can lead us only down the road of demoralization and defeat.[4]

This position was striking in its abstractness, its lack of subtlety, its ex cathedra tone. In addition to demonstrating remarkable ignorance of sexuality–including cross-cultural varieties and ambiguous possibilities that run the gamut between exclusive heterosexuality and exclusive homosexuality–it confused coming out and gay pride with a "strategy for revolution" and suggested that gay liberation was in competition with the revolutionary left. For the RU (as for the ruling class), penis-in-vagina sex represented the apex of human evolution. It saw sexuality in terms of social "contradictions" and dismissed petty-bourgeois individualism, yet its own position reflected a personalistic view of sexuality. Even if homosexuality in the United States could–however unimaginatively–be described as a product of the "decay" of imperialism (an assertion too absurd to refute), the RU offered no theory as to the origin of homosexuality either in the past or in other contemporary cultures (China, Siwa Oasis, tribal African societies, New Guinea, the Zapotecs of Mexico, to name a few). It felt no need for rationalism or evidence to back up its argument. As a basis for a gay-left exchange, this method was a dead end.

Maoist positions on same-sex behavior were rigid and simplistic–simpleminded even. In June 1972, not long after the People's Republic of China was admitted to the United Nations, its Mission to the UN was contacted to inquire about attitudes toward homosexuality in China. "There is no such thing in China," a spokesman responded. When he was told that homosexuality had figured prominently in Chinese history, and that some of China's greatest emperors were homosexual, he persisted: "No, that does not exist in China. In my opinion, it is a completely abnormal and unnatural thing. Oh, perhaps it existed before the Liberation. But after the Liberation our youth acquired a healthy outlook, and they carry out this healthy outlook both in their study and in their work." He expressed surprise upon hearing that the Bolsheviks had decriminalized sex between males and added: "In twenty years of the revolution I have never heard of this kind of curious thing."[5]

Similar to the Maoist position was that of the Communist Party USA. Barely a year after Stonewall, Jarvis Tyner, national chairman of the party's youth group, the Young Workers Liberation League (YWLL), presented a report to its Central Committee in which he reiterated the usual negative views of homosexuality and described gay liberation as a diversion from the "centrality of the struggle for Black Liberation." Women's liberation and gay liberation, he argued, did not belong on the same level as black liberation–but women's liberation was a struggle worth supporting as long as it was approached with "class understanding." An incoherent excursus on gay liberation followed:

> But Gay Liberation is essentially a diversion. And the bourgeoisie picks up on these things and goes to town. The N.Y. Times was talking about "gay ghettoes." Talking about the "gay way of life" and all that. And we really have to examine this, you know. And I don't really understand it fully myself, I have to admit. But I think "sexism" is a misnomer in the first place, as it's projected to parallel racism. There is male chauvanism [*sic*]. There's no question about that, but I don't think "sexism" describes the thing, the phenomenon. We are opposed to the repression of homosexuals on the basis of their being homosexuals. We are opposed to them being treated as criminal problems. But it *is* a psychological problem. It's based on the bourgeois concept of manhood. It's based on all kinds of pressures in the crisis and oppression and exploitation in society with people distorted and so on. But you really can't answer the Gay Liberation movement at this stage by walking up to them and saying "You're sick." They're not ready to accept this. And in every coalition, Gay Liberation has been brought in. Incidentally, the basic line of Gay Liberation is basically a petty-bourgeois line. They've played that role in every single coalition. They were the ones who shouted Nina Simone off the stand at Bryant Park here in N.Y. Gay Liberation was right in the forefront. Shouted her right off the stand. Took over the platform. Then they had this united front with some sections of the Trotskyites and other trends.[6]

The Communist Party lumped homosexuality together with drug addiction and other social problems. In 1972, Roque Ristorucci, chairman of the New York YWLL, "linked the promotion of drugs, including marijuana, with the promotion of prostitution, homosexuality and pornography and pointed to the similarity with Germany during the rise of Nazism," according to a report in the party's daily.[7]

Despite regarding homosexuality as unsavory, and gay liberation as a diversion from more important matters, Tyner omitted the usual "fascist perversion" slander and even voiced opposition to the oppression of homosexuals. This suggested the inroads that gay liberation, barely a year after Stonewall, had made into the youth and antiwar movements. As Tyner noted, heterosexuals could no longer get away with dismissing homosexuals as "sick": "They're not ready [!] to accept this."

Still, the CP was not about to fundamentally reassess its position or embrace gay liberation. In the more than two decades since Tyner's report, the CP has neither been involved in gay liberation nor adopted a more refined position on homosexuality. It never criticized the Soviet Union for its law penalizing male homosexuality, adopted in 1934, nor did it develop a program for sexual liberation. Although individual members expressed support for gay rights (Angela Davis being the most prominent), the party itself remained aloof. Following the demise of the Soviet Union in 1991, the party went into crisis.[8]

THE PANTHERS

As early as 1970, during the heyday of New York's Gay Liberation Front, Huey P. Newton, Supreme Commander of the Black Panther Party, issued a "Letter From Huey to the Revolutionary Brothers and Sisters about the Women's Liberation and Gay Liberation Movements" in which he rejected the Stalinist-Maoist viewpoint and urged black revolutionaries to "form a working coalition with the gay liberation and women's liberation groups" and "unite with them in a revolutionary fashion." "The terms 'faggot' and 'punk' should be deleted from our vocabulary," he advised. While admitting that he did not entirely understand why some people are homosexual, he added:

> Some people say that it's the decadence of capitalism. I don't know whether this is the case; I rather doubt it. But whatever the case is, we know that homosexuality is a fact that exists, and we must understand it in its purest form: That is, a person should have freedom to use his body in whatever way he wants to. That's not endorsing things in homosexuality that we wouldn't view as revolutionary. But there's nothing to say that a homosexual cannot also be a revolutionary. And maybe I'm

now injecting some of my prejudice by saying that "even a homosexual can be a revolutionary." Quite on the contrary, maybe a homosexual could be the most revolutionary.[9]

At a time when the Panthers were still a force in progressive politics, before their leaders had been murdered by the FBI or hounded out of political life, Huey's statement made a strong impression–and not only on gay activists, who welcomed it as a sign of support.[10]

On Labor Day weekend, 1970, many gay activists joined more than ten thousand people attending the Revolutionary People's Constitutional Convention in Philadelphia, sponsored by the Panthers. Discussions were held between gay activists and Panther leaders, and lists of demands were drawn up by gay male and lesbian workshops–only the gay male statement was formally presented. Among other things, the statement recognized the Black Panther Party as "the vanguard of the people's revolution in Amerikkka."[11]

TROTSKYISM

Left-wing attempts to relate to gay liberation made the greatest headway among Trotskyist groups. Their discussions went farther than they did among most leftist groups and, in a few cases, produced analyses that went beyond mere liberal support for gay rights. The discussions inside the Socialist Workers Party (SWP) were the most extensive and the best documented. They did not produce a position as radical as that of some other groups, but they addressed the main issues that have defined the debates between radicals and liberals.

During the sixties, the SWP banned known homosexuals from membership on the ground that they were a "security risk"–an argument adopted from McCarthyism. But the policy had an internal contradiction: by compelling homosexual members to treat their sexuality as a secret not to be told, it not only relegated them to inferior status but also made them more vulnerable to blackmail. The policy did not prevent homosexuals from joining; it just kept them in the closet. The SWP seems to have been the only Trotskyist group in the world to ban homosexuals from membership. This policy was never officially adopted, but it was applied in some party branches in the late sixties. Other branches ignored the ban.[12]

The SWP National Committee first discussed the exclusion of homosexuals from membership at its plenum of February 27-March 1, 1970. No one challenged the argument that it was a security measure intended to protect the party from victimization by the state, or that it was comparable to the ban on use of illegal drugs by party members. Curiously, in August 1970–at precisely the moment when the exclusionary policy was becoming untenable–the party leadership had the National Committee of its youth group formally adopt it for the first time. Ironically, it was a homosexual (and former lover of mine) who was selected to present the report urging adoption of the ban. The policy elicited such ridicule and opposition from youth that it became an obstacle to recruiting on the campuses. Barely three months later, on November 13, the party's Political Committee decided to abolish it. It did so, however, without explaining the policy's origins or admitting that the policy had been discriminatory and wrong. Rather, it rejected it on purely pragmatic grounds, saying that it "is really not viable in that it creates more real problems for the party than it solves." Once it was safe, gay members began to come out.

Over the next six months, the party began to involve itself in the gay movement: it joined gay demonstrations, organized gay participation in antiwar demonstrations, held public forums on gay liberation, and published news and analytical articles in its weekly, *The Militant*. This involvement had barely begun when the brakes were applied. Instead of maintaining its involvement, the party turned inward and held a closed, internal "literary discussion" on gay liberation that resulted in withdrawal from gay liberation until 1977, when Anita Bryant's antigay crusade and the massive gay mobilizations it provoked made abstention impossible; the SWP again joined gay coalitions in a few cities. Then, after two years of sporadic participation, in 1979 the party definitively pulled out of the gay movement.

The SWP's official position on gay liberation was adopted by a party convention in August 1973, following nearly three years of heated internal debate. The party has never publicly released the document, entitled "Memorandum on the Gay Liberation Movement." The Memorandum expressed support for struggles by homosexuals "for full democratic rights, including full civil and human rights, and against all the forms of discrimination and oppression they suffer under capitalism." This represented an advance over the days when gays were banned from membership, but did little more than give the party something to say that would look good in election propaganda. It described gay liberation as relating to a "relatively narrow sector of the population," as lacking the "potential mass" and "social weight" of movements for women's and black liberation, and as being "much more peripheral to the central issues of the class struggle" than those movements. It held that members should not generally be assigned to be involved in gay liberation. It refused to "take a stand on the nature or value of homosexuality," thereby suspending judgment on whether same-sex behavior is an inherent capacity of the human animal or a bizarre deviation from "normal" heterosexuality. To do so, it argued, would alienate it from workers–a reformulation of the idea that "workers hate queers." It justified this stance by claiming that, as a political organization, it could not "take a stand" on "scientific" questions–although it had no trouble doing so when this involved women (for example, its rejection of the notion that "biology is women's destiny").

The SWP was torn by internal debates on homosexuality throughout the seventies, but its position did not change. Altogether, the party held a half dozen such debates, producing scores of documents circulated only to party members.[13] Many gay SWPers opposed the party's position, not only because it meant abstention from the gay movement (gay members were not allowed to attend meetings of gay groups), but because it was considered a liberal approach that reduced gay liberation to a movement for equal rights by a fixed social minority ("gay people") rather than a struggle for sexual liberation–a topic addressed later in this essay. Other Trotskyist groups took positions that were more radical, as well as more consistent with a Marxist analysis: in the United States, both the Spartacist League (SL) and the Revolutionary Socialist League (RSL); in Mexico, the Partido Revolucionario de los Trabajadores (PRT); in France, the Ligue Communiste Révolutionnaire (LCR). In general, these groups went beyond mere support for equal rights and attempted to develop an analysis that would integrate gay liberation and the struggle for socialism. They also tended to hold a more pro-sexual outlook on such issues as prostitution, pornography, and pederasty.[14]

OTHER GROUPS

Among other groups with positions favorable to gay liberation, the most ubiquitous has been the Workers World Party (WWP). Since the early seventies, it has participated in gay demonstrations and coalitions. Its gay members had a high profile as a caucus of its youth group, Youth Against War & Fascism (YAWF), and later as part of its front group, the People's Assembly. The WWP's newspaper, *Workers World*, regularly features articles on the gay movement, including issues of gay and transgender rights. It has published two pamphlets on gay liberation: *The Gay Question: A Marxist Appraisal* (1976) and *In the Spirit of Stonewall* (1979), a compilation of articles from its newspaper.

The WWP's support for gay liberation has been enthusiastic, but it has a tendency to see the world in Manichean terms: good, oppressed groups and socialist or Third World countries versus bad oppressors and imperialism–a worldview that led it to endorse both the crackdown in Tiananmen Square in June 1989 and the botched coup in the Soviet Union in August 1991. It brushed off gay criticism of repression in such countries as Cuba and the Soviet Union:

There is no country in the world today that has an adequate position with regard to ending the oppression of homosexually inclined people. But to single out any of the socialist countries for special attack, as some leaders of the gay movement in the U.S. have done, is to cover over this important fact and, in addition, it lets the U.S. imperialists, the ones who have a real stake in the maintenance of racism, sexism, and anti-homosexual attitudes, off the hook.[15]

Like most groups, the WWP focused on a struggle of "gay people" (or "homosexually inclined people") as a social minority.

Its views on sex in a socialist future do not sound much different from those of other groups, including the SWP:

> Marxism is a potent tool in the struggle for a better world but it is not a crystal ball. Yet Marxists *are* concerned with the questions of love and sexuality. We are confident that with the end of exploitation and oppression will come the possibility of much fuller, richer, and more profound human relationships.[16]

Among the most compelling attempts to develop a Marxist analysis of homosexual oppression and "to encourage in the gay movement an understanding of the links between the struggle against sexual oppression and the struggle for socialism"–as it stated its aims–was that of the Gay Left Collective in England in the mid-seventies. The collective's article "Why Marxism?" is the best in an uneven anthology–published by the New American Movement (NAM), a social-democratic group–that addresses some challenges the left faces in relating to gay liberation.[17]

By the end of the 1970s, most left groups supported the idea that homosexuals ("gay people," "lesbians and gay men") deserved equal rights, whether in capitalist or socialist society. This was also becoming the position of the Democratic Party and several Christian churches. As long as gay equal rights remained abstract and did not cost the state anything, they could be supported. Such a position dovetailed with that of an increasingly assimilationist gay movement: the farther removed from Stonewall, the more its social agenda focused on symbolic issues (gay civil-rights legislation and film portrayals of homosexuality, for example) rather than on sexual freedom, repeal of sodomy and age-of-consent laws, or the release of persons imprisoned for consensual–yet illegal–sexual activity.

It was the issue of consensual sex, or man/boy love, that demonstrated the limitations of the pro-gay positions taken by most left-wing groups.

THE MAN/BOY LOVE ISSUE

Most left-wing groups have had trouble dealing with the taboo against intergenerational love, although a few have taken a libertarian stand on the issue. Some, fearing that any restrictions on free speech could jeopardize their own, have expressed support for the civil liberties of pederasts and their right to organize. When the FBI targeted the North American Man/Boy Love Association (NAMB-LA) in December 1982, several left papers (the *Guardian, Workers Vanguard, Workers World, Torch*) defended the group's rights.[18] On more substantive issues of man/boy sexuality, positions varied.

The WWP, for example, supports age-of-consent laws. "Age of consent laws were a progressive victory that stopped some of the most blatant exploitation of children, such as the selling of young girls into marriage," it asserted, apparently unaware that such laws were instituted to control youth sexuality and in no way protect children from abuse.[19] The WWP sidestepped the fact that the age of consent varies greatly (from twelve to twenty-one, depending on the country or state) and did not say which one it supports. Historically, the age had nothing to do with "protection"–least of all of boys–but rather represented the age at which a young girl was legally marriageable. It would be stretching it, to say the least, to describe the age of consent in, say, Elizabethan England (where it was set at ten) as a "progressive victory." On the age of consent, many leftists defer to prevailing ruling-class or feminist prejudices.

In 1982, the staff of the *Guardian*, an independent weekly, held an internal discussion on the question and, in deference to feminists, adopted the position that man/boy love equals child abuse. Only one staffer–a gay man who came out as a pederast after leaving the staff–opposed the position. The staff rejected his proposal that it meet with radical boy-lovers before deciding on a position.[20] The *Guardian* never reported on this internal discussion. Instead, the editor chose to announce the paper's position in the letters column–without mentioning the internal debate that had produced it:

We strongly support laws protecting children against sexual abuse by adults and reject any suggestion that this position is "puritanical." We would, of course, oppose the use of such laws as a pretext for sweeping attacks on the rights of gays and lesbians, but we don't share the view of some in the gay/lesbian community that the issue of pederasty is mainly one of the civil liberties for the adult involved.[21]

Subsequently, in an article defending NAMBLA against state harassment, the *Guardian* expanded on its position but did not acknowledge the right of a young person to choose sex with an older person. It made no distinction between a small child and an adolescent youth, nor between a young girl and a teenage boy (even though the consent issues involved in sex between a sixteen-year-old gay-identified boy and his twenty-one-year-old gay lover are very different from those, say, between a six-year-old girl and her father):

> The issue of sexual relations between adults and young people is a controversial one within the lesbian and gay communities. Most left groups, including the *Guardian*, do not condone sexual relations between adults and children, arguing that truly consensual relationships are not possible given the disparity in power, experience, and physical and emotional development. The rights of children, they stress, must be paramount and protected.[22]

This surrender to bourgeois morality and antisex feminists avoided obvious questions: What is a "child"? If a state defines a "child" as someone under the age of eighteen, yet sets an age of sexual consent at sixteen, should the age of consent be raised to coincide with the higher age? Since it is legal for a sixteen-year-old to consent to sex in New Jersey but illegal across the Hudson River in New York, should New York sixteen-year-olds wait until they are seventeen? Do gay youths have a right to sex with older gays if they choose (many feel safer with gay men than with other teens)? If laws against same-sex activity between adults–long supported by the left–are now wrong, why are laws setting widely disparate ages of consent more reasonable? Do children have a right to sexual pleasure? If a teenage girl should have the right to an abortion without her parents' consent (a position endorsed by most leftist groups and by NAMBLA), why should a teenage boy not have the right to enjoy his body with an older man (or woman)?

The most vociferous hostility on the left to man/boy love came from the U.S. Socialist Workers Party. In 1979, the SWP abruptly withdrew from activity in the gay movement and reallocated its cadre to jobs in industry. Its involvement in gay liberation had been sporadic in most places (New York being something of an exception). But after two years of involvement during a time of mass mobilization in the gay community, it had recruited no new members from it and was facing yet another internal debate on gay liberation. Its leaders played up the man/boy issue to help justify their decision to "turn to labor" and withdraw from the gay movement.

In 1979, the gay movement went through a wrenching controversy over the age-of-consent issue, especially in New York and New Jersey, where, as a result of lobbying by feminists, the state legislature had adopted a measure that lowered the age of consent from sixteen to thirteen, as well as abolishing the sodomy statute. In the ensuing controversy, the feminists acquiesced in the state's decision to push the age of consent back up to sixteen. This is the context in which the SWP announced its opposition to man/boy love, which coincided with its withdrawal from the gay movement:

> The age-of-consent issue has recently been foisted on gay rights organizations by a small group called the North American Man/Boy Love Association. A central leader of this group is David Thorstad, who ... argues that supporters of gay rights must take up the fight against all age-of-consent laws. . . .
>
> The repeal of age-of-consent laws is a reactionary demand, even though its supporters try to pass themselves off as defenders of adolescents against legal victimization.
>
> The campaign around this demand has nothing to do with the totally progressive stance of defending the right of teenagers not to be penalized for their sexual activity. On the contrary, the advocates of repealing age-of-consent laws are primarily adult men who believe they should be unrestricted in having sex with children.
>
> Saying that children have the "right" to "consent" to sex with adults is exactly like saying children should be able to "consent" to work in a garment factory twelve hours a day. Don't some children "consent" to being used in brutal pornographic films? Don't child prostitutes "consent" to their miserable and terrifying existence? . . .
>
> Laws designed to protect children from sexual and econom-

ic exploitation by adults are historic acquisitions of the working class and should be enforced. An anti-working-class, anti-child, campaign against the age-of-consent laws has nothing to do with gay rights or human rights of any kind. It has no place in the struggle to end discrimination against lesbians and gay people.[23]

The most libertarian views on man/boy love came from two small groups, the Trotskyist Spartacist League and the Revolutionary Socialist League. The Spartacists ridiculed the SWP's position:

Revolutionaries, unlike the social-democratic SWP, oppose any and all legal restrictions by the capitalist state on effectively consensual sexual activity. Get the cops out of the bedrooms! We know that such measures are not designed to protect children but to enforce the sexual morality of the nuclear family which is at the root of the oppression of women, youth and homosexuals. The case of Roman Polanski, the Polish-born director, dragged through the courts, sent to jail and forced into exile for his liaison with a precocious Hollywood 13-year-old, was only a highly publicized example of the reactionary purpose of age-of-consent laws.[24]

Several years later, the Spartacist League defended NAMBLA against FBI harassment:

Perversion, it has been noted, seems to be not what you like, but what other people do. As we wrote five years ago during the persecution of Polish film director Roman Polanski, who was witchhunted for having an affair with a 13-year-old girl: "As communists we oppose attempts to fit human sexuality into legislated or decreed 'norms.' The guiding principle for sexual relations should be that of effective consent–that is, nothing more than mutual agreement and understanding as opposed to coercion . . . the state has no business interfering." This ought to be the guiding principle not just for Marxists but for any democrat on such social questions. Determining what is effective consent is always tricky, and particularly with youth there is a grey area. But such a judgment must be case by case, not categorical as it is with the reactionary age-of-consent laws. The act of sex in itself is not *prima facie* evidence of abuse or coercion. And the NAMBLA activists are being witchhunted for things nowhere close to where their real interests and activities lie.[25]

The Revolutionary Socialist League (RSL), which was active in the gay movement until it disbanded in 1989, went farther than other U.S. groups in integrating sexual liberation into its program. Age-of-consent laws, it said, are "one of the primary ways in which a repressive sexual 'morality' is imposed on young people." Their result "is to take away from a young person any power to give consent, or in fact to play any role whatsoever in making decisions about his or her sexuality at an important age of development. Instead, this power is placed in the hands of the state or, in some cases, the state in conjunction with the parents."[26] The RSL summarized its views in a June 1980 leaflet:

We believe that all consensual sex is the business only of those involved. The state has no business regulating in any way expressions of sexuality between consenting persons of any number, sex, or age. The state's attempt to regulate youth sexuality in particular is rooted in young people's position as property of their parents and/or wards of the state. Young people are jailed in schools, economically exploited, and denied the most basic political rights. Society maintains this oppression by imposing the idea that young people are not capable of determining their own wants and needs, in particular their sexual needs and desires. We oppose age of consent laws. These laws deny the ability of young people to determine their own sexual needs and desires. They maintain the status of youth as property, and reinforce the closet for gay youth.[27]

The SL and RSL positions hold several elements in common with the views of radical boy-lovers: a pro-sexual outlook; a recognition that young people are sexual and have a right to choose their partners; support for individual rights; a recognition that every case is different and should be treated on its own merits; opposition to age-of-consent laws and other laws that discriminate against young people; a rejection of any role for the state in restricting consensual activity.

THE "GAY PEOPLE" CONCEPT

Over the past century and a half, the gay movement has sought to answer the question: What is the nature of homosexuality? Is it an inherent capacity of the human animal, or a quirk of nature affecting only a minority of humans? Is there such a thing as "gay people," or is everyone potentially gay (therefore also potentially straight)? How one responds to such questions not only colors scientific judgments but determines political strategies–whether one sees solutions to sexual oppression and discrimination in terms of radical change or piecemeal adjustment of social structures and attitudes; of combating heterosupremacy and liberating repressed homoerotic potential, or merely increasing spheres of tolerance.

The view that gays constitute a more or less fixed social minority ("gay people") prevails today–in the ruling class, among gay and lesbian activists, among feminists, in the psychiatric, legal, and religious professions, on the left. The concept imposes rigid polarities on an ambiguous reality, forcing a square peg into a round hole while claiming a perfect fit.

Gay leaders purport to represent a group defined as "gay." This constituency must be perceived as large enough to warrant attention by the presumed heterosexual majority, yet at the same time as unthreatening. Gay leaders claim to speak for the minority of people who have come out and identify as gay. Rarely do they address the far larger group of people who have not yet come out, or who are still struggling with their homosexuality; fearful of being seen as proselytizers for homosexuality, they relegate the suppressed homoerotic potential of the presumed heterosexual majority–especially of youth, and even of teenage gay bashers–to off-the-record social chitchat. Pederasts, who take the risk of responding to the sexual needs of youth, are considered anathema by many gay and lesbian leaders.[28]

The concept that homosexuals are a social minority implies that they are a special kind of human being, different from heterosexuals–a contemporary version of the nineteenth-century view that they were a "third sex." Homosexuals are defined as people who love the same sex, and heterosexuals as people who love the opposite sex–two different kinds of people, depending on whom they go to bed with. But this is a political fiction–sexual identity and sexual practice do not necessarily overlap–designed to give definition to yet another liberal pressure group. It is a useful fiction insofar as it allows the gay movement to exploit cracks in the political system, but simplistic in its reduction of the ambiguities of sexuality to bipolar categories of hetero and homo. It has less to do with sexual liberation than with readjusting the status quo; in exchange for minor perks, gay and lesbian leaders keep the flock corralled.

Few have addressed these issues more creatively than Mario Mieli, who has critiqued both gay assimilationism and left-wing heterosupremacy. Speaking of gay liberation goals, he wrote:

> We homosexuals must liberate ourselves from the feeling of guilt (and this is one of our immediate goals), so that homoeroticism spreads and "catches on." We have to make the water gush from the rock, to induce "absolute" heterosexuals to grasp their own homosexuality, and to contribute, through the dialectical confrontation and clash between the minority and majority sexual tendencies, to the attainment of the transsexuality which the underlying polysexual "nature" of desire points towards. If the prevailing form of monosexuality is heterosexuality, then a liberation of homoeroticism, this Cinderella of desire, forms an indispensable staging-post on the road to the liberation of Eros. The objective, once again, is not to obtain a greater acceptance of homoeroticism by the heterocapitalist status quo, but rather to transform monosexuality into an Eros that is genuinely polymorphous and multiple; to translate into deed and into enjoyment that trans-sexual polymorphism which exists in each one of us in a potential but as yet repressed form.[29]

The argument that homosexuals are a social minority goes back to the second half of the nineteenth century. Until then, the notion of "the homosexual" did not exist. Other terms were used: "sodomite" (any male who engaged in anal intercourse, with man or woman), "pederast," "Sapphist." The terms referred to specific acts (or sins), not to a state of being. The nineteenth century saw the birth of a new movement on behalf of "third sexers" (people thought to be born half-man, half-woman). Since then, the concept of homosexuals as a distinct social minority has remained a common feature of gay propaganda. It achieved preeminence with the evolution of the gay movement toward liberal assimilationism since the mid-1970s.

The forerunner of the Mattachine Society, the International Fraternal Orders for Peace and Social Dignity (sometimes referred to as Bachelors Anonymous), described itself in 1950 as "a service and welfare organization devoted to the protection and improvement of Society's Androgynous Minority." Mattachine continued this approach, which had the virtue of defining the unmentionable in terms of civil rights, thereby making it accessible–in theory, at least–to the American melting pot. In the early 1950s, it was radicals who advocated the minority-group concept, and conservatives who opposed it. During the McCarthy witch-hunt, in 1953, one Mattachine member argued during a debate: "Never in our existence as individuals or as a group should we admit to being a minority. For to admit being a minority we request of other human beings that we so desire to be persecuted."[30]

Minority-group partisans today argue that homosexuals are just like everybody else, except for what they do in bed. The argument seems surprising, because in reality homosexuality and heterosexuality do not differ appreciably with regard to either mechanics or emotion. In the sex act, difference in partner gender seems inconsequential; imagination plays the larger role. True, some gay men have pushed the erotic capacities of body orifices to the limit (fistfucking, for example). Although to some their practices may appear far-out, surely they are harmless compared, say, to heterosexually inspired infibulation and female circumcision in some African cultures.

Same-sex and other-sex behavior are both universal aspects of human experience. If sexual pleasure is its own reward, and not merely a trick of nature to get the species to reproduce, then the aim of sexual emancipation would seem to be to free people's capacity to love persons of the same as well as the opposite sex. If the primary purpose of sex is pleasure, not reproduction, then same-sex play cannot be viewed as a practice peculiar to a minority of people defined as "gay," but rather as part of the potential experience of everyone.

Cross-cultural studies confirm what common sense knows: the impulse toward same-sex love lies within the human animal. Its expression is culturally determined, but its biological basis is suggested by the fact that it has evolved as part of the mammalian heritage and becomes more common the higher up the phylogenetic scale one goes. This is not to say that homosexuality (or heterosexuality) is inborn, or that it is a function of the size of one's hypothalamus—but rather that creativity and imagination acquire greater value in more highly evolved species. The idea that homosexuality is a minority phenomenon is culture-bound. Clellan S. Ford and Frank A. Beach demonstrated more than forty years ago what anyone who travels widely, especially in non-Western societies, can easily confirm: same-sex activity is, to a greater or lesser extent, accepted behavior in the majority of societies studied.[31]

The idea that "gay people" are a social minority reassures the heterosexual dictatorship that homosexuality represents no threat. It focuses on gay rights (liberal, symbolic measures that usually add no burden to city and state budgets), not on sex-law reform (which strikes at the heart of the Judeo-Christian, heterosupremacist underpinnings of Western capitalism). It oversimplifies the complexities of human sexuality. It leaves largely intact the tools of state and church control.

Most left-wing groups—and an increasing array of capitalist institutions and corporations—now endorse equal rights for "gay people" and oppose some forms of discrimination. In this, the outlooks of gay leaders, the ruling class, and most left-wing groups largely coincide. Yet more than two decades after Stonewall—especially with the arrival of AIDS—sexual freedom seems as remote as ever. Gay leaders focus on gay rights rather than sex-law reform. They play down issues of sexual freedom and try to sanitize their constituency by cutting loose embarrassing elements. They sometimes claim that sexual orientation is determined by age six, yet they refuse to call for lowering or abolishing the age of consent; they try to distance themselves from pederasty—despite the fact that pederasty is the main form that homoeroticism has taken throughout most of Western (and not only Western) culture. In their rush toward respectability, they are promoting coupledom as a gay ideal. Gay marriage and receiving spousal benefits seem more important to them than repealing Judeo-Christian sodomy laws, which remain on the books in nearly half the states. They have lost sight of the central goal of gay liberation: the right of human beings to love someone of the same sex.

Is sexual freedom a realistic goal? The answer lies outside the parameters of this essay. But even if it is unrealistic, even if a society in which sexual freedom prevailed might not resemble the egalitarian nirvana associated with the dream,[32] the strategies that result from such a perspective–libertarian, antiauthoritarian, multicultural, tolerant–seem preferable to the accommodationist compromising inherent in the gay minority dogma.

AUTHOR NOTE

David Thorstad is a former president of New York's Gay Activists Alliance and a founding member of the North American Man/Boy Love Association (NAMBLA) and New York's Coalition for Lesbian and Gay Rights (CLGR). From 1967 to 1973 he was a member of the Socialist Workers Party (SWP). He is coauthor, with John Lauritsen, of *The Early Homosexual Rights Movement (1864-1935)* (New York: Times Change, 1974).

NOTES

1. Cited in Clara Zetkin, *Erinnerungen an Lenin* (Berlin/GDR: Dietz, 1975), p. 67; translated by the author.

2. An exception to this is the utopian socialist Charles Fourier (1772-1837), a precursor of the hippie counterculture of the 1960s who placed love at the center of his vision of a future society, which he dubbed Harmony. His utopia provided not only for homosexuality (he called it "unisexual" or "same-sex" love), including lesbianism, but also boy-love. For Fourier, sexual variety was built into nature; varieties of sexual behavior were to be welcomed, not feared or combated. He considered laws against sexuality to be "spider webs that stop only the small gnats and let the big ones through." His views on sex were written around 1817 to 1819 in *Le Nouveau Monde amoureux*, but they were suppressed by his epigones

and not published until 1967, a century and a half later. They are presented in more accessible form in the anthology of his ideas on sexuality, *Vers la liberté en amour*, ed. Daniel Guérin (Paris: Gallimard, 1975), as well as in Guérin's *Essai sur la révolution sexuelle après Reich et Kinsey* (Paris: Pierre Belfond, 1969). For a useful discussion, see the contribution by Saskia Poldervaart to this volume.

3. For a discussion of attitudes toward homosexuality among the Bolsheviks, Stalinists, and the German Social Democracy, see John Lauritsen and David Thorstad, *The Early Homosexual Rights Movement (1864-1935)* (New York: Times Change, 1974). On the German Social Democracy, see also James D. Steakley, *The Homosexual Emancipation Movement in Germany* (New York: Arno, 1975), and Wilfried U. Eissler, *Arbeiterparteien und Homosexuellenfrage: Zur Sexualpolitik von SPD und KPD in der Weimarer Republik* (West Berlin: Rosa Winkel, 1980). Proudhon's views on sexuality are elaborated in *De la Justice dans la Révolution et dans l'Eglise*, vol. 4 (Paris: Rivière, 1858), and are summarized in Daniel Guérin's *Essai sur la révolution sexuelle*. Engels's comments are in his *Origin of the Family, Private Property, and the State* (1884). For a discussion of Engels's and Karl Marx's rather silly exchanges on the subject of homosexuality, see Hubert Kennedy's contribution to this volume. Lenin's opinions about sex can be found in Clara Zetkin's *Erinnerungen an Lenin* (Recollections of Lenin), written in 1925 and published in Russian in 1926 and in German in 1929, as well as in A. Kollontai's *The Autobiography of a Sexually Emancipated Communist Woman*, trans. Salvator Attanasio (New York: Herder and Herder, 1971). Aleksandra Kollontai, best known for her writings on women's emancipation and sexuality, was the foremost Bolshevik advocate of "free love." She is believed to have been the first to raise with Lenin what came to be known as the "glass of water" theory, which held that satisfying the sex drive was as simple, and morally neutral, as drinking a glass of water to quench one's thirst. Lenin's sharply critical views on the theory exist in several versions, including in Zetkin. Here is the version from Fannina W. Halle's *Women in Soviet Russia*, trans. Margaret M. Green (New York: Viking, 1933), pp. 112-14:

> Naturally the changed attitude of the young people to sexual questions is "fundamental" and appeals to a theory. Some call their attitude "communist" and "revolutionary." They honestly believe that it is so. I at my age am not impressed. Although I am far from being a somber ascetic, the so-called "new sexual life" of the young people–and sometimes of the old–seems to me to be often enough wholly bourgeois, an extension of the good bourgeois brothel. All that has nothing to do with free love as we communists understand it. You are doubtless acquainted with the capital theory that in communist society the satisfaction of the instincts, of the craving for love, is as simple and unimportant as "the drinking of a glass of water." This "glass of water theory" has driven some of our young people crazy, quite crazy. It has been the destruction of many young men and women. Its supporters declare that it is Marxist. I have no use for such Marxism, which deduces all the phenomena and transformations in the

intellectual superstructure straight from its economic basis. Things are not quite so simple. . . .

I consider the famous "glass of water theory" to be utterly un-Marxian, and, moreover, un-social. . . . Of course thirst cries out to be quenched. But will a normal person under normal conditions lie down in the dirt in the road and drink from a puddle? Or even from a glass with a rim greasy from many lips? But most important of all is the social aspect. Drinking water really is an individual concern. Love involves two, and a third, a new life, may come into being. That implies an interest on the part of society, a duty to the community.

As a communist I have not the slightest sympathy with "the glass of water theory," even when it is beautifully labeled "love made free."

One can disagree with Lenin's comments on free love, but they at least show an intellectual respect for his interlocutor and a tone that would vanish from debate on the Communist left. Left-wing positions on man/boy love, from the utopian socialists to the present, are discussed in David Thorstad, "Man/Boy Love and Sexual Freedom: A Radical Perspective," in *Varieties of Man/Boy Love: Modern Western Contexts* (= *NAMBLA Journal*, no. 8 [1992]), ed. Mark Pascal (New York: Wallace Hamilton, 1992), pp. 85-103.

4. Revolutionary Union, "On Homosexuality and Gay Liberation" (leaflet in author's files). The RU's complete statement is presented (with slight variations and with commentary and illustrations from a radical gay perspective) in the pamphlet *On Homosexuality: A Stalino-Leninist Guide to Love and Sex* (Ann Arbor: by the authors, 1975), which also contains an "Appendix on Cuba," consisting of documents detailing the antigay position of the Cuban regime. The RU's statement is also published (without changes in the original text) in a pamphlet by the Los Angeles Research Group (a Maoist group of "ten communists who are gay women"), *Toward a Scientific Analysis of the Gay Question* (Cudahy, CA: Los Angeles Research Group, n.d.), which presents a critique of the RU and the other main Maoist group of the day, the October League. For a more recent statement of the Stalinist-Maoist viewpoint, see *On the Question of Homosexuality: Reply to the Body Politic Collective*, published by the Canadian Bolshevik Union (Montreal: Lines of Demarcation, 1981).

5. I conducted the conversation in French; translation by the author. The complete exchange appears in David Thorstad, "Antigay Laws in the United States and Some Other Countries," *SWP Discussion Bulletin* 30.3 (July 1972): 8-9.

6. Jarvis Tyner, *Build the Youth Front!* (New York: Young Workers Liberation League, n.d.), a speech to the Central Committee of the YWLL meeting October 17-18, 1970. Tyner's comments about the *New York Times* referring to a "gay way of life" must be inaccurate because it was not until June 1987 that the *Times* began to use the word "gay" in such contexts. The *Times*'s 1979 *Manual of Style and Usage* instructed reporters and editors: "Do not use [gay] as a synonym for

homosexual unless it appears in the formal capitalized name of an organization." In an apparent slip, the November 16, 1980, issue of the newspaper nevertheless printed the headline, "Army Allows Clearances to Gays"–although the *Times* had first used the word "gay" for homosexual in a book review in 1963; see Jonathan Ned Katz, *Gay/Lesbian Almanac* (New York: Harper & Row, 1983), p. 15. It is not clear who Tyner was referring to in his assertion that gay groups made a "united front with some sections of the Trotskyites"; the main Trotskyist group at the time, the Socialist Workers Party, banned homosexuals from membership until the end of 1970, and no other Trotskyist groups were involved in the gay movement at this point. Perhaps Tyner was referring to individual gay activists, but his report reflected the usual Stalinist ploy of tarring opponents as "Trotskyites."

7. Donna Ristorucci, "Drugs Called by YWLL a Ruling Class Weapon," *Daily World* 5.104 (December 9, 1972): 4. Similar warnings were voiced a month later by the chairman of the party's International Affairs Commission, who wrote: "In our present-day society, we have a magnitude of ills–reflecting and resulting from the deterioration of the system in which we live. There is the drug scene with its resultant criminal activities; there is over-drinking and alcoholism, there is sexual promiscuity, there is homosexual behavior. There is white chauvinism, male supremacy, bourgeois nationalism and feminism–and much more. There is over-concern for one's own comforts." This appeared in a section entitled "Social Ills Must Not Seep Into Our Party," in Helen Winter, "Standards for Party Members and Leadership," *Party Affairs* 7.1 (January 1973). In the same issue of the internal party publication, party leader James E. Jackson stated: "It is necessary to remind ourselves that there are those whom we do not recruit." He listed five groups: dope addicts, drug users; alcoholics; racists, white supremacists, national fanatics; common criminals, thieves, hustlers; and "homosexuals, perverts." See "For Safeguards Against the Party's Enemies," from a report to the Central Committee meeting, September 8-9, 1972, on Problems of Security and the Struggle for Higher Standards (ibid., p. 51).

8. On May 27, 1993, Russia (the largest of the republics of the former Soviet Union) repealed its law against homosexual acts (*New York Times*, May 29, 1993, p. 3).

9. Newton's letter was published in *The Black Panther* 5.8 (August 21, 1970): 5, and is reprinted in Donn Teal, *The Gay Militants* (New York: Stein and Day, 1971), pp. 170-71.

10. Assimilationist homosexuals did not welcome Newton's statement. A leading gay journal editorialized: "So Huey Newton wants to be friends. Sorry, Huey, but somehow this fails to elate us. . . . We see some virtue in evolution. We think it is possible to change the 'system'–to make it what it is supposed to be. In fact, we see much more hope this way than in violence and destruction. Sorry, Huey." See Dick Michaels, *The Advocate* 4.17 (October 14-27, 1970): 5; quoted in Teal, p. 172. Huey's statement argued that black militants, regardless of their sexual orientation, should support gay liberation, but made no reference to "violence and destruction."

11. "Statement of the Male Homosexual Workshop," quoted in Teal, p. 174. Teal's account of the Revolutionary People's Constitutional Convention (pp. 169-78) includes a report by Steve Kuromiya of the Philadelphia Gay Liberation Front (originally published as "Gay People Help Plan New World," *Gay Flames*, no. 2), as well as the "Statement of the Gay Male Homosexual Workshop," including its list of eighteen demands, and the "Demands of the Lesbian Workshop." Martin Duberman provides a brief account of the convention in *Stonewall* (New York: Dutton, 1993), pp. 259-60, and also discusses reactions to the Panthers among gay and lesbian activists.

12. The Minneapolis-St. Paul branch of the SWP, for example, had three organizers in a row (including myself) who were gay–all closeted; all three came out once the policy was eliminated in 1970. One was widely assumed at the time to be gay and had friends who clearly were–one of whom was a party member. In the mid-sixties, a friend of mine who was a University of Minnesota student continued to hustle while a member of the party's youth group, the Young Socialist Alliance. Despite his turbulent personal life, he was offered a job on the party's newspaper in New York. (The offer was arranged by Vincent Raymond Dunne, a former member of the IWW, founding member of the CPUSA, and longtime SWP leader famous in Minnesota for his role in the Teamster strikes of the 1930s that made Minneapolis into a union town.)

13. The debates on gay liberation inside the SWP during the 1970s are documented in *Gay Liberation and Socialism: Documents from the Discussions on Gay Liberation inside the Socialist Workers Party (1970-1973)*, ed. David Thorstad, 2nd ed. (New York: by the author, 1981), and *No Apologies: The Unauthorized Publication of Internal Discussion Documents of the Socialist Workers Party (SWP) concerning Lesbian/Gay Male Liberation (Part 2: 1975-79)*, ed. Steve Forgione and Kurt Hill (New York: by the authors, [1981]). The former contains nearly 40 of the 104 documents published during preconvention discussions in 1971 and 1973, and the "literary discussion" of 1972, as well as an epilogue of articles pertaining to the SWP's opposition to man/boy love, which it used to justify its withdrawal from the gay movement in 1979. The latter contains documents from three subsequent discussions–in 1975, 1977, and 1979. During a period of renewed activity in the gay movement in 1977, the SWP published a pamphlet on current movement issues, *Gay Liberation Today: An Exchange of Views* (New York: Pathfinder, 1977). After 1979, no self-respecting homosexuals remained inside the SWP. In 1982, the SWP ceased to consider itself Trotskyist. It has since evolved into a sect on the fringe of a shrinking left. Similar debates took place in the SWP's sister group in Canada, the League for Socialist Action/Ligue Socialiste Ouvrière, which published its own pamphlet of selected documents, *Gay Liberation in Canada: A Socialist Perspective* (Toronto: Vanguard, 1977). Unlike the SWP, the LSA/LSO never banned homosexuals from membership–nor did it expel members for smoking marijuana. It did, however, follow the SWP's line on homosexuality.

14. Most of these groups published leaflets or pamphlets on gay liberation. These include Paul Carson, *Socialism and the Fight for Lesbian and Gay Libera-*

tion (New York: Revolutionary Socialist League, 1982); *Luttes homosexuelles: Quelles perspectives?* (Paris: Commission nationale homosexuelle, Ligue Communiste Révolutionnaire, 1981) and *Le Droit d'être homosexuel/lesbienne* (Paris: Commission nationale homosexuelle, Ligue Communiste Révolutionnaire, 1981); Partido Revolucionario de los Trabajadores, *Liberación homosexual: un análisis marxista* (Mexico City: Folletos Bandera Socialista, 1983). Spartacist League positions can be found in many issues of its magazines, *Women and Revolution* and *Spartacist*, and in its newspaper, *Workers Vanguard*. The SL was not directly involved in the gay movement (it opposed "sectoralism"), whereas the RSL was an active presence in gay groups in several cities. When the California gay group Red Flag Union (formerly called the Lavender & Red Union), having evolved from Maoism toward Trotskyism, dissolved in 1977, one faction joined the SL, the other the RSL. The RSL, which combined elements of Trotskyism and anarchism, disbanded in 1989. The Freedom Socialist Party, a "Trotskyist-Feminist" group, has also maintained a pro-gay stance and involvement in the gay movement in some areas, although it has refused to take a stand on the issue of man/boy love. Other groups resulting from SWP explusions during the 1970s (Socialist Action, Fourth Internationalist Tendency, Solidarity) did not evolve positions on gay liberation sufficiently different from those of the SWP to warrant attention here. (The Fourth Internationalist Tendency dissolved into Solidarity in September 1992.)

15. Bob McCubbin, *The Gay Question: A Marxist Appraisal* (New York: World View, 1976), p. 62.

16. Ibid., pp. 80-81. The WWP originated in a 1956 split from the SWP because it supported the Soviet crushing of the workers' uprising in Hungary, which the Trotskyists opposed. It sees a "global class war" between capitalism and socialism–which can lead to incantatory clichés such as this (now quite dated) one: "For the capitalist class, each passing day deepens the dread and gloom as their system grows weaker and weaker and the socialist countries grow stronger and stronger. For revolutionaries, the future is bright" (p. 81).

17. New American Movement, *Working Papers on Gay/Lesbian Liberation and Socialism* (Chicago: NAM, 1979). The Gay Left Collective article, reprinted from *Gay Left* (Winter 1977), is included because it "recognizes the importance of connecting the personal and the political, and Gramsci's posthumous contribution to our current discussion in NAM" (p. 7).

18. This series of events is recounted in *A Witchhunt Foiled: The FBI vs. NAMBLA* (New York: NAMBLA, 1985), available for $6.95, postpaid, from NAMBLA, P.O. Box 174, Midtown Station, New York, NY 10018. For an analysis of the relationship between man/boy love and the left, see David Thorstad, "Man/Boy Love and Sexual Freedom: A Radical Perspective" (see note 3), which is based on a talk before the New York Marxist School sponsored by the Committee of Lesbian and Gay Male Socialists on January 6, 1983. In addition to discussing the American left, the article analyzes the position of the French Trotskyist group, the Ligue Communiste Révolutionnaire. The positions of foreign groups on man/boy love and homosexuality lie outside the scope of this article. In

her book *Sexual Personae: Art and Decadence from Nefertiti to Emily Dickinson* (New Haven: Yale University Press, 1990), Camille Paglia says this about state harassment of pederasts: "These days, especially in America, boy-love is not only scandalous and criminal but somehow in bad taste. On the evening news, one sees handcuffed teachers, priests, or Boy Scout leaders hustled into police vans. Therapists call them maladjusted, emotionally immature. But beauty has its own laws, inconsistent with Christian morality. As a woman, I feel free to protest that men today are pilloried for something that was rational and honorable in Greece at the height of civilization" (p. 116). For an overview of the relationship between pederasty and gay liberation, see David Thorstad, "Man/Boy Love and the American Gay Movement," in *Male Intergenerational Intimacy: Historical, Socio-Psychological, and Legal Perspectives*, ed. Theo Sandfort, Edward Brongersma, and Alex van Naerssen (Binghamton, NY: Harrington Park Press, 1991), (simultaneously published as *Journal of Homosexuality* 20.1-2) pp. 251-74.

19. Preston Wood, "Frameups Spark Anti-Gay Media Campaign," *Workers World* 24.52 (December 24, 1982): 11. Curiously, the practice of selling girls into marriage–and even of female infanticide–is not uncommon even today in China, despite Mao's "Cultural Revolution," which the WWP welcomed.

20. Private communication to the author. In subsequent public statements of its position, the *Guardian* avoided the explicit and crude equation of pederasty with "child abuse," preferring more roundabout formulations. This equation was feminist-inspired; in October 1980, the National Organization for Women (NOW) had adopted a resolution–submitted by its Lesbian Rights Committee–condemning pederasty, pornography, sadomasochism, and public sex. The *Guardian* staff accepted feminist arguments unquestioningly while sweeping aside those of radical pederasts. The *Guardian* folded in 1992.

21. *Guardian* 34.34 (May 26, 1982): 22. In a letter to the editor (*Guardian* 34.42 [July 21, 1982]: 18), I explained that pederasts did not regard the issue as "mainly one of the civil liberties for the adult" but as a "fundamental question of the civil and human rights of the young person":

We radical homosexuals are fed up with leftist groups reasserting their heterosexism. Do you take your cues from the New Right, the FBI, the Moral Majority, and the Pope? Your attack on man/boy love was not merely puritanical, it was reactionary. . . . In general, man/boy relations are far less exploitative than heterosexual relationships.

22. John Trinkl, "Cops and Media Target 'Man-Boy Love' Group," *Guardian* 35.13 (January 5, 1983): 7. Several months later, the *Guardian* published a discussion piece by Steve Ault, "Man/Boy Love Can Be Defended, But So Can Some Limits," *Guardian* 35.36 (June 8, 1983): 23. However, it did not publish any of the letters it received as part of the "discussion." By the late 1970s, the *Guardian* carried regular news stories on gay rights as well as discussion articles; see, for example, David Thorstad, "Linking the Left and Gay Movements," *Guardian* 31.41 (July 18, 1979): 17.

23. Rich Finkel and Mathilde Zimmermann, "The Class-Struggle Road to Winning Gay Rights," *The Militant* 43.14 (April 13, 1979): 24-25. This statement rivaled the rhetoric of the right wing. Most odd was its comparison of man/boy sex to twelve hours of work in a garment factory–the authors seemed unfamiliar with either man/boy sex or factory work. For an answer to the Finkel/Zimmermann article, see David Thorstad, "The Socialist Workers Party vs. Gay Liberation (or the Cuckoo Builds a Strange Nest)," in *Gay Activist* 8.3 (June-July 1979): 12-16, and in *Gay Insurgent*, no. 7 (Spring 1981): 17-23. Both are reprinted in Thorstad, *Gay Liberation and Socialism* (see note 13), as is David Thorstad, "A Statement to the Gay Liberation Movement on the Issue of Man/Boy Love," *Gay Community News* 6.23 (January 6, 1977): 5, which Finkel and Zimmermann denounce.

24. "SWP: From 'Gay is Good' to 'Save Our Children,'" *Young Spartacus*, no. 74 (Summer 1979): 5.

25. "Defend NAMBLA!" *Workers Vanguard*, no. 321 (January 14, 1983): 14. Nine years later, during another media frenzy that attempted to get NAMBLA thrown out of the Potrero Hill public library in San Francisco, where it had been meeting for two years, the Spartacist League published an article under the same title defending the group; see "Defend NAMBLA!" *Workers Vanguard*, no. 544 (February 7, 1992): 2. During this struggle, NAMBLA was also actively supported by another small leftist group, the Revolutionary Workers League. The RWL participated in NAMBLA's 1991 Membership Conference in San Francisco, the first non-boy-love group to do so.

26. Ian Daniels, "NAMBLA, Age of Consent, and Human Sexuality," *Torch* 10.1 (January 15-February 14, 1983): 5.

27. Revolutionary Socialist League, "Lesbian and Gay Liberation Through Socialist Revolution," June 1980. Copy in author's files.

28. In the years following Stonewall, the gay movement seemed more willing to acknowledge the ambiguities of sexuality. Nowadays, image matters more, so gay leaders seek to rein in "politically incorrect" tendencies. For example, gay youth at the June 30, 1985, New York City Gay Pride March were quickly shushed up by an adult mentor when they broke into a chant of "2, 4, 6, 8–How do you know your wife is straight? 3, 5, 7, 9–Hey, lady, your husband's mine!"

29. Mario Mieli, *Homosexuality and Liberation: Elements of a Gay Critique*, trans. David Fernbach (London: Gay Men's Press, 1980), pp. 120-21.

30. John D'Emilio, *Sexual Politics, Sexual Communities: The Making of a Homosexual Minority in the United States, 1940-1970* (Chicago: University of Chicago Press, 1983), p. 79n. D'Emilio discusses the Mattachine's debates over the gay minority concept on pages 79-81.

31. See Clellan S. Ford and Frank A. Beach, *Patterns of Sexual Behavior* (New York: Harper & Brothers, 1951), who report that the majority of societies studied approved some form of homosexuality: "In 49 (64 percent) of the 76 societies other than our own for which information is available, homosexual activities of

one sort or another are considered normal and socially acceptable for certain members of the community" (p. 130).

32. This is the view of Camille Paglia, for instance, who argues that "whenever sexual freedom is sought or achieved, sadomasochism will not be far behind"; see *Sexual Personae*, p. 3. C. A. Tripp describes as standard violent sexual encounters in several societies that are nonrestrictive in permitting sexual liaisons; see Tripp, *The Homosexual Matrix* (New York: McGraw-Hill, 1975), p. 40.

The Church, the Stasi, and Socialist Integration: Three Stages of Lesbian and Gay Emancipation in the Former German Democratic Republic

Denis M. Sweet

Bates College

SUMMARY. Organized groups of homosexuals began forming in the East German Protestant Church beginning in 1982. They constituted a rapidly spreading nucleus for a lesbian and gay emancipation movement. As such, they were viewed with suspicion by the state security apparatus which heavily infiltrated them. As an attempt to outmaneuver the church groups and raise political capital, the East German state by the last years of its existence in the late eighties embarked on a program of tolerance and integration of homosexuals into socialist society.

Queerness makes no sense as a special preserve; it only makes sense to the extent that it paralyzes bourgeois "heterosexuality."

Olaf Brühl[1]

Correspondence may be addressed: Department of German, Russian and East Asian Languages and Literatures, Bates College, Lewiston, ME 04240. E-mail: dsweet@abacus.bates.edu

[Haworth co-indexing entry note]: "The Church, the Stasi, and Socialist Integration: Three Stages of Lesbian and Gay Emancipation in the Former German Democratic Republic." Sweet, Denis M. Co-published simultaneously in *Journal of Homosexuality* (The Haworth Press, Inc.) Vol. 29, No. 4, 1995, pp. 351-367; and: *Gay Men and the Sexual History of the Political Left* (ed: Gert Hekma, Harry Oosterhuis, and James Steakley) The Haworth Press, Inc., 1995, pp. 351-367; and *Gay Men and the Sexual History of the Political Left* (ed: Gert Hekma, Harry Oosterhuis, and James Steakley) Harrington Park Press, an imprint of The Haworth Press, Inc., 1995, pp. 351-367. Multiple copies of this article/chapter may be purchased from The Haworth Document Delivery Center. [1-800-342-9678 9:00 a.m. - 5:00 p.m. (EST)].

351

I

The April 20, 1990, celebration of "Führergeburtstag" (i.e., Hitler's birthday) on East Berlin's Alexanderplatz by hundreds of young men raising their right arms in the Nazi salute, attacking passersby, and shouting "Jew swine!" or simply "Foreigners get out!" was up to then the largest and most violent neo-Nazi demonstration in the dying East German state.[2]

The Alexanderplatz demonstration, one of many in both East and West Germany that day, marked the rising tide of racist and xenophobic violence in both halves of Germany that has continued and increased substantially since. On that birthday, knife- and truncheon-sporting skinheads shouting "Queers get out!" trashed a well-known gay watering place on the Alexanderplatz,[3] but such events in the then still existing German Democratic Republic (GDR) pale in the light of subsequent experience.

In May, 1991, for example, some seventy young men, many of them skinheads wielding tear-gas pistols and sporting knives, chains, and baseball bats, attacked a lesbian and gay fundraiser in Mahlsdorf, East Berlin, causing some of the guests to be hospitalized. Shortly before in Dresden, a black man was thrown out of a moving streetcar and killed. In Wittenberg, young black men were pushed off a fourth-floor balcony by knife-wielding youths–all events from the new states in eastern Germany within the year after German reunification.

The conjunction of hatred against Jews, foreigners, and gay people is an old one in Germany. Forty years of an officially "antifascist" East German nation had not plucked out the roots of xenophobia, anti-Semitism, and racism. In contradistinction to an official policy on anti-Semitism and racism, however, there never was a socialist policy to address the issue of hatred of gays. Quite the contrary. "We will have nothing to do with all those who have a false relationship to our state, to work, and to the opposite sex."[4] This quotation, with its characteristic arrogance, was repeated by the middle cadres in Party meetings as a clear and welcome indication of Party sensibility. It sums up an entire way of thinking: These are the values our state incorporates. The words and sentiments do not, as one might suppose, stem from the heyday of Stalinism but from 1984, and come from Hermann Axen, the member of the Politbüro and former concentration camp inmate who was responsible for ideological purity.

One clear-cut corollary was, however, encoded in the administrative practice of the GDR. With the signing of the Helsinki Accords in 1974, the GDR formally committed itself to a range of human-rights provisions that for the first time granted GDR citizens the right to apply to emigrate. Processed in a secretive and seemingly capricious manner, applications were not only denied in the overwhelming majority of cases but led to government reprisals against the applicants. As we now know, the bureaucrats handling these applications followed a confidential set of guidelines that set forth various criteria for granting permission to emigrate from the GDR. Article 5 listed homosexuality, nothing more.[5]

The first impulse to rethink the issue of homosexuality came from an unlikely source: the Protestant (Lutheran/Evangelical) church.

II

The September 15, 1983, issue of the church paper *Die Kirche* published a large number of letters to the editor from readers who were responding to a series of articles concerning homosexuals under such characteristic headings as "Tolerance for Minorities," "Accepting Others as Different," "Living with Each Other," and "Normalization and Acceptance." The editorial staff had broken the reader responses down into four main groups.

To the first group belong those readers who found that the mere mention of this subject was unnecessary:

"I am terribly upset to find such an article in a church newspaper."
"The church is not a sex bar."

The second–and largest–group was entirely condemnatory and made no bones about it:

"Homosexuality is an orientation acquired by living a life separated from God."

"This vice originates in the cities with their unnatural conditions."
"Homosexuals who persist in their sin and do not desist and repent, stand under the judgment of God."

The readers of the third and relatively small group showed a certain thoughtfulness, even compassion:

"I was very much moved by the article."
"It has become clear to me that these differently fashioned human beings cannot act any differently."
"The article certainly means well–and is also right. May many others come to the understanding that one may not accuse these people, but must help them come to terms with their diseased orientation."

Those in the fourth group–gay men and lesbians among them–found public discussion of this touchy topic absolutely indispensable:

"After the striking of the old § 175 from the criminal code of the GDR in 1968, it is crucial to overcome remaining prejudices."
"It is my opinion that something like this absolutely belongs in a Christian newspaper."[6]

This first public discussion of homosexuality had begun with a conference of the Evangelical Academy Berlin-Brandenburg in January, 1982: "Can One Speak about It? Homosexuality as a Question for Theology and Pastoral Care."[7] The conference was, as Manfred Punge explained in his discussion of it, the first not only to tackle issues connected with gayness but also to include lesbians and gay men among the participants. The discussion concentrated on two main issues: using the insights of modern sexology to diminish prejudice and widespread, fallacious conceptualizations of homosexuality; and providing a framework for lesbians and gay men to meet and discuss issues concerning them, with a view toward furthering self-acceptance.
As a measure of the needs that this conference addressed, and of

its success, working groups ("Arbeits- und Gesprächskreise," in the terminology of the Church) were formed that same year in Leipzig and Berlin. Other groups were quickly constituted in other cities of the GDR. They soon grew in number to over twenty and were established not only in all the large cities and in the lesser metropolitan areas such as Magdeburg, Chemnitz, and Rostock, but also in such smaller, provincial towns as Zwickau, Plauen, and Neustrelitz. Two of the most influential groups, in Leipzig and Dresden, were founded by schooled theologians denied ordination because they were an out gay man and an out lesbian, respectively.

These working groups did not advance without concerted resistance from within certain well-situated Lutheran and charismatic factions within the Church, particularly from the south of the GDR with its own traditions of theology and piety–so much so that the Church authorities in Saxony felt obliged to append within the territory of their administration a publication that countered the largely positive and tolerant brochure *Homosexuelle in der Kirche?* (Homosexuals in the Church?) issued in 1984 by the central office of theological study of the East German Church (Theologische Studienabteilung der Evangelischen Kirchen). This Saxon alternative brochure warned about "militant homosexuals" forcing an entry into the Church to advance the "ideology of homosexual emancipation." This excerpt is characteristic of its tenor:

> The homosexual, whatever the way he may be fashioned, should be made aware of the life-transforming power of the Holy Spirit in the saving name of Jesus. If the Church neglects this offer of grace and instead confirms the homosexual in his orientation and calls upon him to accept himself, to the extent of even practicing homosexual behavior, then the Church itself is practicing a godless work and departing not only from the framework of the law, but also from that of the Gospel.[8]

Despite such resistance by Church hierarchies, and not always with the widespread support of their local communities, lesbians and gay men continued to organize working groups on homosexuality within Church precincts.[9] These efforts were not only viewed as threatening by those within the Church, as the quotation above evidences, but immediately attracted the attention of agents from the Ministry of State Security (Ministerium für Staatssicherheit, or Stasi).

III

Surveillance of homosexual working groups operating under the aegis of the Church was systematic and all-encompassing, carried out by a Stasi office in each of the major cities.[10] They in turn were coordinated by a Stasi office for homosexual affairs in Berlin, which was staffed by five full-time officers under a Stasi colonel.[11] Informants constituted a massive presence in the working groups on homosexuality. One group estimates in hindsight that over sixty percent of its members were paid Stasi informants ("informelle Mitarbeiter," or IMs). One of the informants in the working group in Magdeburg whom I interviewed in March, 1991, a young grade-school teacher and himself a gay man, related to me how he came to inform on the other members of the working group, many of them longtime friends, for a period of about three years up to the final denouement of the "Wende" (turnabout) in the fall of 1989, when the Wall was breached.

This individual had first been approached by the Stasi, he related, some time after he had been detained in a police raid on a public restroom in a big city. "We know you're queer," they said, "but we think you can do something worthwhile for your country anyway." And he agreed. He was told that the working groups were engaging in anti-GDR activities, and that keeping track of them was a patriotic duty. He wanted to be a good citizen. When, after a while, he began to see that the working groups were not engaged in anti-government activities, the Stasi told him that his spying could help the cause of gay liberation in East Germany. He did not do it for the money (he received 500 Marks a year), nor because he felt threatened, blackmailed, or coerced. His motive, he said, was to serve his government, which he believed in. He wanted to demonstrate that he was a patriot.

Another example typical of prevailing attitudes and the practices of the GDR authorities is provided by the following report by a group of eleven lesbians who set out in 1985 to honor the memory of lesbians killed at Ravensbrück, a Nazi concentration camp specifically for women:

For the second time now, women have been forced to learn that it is apparently impossible to honor the victims of fascism. On March 10, 1984, on the occasion of Women's Day, the homosexual self-help working group Lesbians in the Church registered and was given permission to make a trip to Ravensbrück. After their visit to the National Memorial of Warning, the wreath that they had left and their inscription in the guest book were removed. After they protested this, they were told among other things that while each citizen of the GDR as an individual would be permitted to honor the victims of fascism, a group or organization unrecognized by the state would not.

On April 20, 1985, eleven of us women, all friends of one another and most of us lesbians, tried to go to Ravensbrück in order to attend the large, state-organized public ceremonies to mark the fortieth anniversary of the camp's liberation. . . .

For this occasion we ordered a wreath from a florist in Gaudystraße, on whose ribbon we recalled the sorrow of our lesbian sisters and which we signed with our first names. On April 19th, the woman who had ordered the wreath was visited at about 11:00 a.m. in her apartment and asked to come along to the police station to explain the matter. After an interrogation lasting one hour, she was informed that our honoring the victims of fascism was not going to be permitted. Putting our names on the ribbon denoted us as a group–a group that was not recognized by the state. As she left the interrogation room, they yelled, "Don't differentiate among the victims of fascism!"

. . . When the women stepped out of the house early Saturday morning, two men dressed in civilian clothes were already waiting for them on the other side of the street. They followed them to the train station and accompanied them in a way clearly meant not to attract attention.

At the Fürstenberg train station, we eleven women were singled out and detained with the excuse that the transportation police were conducting a search. Our identity papers were collected, and we were told to wait in the main hall of the station that had been cleared of other travellers. Only the eleven of us, twenty transportation police, and the two men in civilian clothes already mentioned remained. After about a quarter of an hour we were encircled by about thirty riot police and driven with insults, pushes, shoves, and arm holds to a police truck about 100 meters off.

With language like: "Get on up there, go on, go on, hurry up! You'll be able to sit your ass flat enough later on!" We were driven up onto the flatbed truck under constant verbal and physical abuse.

Once on the truck, we first waited for a long time and then began to be driven through Fürstenberg and environs, watched over by five men in uniform. . . . They regaled us with such bon mots as: "I'd rather fuck a dead pig." When we asked them where we were headed, they answered, "Where you belong, to the concentration camp."[12]

The regime and its state security apparatus viewed the Church working groups as a potential threat to socialist order. The Magdeburg Stasi office wrote in an official report dated 1983 that certain "politically negative and adversarial forces" regarded the working groups as "grassroots organizations for underground political activities" and planned to make use of them to foment "internal opposition."[13]

Eduard Stapel, one of the main organizers of the Church working group movement in the early 1980s and founder in 1990 of the (East) German Gay Association (Schwulenverband Deutschlands), related to me how a young man imprisoned on a manslaughter conviction was released early by the Stasi specifically to spy on Stapel and his church group.

An official Stasi memorandum on the infiltration and destruction ("Zersetzung") of groups provided detailed instructions on how to destroy a group from within by, among other things, sowing mistrust and the suspicion that other members of the group were Stasi spies. In 1990, after citizens' groups had broken into and occupied Stasi offices throughout the country, one such Stasi report on surveillance methods for Church working groups made its way to Stapel anonymously: it simply appeared in his mailbox one day. It directed that correspondence with West Germany was to be systematically opened, the identities of those present at group meetings were to be recorded, and, most importantly of all, the sense of a secret conspiratorial movement fundamentally opposed to the interests of the state was to be invented and fostered.[14]

In view of this, the positive attitudes propagated by the East German state towards homosexuality that began to emerge in the last years of the GDR appear to be somewhat paradoxical.

IV

The watershed for open discussion of homosexuality outside of the Church came in 1985. Sponsored by the Marriage and Family Section of the Society for Social Hygiene of the GDR and the Andrology Section of the Society for Dermatology of the GDR, a series of interdisciplinary conferences on the "psychosocial aspects of homosexuality" was initiated. Held at Leipzig in 1985, Karl-Marx-Stadt in 1988, and Jena in 1990, these conferences had far-reaching ramifications for social policy. Although hosted by the medical profession, each conference was broadly interdisciplinary in intent. Invited participants included not only medical doctors, but also psychologists and sexologists, Marxist philosophers and journalists, and especially important, as in the Church conference that had preceded it, lesbians and gay men who spoke for themselves in their own voices.

Equally important is who did not attend. Conspicuous by his absence was Günter Dörner, an internationally prominent endocrinologist at the Humboldt University in East Berlin, who for decades has conducted laboratory research with rats and advances the hypothesis that human homosexuality is caused by hormonal imbalances brought on by prenatal stress in the mother and affecting the fetus, which opens the prospect that pregnant women could potentially be tested for such hormonal imbalances and encouraged (or compelled) to abort a gay fetus. His standpoint was repeatedly mentioned–and massively criticized. The firm repudiation of Dörner's ideas by conference participants signalled a break with nineteenth-century notions of homosexuality as pathology; the emerging public discussion of the issues surrounding homosexuality was thus set on a track both morally and socially responsible.

What began to emerge during the three conferences was an understanding of sexuality as a socially constructed given, one with a social history marked by forms of policing and punishment under an apparatus that seeks to protect certain forms of sexuality while prosecuting others. The sociologist Rainer Warczok formulated it in this way:

> The presence of prejudices concerning homosexuality results basically from the material and intellectual conditions of pre-socialist society. At various times the then ruling classes . . . made use of the rejection of same-sex behavior in order to accomplish their political goals all the more easily. They discriminated against homosexuals and claimed that they were responsible for a variety of social ills.[15]

Two themes emerged here, as they did from the conferences as a whole: prejudice had no place in socialist society; discrimination against homosexuals has historically been connected to ways of maintaining certain political and social orders.

The social consequences of these conferences were immediate in the GDR. In their wake ensued a proliferation of lesbian and gay youth groups connected to the communist youth organization Free German Youth (Freie Deutsche Jugend, or FDJ) and Jugend Klubs, as well as of other, independent lesbian and gay organizations.[16] An unprecedented discussion of homosexuality followed in the media, based on the twin key concepts of tolerance and integration into socialist society.

Gerhard Schöne's songs, heard on GDR radio, pleaded for tolerance of those who are different by reciting everyday forms of homophobic language and conduct:

"They're scum,
people like that should be shot.
If that were my son, I'd know what to do!"
Someone says, "He's a runaway."
Someone says, "Beat it, get out of here."
Someplace someone mumbles, "Ya fuckin queer."
Someone spits at his feet,
someone throws food after him.

A drunk grabs him and starts to pummel him.
  Refrain:
When my yellow parakeet flew out the window,
a pack of sparrows started to peck at him.
He sang a bit different
and wasn't as grey as they.
Unacceptable things to a sparrow brain.[17]

A welter of articles in the print media acted as accompaniment. The popular *Das Magazin*, which regularly dealt with issues of sexuality, ran a series on homosexuality including life stories and interviews, in particular with troubled young gay men.[18] Lesbians, as one letter from a reader pointed out, remained largely invisible. Themes from coming out to teen suicide made their appearance, but the overriding message was simple: Social ostracism was to be countered by tolerance, aiming at the full integration of gays and lesbians into socialist society.

Directed toward a general audience, this programmatic message expanded to other media, most notably in Heiner Carow's DEFA feature film *Coming Out* (1989), whose subject matter alone won it a Silver Bear at the 1990 West Berlin Film Festival. Didactic in intent, the film presents a broad panoply of characters and events, ranging from the suicide attempt of the young gay male character (with which the film opens) to East German skinheads attacking a black man in a commuter train. The film includes narratives of all sorts of unjustifiable social suffering, including that of a former gay concentration camp inmate. Both this film–a box-office hit–and the rapidly increasing publications on homosexuality in the GDR were authorized by the regime, which was implicitly calling upon society as a whole to restructure its sexual economy in order to make a little more room for those stigmatized by their difference.

In view of German history, the message of tolerance and integration propounded in the closing years of the GDR's existence was doubtless a progressive one. But by presenting this message as programmatic policy, the state used it to mask underlying issues of social control and hegemony. No questions were or could be raised about the nature of the existing patriarchy (within which homosexuals were to be tolerated and integrated), about the nature of the family, the function of homophobia as a form of social control, or the social valuation of heterosexuality that makes it compulsory social behavior. There was no discussion of the extent to which all these issues were grounded not on concrete "natural facts" but on social valuations, prevailing thought, customs, folklore.

Yet one of the most thoughtful critical thinkers who emerged from the homosexual emancipation movement in the GDR pursued just this question of the ideological roots of the social valuations surrounding sexuality. Speaking at a conference convened at the Waldschlößchen (near Göttingen) just eight days after the Wall opened, Hubert Thinius, an instructor in the Department of Marxist-Leninist Philosophy at Humboldt University in East Berlin, began by quoting a poem by Heinz Kahlau that had just appeared in the *Berliner Zeitung*:

The State of My Knowledge

Since at least the end of the last ice age,
the male principle
in contrast to all other principles
of human beings living together
has prevailed as the victorious principle
and has surpassed its high point
with the money economy.

It still holds for humankind:
whoever wins is right and determines
what truth is,
As a natural law.
Wealth and power and violence
raise the victor
above death
until it extinguishes him.

But now
the victor can no longer
be determined by war.
But now
nature no longer withstands
our exploitation.

She succumbs.
From now on
consciousness determines
being. Every attempt at rescue
must be undertaken
without the male principle.
Because it has led us
to the edge of this abyss.

Socialism itself has failed
because it has not renounced
this principle.

Power to the people
is the sole way
is the human principle
of democracy.[19]

What is here described as "the male principle" points to a far-reaching and fundamental dilemma of power, one that feminists have focused on for some time and which the ecological movement has increasingly brought to public attention, one that finally, as here in the first euphoria after the fall of the Wall, came to be a central point of discussion—with a view to understanding and challenging the ideologies and administrations surrounding sexualities and difference.

This last stage of discussion, it should be noted, was inspired by the aim not of eliminating but reforming East German socialism. It was the culmination of more than a decade when lesbians and gay men had been organizing for their rights in Church working groups, creating new social and personal spaces for a discourse of liberation within the confines of a totalitarian state.

That regime and its official organs had initially reacted with denial and repression, then with surveillance and cooptation, before finally coming to see that the working groups could be exploited to meet state interests: out in the open, lesbians and gay men could all the more easily be subjected to surveillance. The working groups provided an ideal funnel for intelligence gathering, and the Church itself played a "domesticizing" role vis-à-vis the working groups.[20]

Further, it was in the interests of this regime to take the wind out of the sails of the working groups. As shepherd of a new openness, the Church was repugnant. Thus the interdisciplinary conferences and the ensuing non-Church (and in some cases pro-Party) gay and lesbian groups were at first grudgingly permitted and ultimately promoted, for they demonstrated to the world that socialism cared for its minorities and thus produced political capital. Notwithstanding the decriminalization of homosexual acts in the name of tolerance and integration into socialist society, the interests of this regime and the interests of its lesbian and gay citizens were by no means in harmony at the time "really existing socialism" came to an end.

V

Unification with West Germany has brought a new social order. Theodor Adorno once wrote that "in truth one cannot argue against the criminalization of homosexuality; one can only recall the sheer insult [that criminalization represents]."[21] Same-sex acts between consenting males were decriminalized in the 1989 penal code of the GDR, but the law is still on the books in the Federal Republic and threatens now to expand eastward.

The Round Table's 1989-90 draft of a new constitution for the GDR specifically called for an end to legal discrimination on the basis of sexual orientation,[22] but in the rush toward unification this constitutional draft was neither discussed nor adopted by the East German Parliament (Volkskammer) seated by the March, 1990, elections. Barring the now unlikely eventuality of a constitutional congress comprised of members from all the states to draft an entirely new constitution for a united Germany which would extend rights to sexual minorities, the future seems to hold continued social discrimination. The full-scale adoption of West German values certainly will not bring the protection of civil liberties fundamental to human dignity. The epigraph of this article–the programmatic cry voiced by Olaf Brühl shortly after the Wall came down–seems formulated in another age. It was.[23]

AUTHOR NOTE

Denis M. Sweet spent a year in East Berlin researching the lesbian and gay emancipation movement in the former East German state as a Senior Fulbright

Research Fellow. He is currently conducting research on homosexuality in other post-communist societies in Europe and Russia, and would welcome correspondence and contacts in that area.

NOTES

1. Olaf Brühl, interview by Ulli Klaum, in *Die DDR–Die Schwulen–Der Aufbruch: Versuch einer Bestandsaufnahme*, ed. Jean Jacques Soukup (Göttingen: Schriftenreihe des Waldschlößchens, 1990), p. 114. The panel discussions and reports by and interviews with politically active gay men from the GDR contained in this volume stem from "Schwule in der DDR," a German-German conference sponsored by the Waldschlößchen held November 17-19, 1989, near Göttingen.

2. M. Habersetzer and P. Plarre, "Rechtsradikale Randale in Ost-Berlin," *die tageszeitung*, April 23, 1990, p. 1.

3. "Happy Birthday," *Magnus* 2.6 (June 1990): 3.

4. Hermann Axen, as quoted by Klaus Laabs, in *Die DDR–Die Schwulen– Der Aufbruch*, p. 78; see also p. 120.

5. See Günter Grau in *Die DDR–Die Schwulen–Der Aufbruch*, p. 78: "In the criteria for leaving the country, after family members in the West, etc., came Article 5. It listed homosexuality, nothing more."

6. Günter Grau, "Beginn des Dialogs," in *Und diese Liebe auch: Theologische und sexualwissenschaftliche Einsichten zur Homosexualität*, ed. Günter Grau (Berlin/GDR: Evangelische Verlagsanstalt, 1989), pp. 18-19.

7. Manfred Punge, "Das gebrochene Tabu: Zu Gang und Stand der Homosexualitäts-Debatte in den evangelischen Landeskirchen der DDR," in *Und diese Liebe auch*, pp. 93-94.

8. Ch. Richter, *Hilfe in Sicht? Ein Alternativ-Beitrag zum Papier der Theologischen Studienabteilung beim Bund der Evangelischen Kirchen in der DDR "Homosexuelle in der Kirche?"* (Albernau: reproduced as manuscript, 1984), p. 5; as quoted by Punge, p. 98.

9. See Raelynn J. Hillhouse, "Out of the Closet behind the Wall: Sexual Politics and Social Change in the GDR," *Slavic Review* 49 (1990): 585-96.

10. See Detlef Grumbach and Günter Grau, "Aktenvermerk: 'Homosexuell.' Die Stasi und die Schwulen," *Magnus* 6.2 (February 1994): 10-17.

11. This information was provided by Christina Wilkening, author of *Staat im Staate: Auskünfte ehemaliger Stasi-Mitarbeiter* (Berlin and Weimar: Aufbau, 1990), at a meeting of the gay working group of the Advent-Kirchengemeinde, East Berlin, on February 26, 1991. Ms. Wilkening spoke in the place of the Stasi colonel who had originally been scheduled to appear himself but, we were told, was afraid that the publicity would cause him to lose his job with the railroad. Ms. Wilkening did not respond to my request to help arrange a direct meeting with the ex-colonel.

12. Ute Postler, "A Report by the Women to Whom It Happened Concerning Their Attempts to Honor the Victims of Fascism," mimeographed document marked "For Church-Internal Use Only." Reprinted in: Ursula Sillge, *Un-Sicht-*

bare *Frauen: Lesben und ihre Emanzipation in der DDR* (Berlin: LinksDruck, 1991), pp. 139-41. From information received verbally on March 13, 1991, from Ilse Kokula in the Berlin government's "Referat für gleichgeschlechtliche Lebensweisen," one of the organizers of this trip was a Stasi informant. See Irena Kukutz and Katja Havemann, *Geschützte Quelle: Gespräche mit Monika H. alias Karin Lenz* (Berlin: BasisDruck, 1990).

13. Eduard Stapel, "An meine pensionierten Überwacher! Zur Auseinandersetzung mit den Stasi-Akten," *mini slib* [der Homosexuelleninitiative Leipzig], no. 8 (October 1990): 6.

14. One of the myths about gay people to which the Stasi subscribed was that they were fundamentally asocial and easy prey for foreign information-gathering services. Yet according to the coming out studies by Professor Erwin Günther at the Universität Jena, the first fairly large-scale questionnaire sent out to homosexuals in the mid-1980s, around twenty percent of the respondents indicated that they were members of the East German Communist Party (SED), and others were members of other state and party organizations, indicating far more social integration and involvement than the Stasi myth allowed for.

15. Rainer Warczok, "Soziologische Aspekte der menschlichen Sexualität unter besonderer Berücksichtigung des gleichgeschlechtlich ausgerichteten Empfindens und Verhaltens," in *Natürlich anders: Zur Homosexualitätsdiskussion in der DDR*, ed. Günter Amendt (Cologne: Pahl-Rugenstein, 1989), p. 133.

16. The significance of a position paper put out by the interdisciplinary working group on homosexuality at Humboldt University (spring, 1985) as a precipitating factor in these developments should be underscored. See Dietmar Bsonek, "Individualität und Freiheit–Gedanken zu aktuellen Fragen der Emanzipation der Homosexuellen in der DDR," paper read at the 1988 conference in Karl-Marx-Stadt, in *Natürlich anders*, p. 156.

17. " 'Das ist der Abschaum, / sowas müßte man erschießen, / wenn das mein Sohn wär', ich wüßte, was ich tät!' / Jemand sagt: 'Der ist entlaufen!' / Jemand sagt: 'Hau ab, zieh' Leine!' / Irgendwo ruft einer halblaut: 'Schwules Schwein!' / Jemand spuckt ihm vor die Füße, / jemand wirft nach ihm ein Brötchen, / ein Besoffner packt ihn und schlägt auf ihn ein. REFRAIN: Als mein gelber Wellensittich aus dem Fenster flog, / hackte eine Schar von Spatzen auf ihn ein. / Denn er sang wohl anders / und war nicht so grau wie sie / und das paßt in Spatzenhirne nicht hinein." Gerhard Schöne, "Der gelbe Wellensittich," transcribed from a transmission from GDR radio by Gudrun von Kowalski. A slightly different version of this song is found on Schöne's album *Menschenskind* (Amiga, 1985) as "Wellensittich und Spatzen."

18. Ursula Hafranke, "Ungestraft anders?" *Das Magazin*, nos. 1, 2, 5 (1989); no. 2 (1990).

19. "STAND MEINER ERKENNTNIS. Wenigstens seit Ende der letzten Eiszeit / hat sich das männliche Prinzip / gegenüber allen übrigen Prinzipien / des Zusammenlebens von Menschen / als das siegreiche Prinzip / durchgesetzt und hat seinen Höhepunkt / in der Geldwirtschaft / überschritten. // Noch gilt der Menschheit: / Wer siegt, hat recht und bestimmt, / was die Wahrheit ist. / Als Na-

turgesetz. / Reichtum und Macht und Gewalt / stellen den Sieger / über den Tod. / Bis der ihn auslöscht. // Doch nun / kann der Sieger nicht mehr / durch den Krieg ermittelt werden. / Doch nun / widersteht die Natur / unserer Ausbeutung nicht mehr / und erliegt. / Von nun an / bestimmt das Bewußtsein / das Sein. Jeder Rettungsversuch muß / ohne das männliche Prinzip / unternommen werden. / Denn es hat uns / an diesen Abgrund geführt. // Selbst der Sozialismus scheiterte bisher / weil er sich nicht von diesem Prinzip / losgesagt hat. // Volksherrschaft / ist der einzige Weg / ist das menschliche Prinzip / der Demokratie."

20. From an interview with Church Superintendent Christof Ziemer, Dresden, June 18, 1991.

21. Theodor W. Adorno, "Sexualtabus und Recht heute," in *Eingriffe: Neun kritische Modelle* (Frankfurt a.m.: Suhrkamp, 1963), p. 111.

22. Draft for "Die Verfassung der Deutschen Demokratischen Republik," *Neues Deutschland*, April 18, 1990, p. 7.

23. After this article was written, the German Bundestag on March 10, 1994, repealed the anti-sodomy § 175 of the penal code, whose repeal had long been a goal of the German gay liberation movement. At the same time, however, § 182 was revised so as to set a (gender neutral) de facto age of consent of sixteen for all of Germany. See *Frankfurter Rundschau*, March 12, 1994, p. 1. [Manuscript Editor]

From Revolution to Involution: The Disappearance of the Gay Movement in France

Jan Willem Duyvendak

Universiteit van Amsterdam

SUMMARY. This essay sketches the development of the modern French gay movement in relation to its political context, in particular to the French Socialist Party. The author argues that its curvilinear development–the movement started very modestly in the 1950s, spread within small, radical left-wing circles in the late 1960s and early 1970s, peaked around 1980, and declined rapidly in the course of the 1980s–can be explained by the ups and downs in political repression on the one hand and political support and success on the other.

Those men and women who do not reproduce but are always more numerous. . . .

Georges Pompidou

Correspondence may be addressed: Van Ostadestraat 333a, 1074 VV Amsterdam, Netherlands.

[Haworth co-indexing entry note]: "From Revolution to Involution: The Disappearance of the Gay Movement in France." Duyvendak, Jan Willem. Co-published simultaneously in *Journal of Homosexuality* (The Haworth Press, Inc.) Vol. 29, No. 4, 1995, pp. 369-385; and: *Gay Men and the Sexual History of the Political Left* (ed: Gert Hekma, Harry Oosterhuis, and James Steakley) The Haworth Press, Inc., 1995, pp. 369-385; and *Gay Men and the Sexual History of the Political Left* (ed: Gert Hekma, Harry Oosterhuis, and James Steakley) Harrington Park Press, an imprint of The Haworth Press, Inc., 1995, pp. 369-385. Multiple copies of this article/chapter may be purchased from The Haworth Document Delivery Center. [1-800-342-9678 9:00 a.m. - 5:00 p.m. (EST)].

369

The homosexual movement may be considered a subcultural movement par excellence. As we shall see, an instrumental, activist wing developed within this movement in France during the late 1970s and first half of the 1980s, but the subcultural side has remained preponderant. The homosexual subculture, the gay and lesbian "scene," has figured as the indispensable substrate of activism largely because identity production has been one of the movement's main goals. To the extent that a positive gay or lesbian identity is formed in subcultural settings, shared sexual preference has provided an incentive for individuals to mobilize and organize collectively.

In this essay, I will mainly be concerned with the gay male side of the French homosexual movement. Whereas mixed (lesbian and gay male) organizations dominate the stage in some countries (for instance in the Netherlands), homosociality has been and remains the norm in France. It is, of course, an interesting question why non-mixed organizations dominate in France. Apart from broader cultural aspects (e.g., polarized relations between the sexes in general), a more specific answer may be possible. To the extent that a homosexual movement has a more instrumental orientation, i.e., focuses mainly on representing interests, a mixed organization may develop provided that discrimination against lesbians is seen primarily as a form of homosexual and not of women's oppression. In a subculture-oriented organization, on the other hand, homosociality will prevail because men and women exclude each other in their homosexual desires. Since, as we will see, the period of instrumental-oriented interest representation in France was rather short-lived, non-mixed, pleasure-oriented organizations have predominated.

Gay movements need to strike a balance between desires and interests: when desire prevails, a pure subculture may result;[1] but when interest advocacy comes to predominate and the link with the subculture is loosened, the movement may dwindle to insignificance, since identity production will no longer take place and the main incentive for most people to participate will disappear in the process.[2]

A subcultural movement that aims solely at the collective good for its participants—and, in this case, produces it through activities—does not suffer from free-riders. This is true, however, only in the short term: although direct participation is an indispensable prerequisite for sharing in any collective benefits at the start of the emancipation process, "parasitic" behavior may arise as an option later on, when a collective identity has been produced and the position of gay men and lesbian women is starting to improve. This is particularly true as subcultures become increasingly professionalized (in this instance, commercialized) and people can share a collective identity outside the movement purely on the basis of pleasure.

In this essay I seek to show that the development of the gay movement depends strongly on its political context. Subcultural movements are generally less influenced by politics than are instrumental movements, since the latter are wholly dependent on interaction with the authorities to reach their goals. Yet the history of the gay movement in France shows that, even for its subcultural wing, the power of politics has been overwhelming. As we shall see, this means that in the polarized, left/right political situation specific to France, *left-wing* parties have played a decisive role in the development of the gay movement.

PROLOGUE

It is difficult to fix the precise date when the French gay movement came into being. Surveying the period after World War II, we can detect (as in Germany, the Netherlands, and Switzerland) a very cautious beginning with the publication of a journal, *Futur* (1952-55). This remained almost unknown to the outside world, however, since publicity for it was forbidden by the state. Homosexuality was simply not regarded as a public political category–in contrast to its place in French cultural life, in which it was a source of inspiration.[3] Contacts between gays and the authorities during these years were quite one-sided: any interaction was consistently initiated by the authorities, with repressive intentions and tactics.

This desolate situation improved slightly in 1954, when the journal *Arcadie* was launched. Some authors regard this event as the starting point of the modern gay movement,[4] while others, who would define a movement as essentially outward-directed and change-oriented,[5] refuse to ascribe the status of a full-fledged movement to either the journal or to the Literary and Scientific Club of the Romance Countries (Club littéraire et scientifique des pays latines, or CLESPALA), the apolitical social club that was affiliated with it.[6] The *Arcadie* circle was nonetheless important, since all subsequent organizations had to relate to this highly autocratic institution. André Baudry was its leader from start to finish, and he dictated its (a)political line.[7] A self-help organization (*"Arcadie* permits homosexuals to meet each other, to come out of their solitude"), *Arcadie* stressed the equality of hetero- and homosexuals: "the homosexual is also a social human being."[8] In its slowly developing contacts with the outside world, *Arcadie* followed a so-called key-figure policy, with designated spokesmen.[9] Under the prevailing conditions of repression, public activities were absolutely impossible. But even when the political climate became a bit less wintry following the May events of 1968, *Arcadie* clung to its strategy of advising homophiles to behave as normally as possible in order to improve the status of homosexuals.[10]

The highly confrontational style of the Revolutionary Pederastic Action Committee (Comité d'Action Pédérastique Révolutionnaire) which emerged at the Sorbonne in May 1968 and, more importantly, of the Revolutionary Homosexual Action Front (Front Homosexuel d'Action Révolutionnaire, or FHAR) from 1971 on ran directly contrary to *Arcadie's* approach. These new formations stressed not only the political character of homosexuality and its repression but also its revolutionary potential. In contrast to *Arcadie*, they considered *"la différence"* a positive quality. "Abnormal" sexuality was no longer to be hidden, but instead exhibited in public. "Our asshole is revolutionary," proclaimed FHAR spokesman Guy Hocquenghem. The public display of homosexuality on the streets, disrupting the May 1st demonstration of the Communist Union (Confédération Générale du Travail, or CGT), was the start of the gay movement as a "new social movement," although–like other such movements–it remained colored by conventional Marxist ideology and rhetoric in its early days: "In a world based on sexual repression and on that repulsive filthiness–labor, all those who do not reproduce and who make love solely for pleasure rather than to produce a reserve army of factory workers have no alternative other than to be smashed or to revolt."[11]

This development signalled a split within the French movement between the radical *"pédés"* and the homophile *Arcadie* circle; by contrast, the main homosexual organization in the Netherlands, the COC, proved capable of incorporating such oppositional tendencies.[12] The new French organizations of the 1970s were more radical than their counterparts in other countries, due not only to the climate which was still rather repressive, but to interorganizational relations as well. The new organizations strongly opposed the "dignified and virile clandestineness" of the old guard. "While *Arcadie* broadly rejected effeminates, inverts, queers, transvestites, and transsexuals, FHAR on the other hand brought together a rich variety of conducts and behaviors."[13]

In addition, this movement made it clear that autonomous organizing by new social movements was virtually impossible in France. Although the prominent left parties, the Socialist Party (Parti socialiste, or PS) and French Communist Party (Parti communiste français, or PCF), ignored homosexuality during the first half of the 1970s, smaller leftist and especially Trostkyite groups such as the League of Revolutionary Communists (Ligue communiste révolutionnaire, or LCR) integrated gay demands to the extent that they were conceptualized in class terms. In fact, the gay movement in France became politicized rather early on because of the overall climate of repression and *Arcadie's* absolutely apolitical character:

Thanks to FHAR, homosexuality erupted within politics; in this country where social struggles have traditionally been fierce, where the division between the left and the right is quite pronounced, where the spectrum of political parties is very broad, the homosexual movement will be entangled in a web of political divergences which probably runs counter to the essential nature of the homosexual condition.[14]

FHAR sought to balance the promotion of pleasure with a policy of advancing gay interests by organizing events which combined the qualities of a party and a political meeting. Its journals *Le Fléau Social* (Social Plague) and *L'Antinorm* were likewise interesting mixtures of anarchistic chaos and Trotskyite order. But as new organizations came into being, they increasingly tended toward a one-sidedly political agenda, a development encouraged by the continuing police repression of pleasure-oriented institutions of all kinds (e.g., bars, journals, saunas, etc.). This repression was, however, less harsh than in earlier times, giving the organizations some "space" to express themselves. It was exactly this combination of some repression and a certain opportunity which fueled the starting liberation movement.

After FHAR faded away in 1973, the Homosexual Liberation Group (Groupe de Libération Homosexuelle, or GLH) came to the fore and a factional struggle developed among its members: some favored a political line in the new tradition of "anti-normalcy,"[15] while others called for greater pragmatism. This demonstrated that if a subcultural movement becomes more externally oriented, it has two options: to choose either a countercultural profile, challenging authorities with highly confrontational tactics, or an instrumental profile, dealing with politics in the manner of the environmental or peace movements. If the climate is not too repressive, countercultural organizations often tend in the long run to deradicalize and adopt a more instrumental attitude.

This is exactly what happened with the winner of the struggle within the GLH. Of all tendencies, GLH-Politics and Everyday Life (GLH-Politique et Quotidien, or PQ) survived and even succeeded in building a network of local organizations. Besides organizing a great number of activities with other new social movements (concerned with such issues as abortion rights and the risks of nuclear energy), PQ also mobilized the first massive demonstrations in the streets of Paris and put forward openly gay candidates in local and national elections. In its political discourse, PQ struck a balance between new and old leftist points of view, which reflected its repudiation of the Communist Party of France (PCF). The PCF was still opposed to gay liberation, even when it was couched in class terms.[16] Nevertheless, the gay movement garnered support from the more moderate left parties such as the PS during the second half of the 1970s, and this success tempered the radical discourse of the movement: the total politicization of homosexuality (countercultural orientation) was replaced with a more reform-oriented tack (instrumental orientation).

DIALOGUE

It is state power that has primarily preoccupied the gay and lesbian movements of the 1980s.

Barry D. Adam[17]

At the end of the 1970s, an umbrella organization was established comprising sixteen gay and lesbian groups, excluding *Arcadie*. This Emergency Committee against the Repression of Homosexuals (Comité d'Urgence Anti-Répression Homosexuelle, or CUARH) openly supported the candidacy of François Mitterrand in the 1981 presidential election. On the one hand, this showed a certain moderation in the political outlook of many gay activists; on the other hand, it clearly indicated that the movement was still highly politicized. In the specific context of France, this implied that the CUARH was still dependent on the left, and particularly on the Socialist Party (PS). Whereas in other countries it was also liberal parties–such as the Free Democrats (FDP) in Germany and both the VVD and D'66 in the Netherlands–that showed a degree of interest in gay issues (to the extent that they were formulated in terms of equal rights), in France only the PS opened itself to the gay and lesbian movement in the late 1970s.

Apart from this umbrella organization, some other new organizations emerged that provided structure and publicity for the subculture. While lesbians and gay men cooperated in advancing their common interests in the CUARH, only gay men were behind the founding of the most important new journal *Gai Pied*. Although the instrumentally and more subculturally oriented wings of the movement maintained some connections in the early 1980s, these disappeared afterwards due to the success of the instrumental side. What brought this about?

Between the two rounds of the presidential elections, François Mitterrand promised to put an end to all "discrimination on grounds of the nature of morals." For the first time the issue of homosexuality became a political question that figured in the political platforms of presidential candidates in the same way as the death penalty or education. This "eruption at the summit," widely covered by the media, transformed the social standing of homosexuality: it signalled recognition by governmental authorities who were willing to discuss with homosexual organizations. All this was facilitated by a homosexual movement which increasingly renounced its leftist and radical discourse in favor of precise requests.[18]

The prospect of success offered by PS backing powerfully reinforced the instrumental wing of the gay movement. This process was accelerated by the founding of gay groups within or closely linked to political parties, such as Homosexuality and Socialism (Homosexualité et Socialisme) and Gays for Liberty (Gais pour la Liberté), both PS-oriented, as well as the right-wing Movement of Liberal Gays (Mouvement des Gais Libéraux).

On the other hand, the climate of reform which came to prevail was not particularly conducive to mass mobilization. The French gay movement proved capable of the strongest mobilization in Europe in the late 1970s and early 1980s (with two 1981 demonstrations drawing about 10,000 people), but subsequent decline was even more dramatic. From this time on, the hard core of the movement concentrated on parliamentary politics, and successfully so:

> Between 1981 and 1986, the government and the parliamentarians put an end to discrimination directed against homosexuals and even went so far as to start setting forth protective measures in several legal and regulative decisions. In December 1981, [Minister of Justice] Robert Badinter declared: "It is time that France recognize what it owes to the homosexuals as to all other citizens."[19]

Since the government of a "strong," centralized state has the capacity not only to make decisions but to implement them as well, the CUARH quickly scored substantive and procedural successes.

This breakthrough, coming at the very moment that both an instrumental orientation was absolutely dominant within the movement and a commercial subculture was beginning to flourish, brought about a rapid decline of the gay movement. Notable political advances without facilitation–in this case, subsidization–of any organization by the government necessarily brought an end to the instrumental wing of the gay movement. This wing had already become isolated, insofar as the gay community was increasingly inclined to prioritize pleasure. This was possible because the left-wing government itself was now protecting homosexual interests by dismantling all the legal barriers that had heretofore prevented the gay subculture from developing. CUARH membership declined after 1982, and provincial groups disappeared. While its journal *Homophonies* survived until 1986, it faced growing competition from other magazines aimed exclusively at either lesbians or gay men. And because these magazines were non-mixed, they were better able to strike a balance between pleasure and political issues.

Good relations between the CUARH and incumbent politicians were the main reason for the disappearance of *Arcadie* in 1982, which had increasingly found itself isolated and hopelessly out-dated. *Arcadie*'s obsolete character was vividly revealed in June 1981, one month after Mitterrand's election, when it protested against the closing of the police bureau which had specialized in the surveillance of gays. *Arcadie* complained bitterly about the loss of the good contacts it had developed with some key figures within this (repressive!) agency:

> *Arcadie* did not understand that the homosexual movement had to build upon a non-discriminatory attitude on the part of all policemen; and even if that required a major commitment of time and frequent consultations with the movement, it was preferable to the prison, however golden it may have been, that this kind of police surveillance stood for.[20]

The *Arcadie* circle also ceased to function as a meeting place at this time, because the commercial scene was booming and people were no longer forced to meet behind closed doors.

It is interesting to note that the commercial scene also became too competitive for the *"lieux associatifs"* (community centers) which, with subsidies from the Ministry of Culture,[21] had developed during the first half of the 1980s but faded away during the second half of the decade. This period also witnessed the demise of the rather intellectual journal *Masques*,[22] which was neither commercial nor political in a partisan sense. The success of the CUARH's "equal rights" program not only outstripped the anti-normality discourse so eloquently formulated by FHAR and its successors,[23] but all collective sexual identities, either normal or abnormal, as the staff of *Masques* finally concluded: "Even more fundamentally, the future of homosexual men and women resides in the disappearance of the very concept of homosexuality, which ipso facto brings with it the end of heterosexuality and thus all sexual normality."[24] It is important to note that this Foucauldian "deconstruction" of sexual identity could only take place in a setting in which gay men and lesbians were experiencing less discrimination. The relativization of identities presupposes relative freedom.

Apart from commercialization, the pure subculture was characterized by territorial concentration, especially in Paris, and a strong emphasis on sex: pleasure became an even stronger binding element than it had been heretofore, and all kinds of sexual substyles came into being as restrictions eased. Although this newly acquired sexual freedom was still displayed to the outside world at the outset, it turned out some years later that the drive to show just how "gay" gay life can be no longer generated sufficient incentive for mobilization. This can be illustrated by the decline of the Gay Pride March. As stated, the number of participants had sunk from 10,000 at the start of the 1980s to 2-3,000 by the second half of the decade. The character of the march underwent both a quantitative and qualitative change: whereas political demands were expressed during the early years, the element of fun became more important as time went by. In 1985, the most prominent gay entrepreneur of those days, David Girard, wrote in an open letter to *Gai Pied*:

> Everyone to the demo! What is certain is that we are not coming to the demo in the same spirit as the people of the CUARH. They want to parade to denounce the anti-homosexual racism? That is their right. But you will permit me to think that putting up a banner and parading underneath it while saying 'No to anti-homosexual racism!' will change absolutely nothing and will not even attract sympathy. That's depressing. That's gray. We, we will come to have a party. And what we defend is the right to party. It is certainly more communicative (and communicating), more exciting for the participants,

and therefore more impressive and remarkable for the on-lookers and the media.[25]

The same development from an outer-directed, largely political orientation towards a subcultural one can be traced in the pages of *Gai Pied*.[26] This magazine was founded in 1979 by former members of the GLH-PQ who had discovered the impact of media use by the gay movement. From its beginnings, however, there was tension between political purity and sexual pleasure, resulting in several shake-ups within the editorial board. The expansion of the subculture and the growing number of people who considered themselves openly homosexual nevertheless provided a basis for a profitable project. A price had to be paid, however: the magazine dealt increasingly with issues related to pleasure, as its readership was no longer very interested in politics.[27]

It was in this environment of a very weak instrumental movement wing and an increasingly sex-oriented, inner-directed subculture that HIV started to circulate.

THE AIDS CRISIS

While the influence of AIDS upon the gay movement is difficult to gauge, it should not be underestimated—especially in France, which has the largest number of HIV-infected homosexuals and highest percentage of AIDS patients of any European country.[28] Although prevention measures have not been any less effective here than in comparable Western European countries,[29] the lack of a strong French movement in the years between 1983 and 1986 hindered the treatment of patients, the establishment of support networks, lobbying activities, and so on. During the second half of the 1980s, however, a network of groups did develop, within which AIDES was the single most important organization.[30] Although it did not want to be considered part of the gay community, AIDES was clearly linked to several more or less political gay organizations. Contacts between AIDS organizations and the government have come about only recently with state recognition of the seriousness of the crisis. Apart from the general lack of interest shown by the government during the first years of the epidemic, one of the main reasons for the isolation of the AIDS/gay organizations was the weakness of the gay movement's instrumental wing: the government was not confronted with a strong organization capable of speaking on behalf of the gay community as a whole.

Together with this lack of an adequate reaction from all the parties concerned, the enormous number of infected homosexuals and registered AIDS patients has resulted in a new kind of radical militancy in ACT-UP groups, which seek confrontation with the authorities in order to stress the systemic failure in containing the epidemic. Although the AIDS crisis has broadly had the effect of both increasing awareness about homosexuality in official politics[31] and (re)politicizing the gay community,[32] this latter effect caught French gays by surprise. Their agenda had been devoid of politics during the 1980s, and its sudden reappearance revealed their inability–inherent in this pleasure-oriented community–to deal politically with a crisis related to their sexual behavior.

EPILOGUE

Apart from the rise of many kinds of AIDS-related organizations (varying from support networks to safe-sex groups), we can discern a double reaction to the AIDS crisis within the gay community. On the one hand, many pleasure-oriented (but not sexual-oriented) organizations have come to the fore, such as sport clubs (*"randos"*; Gay Games), choral groups, radio programs, bars, and restaurants; on the other hand, political activism has undergone a form of revival in the Gay Pride March, the opening of a community center, and a more outward orientation on the part of, for instance, *Gai Pied.*

In addition, AIDS organizations have finally begun to receive some financial support, and taken together all these developments have contributed to a small revival of the movement–despite the deaths and illness of many of its members. The generation of 1970s militants has been particularly hard hit, and since the swinging start of the 1980s did not bring about the the socialization of a younger generation of militants, the mobilization level of the community was significantly reduced.

This political reactivation–or at least political vigilance–has gained extra impetus from national political changes. The era of reform ended once Chirac's cabinet came to power in 1986. *Gai Pied*'s existence was particularly threatened, as the right-wing Minister of the Interior Pasqua was of the opinion that it and other homosexual journals posed "a danger to youth by reason of their licentious and pornographic character."[33] *Gai Pied* was forced to (re)act in a very interesting way, since it could no longer rely on instrumental gay organizations that had disappeared. By now the most important organization within the gay community, *Gai Pied* was forced to look for support outside the movement.[34] It launched a publicity campaign stressing fundamental civil rights, such as freedom of the press, and succeeded in gaining support from other organizations within the new social movements (SOS Racisme, Ligue de Droits de l'Homme) as well as many important intellectuals. Divided, the government finally halted the campaign.

Gai Pied nevertheless folded in 1992, a demise due not to the politics of the authorities, but to the politics of its publisher who responded to a continuing decline in sales. This turn of events should be understood in relation to the journal's repoliticization. While its readership remained interested primarily in sex and to a lesser degree in political and social coverage, the editorial staff felt it urgent to devote full attention to the interests of gay men and, increasingly, of lesbians as well. This time the readers did not follow the switch in the journal's policy, and *Gai Pied*, a commercial enterprise, was forced to cease publishing.

The AIDS crisis and the threat of the right-wing government in 1986-88 stirred the gay movement after its long sleep. Direct crackdowns and the generally more repressive situation forced homosexuals to organize and mobilize. In the political context specific to France, this did not mean simply attention to politics in general, but to party politicization. Since 1986, the number of gays positioning themselves to the left on the political spectrum has increased. Because the PS was considered the one party that really protected minorities and individual liberties, "*la vote rose*" took on a double meaning: the gay ("pink") vote for France's moderate left-wing ("red") party. Political polarization remained so strong and support for gay rights within the right-wing parties so weak that the right-wing Movement of Liberal Gays disappeared from the political arena after "its" government menaced *Gai Pied*.

In contrast to other European countries, France stills lacks an umbrella organization representing common gay interests in a unified fashion, in particular since *Gai Pied* disappeared.[35] The situation is perhaps even more difficult because the feeling of belonging to a community, of having common interests and identities, is rather underdeveloped in France.[36] Of course, this may change under the influence of a new political situation. But as long as the majority of gays identifies with the PS and a PS president is in power, the demobilization of the movement will not be easily overcome.

AUTHOR NOTE

Jan Willem Duyvendak was born in the Netherlands in 1959, studied sociology and philosophy in Groningen and Paris, and completed his doctorate in political science at the Universiteit van Amsterdam in 1992. He currently teaches in the Department of Political Science of the Universiteit van Amsterdam. He is the author of *Le Poids du politique. Nouveaux mouvements sociaux en France* (Paris: L'Harmattan, 1994). He has also coauthored one book on new social movements in the Netherlands and another on the issue of the "normalization of homosexuality" in the Netherlands in the 1980s.

This essay is based on a chapter of the author's dissertation dealing with new social movements in France: J.W. Duyvendak, *The Power of Politics* (Boulders, CO: Westview, 1995).

NOTES

1. If outsiders consider the mere existence of this subculture provocative and start to "interact" with homosexuals whose intent is not to provoke any reaction by their behavior, this pure subculture may, however, develop into a movement.

2. Naturally, the production of a gay identity is not the most important factor motivating all members of the movement to participate. However, even the hard core for whom interests predominate has a subcultural identity as well. Their strong conviction that "this work has to be done" may be considered a form of "interest identity."

3. Famous authors and other artists (Proust, Gide, Jouhandeau, Cocteau, Genet, Foucault, Colette, Fernandez, Tournier, Guibert) could deal with issues related to homosexuality relatively openly. This openness, however, has little bearing on the broader hostile public attitude toward homosexuality. Those who one-sidedly stress this cultural tradition are overlooking the fact that these extraordinary people have rather exceptional points of view not generally shared by society at large. Although writers and artists may have contributed support to the emancipation movement as a

whole, most of them did not become actively involved in it. Because they enjoyed artistic freedom, they were not directly confronted with discrimination and related problems; as a consequence, the category of "gay writers" has not developed in France along the lines of, for instance, the USA.

4. See Gérard Bach-Ignasse, *Homosexualités: expression/répression* (Paris: Le Sycomore, 1982); idem, *Homosexualité: la reconnaissance?* (Paris: Espace Nuit, 1988); Jean Cavailhes, Pierre Dutey, and Gérard Bach-Ignasse, *Rapport gai: enquête sur les modes de vie homosexuals en France* (Paris: Persona, 1984).

5. See, for instance, Jacques Girard, *Le mouvement homosexuel en France 1945-1980* (Paris: Syros, 1981).

6. Under repressive circumstances, homosexual organizations in all countries favor names with a high protection value, suggesting that the organization deals either with literature (e.g., the Shakespeare Club in the Netherlands) or science (e.g., the Scientific-Humanitarian Committees in Germany and Holland prior to World War II).

7. "*Arcadie* seeks to be apolitical: it does not believe that improvements in the fate of homosexuals should automatically be linked to the victory of any party or of any economic doctrine." This platform was repeated in every issue of the journal.

8. *Arcadie*, no. 273 (September 1977): 14.

9. It has been pointed out that a key-figure policy developed in the Netherlands because of the division of Dutch society into so-called "pillars"; see Rob Tielman, *Homoseksualiteit in Nederland* (Meppel: Boom, 1982), p. 163. Using this approach, representatives of the Dutch national organization COC entered into discussions with the leaders of other pillars. France illustrates, however, that the key-figure model was also used in other countries; this model seems to develop in all repressive but non-dictatorial societies. The effectiveness of this approach in the Netherlands may be attributable to the fact that not just homosexuals but other groups as well were pillarized.

10. *Le Regard des autres* (Paris: Arcadie, 1979).

11. Pamphlet cited in Hervé Hamon and Patrick Rotman, *Génération. Les années de poudre* (Paris: Seuil, 1988), p. 329.

12. Tielman, p. 165, and Hans Warmerdam and Pieter Koenders, *Cultuur en Ontspanning; het COC 1945-1966* (Utrecht: Interfacultaire werkgroep homostudies/NVIH-COC, 1987), p. 341.

13. Girard, p. 91.

14. Ibid., p. 116.

15. The booklet *Rapport contre la normalité* (Paris: Champ Libre, 1971) was, for instance, published by the FHAR.

16. Juquin, who in those days was spokesman for the PCF, formulated the party's position in the first half of the 1970s as follows: "I did not know that homosexuality, glorified in the leftist movement, has an especially radical position. . . . The cover of homosexuality or drugs never had anything to do with the workers' movement. Each of them actually represented the opposite of the workers' movement" (cited in Girard, pp. 96-97). By 1977, the PCF position had become some-

what more liberal: "We must revise the law, not because homosexuality in itself would have either a liberating or revolutionary value (that would seem absurd to me), but because homosexuals have as much right to live in peace as all the other citizens of our country" (ibid., p. 138).

17. Barry D. Adam, *The Rise of a Lesbian and Gay Movement* (Boston: Twayne, 1987), p. 121.

18. Report of the Socialist Party's Commission on Gay Issues preparing the party's 1988 election platform, p. 1. Mimeographed copy in the archive of the author.

19. Ibid., pp. 1-2.

20. Bach-Ignasse, p. 71. That the closing of this department was not a guarantee against police homophobia was illustrated in 1990, when a policeman, who was backed by his colleagues, harassed (and murdered) Father Doucé, one of the leaders of the French gay movement.

21. Whereas the left-wing government subsidized gay organizations oriented toward pleasure, more interest-oriented organizations, which desperately needed support for their survival, did not get much money. This shows that this government placed scant value on the intermediary organizations of civil society: only such inward-oriented organizations as the *"Fédération des Lieux Associatifs Gais,"* based on participation and not on representation, were in fact subsidized.

22. See in particular three *Masques* publications: *Homosexualités 1971-1981* (no. 9/10), *Années 80: Mythe ou libération* (no. 25/26), and *Homosexualité & Politique* (Spring 1986).

23. Jan Willem Duyvendak, "De uitdaging van de homoseksuele subcultuur. De normen van de marginaliteit, de marges van de normaliteit," in *Over normaal gesproken: hedendaagse homopolitiek*, ed. Irene Costera Meijer, Jan Willem Duyvendak, and Marty P. N. van Kerkhof (Amsterdam: Schorer-imprint, 1991).

24. *Homosexualité & Politique*, p. 31.

25. *Gai Pied*, no. 174 (June 1985), p. 61.

26. On the development of *Gai Pied* from 1979 to 1989, see Jan Willem Duyvendak and Mattias Duyves, *"Gai Pied* After Ten Years: A Commercial Success, A Moral Bankruptcy," *Journal of Homosexuality, 25(1/2)* (1993).

27. Data from *Gai Pied*'s annual readers poll, conducted in cooperation with Michael Pollak, showed that in 1983, 25% of the readers considered *Gai Pied* too political, 30% would have liked to see more erotic or pornographic pictures, and 36% wanted more "pictures" in general. These heretofore unpublished figures, based on a survey in *Gai Pied*, nos. 80/81/82 (June 30-September 1, 1983), were provided by Michael Pollak. The 1986 results indicated that the readers thought too much attention was still given to politics–even though the journal's political coverage had already diminished considerably. See Michael Pollak, "Ce que veulent les gais," *Gai Pied*, no. 257 (February 14, 1987): 25-27.

28. This section is mainly based on Michael Pollak, *Les Homosexuels et le SIDA* (Paris: A. M. Métailié, 1989); Emmanuel Hirsch, *AIDES, solidaires* (Paris: Cerf, 1991); Michael Pollak, Rommel Mendès-Leite, and Jacques Van Dem Borghe, *Homosexualités et SIDA* (Lille: Cahiers Gai-Kitsch-Camp, 1992); Jan Willem Duyvendak and Ruud Koopmans, "Résister au SIDA: destin et influence

du mouvement homosexuel," ibid., pp. 195-224; reports about AIDS organizations; and discussions with the late Michael Pollak and with Rommel Mendès-Leite. See also Frank Arnal, *Résister ou disparaître? Les homosexuels face au sida. La prévention de 1982 à 1992* (Paris: L'Harmattan, 1993).

29. Duyvendak and Koopmans, "Résister au SIDA: destin et influence du mouvement homosexuel." Data shows that HIV prevention among homosexuals has been (almost) as effective in France as in other countries, which implies that the weakness of the gay movement was compensated for by the infrastructures of bars, restaurants, newspapers, etc. Countries such as Italy, Greece, and Spain that lacked a functional equivalent of this nature were at a disadvantage.

30. On the development of AIDES, see Hirsch.

31. See, e.g., Janine Mossuz-Lavau, *Les lois de l'amour: Les politiques de la sexualité en France de 1950 à nos jours* (Paris: Payot, 1991).

32. Dennis Altman, "Legitimation through Disaster: AIDS and the Gay Movement," in *AIDS, the Burdens of History,* ed. Elizabeth Fee and Daniel M. Fox (Berkeley: University of California Press, 1988), and John D'Emilio and Estelle B. Freedman, *Intimate Matters: History of Sexuality in America* (New York: Harper and Row, 1990).

33. *Gai Pied,* no. 264. Information about the action campaign against the ban can be found in ibid., nos. 264, 265, 266, all of March 1987.

34. The distance between *Gai Pied*'s journalists (often former militants) and the last old-style militants, who organized the campaign of support, was evidenced in the reporting about this mobilization in *Gai Pied.* The latter wrote: "The contrast between impotent anger and powerful mobilization stirred up by *Gai Pied* in those last days was indeed compelling. . . . Though the demonstration pleased the old militants, they once again displayed their inability to mobilize the people. GPH won because it understands the media age." Marco Lemaire, "Censure," *Gai Pied,* no. 264 (April 9, 1987): 9-10; here, p. 10.

35. I am not dealing here with an important part of the gay movement that is rather unrelated to politics: the Christian organizations, such as "David & Jonathan." These organizations are nonetheless important, not only for individual help, but also for the continuity of the movement. Although these organizations are virtually invisible to the outside world, their decentralized infrastructure is impressive and their activities–with regard to AIDS, for instance–are important. These organizations are based on a kind of double-identity: homosexual identities are produced within the context of a shared "external" identity as members of a religious community, providing considerable stability to these organizations. After other organizations had disappeared during the 1980s due to the quick successes at the start of Mitterrand's first period, David & Jonathan even became one of the most important groups within the field of homosexual organizations. Due to its denominational character, however, it will never function as an umbrella organization.

36. In 1985, the *Gai Pied*/Pollak survey showed that forty-five percent of the readership did not consider itself as belonging to a "special social group."

Index

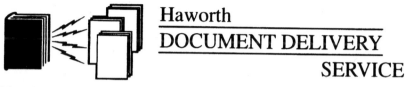

Haworth
DOCUMENT DELIVERY
SERVICE

This valuable service provides a single-article order form for any article from a Haworth journal.

- *Time Saving:* No running around from library to library to find a specific article.
- *Cost Effective:* All costs are kept down to a minimum.
- *Fast Delivery:* Choose from several options, including same-day FAX.
- *No Copyright Hassles:* You will be supplied by the original publisher.
- *Easy Payment:* Choose from several easy payment methods.

Open Accounts Welcome for . . .
- Library Interlibrary Loan Departments
- Library Network/Consortia Wishing to Provide Single-Article Services
- Indexing/Abstracting Services with Single Article Provision Services
- Document Provision Brokers and Freelance Information Service Providers

---

MAIL or *FAX* THIS ENTIRE ORDER FORM TO:

Haworth Document Delivery Service
The Haworth Press, Inc.
10 Alice Street
Binghamton, NY 13904-1580

or FAX: 1-800-895-0582
or CALL: 1-800-342-9678
9am-5pm EST

PLEASE SEND ME PHOTOCOPIES OF THE FOLLOWING SINGLE ARTICLES:

1) Journal Title: _____
    Vol/Issue/Year:_____Starting & Ending Pages:_____
    Article Title:_____
    _____

2) Journal Title: _____
    Vol/Issue/Year:_____Starting & Ending Pages:_____
    Article Title:_____
    _____

3) Journal Title: _____
    Vol/Issue/Year:_____Starting & Ending Pages:_____
    Article Title:_____
    _____

4) Journal Title: _____
    Vol/Issue/Year:_____Starting & Ending Pages:_____
    Article Title:_____
    _____

(See other side for Costs and Payment Information)

COSTS: Please figure your cost to order quality copies of an article.

1. Set-up charge per article: $8.00

               ($8.00 × number of separate articles) _____

2. Photocopying charge for each article:

               1-10 pages: $1.00 _____

               11-19 pages: $3.00 _____

               20-29 pages: $5.00 _____

               30+ pages: $2.00/10 pages _____

3. Flexicover (optional): $2.00/article _____

4. Postage & Handling: US: $1.00 for the first article/

               $.50 each additional article _____

               Federal Express: $25.00 _____

               Outside US: $2.00 for first article/

               $.50 each additional article _____

5. Same-day FAX service: $.35 per page _____

               GRAND TOTAL: _____

METHOD OF PAYMENT: (please check one)

❏ Check enclosed   ❏ Please ship and bill. PO # _____

               (sorry we can ship and bill to bookstores only! All others must pre-pay)

❏ Charge to my credit card: ❏ Visa; ❏ MasterCard; ❏ Discover;

               ❏ American Express;

Account Number: _____ Expiration date:_____

Signature: **✗**_____

Name: _____ Institution: _____

Address: _____

_____

City: _____ State:_____ Zip:_____

Phone Number: _____ FAX Number: _____

MAIL or *FAX* THIS ENTIRE ORDER FORM TO:

Haworth Document Delivery Service	**or FAX:** 1-800-895-0582
The Haworth Press, Inc.	**or CALL:** 1-800-342-9678
10 Alice Street	9am-5pm EST)
Binghamton, NY 13904-1580	